National and International Conflicts, 1945–1995

The information flow about crises and conflicts is highly selective. The media can focus only on a few major conflicts at a time. Many conflicts are neglected, others soon forgotten after the fighting ends. This book fills the gaps and offers a systematic overview of all crises and conflicts in and among states during the fifty-year period 1945–95 and traces the global trends of conflict development.

This book contains descriptive generalizations, hypotheses on trends and patterns of conflicts and discussions of current conflict theories – all based on the broad empirical basis of the Conflict Simulation Model KOSIMO – a databank which contains 661 conflicts, both peaceful and violent as well as internal and international. Where ordinary conflict research has a bias towards violent international conflicts, this book, on the other hand, uses an integrated approach to cover many other forms and types of political conflicts.

The KOSIMO approach reveals new insights into the trends, both nationally and internationally, of conflicts since 1945. Its major diachronic findings include for example the fact that domestic, ethnopolitical and religious conflicts were on the rise long before the end of the East–West conflict, and democracies may not be as peaceful as Kant's theorem on democratic peace might suggest. With conflict studies being a growing field of interest in international relations, this book will provide solid empirical and theoretical research for scholars and researchers in political theory, political science, international relations, peace and conflict studies, and modern history.

Frank R. Pfetsch is Professor of Political Science at the University of Heidelberg with Jean-Monnet Chair. His main research fields are science policy, foreign policy and international relations, political theory and constitutional law. **Christoph Rohloff** is Research Fellow at the Institute for Development and Peace INEF, University of Duisburg. He has published on topics in empirical peace and conflict research. He is also director of the Heidelberg Institute of International Conflict Research HIIK.

Routledge Advances in International Relations and Politics

National and International Conflicts, 1945–1995

New empirical and theoretical approaches

Frank R. Pfetsch and Christoph Rohloff

Routledge
Taylor & Francis Group

LONDON AND NEW YORK

First published 2000
by Routledge
2 Park Square, Milton Park, Abingdon, Oxfordshire OX14 4RN

Simultaneously published in the USA and Canada
by Routledge
711 Third Avenue, New York, NY 10017

First issued in paperback 2014

Routledge is an imprint of the Taylor and Francis Group, an informa business

Typeset in Times by
MHL Typesetting Ltd, Coventry

British Library Cataloguing in Publication Data
A catalogue record for this book is available
from the British Library

Library of Congress Cataloging in Publication Data
Pfetsch, Frank R., 1936–
    National and international conflicts, 1945–1995: new empirical
and theoretical approaches/Frank R. Pfetsch and Christoph Rohloff.
        p.   cm. – (Routledge advances in international relations and
politics)
    Includes bibliographical references and index.
    1. World politics – 1945– 2. International relations.
I. Rohloff, Christoph. II. Title. III. Series.
D843.P4795   2000
303.6'09'045–dc21   99–40347
                                                           CIP

ISBN 13: 978-1-138-88222-5 (pbk)
ISBN 13: 978-0-415-22344-7 (hbk)

Publisher's Note
The publisher has gone to great lengths to ensure the quality of this reprint
but points out that some imperfections in the original may be apparent

Contents

Figures

Tables

x *Tables*

Preface

This book analyses trends and patterns of political conflicts in and among states on a global scale. We will present systematized data on more than 650 domestic, international, non-violent and violent political conflicts that have occurred between 1945 and 1995 and that have been recorded in the KOSIMO databank at the University of Heidelberg. We will present in this book descriptive generalizations and hypotheses on trends and patterns of conflicts, and we will discuss current conflict theories and test their validity on the broad empirical basis of the KOSIMO ('Conflict Simulation Model' *Konflikt-Simulations-Modell*) research project.

This project was initiated in 1988 with financial support from the German Ministry of Research and the German Research Foundation. The goal was to develop a model of conflicts that included both non-violent and violent conflicts, domestic and international conflicts, state and non-state actors as well as structural and behavioral determinants, issues in dispute, domestic systemic conditions of actors and external constellations of the international system. This challenge has in part been taken up by earlier researchers. Sorokin (1937) and Wright (1942) provided the theoretical and empirical foundations for more elaborate databanks such as the correlates-of-war project by Singer and Small (1972), Singer (1979, 1980), and Geller and Singer (1998) and the data on conflicts compiled by Butterworth (1976), Holsti (1991), and Gurr (1993). Kende (1971), Gantzel and Meyer-Stamer (1986) and Gantzel and Schwinghammer (1995) established this tradition of empirical quantitative research in the German social-science community.

Despite the existence of a considerable amount of research already done in this field, we still found reasonable arguments for the compilation of a new databank on political conflicts. The first reason was that the existence of several databanks on conflicts has not solved the problem of their incompatibility. Each databank uses its own definitions for basic terms such as conflict, party, state, war, violence, victims and regions. Some observe only international conflicts (CIA fact book) and others separately international and domestic conflicts. Some focus on certain issues, for example, ethnicity, minorities and conflict (Gurr 1993) or conflicts induced by environmental degradation (Bächler *et al.* 1996). Obviously, we cannot overcome the lack of a common quantitative database for such complex social phenomena as political conflicts, but we have tried to integrate as many cases and variables as methodologically permissible from earlier research into our databank. KOSIMO is thus an integrated and completely revised compilation of cases from existing databanks on conflicts and cases from our own empirical research. The periodic updating of the databank is done at the Heidelberg Institute for International Conflict Research at the University of Heidelberg.[1]

Related to the difficulties in defining generally accepted cases is the general vagueness of central terms like 'war' and 'violence'. Singer and Small are using a quantitative definition for the term 'war', i.e. at least 1,000 people must have been killed in a conflict to qualify as a 'war'. Gantzel and Meyer-Stamer (1986) have used a qualitative definition, i.e. 'war' is defined as military fighting over a considerable period of time and with a certain intensity. All wars are, obviously, acts of violence, but not every act of violence seems to be a war. However, the existing databanks on wars do not clearly distinguish between the various forms of violence in political conflicts. We assume that it will impair the validity of one's propositions when a sporadic and peripheral unrest with 1,500 deaths over several years is grouped together with, for example, the first Gulf War. The lack of a systematic differentiation in empirical conflict research between these forms of violence led us to distinguish two degrees of intensity in violent conflicts: sporadic, unorganized, irregular violence in severe crisis situations and organized, collective, regular use of force in wars. The obvious advantage of this differentiation is the avoidance of an inflated use of the term 'war.' On the other hand, this differentiation does not intend to marginalize or minimize the effects of sporadic, irregular or unorganized violence. While classical inter-state wars, such as the first Gulf War in the 1980s or the wars between Eritrea and Ethiopia in 1998 and 1999, have become exceptional cases in the modern global conflict profile, irregular, sporadic and unorganized violence by gang fights, drug-related violence, warlordism, ethnopoliticized or religious group rivalries have become the new dominant source of violent conflict at the end of this century. KOSIMO tries to reflect and react to these and related trends by maintaining the term 'war' in its 'classical' meaning, and by introducing the term 'sporadic, irregular or unorganized violence in severe crises' as a means to capture the change in today's global conflict profile.

Also, the dynamics of conflicts over time should be awarded more attention in empirical conflict research. Many databanks in the field regard conflicts on a formal level as unitary acts or as singular events. Conflicts are labeled as, for example, 'the Vietnam War' – although *the* Vietnam War obviously passed through many different phases from a latent conflict over a crisis situation to sporadic use of force and all-out war that was interrupted by innumerable cease-fires. Empirical quantitative conflict research has not yet developed more adequate models to differentiate more accurately and systematically between these phases. Related to this aspect is the fact that many conflicts escalate and de-escalate more than just once. For example, massacres in the Great Lakes region of Central Africa have been observed in the 1960s *and* in 1994. To capture the escalations and de-escalations of conflicts systematically over time, KOSIMO introduced the new concepts of basic and partial conflicts. A basic conflict is, for example, the Vietnam War. It is understood as the entire conflict, that begins with the first formulation of certain national interests against a second actor and that continues on different levels of intensity until the consensual conclusion of a binding accord. Thus, our databank is not based on a simple listing of conflicts, but on a conflict simulation model that allows conflicts to shift from potential conflicts and non-violent crisis situations on to severe crises and wars and back. The inclusion of non-violent and violent conflicts in one databank is therefore a unique feature of KOSIMO and, in our understanding, an essential component to allow for meaningful propositions on peace, conflict and war on the basis of quantitative research. In other words, databanks on wars are limited to an important yet marginal subset of all political conflicts. As such, they are likely to lead to under-dimensioned conclusions on a much more complex social phenomenon. Databanks can offer information about conflicts on a scale that reaches – in theory – from positive peace to war. Between these extremes KOSIMO differentiates negative peace or the mere absence of war, verbal disputes in latent crises and crisis situations, spontaneous or irregular use of force and finally collective and organized use of force. Figure P.1 illustrates the possible dimensions of conflicts on a peace–war continuum and indicates the scope of the KOSIMO data.

Initial sketches of the databank were published as working papers in 1990. Theoretic aspects relating to the KOSIMO databank have been published in *Conditions for Nonviolent Resolution of Conflict* (Pfetsch 1990), *Internationale und nationale Konflikte nach dem Zweiten Weltkrieg* (Pfetsch 1992) and *Eskalation und Deeskalation internationaler Konflikte* (Billing 1992). The first version of the databank (1945–1990) was published in: *Datenhandbuch nationaler und internationaler Konflikte* (Pfetsch and Billing 1994). We also published a qualitative five-volume edition *Konflikte seit 1945* (Pfetsch 1991) where the project members verbally described the development of – at that time – 546 conflicts between 1945 and 1990. All of

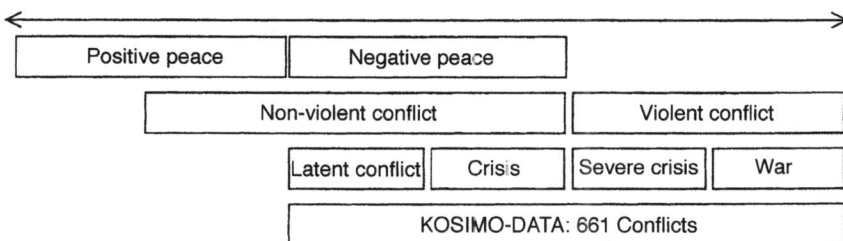

Figure P.1 Dimensions of conflict.

these conflicts can be found in the KOSIMO databank as operationalized record-sets. In 1996, we presented a descriptive follow-up of the one hundred newly escalated conflicts for the period between 1990 and 1995 followed by two comprehensive area studies for the Middle East (Trautner 1997) and South America (Schindler 1998). The present volume is the first comprehensive publication of the databank for the English-speaking social-science community. The KOSIMO version II, on which this book is based, contains 661 conflicts. The latest version, KOSIMO III, covers the period from 1945 until 1998 and is available on the Internet at http://www.kosimo.de

This book can be used as a general work of reference on political conflicts, as a textbook for students in International Relations or Peace and Conflict Studies and as a basis for further studies in empirical conflict research.

We would like to thank the KOSIMO team, Peter Billing, Sabine Klotz, Christof Hartmann, Marianne Rinza, Hardi Schindler and Bernhard J. Trautner for their valuable input. The project would not have succeeded without their skilled research and their regional expertise. This book has profited from university seminars and discussions at the Third Pan-European Conference on International Relations, Vienna 1998 and the Third International Security Forum, Zurich 1998.

Heidelberg, October 1999

1 Introduction

At the doorstep to the third millennium, political violence and wars are still threatening and killing people in numerous countries. This fact serves as the most obvious justification for our critical and systematic analysis of the major trends and patterns of political conflict over the second half of the twentieth century. The underlying and crucial question for such an endeavor is old and still unchanged: How can people organize and maintain peaceful relations among and within modernizing pluralistic societies? Our underlying assumption is that in and among societies, where this question is not properly addressed and answered, the risk of violent conflicts will not diminish. Whereas many Western, Latin American and Asian states have successfully managed to build a modern nation state, other countries are still struggling along the dangerous road from traditional societal structures to political, economic and cultural modernization.

For our empirical project, the trends and patterns of political conflicts since 1945 are observed and interpreted in the light of continuously changing international and domestic constellations and conditions. The global political map has in effect changed dramatically throughout the twentieth century. These changes had in turn far-reaching effects on the actors, issues and structures of political conflicts. What are these major changes in the international system and how are these changes related more specifically to the field of political conflict research?

Global changes since 1945

From a global viewpoint, the international relations among states in the twentieth century can be divided into three major periods. In the first period, which lasted until the Second World War, states competed for the maximization of power, prestige and influence. It was the period of classic *realpolitik* which continued from the nineteenth century. The second period was dominated by the United States and the Soviet Union who had reached an uncontested status as superpowers after the Second World War. Most of the states in the northern hemisphere, including Central America and the Middle East, were allies to one or the other bloc in a bipolar world. The non-aligned movement, prominent as it was, lacked the bases of power to challenge the superpowers. In the third period, that began in the early 1970s, multinational corporations and non-governmental organizations entered the international arena. The appearance of politically influential non-state actors reflects a world of increasing interdependence. Until now and for the foreseeable future, the traditional geopolitical state-centric and power-dominated international system is evolving into a geo-economic societal system of coordinated regional politics. Within these three major epochs of a dynamic international system several more specific changes with significant positive or negative affects on conflict patterns can be observed. We will highlight those changes which we believe to have the most influential impact on conflicts and conflict analysis. Among these changes are the decline of power- and prestige-politics that was typical of nineteenth-century foreign-policy styles, the decline of territorial expansionism, the multiplication of the number of states, the population growth, the spread in number and scope of international and transnational organizations, the growth of economic production and world trade leading to globalization and regionalization and the consequences of the end of the East–West conflict.

Decline of power and prestige-politics

When compared to the period between the Westphalian Peace treaty until the end of the Second World War, the foreign policies of most states since 1945 have obviously undergone a fundamental change in their political behavior and style. Foreign policies of many mostly Western states have moved away from self-centered prestige- and power-politics, from colonial and imperial politics and from zero-sum games; they are now moving towards an increasingly multilateral and cooperative disposition. A collective insight into the regional and global interdependencies on virtually all fields of modern human existence has led to an unprecedented appreciation of cooperative patterns of behavior and of relative gains and comparative advantages. The underlying mood and motivation for the evolution of reliable multilateral cooperative patterns in the second half of twentieth century Europe can be found to a large extent in the experience of two World Wars.

The most apparent effect of this fundamental structural change in foreign policy conduct on political conflicts since 1945 is a steady decrease in the number of international wars initiated by states. By today, we must consider international wars initiated by governments and directed against other governments as exceptionally rare phenomena. The Iraqi invasion into Kuwait in 1991, Eritrea's 1998 invasion into Ethiopia and the inter-nationalization of the Congo regime crisis since 1997 face the univocal opposition of the international community. Nevertheless, the conflicts between India and Pakistan since 1947, between the two Yemens in 1964 and 1991/94, between Yemen and Saudi Arabia in 1998, between the two

Koreas since 1950, between Israel, Syria and Lebanon since 1948, between Iraq and Iran between 1980 and 1998, between Peru and Ecuador since 1942 or between Great Britain and Argentina in 1982 illustrate the destructive potential that will continue to reside within inter-state relations.

The point here is to underline the steady trend against overt aggressive international behavior among states. Although states will obviously continue to weigh the costs and benefits of cooperative against conflictive international behavior in the future, wars in the nineteenth century were a more or less calculable risk with limited scope and effects. At the beginning of the twentieth century, this picture began to change. Weapons capable of mass destruction on the one hand, and, on the other hand, the formulation of the principle of collective self defense changed the cost–benefit rationale of international aggression. The institutionalization of this principle in the United Nations Charter in 1945 and the empowerment of the Security Council and regional organizations to sanction malicious states can be considered as the epochal safeguard against a general fallback into the aggressive patterns of the nineteenth and first part of the twentieth century.

Decline of territorial expansionism

In the era of European hegemony, territories within and outside Europe were continuously subject to occupations, annexations, conquests and colonization until this practice and the underlying ideologies and worldviews culminated in the disastrous experience of two World Wars. Hence, rivalries among states about territories have become significantly less frequent. Within the European Union, for example, territories and frontiers have almost completely lost their former significance. This is not to say that there will be eventually no more conflicts about national boundaries – it is the objective that has changed. By today, the economic, political and human costs of violent territorial conflict have become exorbitantly higher than the gains that could ever be expected from the aggressively acquired additional resources, people or territory. Most border conflicts today arise about uncertainties and disagreement over a specific delineation rather than about threats of annexation and conquest. Ironically the new Law of the Sea which went into effect in 1994 has caused a number of new conflicts to erupt despite the intention ultimately to clarify the delineation of maritime borders. Hence, the size of territories has, on the one hand, lost its former significance as an object of national prestige. On the other hand, borders will remain objects of conflicts. Yet, for the reasons mentioned above, they will be carried out in a more legalistic and civilized manner than before.

The multiplication of the number of states

A further change on the political map is the increase in the number of states. In 1945 fifty states signed the United Nations Charter. By 2000, this number had increased to 188 member states. Two waves of decolonization, immediately after the Second World War and during the 1960s, were mainly responsible for this increase. A third group of states joined the international community with the dissolution of the USSR and the former Yugoslavia. The arithmetic increase in states is coupled with an increase in national interests and, in consequence, an exponential increase in possible conflict relations. Despite this increase in the global conflict potential, as we will show in the empirical part of this book, the number of violent international conflicts is overall lower than the overall number of violent domestic conflicts. In fact, international violent conflicts have become exceptional and short-lived phenomena in the 1980s and 1990s.

Contrary to what was envisioned by the former colonizing states, the increase in the number of states did not result in a proportional increase in the number of democracies. Still, we can identify four waves of democratization,[1] i.e. in Europe and Asia after the Second World War, in Southern Europe in the 1970s, in Latin America in the 1980s and in Eastern Europe since 1989. Democratic regime changes in Africa were promising between 1989 and 1992. Yet, many regimes returned to authoritarian rule. A long-term democratization in the Far East is most promising in Taiwan, South Korea and Thailand, while many Southeast Asian nations are still struggling with autocratic regimes.

If not democratization itself, it is an increasing degree of fundamental politicization of peoples that has led to a much greater awareness of human, political, social, economic and cultural rights. These rights are increasingly codified in the United Nations system; for Europe these rights are codified by the Council of Europe. Yet it is the realization of these rights either through enforcement or through non-state actors such as opposition movements, non-governmental organizations, churches, conventions and others, that puts authoritarian states under increasing public pressure. This politicization of peoples as a result of the globally effective pressure for modernization has led to an increasing number of violent conflicts that involve ethnic, religious and regional minority conflicts. Thus, states that suppress minority rights are a much greater source of contemporary violent conflict than states that behave aggressively against their neighbors.

Population growth

A fourth factor influencing conflict patterns is the dramatic increase of the global population. World population doubled between 1950 and 1997. In 1999, we count 6.0 billion people on earth. Estimates by the United Nations say that this increase will continue until approximately the year 2025. Then, the earth's population will amount to 8.2 billion people (Globale Trends 1998: 119).

How does population growth relate to political conflict? Classic realist political scientists proposed that population is a central requisite of state power albeit not the only one (Morgenthau 1948). Whereas the increase of a nation's population was a political goal in terms of power acquisition in the nineteenth century, today we observe the reverse course. Overpopulated nations desperately try to curb their demographic growth which they regard as a prime obstacle to modernization and general economic prosperity. Still, population growth by itself is not a direct cause of violent conflict. It is a catalyst if combined with economic and social deprivation or marginal-ization of certain groups or in combination with degraded eco-systems. In addition, migration of refugees in already densely populated areas has led to violent conflicts over access to and distribution of scarce resources, be it land or labor.

International and transnational organizations

The fifth change since 1945 that affects conflict behavior and patterns is the proliferation of international and transnational organizations. By today, these official and private organizations can be regarded as the most influential international actors next to the states themselves. Three aspects can describe their development: firstly, the exponential increase in the mere number of international and transnational organizations; secondly, the increase in the number of members within these organizations to the level of regional or global completion and, thirdly, the inclusion of many new policy fields in addition to the traditional field of international security, like human rights, women, housing or the environment.

Since 1945, the United States have vigorously pursued both military containment of the communist countries and the preservation of the economic free-trade system. The existing international institutions reflect this dominant military, political and economic position of the United States. They endorse the idea of a United Nations against a decentralized or regional model of international security proposed by Winston Churchill. Theodore Roosevelt opted for a comprehensive and universal political model as an authority primarily responsible for world peace and international security. On regional levels, the United States secured their military supremacy through various bilateral and multilateral defense alliances and pacts (NATO, SEATO, ANZUS, CENTO). The gradual institutionalization of the military power balance after 1945 led to a relatively stable international system when compared with the systems prior to the Second World War. On a regional and local level, the bipolar system had the effect that many potential and latent conflicts remained below the threshold of violent conflict. As such, it had an appeasing and pacifying effect on the respective allies. However, outside these blocs conflicts occurred which have been influenced by respective bloc members.

In global economics, the international system was structured through a multitude of trade agreements and financial institutions such as the Bretton Woods system, the World Bank and the International Monetary Fund, the

General Agreement on Tariffs and Trade (today's World Trade Organization). With the end of the East–West conflict and the collapse of the communist regimes, this liberal free-trade model seems to be without an alternative.

On the regional level, economic and security arrangements have been initiated by the superpowers, by regional powers and by the Organization of American States (OAS), the Organization of African Unity (OAU), the Arab League (AL), the Council for Mutual Economic Relations (COMECON), the Association of Asian States (ASEAN), the North American Free Trade Area (NAFTA), the Association of Pacific Economic Cooperation (APEC) and the South American Market (Mercosur). The Council of Europe, the Organization for Security and Cooperation in Europe (OSCE) and the European Union (EU) are forming stable peace structures in Europe. All these organizations are regional cooperative integration arrangements for common security, mutual confidence building and economic cooperation. They can also function as mediators and impartial authorities in political conflicts, and, in effect, they have evolved as indispensable organs for regional peaceful cooperation.

It seems plausible to assume that these agents in international and transnational politics are contributing to the pacification of conflicts; the common bond of these organizations is their mission to enhance cooperation, to facilitate mutual understanding and to pacify relations among their members. We observe among the activities of international and transnational organizations an evolution of a new regional conflict culture with its focus on preventive diplomacy, early warning and improved negotiation capacities. Despite several setbacks, as in Bosnia-Herzegovina, Somalia or Kosovo, the concept of peaceful conflict resolution through concerted humanitarian interventions, mediation and preventive and consolidating measures is being institutionalized on societal, state and international levels. The Organization for Security and Cooperation in Europe (OSCE) became the organization next to the UN which has in its hands the most versatile instruments for preventive and de-escalative interventions in explosive conflict situations. Despite or because of this positive development, the actual number of ongoing conflicts per year since 1994 remains at a level of about thirty violent conflicts (*Konfliktbarometer* 1998). However, this level might rise again in the future and inter-state conflicts might reappear over access to arable land and water sources in regions with scarce resources, overpopulation and environmental degradation (Biermann, Petschel-Held and Rohloff 1998: 273).

The integrative forces within the international and the regional systems and the trend towards the institutionalization of international politics gave rise to the theory of 'New Institutionalism' (Keck 1993: 35) which states that by the very nature of their existence international institutions can guarantee cooperation among states, and undermine the classic security dilemma. As a consequence for conflict research, we assume that the institutionalization of rules in international politics has altered the states' policy styles away from zero-sum games of *realpolitik* towards positive-sum games of cooperation and strengthened the capacity for non-violent conflict behavior in international organizations as well as in the foreign policies of the member states.

Globalization and regionalization

In 1945 the United States was the driving force behind the institutionalization of what was called 'embedded liberalism' (Ruggie 1983: 185–231, Rittberger 1994: 185). After the war, when the chapters on the institutionalization of international social and economic relations were written into the United Nations Charter, there was a consensus that, in response to the great economic depression in the early 1930s, the protectionist reflexes of the affected states and the lack of coordinating organizations contributed to the radicalization of politics, the rise of fascism and the outbreak of the Second World War. In the West the idea was to pursue the general advantages of free trade while avoiding its implicit disadvantages during recessions by the help of interventionist fiscal, monetary and tariff-related instruments.

Over the decades, the Bretton-Woods institutions and the periodic General Agreements on Tariffs and Trade (GATT) have effectively adapted to many new challenges, like the increase in the number of developing economies during the decolonization period in the 1960s. By the end of the 1980s, the attraction of liberal democracies coupled with the persuasive powers of international and regional political and economic organizations as well as the monetary powers of multi- and transnational corporations and trading partners, have overwhelmed the model of centrally planned economies along with the communist ideology behind it. Today, free-market democracies have evolved as the unrivaled global economic-political model. During the 1990s we observe an ongoing trend towards globalization; a phenomenon which is paralleled by an intensified economic and regional integration process in the Americas, Asia and Europe. The severe financial crises in Japan, Southeast Asia and in Russia in 1997 and 1998 are forcing inept or reluctant governments either to adjust to the demands of free capital flow, round-the-clock stock exchanges or to abdicate, as was the fate of Indonesia's former President Suharto. The moral righteousness and the effectiveness of the World Bank and IMF's policy to condition credits on political reforms is often debated (Tetzlaff 1996). But with regard to the effects on conflict behavior, the need for economic performance and world market compatibility and integration leaves governments with little means to divert internal frustration into external aggression (Brock 1997: 399). Although not envisioned in today's dimensions by Immanuel Kant, Adam Smith or David Ricardo, we conclude that since 1945 the theorem of free-trade peace can be empirically supported under the condition of institutionalized forms of international regulation and cooperation.

Regional cooperation has not only been helped by state-membership organizations. Many non-state actors play a major role in international and transnational relations. The investments of multi- and transnational enterprises disregard national boundaries. Today, they make up an important part of the global village; economic transnationalism has led to political regionalism. The European Union, the Mercosur and various African and Asian zones of economic cooperation networks are an expression of regional liberalization. The intention is to enhance the competitiveness through integrated regional markets. The aim of economic regionalization is the general welfare of the people, although the integration into the world market system may lead to the marginalization of peoples and regions. This economic marginalization has the potential to lead to social unrest and even violent conflicts.

On the state level itself, traditional power rivalry at the expense of neighboring states in a costly search for a balance of power is being replaced more and more by institutionalized bi- and multilateral patterns of cooperation. The insight into the logic of global, regional and neighborly interdependence in most fields of national interest, like security, energy and food, has furthered this trend toward mutual cooperation. This trend is strongest among states with developed economies.

The end of the East–West conflict

The collapse of communist regimes in 1989 and 1990 accelerated the trends described above in the international system toward an internalization and privatization of potentially violent conflicts. The major threat to world peace and international security does not derive from inter-state conflicts but stems from internal conflicts along ethnic, religious and regional formations. On the positive side we find a strengthened United Nations and many governmental and private regional organizations working on the professional prevention, mediation and resolution of conflicts and the long-term consolidation of peace agreements. The end of the East–West conflict in 1989/90 affected conflict potentials in both aggravating and restraining ways.

On the international level:

- it ended the era of mutually exclusive doctrines, like the doctrine of spheres of influence and of mutual deterrence
- it ended open military interventions by proxies
- it ended the arms race of the superpowers
- it led to the dissolution of the communist bloc and to the expansion of Western liberalism
- it led to German unification.

On the internal level:

- it helped the emergence and stabilization of democratic movements and regimes and made the superpowers more cooperative long before the end of the East–West conflict
- the end of the East–West conflict led also to the violent escalation of many latent internal conflicts, especially on the territory of the former USSR; some of these violent conflicts have yet to be resolved.

The East–West conflict and its ending are political phenomena that by popular opinion have had profound impacts on former and present-day political conflict patterns. It is self-evident that nuclear deterrence as an expression of the unrestrained rivalry between the two superpowers was the biggest threat ever to mankind's survival. The polarization of ideological disputes to 'capitalism' versus 'communism' was a source of internal upheavals in many societies around the globe. Between 1947 and 1990, on the other hand, ethno-political, secessionist and minority conflicts seem to have become widespread only after the end of the East–West conflict. Many historians claim that these conflicts had been 'iced' during the East–West conflict, or even since the First World War, and resurfaced when the authoritarian communist lid was lifted.

Are these statements and observations accurate and can they be validated by empirical research? First, we have to look at the East–West conflict itself and its effects on conflict patterns, before we ponder on the consequences of its ending. Two opposing theories try to explain the fact that the Cold War did not escalate into a 'hot' war: on the one hand, the realist theory of 'Cold War peace' (Mearsheimer 1990) claims that the Cold War gave stability and accountability (*Erwartungsverläßlichkeit*) to actors in the international system; it prevented a hot war not only between the superpowers, but also between and within smaller states. A more liberal theory states that, while inside of the bipolar system peace prevailed, war was and continues to be a widespread phenomenon in the peripheries. In contrast to what might be expected from the theory of 'Cold War peace', our empirical findings suggest that, in accordance with the second theoretical version, the end of the East–West conflict had little additional impact on the overall global number and patterns of violent conflict.

The end of the arms race

Foreign-policy doctrines and military strategies have changed with the end of the East–West conflict. Both the US and the USSR have given up their Cold War doctrines and in 1985 they began to cooperate in selected policy fields, e.g. the first Gulf War, Angola and South Africa. Furthermore, in the second half of the 1980s the superpowers agreed to effectively reduce parts of their nuclear missiles arsenal and to cut back on defense expenditure.

There was a measurable peace dividend as a result of the end of the arms race and the ideological rivalry, although the extent of this dividend is much debated (BICC 1996, Debiel and Zander 1992: 9). Military spending today is about two-thirds below the mid-1980s. In 1987, the world's military expenditure as a share of global GNP amounted to 5.4 percent; by 1994, this percentage had fallen to below 3 percent. Employment in the military sector decreased between 1987 and 1996 from 17.5 million employees to 9.2 million. The general trend to reduce military spending seems to continue in the second half of the 1990s with a decrease of 4 percent from 1995 to 1996. These figures have to be differentiated along high- and low-income countries. In many high-income countries, the percentage dropped even below 1 percent while, e.g., Indonesia increased its military spending to 10 percent of its GNP. The 1998 BICC conversion survey finds that out of 157 observed states, 85 states reduced and 69 states increased their military spending. Industrialized and Eastern European states were prominent among the former group, whereas many low-income countries overburden their budgets with high military spending. Countries engaged in ongoing violent conflicts are among those with the highest increase in military spending, i.e. Turkey, Indonesia, Papua New Guinea, Colombia, Sierra Leone, Myanmar, Armenia, Sudan, Burundi, Sri Lanka and Rwanda (all figures: BICC 1996, SIPRI 1997). In the industrialized countries, the resources that were used by high defense budgets are now being allocated to balance the state budgets and to counterbalance the social effects of economic globalization processes. In developing countries and in states with ongoing violent conflict, a peace dividend is less tangible. Many defense budgets still consume too much capital that would be better spent on economic incentives and social or infrastructural needs.

There is also debate on whether the official ending of nuclear deterrence among the superpowers has actually reduced the risk of nuclear warfare (Krause 1998). The risk of the proliferation of enriched plutonium and nuclear weapons technology as well as nuclear conflict escalations, possibly between Israel and Iraq, India and Pakistan or between North and South Korea, may be the world's greatest threat in the future. Yet, progress has been made in the fields of biological and chemical weapons reduction (1994 and 1997 UN treaties), the production, sale and possession of land mines has been restricted and the UN continues efforts to reduce the number of small weapons in conflict regions (UNIDIR 1995).

Internal conflicts and the privatization of violence

The most recent major change concerns the official end of the superpower rivalry in 1990. Between 1990 and the debacles of the United Nations blue-helmet missions in Somalia and in Bosnia-Herzegovina, there was a real euphoria about a new peaceful world order. This hope has definitively been disappointed. The revitalized

United Nations could not successfully fulfil its peace-enforcing mandates, as it was hoped by the world community. Within only a short period, this vacuum was filled by the US as the only remaining superpower that is still able and willing to intervene in armed conflicts. Nevertheless, the proficiency and efficiency of international and non-governmental conflict resolution organizations continues to grow especially in negotiable conflict situations. The peaceful transitions in Eastern Europe and in many parts of the former Soviet Union, the peaceful separation of Czechoslovakia, the ending of the conflicts in Guatemala, in El Salvador, in Nicaragua, in Mozambique and partially in Angola, the end of apartheid in South Africa, the independence of Namibia and Eritrea or the unification of divided Germany and Yemen could have been accomplished neither during the East–West conflict nor without the world community's effort to help the difficult conflict resolution and peace consolidation processes.

The trend away from international towards internal conflicts finds a continuation in what can be called 'privatization of violence'. For instance, in certain regions in today's Guatemala, the level of crime-related violence is exceeding the violence experienced during Guatemala's civil war. The issues in private violence do not directly concern state power, autonomy or other classic political issues. These groups are rather driven by criminal energy and an indiscriminate use of violence (Butterwegge 1997). Private violence appears in the forms of Mafia crime, drug trafficking, gang war, juvenile crime and large- and small-scale terrorism. The German writer Hans Magnus Enzensberger (1993) called this phenomenon 'molecular war'. The theory of weak states (Holsti 1996) tries to capture this phenomenon by stating that the absence of a strong state, especially in developing countries, allowed for the dissolution of social cohesion and promoted the privatization of violence. He calls them conflicts 'of the third kind'. Kaplan's 'chaos-theory' (1996) is headed in the same direction. The inclusion of this type of violence into political conflict research poses several problems: actors and their ambitions are difficult to grasp and define, the difference between political conflicts and criminal activity is diffuse, the avoidance and management of private violence poses great obstacles to conventional modes of political conflict resolution. There are no easy answers to these difficulties, and we suggest that it might be useful to re-discover theories on social and political change (Parsons 1961 and 1964, Eisenstadt 1964, Bendix 1971) and theories on revolutions (Gurr 1970) which were more prominent in the 1960s and 1970s.

Overview of major changes since 1945

Table 1.1 summarizes the areas of change which we believe to have or have had effects on the dynamics of political conflict. They can be grouped by

Table 1.1 Global changes and conflict patterns (+ denotes restraining effect on conflict behavior; − denotes aggravating effect on conflict behavior)

	Political	Military	Economic	Socio-cultural
Actor and actor-related level of analysis: concrete, material and manifest changes	• (−) quadrupling of number of states • (+) growth of IOs and NGOs • (+) increasing memberships in IOs and NGOs • (−) evolution of diverse subnational political actors (guerillas, liberation armies, terrorists, ethnic, religious or tribal groups *et al.*)	• (+) increased regulation on arms-production and arms-trade (Non-Proliferation Treaty, biological and chemical weapons conventions, convention on the ban on landmines etc.) • (−) proliferation of nuclear technology and material, small weapons etc. • (−) resurgence of private political actors • (−) privatization of violence	• (+) advance of multi- and transnational enterprises • (+) communication-technology revolution • (+) global networking	• (+) codification of human and civil rights standards • (+) codification and application of international law (tribunals) • (+) world opinion ('CNN-factor')

Structural level of analysis/ideology, strategy				
• (+) decline of power- and prestige politics • (+) decline of territorial expansionism • (+) advance of international and multilateral cooperative patterns (e.g. political regionalization) • (−) end of Cold War • (−) dissolution of communist bloc, • (+/−) expansion of Western liberalism (modernization) • (+) stabilization of new democratic regimes • (+) end of Cold War doctrines	• (+) end of superpowers' arms race • (+/−) end of nuclear deterrence • (+/−) decline of regional defense mechanisms except NATO and bilateral alliances, e.g. Japan-US)	• (+) global-ization of cash flows, trade, production and information • (+) economic regionalization (market integration) • (+) continuation of embedded liberalism (WTO)	• (+) advance of global village thinking ('Weltinnenpolitik', 'Gesellschaftswelt') • (+) de-ideologization • (+) post-modernism • (−) politicization of ethnic, religious and language differences • (−) increasing demands by minorities for self-determination • (−) advance of fundamentalism • (−) clash of civilizations? • (−) growth of population	

⇒ Towards a new conflict resolution culture?

⇒ New challenges for conflict theory and future conflict developments?

⇒ Consequences for conflict research?

political, military, economic and socio-cultural issues (columns) and by actor-driven and structure-related changes (rows). The aggravating and restraining effects on conflict behavior are marked by minus and plus respectively.

At the bottom of the table, the matrix points at three fields that are directly affected by the consequences from the global changes since 1945. Is there a new conflict resolution culture? How can existing theories explain conflict behavior and what do they tell us about future developments? Finally, what are the consequences for conflict research?

Towards a new conflict resolution culture?

Can the changes mentioned so far contribute to a new conflict resolution culture? Weighing the restraining against the aggravating factors as listed in Table 1.1, we came to the conclusion that overall the restraining forces on the causes and the development of conflicts are stronger than the aggravating factors. In particular, the constraining effects of international organizations on the foreign policy of states may lead to a decrease in violent conflicts and eventually to a new conflict resolution culture.

The empirical finding that the number of violent inter-state conflicts is decreasing can be related to a change in conflict-culture on the domestic level. How society conceptualizes conflict and violence is a scale to measure world trends towards a more civilized future (Vogt 1997:11). In this sense, peaceful conflict resolution as a holistic concept reaching from conflict prevention to peace consolidation is evolving as an overarching concept that is beginning to govern the international community in the post-Cold War era. In a world beyond the ideological East–West system conflict, international conflicts are perceived as, in principle, solvable by rational and creative problem-solving approaches. The creation of mutual interest constellations and the promotion of win–win solutions have been formulated at length by various negotiation theorists and have been applied to many peace processes in the 1990s. As a consequence of changes in the nature and perception of conflicts and their threat potential, modes of conflict resolution have been changing accordingly. It is not the conflictive constellation of values and belief systems that are solely in the center of the affected parties' attention and that must be resolved by all means – as suggested by Huntington (1993) – but 'only' their violent pursuit. Regardless of differing values, a common-interest-based approach toward win–win solutions and formula deals, such as 'land for peace', seem to be a promising approach for peaceful conflict resolution (Zartman 1985).[2]

Crisis management beyond traditional diplomacy

Conflict management can be performed by the conflicting parties themselves. However, the development of conflicts is also affected by external constellations. Therefore, we need to ask about the behavior of neighboring states, allies, and the superpowers toward the conflict, the disputed issues, and the parties involved. When did external parties intervene by military means? What are typical patterns of these conflicts that became internationalized through external military intervention? What strategies and instruments have been used in what kind of conflict situation? Were they effective or successful? Offers from third parties to meditate or arbitrate have been seen to increase over time (Bercovitch 1986). The focus of conflict research is shifting from the causes of war to negotiation efforts. The United Nations has extended its responsibilities from acute crisis management in its earlier decades to early warning and peace consolidation in the 1990s. Today, conflict management and conflict resolution programs attempt to embrace the entire horizon of a conflict from its beginning to its end. Has the academic emphasis on management techniques and problem-solving capabilities led to higher rates of peaceful conflict resolution than previously? KOSIMO traced mediation efforts of international third parties in conflicts and coded the forms of resolution and the political, military, and territorial outcomes of conflicts. Since our focus is on conflicts and not on mediation, we can only recommend, for example, Bercovitch's (1986) comprehensive empirical study of several hundred mediation attempts. However, our databank allows us to compare mediated and non-mediated conflicts and their respective regions, frequencies, intensities and durations, issues and actors.

The conflict cycle (Figure 1.1) illustrates a comprehensive management and resolution approach to conflicts. Each stage in the development from peace to war requires different management and resolution instruments. For instance, a cease-fire must be secured by peace-keeping forces, peace treaties need to be accompanied by peace-consolidating measures, latent conflicts need preventive action, a crisis calls for non-violent measures as provided by chapter VI of the United Nations Charter, violent crisis can be countered with deterrence, interventions and peace-enforcing measures under chapter VII of the UN Charter. Note that Figure 1.1 reflects only third-party instruments at the UN level. In reality, regional organizations, NGOs, churches and other societal and individual actors play an indispensable part in peace-keeping, peace-making and peace consolidation. In the identification of new challenges for the UN, former Secretary General Boutros Boutros-Ghali endorsed in his *Agenda for Peace* (1992) four measures: preventive diplomacy, peace-keeping, peace enforcement and peace consolidation. These proposals are also reflected in the conflict-cycle.

The current discussion in modernization theories about the so-called civilizing processes (*Zivilisationsprozesse*) can help us to place the changes discussed above in a historic context. Civilizing processes as envisioned by Norbert Elias (1976) and applied to conflict research by Dieter Senghaas (1995) are specific historical developments that have resulted in peaceful and reliable relations among people in a given society. Senghaas has identified

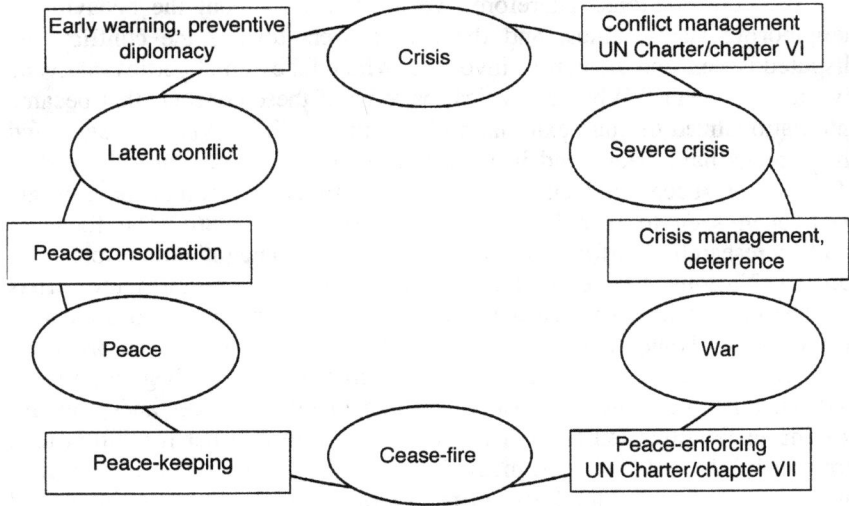

Figure 1.1 Cycle of conflict development with conflict management instruments.

six elements which he assumes to be essential for such reliable non-violent conflict management in modern societies, namely a state monopoly on violence, the rule of law, political participation, social welfare and security, emotional self-control (*Affektkontrolle*) and a constructive conflict culture. The individuals in modern societies would otherwise be forced to live in anarchy or in a Leviathan-type of authoritarianism. Such civilizing processes will, if at all, proceed from within states to the international level. According to Senghaas, we can observe civil structures today only within the relatively few liberal democracies that evolved from a specific European historical experience. In this sense, the advance of civilizing processes on the international level depends on the increase of the number of liberal democracies. Conversely, we assume that civilizing processes can also occur in the opposite direction. They can be a product of international arrangements that positively affect the foreign policies and internally induce changes in political state behavior. At least the empirical evidence suggests that there is a reverse pacifying and civilizing course, namely from the international arena into the internal affairs of states. This effect, as mentioned before, is caused by the growth and strength of global, regional and local, official and private international and transnational organizations, through the codification of human rights and international law standards, the establishment of several *ad hoc* tribunals and plans for a permanent tribunal, and finally by the influence of public opinion in a global media-village onto the foreign and internal policy decisions by governments.

Challenges to theories and conflict analysis

Having highlighted the changes on the global political map and, on this
basis, the chances for a new conflict resolution culture, we now turn to the
resulting challenges for conflict theory. To this end, we will selectively
discuss prominent propositions in current conflict theories and relate their
findings and scenarios to current and possibly future conflict patterns. The
test of theories with data of the KOSIMO project will be provided in later
chapters. The selected theories are discussed with respect to their
propositions for and their relevance to trends and patterns of political
conflicts.

Democratic peace

The theory of democratic peace states that democracies are more peaceful
than authoritarian states and that democracies do not fight each other. In the
words of Immanuel Kant, who first postulated this theorem: 'The republican
constitution (which is based on the principle of the freedom and the
dependence of all upon a single common legislation and the equality of all
citizens) has the prospect of the desired purpose, namely eternal peace'
(Kant 1948: 250–1). And: 'If the consent of the citizens is required in order
to decide whether there should be war or not, nothing is more natural than
that those who would have to decide to undergo all the deprivations of war
will very much hesitate to start such an evil game' (Kant 1948: 251). This
theory is clearly related to the idea of direct democracy, an idea Kant had
taken from Rousseau. The empirical fact that democracies went to war
throughout the twentieth century does not necessarily contradict this theory,
since none of these democratic states possesses a referendum democracy,
and the explicit consent of every individual citizen is not asked for. Those
democracies that have been going to war after 1945, the US, UK and France,
are all members of the Security Council. As such, they claim global interests,
and they cannot directly be held responsible by the world community for acts
of violence due to the veto power.

Nevertheless, a prominent empirical conflict researcher of the twentieth
century concluded optimistically: 'Summarizing we see that absolutistic
states with geographically and functionally centralized governments under
an autocratic leadership are most likely resorting to war, while constituted
states with geographically and functionally federalized governments under a
democratic leadership probably are the most peaceful states' (Wright 1969:
169).

States as aggressors

States continue to be the principal actors in international politics, and the wars
which have occurred since 1945 have been initiated by the governments of

these states. With reference to Tolstoy, Krippendorff takes an extreme position by regarding any state organization as inherently driven to war: 'As long as governments (states) and armed forces (military) exist, there is no end to the arms buildup and war.' In other words, any state, regardless of its constitutional form, is equivalent to military power, military equals arms buildup, and arms buildup ends in war. The state is understood as a result of power struggles and cannot overcome its origins. Whereas war expeditions were once the origin of the state, today the state is the origin of war (Krippendorff 1985). This disregards the fact that in history violent struggles also occurred in pre-state societies, and that even today we still find some peaceful states. People generally tend to be more peaceful than their governments. Therefore, constitutions which reflect the will of the people in the formulation of (foreign) policy should restrain the states from the use of force.

Weak states theory

Holsti's weak state theory (1996) claims that violence occurs as a result or parallel to the weakening or collapse of states especially in the developing world. Weak states are defined as states with weak vertical and horizontal legitimacy and a personalized political culture. Hence, they do not have a truly effective rule and the polity is fragmented into numerous ethnic, religious or regional communities with no binding common identities. These states, according to Holsti, are faced with a state-strength dilemma. In their effort to gain strength they generate resistance which weakens the state. In order to overcome this weakness they resort to coercive measures which, as a reaction, undermines their right to rule. Their discriminatory policy against local power centers and communal, ethnic or religious groups destroys horizontal legitimacy. Hence, by their very policy they undermine their vertical and horizontal legitimacy. Anarchy may be the result of such a policy or even the dissolution of the polity.

'Cold War Peace' (1947–1989)

The 50 years since the end of the Second World War can be divided into a number of periods. We focus here on two phases that show distinct patterns of conflict structures and conflict behavior by certain states, namely the Cold War era and the post-Cold War period. The years 1945 to 1947 mark the end of the Second World War, the end of Allied cooperation, and the beginning of the Cold War. During this short period of time, the global positions of the United States and the Soviet Union shifted from that of allied powers against fascism to nuclear enemies in an ideological struggle that was to last for over forty years. The realistic school of political thought holds the idea that the bipolarity during the Cold War stabilized the overall international system and prevented the outbreak of a 'hot war'. In the words of its most outspoken proponent, Mearsheimer: 'One can establish that peace in Europe during the

Cold War has resulted from bipolarity, the approximate military balance between the superpowers, and the presence of large numbers of nuclear weapons on both sides ...' (Mearsheimer 1990: 13).

New world disorder?

The years since the end of the Cold War have seen global political, ideological, and economic transformations. In international relations theory this new period is regarded as unstable, unpredictable, chaotic, and turbulent. Conflict researchers can identify many new types of conflicts, conflict management facilities and resolution capabilities. The Yugoslav President Milosevic, for example, initiated domestic conflicts on the periphery of Europe of a sort which had not been imaginable in Europe during the East–West conflict. The political exploitation of ethnic and religious cleavages have also driven many African states to the brink of anarchy and to the frequent use of state violence. Conflicts over access to resources are on the rise. Corruption, drug trafficking, the growing gap between rich and poor and international crime syndicates paralyze to a great extent continued political and economic development in the Third World. In the words of Mearsheimer (1990, 6): 'I argue that the prospects for major crises and war in Europe are likely to increase markedly if the Cold War ends. ...'

Issues-related conceptions

Conflicts can be analyzed according to tangible interests, issues, values and objectives. We consider that the objectives in a dispute co-determine the course of a conflict as much as the domestic and external conditions and configuration of the actors. Certain issues in conflicts show distinct patterns of development and resolution, i.e. conflicts about economic goods are easier to manage, e.g. by division or coalition techniques, and, therefore, they are in most cases less violent than conflicts over ideology and values (Fisher and Ury 1981).

Theories on environment and security (wars over resources)

Authors on environmental security state that in the future, scarce and degraded resources may become a new source of conflict (Bächler *et al.* 1996). The authors differentiate between different types of resources; e.g., resources needed by the industrialized world for production or resources needed for subsistence in the rural areas of developing countries. Although the pessimistic scenarios of coming water wars and fighting for arable land arouse public attention, there is still little empirical evidence that supports this outlook (Homer-Dixon 1994, Barandat 1997, Gleditsch 1998). It has been said that struggles over increasingly scarce resources may become predominant types of conflicts in the future (Bächler *et al.* 1996). In fragile regions, such as the Aral Sea, parts of the Middle East, the Northern African

Sahel and elsewhere, quarrels over access to and the distribution of water and fertile land may arise and cause violence. Environmental degradation may become an additional factor that fuels already existing tribal or ethnic political feuds and rivalries. The control over resources for energy and industrial production such as oil, gas, minerals and metals may be contested by neighboring states or subnational groups. Foreign, private, governmental or World Bank investments may affect the course of events in environmentally degraded or contested areas. The civil war in the former Zaire in 1996 exemplifies the way in which the control of resources can serve as both the cause and the catalyst of conflict in an authoritarian political setting with significant economic interests from abroad.

An interesting conceptual approach is pursued by the Scientific Council on Global Change (WBGU 1996) sponsored by the German government. Introducing the concept of 'syndromes', it tries to grasp the various feedback effects on and conflictive interrelations among local, regional, and international groups caused by environmental degradation or depletion. In its extreme form environmental degradation may cause already existing ethnopolitical tensions to turn violent. We assume that neither ethnicity nor environmental degradation by itself constitutes a cause of conflict, but rather the syndrome-like aggregation of various aspects of degradation and discrimination in a political environment with little capacity for the channeling and resolution of conflict.

Clash of civilizations?

The once popular thesis of a 'clash of civilizations' by Samuel Huntington (1996) suggests that classic wars among states belong to the past; instead clashes of civilizations will determine the future. This is certainly an appealing thesis for pessimistic contemporaries, but theoretical arguments and empirical evidence support only parts of Huntington's thesis. The well-known thesis of Samuel Huntington (1996) is often quoted that wars between different civilizations will become a dominant type of violent conflict in the future. Yet, civilizations will become the main pattern of coherence as well as of disintegration and conflict. Civilizations with cultural affinities will cooperate whereas cultural differences among civilizations will lead to conflict. Huntington lists seven civilizations among which these clashes may take place, namely the Japanese, Hindu, Islamic, Western, Latin, African, and Chinese civilizations.

Ethnopolitical conflicts

One can observe on a global scale the decline of 'classical' types of international violent conflicts and the spread of domestic violent conflicts, either between a state or government and its internal opposition groups or among internal groups when the central power is too weak. Empirical conflict research indicates that since the early 1970s more violent conflicts have been fought between a state and internal groups than between two sovereign states. Gurr (1993) has extensively analyzed the ethnopolitical features of domestic conflicts, and his research has been integrated in KOSIMO where the parties fit our definition of conflict, i.e. at least one party in a conflict must be the state or government. The findings of qualitative and comparative empirical studies suggest a net structure of various intertwined causes and effects rather than linear phase developments.

Institutionalism

Since the end of the Second World War a continuously rising number of regional and universal, non-governmental and governmental organizations have been founded. How efficient are these organizations in preventing violent conflicts? What are the capacities of these organizations in conflict management when the conflict escalates into violence? Do the organizations reach their goals, i.e., preserving peace and preventing war? Do these institutions, especially the United Nations, by their mere existence discourage states from the use of violence? Both the theory of neo-institutionalism (Keck 1993) in international relations and the international regime theory (Krasner 1987, Rittberger 1995) answer this question in the affirmative. The peaceful relations among countries in Western Europe and their increasing political and economic integration in the European Union is often quoted as a confirmation of this theoretical approach.

Theories of the negotiated peace

What can we say about the various forms of conflict resolution and conflict outcomes? How and why did a conflict come to an end? What kind of mediation strategy was successful? Did the end of war also become the end of the conflict? What were the territorial, military, and political outcomes? What do we learn from cases of successful conflict resolution, and what from cases of failure? Which conflicts have the potential of being resolved through negotiations and which not? How are conflict developments and negotiation processes linked? Do institutions or committees matter for the peaceful solution of conflicts? And, what is the role of justice in negotiations?

The theory of the negotiated peace assumes that the end to a quarrel that was reached by negotiations without pressure and by consent of all parties involved and of all disputed issues without reservations has a greater chance of durability than non-consensual resolutions. In other words, the level of consent is decisive for the durability of an agreement; the greater the consent, the more durable is the solution. If these conditions are not fulfilled, then the war may end while the conflict goes on.

Future conflict developments

After the end of the East–West conflict, new theories on the causes of conflict appeared in the literature. Hans Magnus Enzensberger (1993) states that violence is not bound to ideology, culture or the state. For him, violence can occur independently from the economic and political situation anywhere in the world in densely populated regions, in suburbs and in zones with high rates of unemployment. 'Privatization of violence' is one expression of this phenomenon where private, public and political motives for violence are mixing. Francis Fukuyama (1994) states that at 'the end of history' conflicts between the capitalist democracies of the West and the non-democratic world will determine the future. In addition, the economic competition among the industrialized countries will become fiercer. Fukuyama's assumption is likely to be of little use as a thesis for the occurrence of wars at the end of the twentieth century, since economic North–South dependencies have never escalated into violent conflicts between an industrialized and a developing state, whereas the relations among democracies in economic competition can be explained more meaningfully by the 'democratic peace theorem'. Another hypothesis by Robert Kaplan (1996) may be called 'chaos theory'; it states that the breakdown of social institutions and political authorities will lead to 'small wars' among gangs and subgroups. This theory resembles the hypothesis of molecular wars by Enzensberger. While the thesis sounds convincing at first sight, it is difficult to validate on the empirical level. Future conflicts may also be caused by the proliferation of nuclear, biological and chemical technology and material. This danger certainly exists when rivaling local or regional powers eclipse control by the world community. Ethnic, religious, and cultural cleavages – enriching as they are in a non-political context – have been instrumentalized in many conflicts by politicians for their personal or their parties' ambitions and have thus become the basis for violent conflicts.

In summary, on our selective survey for future conflict potentials, we can already find existing sources of conflict that can be assumed to occur in the future. These are the risks stemming from the proliferation of weapons of mass destruction and the instrumentalization of ethnic, religious and cultural differences among peoples. Fierce competition over access to the resources for industrial production will continue to be a source of conflict in the future – although this type is unlikely to escalate into violent North–South or North–OPEC conflicts. We can expect new cleavages and sources of conflicts from tensions and clashes of civilizations and from weak and collapsing states. Many governments and societies will increasingly face violence and unidentifiable activism by private, mostly younger groups and gangs on the sub-national level. Environmental degradation will become an underlying factor to social conflicts over access to resources needed for subsistence in many developing countries. These observations underline our argument for the widening of perspectives in conflict research. We need to add non-state actors and unorganized groups as well as new issues and cleavages to the research agenda.

Consequences for conflict research

Keeping the above-mentioned changes and the theses for future conflicts in mind, what can be the contribution of quantitative empirical conflict analysis to our understanding of the world of political conflicts? One motive for writing this book is to show that the general perception of conflicts and changes in conflict trends depend on weighted information. Mass media focus on very few selected conflicts. Thus, Somalia, Rwanda and Yugoslavia have become new synonyms for extremely violent conflict; yet what do we know about other violent conflicts in the world? Are ethnic or religious conflicts the dominant type of conflict? How about wars over resources, borders, water and arable land? Mass media coverage of conflicts often creates the impression that violent internal conflicts are phenomena that have appeared only with and after the end of the East–West conflict. In contrast to this assumption, our findings suggest that internal conflicts have been on the rise since the early 1970s. This example nicely illustrates that it is the normative assumption and general intention of quantitative empirical analysis in general and this book in particular to suggest findings that correct and complete our perceptions of ever-changing global conflict patterns.

Quantitative empirical analysis in the social sciences is sometimes under attack from case study specialists and regional experts who deny the comparability of quantitative data of political and social phenomena such as political conflicts. Figuratively speaking and with simplification, the argument states that one must not compare apples and oranges. Yet both belong to the category of fruit and as such can be compared with vegetables. Quantitative empirical analysis needs a certain degree of abstraction from the reality of political conflicts. But did quantitative conflict researchers react adequately to the above described changes in the global political system? Especially in the late 1980s several shortcomings of existing conflict databanks became obvious. Three types of new data are necessary in order to tackle the changes on the global map and their effects on political conflicts.

Non-violent conflicts

The major shortcoming is a lack of *data on non-violent conflicts*; most available information concentrates on violent conflicts, i.e. wars. Yet, many potentially violent conflicts never escalate into violent and military conflicts. In our view, the results of the empirical gathering and analysis of exclusively violent conflicts are not useful when examining global trends in conflicts and in violence in general. Empirical inquiry into the causes of wars that relies on data that include only wars must lead to limited, one-dimensional answers. In order to build stable structures for reliable and peaceful conflict resolution, the inquiry into the 'causes of peace' is as important as the inquiry into the 'causes of war' (Matthies 1996). In this line of thinking, war-databanks should function only as a control-sample to the group of all potentially violent conflicts.

From international to domestic conflicts

A second reason for a new databank was the lack of information on domestic conflicts; until the 1970s international conflicts dominated both the political arena and the research agenda. Since then, there has been a shift from international to domestic conflicts. A commonly cited explanation is that many states have failed in the nation-building process, and increasingly politicized subnational groups strive for more autonomy and self-determination.

Non-state actors

Thirdly, associated with the shift from international to domestic conflicts, there has been a significant trend from states serving as dominant actors in conflicts to non-state actors and international organizations serving as parties or disputants in conflicts. The claim for minority rights, for cultural or religious self-determination brought non-state actors like liberation movements, minority groupings or religious groups onto the political stage.

Over the past 50 years we can observe conflicts at three levels. From 1945 until the late 1960s international conflicts among sovereign states dominated international relations. Thereafter, conflicts over national power positions and ethnic, religious or regional issues became more frequent than genuinely international conflicts. In the 1990s subnational conflicts have emerged as a new type; these conflicts appear as local or regional upheavals and strife, war lordism, gang war, drug-related violence, organized crime, 'taxi wars' and 'molecular wars' (Enzensberger 1993). All these manifestations of violent conflicts signify a trend toward the re-privatization of violence.

The progression from international to national and subnational conflicts corresponds to a system of nation-states in an anarchic setting, interdependence of states and, in our days, a new focus on societal and local perspectives within a globalizing world system (*Gesellschaftswelt*). While the present book focuses on the first and second phase, i.e. international and national conflicts, the third phase should become the topic of systematic quantitative and qualitative research in the future.

2 Methodology

Quantitative research

In the study of conflicts we can discern two main strategies: the genetic-historical case study and the generalization via hypotheses, models and theories. They can be labeled monographic or nomothetic, and thus be related to the traditionally different communities of science, the Humanities and the Natural Sciences. Though there is no longer any sharp differentiation between these two, the scientists of the respective communities still evaluate problems according to the scales of their field. The degree of satisfaction with the results of an inquiry differs correspondingly. The descriptive enumeration of the frequency of certain aspects of a conflict can stand as a result for itself, when the question is directed to this end. When the question is directed to an explanation of the observed frequencies, we have to argue with hypothetical or theoretical statements. In varying degrees, the four forms of empirical research (description, formulation of hypotheses, testing of theories and prediction) pay respect to the needs of each community. Still, in the context of the overall interest in results, they must be judged and valued as equal. This type of empirical inquiry excludes and denies the comprehension of such facts and intentions that cannot be reduced to operational quantities, and thus, cannot be verified.

Definitions

What are conflicts?

The simplest, but most difficult problem in empirical conflict research is to distinguish between conflict and non-conflict. When does a conflict begin? When does it end? Do states, and for that matter does mankind, interact without conflicts? Must we assume society to be inherently conflictual, as the Hobbesian tradition maintains? Is conflict the driving force for social development? (Dahrendorf 1958). In the study of conflicts, it is the very word 'conflict' that needs to be explained. Though the term has many meanings and dimensions, it always seems to refer to one specific event that has happened and that needs to be explained through understanding. The essence and meaning of conflicts usually become apparent in a confrontation, an opposition, a contradiction or an exclusiveness. As such, conflicts occur on all societal levels, within an individual, in a family or among political groups. The political theoretician Carl Schmitt (1932) has driven this definition to the extreme when he stated that the polarized and radical friend–foe alternative was the essence of politics. Hobbes was equally radical when he saw war as a normalcy and peace as an exception. Contemporary authors are less radical. Luhmann defines conflict as a 'contradiction' (*Widerspruch*) and Czempiel understands conflict as a 'positional difference'.

Another approach to 'conflict' is the focus on opposing interests. 'Interest is where there is opposition' says Hegel in his philosophy of history. Vice versa, it is possible to say that interest is, first of all, generated through opposites. And, as Holsti (1983: 273) adds, these interests must be threatened. Empathy and the recognition and analysis of the intensions of the 'other' are the means to comprehend a conflict.

It is possible to emphasize the disadvantages, e.g. the costs and victims of a conflict, and take the degree of damage and suffering as a criterion for different stages of conflicts. War is associated with the collective use of military force; conflicts with less intensity are often called latent conflicts or crises. The number of casualties is obviously a defining criterion for a war. Still, we cannot explain or comprehend wars by looking only at its material and human costs; we must also look at the causes of wars and the issues in dispute, e.g. territorial conflicts, nationality conflicts or power conflicts. Another way to give meaning to the term 'conflict' is to look at the instruments that the actors are using to escalate, to contain or to resolve a conflict. A definition of 'conflict' also must take into account subjective evaluations and strategic intentions. Three evaluations can be discerned. First, a conflict can be perceived as negative in nature, as something that has to be overcome in order to reach a state of harmony; second, the existence of a conflict can be acknowledged as a social fact, and the participants look for a solution by negotiations, agreements and consensus; third, a conflict can be regarded as unavoidable and it has to be settled 'by all means'. Structural or configurational theories understand conflicts as the discrepancies in the position of actors. Actor-oriented theories concentrate on perceptions of such discrepancies and how they are transformed into action.

We base our analysis on the following assumptions:

- Conflicts result from discrepancies in the position of participants over certain interests or values and they must refer to the same object.
- Such discrepancies or incompatibilities must be recognized or perceived by political actors and put into the political arena.
- Then – and only then – diverting interests are transformed into political issues and, when pushed by one or the other actor, conflicts become manifest.

- Whether incompatible interests lead to crises or more severe consequences depends on the internal and external conditions (support or pressure), the perceptions and actions of actors and the established rules for conflict channeling.

Therefore, we define conflict:

> as the clashing of overlapping interests (positional differences) around national values and issues (independence, self-determination, borders and territory, access to or distribution of domestic or international power); the conflict has to be of some duration and magnitude between at least two parties (states, groups of states, organizations or organized groups) that are determined to pursue their interests and win their case. At least one party is the organized state. Possible instruments used in the course of a conflict are negotiations, authoritative decisions, threat, pressure, passive or active withdrawals, or the use of physical violence and war.

This definition acknowledges the conditions for the emergence of conflicts, i.e. the opposition of interests around certain values or issues, as well as the participating actors and their instruments. As was illustrated in Figure P.1, many databanks that contain only violent conflicts miss the vast majority of all observable cases of conflict. Since conflicts are an inherent feature of societies and in international relations, they occur in peaceful as well as in tense or war-torn times. Underlying our definition of conflict, we assume that it is not the conflict *per se* that creates violence and war, but the poor, ineffective or purposeful handling or mishandling of conflictive constellations of interests by the actors.

As discussed above, conflicts can be grouped according to various criteria. In our project, we are using the following distinctions:

- Depending on who initiates the conflict and who is affected, we can differentiate between aggressive, defensive or preventive conflict behavior.
- A conflict can be called an objective or subjective conflict depending on the existence of a concrete or perceived issue in dispute.
- In terms of the degree of coercion, we can distinguish between latent conflicts, crises, severe crises, and war; the latter two are violent and the former two non-violent conflicts.
- In terms of the geopolitical range and level of analysis, we can distinguish between national/domestic and international/regional conflicts.
- In terms of the issues, we can distinguish between boundary conflicts, territorial disputes, minority conflicts, struggles for autonomy and independence, ideological conflicts, domestic and international power conflicts and conflicts over resources.

- In terms of the parties involved, we can distinguish bilateral from multilateral conflicts, and mediated and non-mediated conflicts.

Thus, we operationalize the terms 'internal' and 'international' from the participants' perspective on different levels of analysis with the following distinctions.

Level of analysis

Internal conflict   Internal conflicts are disputes in which, in general, a non-governmental opposition group or movement challenges the government. The disputed issues must be related to central state or government powers and functions. Internal conflicts are carried out with or without little political or economic help from an external power. When external powers are actively engaged in the conflict with diplomatic, economic or logistical instruments short of a military intervention we call the conflict, for analytical purposes, an internal conflict with external influence.

Internationalized conflict   The term 'internationalized conflict' remains blurred and has not been coded explicitly in the KOSIMO project. An internal conflict can reach international dimensions under the following conditions:

- the conflict escalates with help of foreign weapon imports
- one party is politically and diplomatically supported by a foreign power
- the issues of the conflict become the cause for dispute in another country
- a foreign power intervenes with military action; the foreign power can be a neighboring state, a regional power or an internationally recognized greater power.

The degree of internationalization of a conflict can be measured by the number of intervening powers and the instruments with which they support the parties. When an external power intervenes with troops in another country, this conflict can be called an internationalized violent conflict. Weapon sales or political and logistic support by an external power to one party do not necessarily qualify the conflict as an internationalized conflict.

International conflict   In international or inter-state conflicts, two states must clearly oppose each other over a substantial issue. Cases in which a formerly non-governmental movement, i.e. a national independence movement, has reached sovereignty in the course of the conflict are also counted as international conflicts.

Aggregate status of conflict (intensity)

According to the intensity of the encounters between the conflicting parties, we differentiate between latent conflict, crisis, severe crisis and war; latent conflicts and crises are grouped together as non-violent conflicts, severe conflicts and war are grouped as violent conflicts.

Peace   Similar to 'war', the term 'peace' in everyday language is associated with a variety of intentional connotations. Peace can be the objective of military alliances, it can be the object of the Nobel prize or the name of a popular movement. The saying 'deceptive peace' points at an escalating, but still latent, tension-loaded situation; 'clouds on the horizon' indicate a coming crisis. In his introduction to *Perpetual Peace*, Kant notes that this title came from the sign of a Dutch inn that depicted a cemetery. A cemetery is a fenced-in space, a peaceful place and it is associated with tranquility ('Friedhofsruhe'). Since it is a place for the deceased, there is a close association of peace and its fulfillment in eternity (biblical understanding). 'In a cemetery, peace is associated with death and rest in tranquility; in a home peace is identified with rest at home and silence, with silently giving-in' (Pasierbsky 1983: 13).

The historic etymology associates peace with the *Pax Romana* as a cosmic order; and the Gothic word 'fri' with a state of friendship, forbearance and a type of social order. In Augustine's days and in the Christian Middle Ages the Christian meaning of peace was identified with justice (*pax et iustitia*). The age of enlightenment eventually adopted this linkage. A peace order is a legal order (*pactum pacis*). Kant and Fichte connect an internally legal order with externally peaceful conduct. The age of economic liberalism and political enlightenment associates peace with a certain economic order, namely free trade of politically free people. The Congrès des amis de la paix universelle, Paris 1849, stated: 'L'économie politique est la science par excellence de la paix'. Clausewitz's understanding of peace is a deduction of the transition from war to peace. Peace comes after the defeat of the armies, the occupation of the enemy's territory and his capitulation. Without the decisive and successful conclusion of a war, there is no peace. A state of peace presupposes the concluded objectives of war. In other words, peace is the recognition of the status quo without further demands. The formulation 'peace is the absence of war', derived from this school of thought.

The school of critical peace research was less than satisfied with this definition. Johan Galtung (1968: 520) says: 'Peace is a state within a system of larger groups of people, especially nations, without any organized, collective threat or use of force.' Ernst-Otto Czempiel (1981: 33; 1986: 35) defines it thus: 'Peace is a process (*Prozeßmuster*) in the international system that is characterized by a decrease in violence and an increase in justice.' The consequence of this basic definition is: When you want peace (*si vis pacem*), change all societal conditions that so far have led to war. A positive peace as 'a state of brotherly harmony of all people' (Erich Fromm) is added to the former, negative definition ('absence of war'). Senghaas (1994) emphasizes the procedural aspect of peace by saying that states or nations that have found conventional or institutionalized rules for day-to-day conflict-behavior will in general resolve their conflicts in a 'civilized' manner, i.e. peacefully.

Our operational definition reduces the state of peace to the observable behavior:

> For the internal and external realm of nations, peace is a situation that remains unquestioned (and far from a violent change) for both, all organized groups within that nation and all members of the state-system.

This definition contains an inner and outer component; internal peace is given when the relevant social groups are satisfied with their political status and observe their constitutional rights and duties. External peace depends on the observance of international law and other treaties that have to be accepted without a *reservatio mentalis* (Carl von Clausewitz) or secret clauses (Immanuel Kant). National and/or international communities must support this system with high consensus; thus, it is a highly legitimized state. Peace as a political state of affairs can be identified within a state, when relevant groups in a society are satisfied with their political status and agree with their constitutional rights and duties. Peace in the international relations among states is attained when conventions of international law or other international treaties are being respected and recognized without *reservatio mentalis*, that is without further demands and without hidden reservations.

Latent conflict   Latent conflict is a stage in the development of a conflict where one or more groups, parties or states question existing values, issues or objectives that have a national relevance. Latent conflicts must carry some identifiable and observable signs in order to be recognized as such. The positional differences and the clashing interests in a latent conflict must be articulated as demands or claims. The other party must be aware of these demands. The main feature of latent conflicts is that the positional differences do not top the political agenda. A conflict can remain latent for long periods of time and get comparatively little public attention. When one party starts pushing for new negotiations, the conflict can intensify for a certain time before it falls back to its latent status.

Crisis   A crisis is defined as tensions that are expressed by means that are below the threshold of violence. Tense relations between the parties can reach a turning-point from where the use of force may become more likely. At this point, many decisions are based on incomplete information and made under time-pressure. Economic sanctions, for example, are a means by which a latent conflict can be turned into a crisis. A crisis is – like a latent conflict –

at all stages carried out by non-violent means. In a crisis, the accused or confronted party or parties react in a permissive, enduring or de-escalating manner, and they do not (yet) resort to violence.

Severe crisis A severe crisis is defined as a state of high tension between two parties; they either threaten to resort to the use of force or they actually use physical or military force sporadically. The use of force is rather spontaneous and cannot be compared with a collectively organized use of force. Military threats include the mobilization of regular troops, guerrillas or liberation-armies, the implementation of economic or military sanctions, the partial occupation of land, border territories or security zones and the threat or declaration of war. Different from the category 'war', the use of force in severe crisis must be limited to occasional border incidents, sea or land blockades, partial territorial occupations, brief arrests of people, e.g. opposition leaders, or the confiscation of goods.

War In everyday language, the term 'war' has a wide meaning; this must be differentiated from the narrower, scientific use of the word. For example, the 'chicken war' between the US and the EEC in the 1960s, of course, concluded without casualties, and the 'Cold War' did not end in a direct physical confrontation of the super-powers. Like most political terms, the definition of 'war' and, likewise, the definition of 'peace' is bound to a certain guiding interest; thus, it is connected with what we think of as just or unjust in history.

In the Old Testament war is retaliation, an eye for an eye, a tooth for a tooth. Clausewitz understands war as a rational strategy and Krippendorff as the result of unreasonable state-policies; Glucksmann holds the position that war is a result of the 'power of ignorance' (*Macht der Dummheit*). Kant defines war as an anarchic state and postulates a republican order. The power politics of the nineteenth century regarded war as a 'healthy' event, a 'sobering thunderstorm' and added an almost religious connotation; Beaufre's argument is similar when he defines war as a power-test where one party tries to make the other submit to it. Hans Speier emphasizes the rivalry for a political order: war is an unordered state in which a new and peaceful order, though again not a completely just one, is pursued by means of force. 'War begins in the minds of the people', 'war begins in their bellies': these are just a few examples to illustrate the variety of meanings given to war.

There are also many criteria that have been used to typologize the phenomenon 'war'. For example, a war by proxy that is fought by two minor powers that represent greater power interests. Another type is civil war, where government troops are involved in the fighting among different citizens' militias. There are 'genuine' wars, where one country invades and occupies parts of the other state. Typical for the decolonization period were liberation or guerrilla wars, where armed members of a minority group or a colonized people fight central government troops in the peripheries of a country or society. Again, these categories of war are ideal types, and they occur in more or less mixed forms. In a more formal way, wars can be grouped by:

- the initiator or the affected (offensive or defensive wars)
- morality (just or unjust wars)
- magnitude (total or limited wars)
- the type of armaments (conventional or nuclear war)
- the values and issues in dispute (colonial or imperial wars, border wars, religious wars)
- the threat of use of force or actual use of force (cold war vs. 'hot' war)
- the parties' position (civil war, internationalized or international war)

There is no commonly accepted definition of war in the field of empirical conflict research. The study of the causes of war reduces the term to operational quantities: 'War is a conflict among political groups, especially sovereign states, carried on by armed forces of considerable magnitude and for a considerable period of time' (Wright 1960: 483). Singer and Small (1972: 30) define war as the: 'participation of states with at least 1,000 troops in battle-related activity with at least 1,000 battle-related deaths.'

For operational reasons, we define war as a form of violent mass-conflict that is characterized by:

- the fighting of at least two opponents with organized, regular military forces
- the fighting is not sporadic; it lasts for a considerable period of time
- the fighting is intense, that is, it leads to victims and destruction. The number of victims and the scope of destruction is high.

Sporadic upheavals, revolts or terrorist attacks that are not supported by a recognizable segment in the population are not listed in the KOSIMO set. For example, the conflicts caused by the Irish or Basque separatist terrorist organizations, IRA and ETA, are included, while the attacks from isolated left-wing terrorist groups in Germany, Italy or Japan ('Red Army Factions' or 'Red Brigades') are excluded.

Non-violent conflict   The categories 'latent conflict' and 'crisis' put together are grouped as non-violent conflicts. This term is essential in order to investigate the causes of conflicts which have been resolved without the use of force and to separate them from violent conflicts.

Violent conflict   In political theory Thomas Hobbes and John Locke were the first to distinguish between consensual power and coercive power. They meant the ending of divergence by means of conviction or coercion. Parties with conflicting interests may try to resolve latent conflicts and crises peacefully through bi- or multilateral negotiations; parties in severe crises have resorted to coercive measures such as pressure, threats and military operations. The risk of imminent hostilities must have been perceived by at least one party.

A dynamic phase-model

The very basic and crude form of our dynamic conflict model is shown in Figure 2.1. Each conflict passes through three phases, initiation, escalation and resolution.

The initiation phase is characterized by influencing factors and the reactions by the government or the internal group. Specific demands are formulated by domestic or external parties and directed at the government or the regime in power. The main parameters for the decision-making of a government in such a conflict situation are:

- domestic pressure (or support)
- external, i.e. international pressure (or support)
- the perception of its own interests or policy options
- the action or reaction according to this perception.

There are different sets of factors at the origin of each conflict; they may be structural or configurational, i.e. demographic, economic, military, geographic, domestic or international factors. Structural factors become relevant in political theories in the Marxist tradition, i.e. imperialist theories, dependence theories, or structural violence theories. Other factors are action-oriented. These can be behavioral attributes and attitudes of actors like the type or skills of actors, perceptions or misperceptions, capabilities or decision-making capacities. These factors are central to action-oriented theories like Gurr's deprivation theory, Dollard's frustration-aggression theory, Lasswell's substitution theory, Russett's misperception theory, Hermle's mobilization theory or Morgenthau's power theory. Finally, there

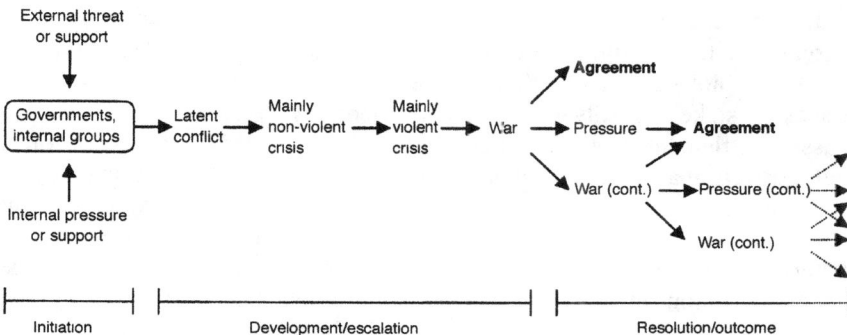

Figure 2.1 Dynamic phase model.

Time

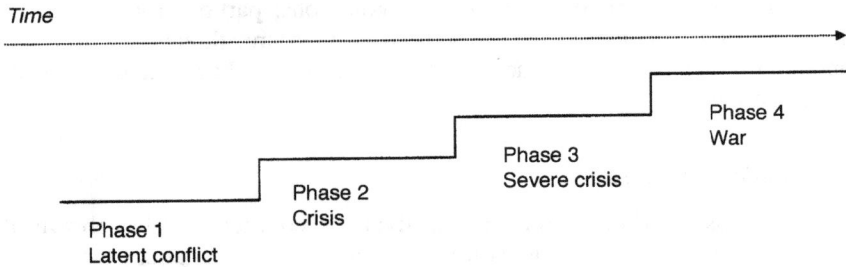

Figure 2.2 Dynamic model of conflict intensity.

are sets of factors for the interaction between structures and actors, i.e. decision-theories or system theories.

For two reasons, the actor level and the institutional framework are central to our analysis. On the one hand, there is only limited explanatory power in global structural theories, on the other hand, management techniques, diplomatic skills or the psychology of actors are notions too vague to lead to more general conclusions.[1] In the escalation phase we assume a regular pattern in the sequence of events of a conflictual interaction, namely latent conflicts, crises on a relatively low level of conflictual behavior, high-intensity crises and violent conflicts, some of which are wars in the classical definition of the term.

Conflicts do not necessarily need to pass through all these stages. A latent conflict like the discussion on border demarcations or the unification of divided countries may remain at that stage for a certain period of time or be terminated by an agreement between the conflicting parties before escalating toward a more severe phase. The same is true for crises like the Cuban Missile Crisis, an example which demonstrates that the worst case did not occur. This dynamic-phase approach makes it possible to discern those conflicts that remain non-violent from those with a high potential for violent escalation. The phase concept can also identify successful conflict-management activities and modes of conflict resolution on a time-scale.

In the resolution phase the conflict can lead to either a consensual agreement, to an imposed outcome or continued violence. The latter two outcomes, not being a solution, will end up in further quarreling until the issues at stake are solved by an agreement, by voluntary withdrawal or passive settlement. Non-violent conflicts are not decided by the use of force, but are terminated either by agreement, threat (imposed termination) or withdrawal. Such a termination does not necessarily lead to a political solution in which case all parties involved voluntarily agree to the decision without reservations. Only a consensual decision to resolve a conflict can be called a solution. In all other cases, the conflict may have lost its intensity or it may have been ended by force, threat, (voluntary) withdrawal or passive settlement.

Identifying conflict (operationalization)

For the purpose of this project, we have developed inclusion and exclusion criteria for conflicts. The most important criterion for defining a conflict is the set of parties involved. For inclusion, at least one party must be a state or government. The other parties may be either states, governments or a non-governmental opposition movement. To qualify in KOSIMO as a non-governmental group or movement, it must have a broad base and it must be able to 'move the masses'. As mentioned before, terrorist groups such as the Red Army Factions in many European countries and Japan do not qualify in KOSIMO as conflict parties because of their lack of broad public support. On the other hand, opposition movements such as the IRA in Northern Ireland and ETA in the Basque region of northern Spain do qualify because of their broad support in large segments of the population. However, these conflicts do not qualify as wars despite the destructive use of force. Most non-governmental groups that are included in the KOSIMO databank are minorities' organizations seeking – violently or peacefully – autonomy, separation, or national independence.

A conflict must involve national issues such as statehood, territorial boundaries, people, and government. These criteria exclude such conflicts as those over the construction of nuclear power plants and international conflicts over car imports – although these may rank prominently on the national agenda or in popular political perceptions. Still, any nationally perceived issue may eventually escalate into a violent conflict. When tensions are already high, for example, even the results of a soccer match can be the trigger that leads to mobilization and even to war. During the Cold War, the accidental violation of foreign air space by a civilian airline might have led to a major political crisis between the superpowers.

Coups d'état may qualify as a conflict since they induce governmental change and involve national power resources. Due to the fact, however, that most coups are extremely brief, they are not included as separate events in the databank.

Another, softer criterion for the inclusion of conflicts in the databank is public reaction to a conflict. Conflicts must be noticed and recognized by the outside world. KOSIMO, in this regard, did not add new conflicts to those already mentioned in the literature and media.

The availability of information is a major element in the evaluation of a conflict. Hidden reprisals in North Korea cannot be documented in the same depth as a British police action in Belfast. The extent of United States involvement in Latin American politics is still largely unknown. The unit of analysis in KOSIMO is discrete conflicts. States become relevant only as parties to a conflict. For example, North Korea is certainly a problematic state and the cause of many tensions and security concerns in the region. Yet, it is not considered as a conflict, but as a party to these two conflicts: 'separation of Korea' (together with South Korea and the United States and the Soviet Union as external parties) and 'control of North Korea's nuclear installations' (together with the International Atomic Energy Agency, the United States and South Korea).

Another problematic issue in conflict research is identifying the initiator and the aggressor in a conflict. The adoption of the United Nations Charter in 1945 universally outlawed war as a legal instrument, as it was intended by the Kellogg–Briand Pact in 1928. Subsequently, violence between states could be justified only on the basis of individual or collective self-defense. Thus declarations of war disappeared, and states began to legitimize the use of force in terms of self-defense and preventive strikes. The USSR legitimized its intervention in Afghanistan in 1979 as an ally's assistance to a government in need. For the KOSIMO databank, the initiator of an international conflict is the first party to raise claims or demands over a given issue against another party. In domestic conflicts the initiator is usually the non-governmental side in the conflict. This definition is based on the assumption that, internally, a state seeks to preserve the status quo, while opposition groups reject it. It is important to keep in mind that we do not code moral or legal aspects of a conflict. While it may be legitimate and morally correct and noble for repressed groups to revolt, these groups remain – in KOSIMO terms – the initiators of a conflict.

KOSIMO attempts to encompass the dynamics of conflict development over time. The key variable is conflict intensity. When the intensity of a conflict increases from a non-violent crisis to a military confrontation – while the direct parties to the conflict remain the same – the conflict is split in two: 'crisis' and – after the outbreak of hostilities – 'violent or severe crisis'. How do we evaluate conflicts that escalate and de-escalate periodically, for example, as do the myriad conflicts between various Kurdish independence movements and the Iraqi, Iranian and Turkish governments? For the period between 1945 and 1986 Gantzel and Meier-Stamer (1986) consider eight separate violent conflicts in which Kurdish independence movements were directly involved; Butterworth (1976) mentions only three separate conflicts between 1945 and 1976. KOSIMO counts ten separate conflicts over the past fifty years. Each of these is based on reasonable assumptions and evaluations of the conflict, and in this case each of the three research teams offer written descriptions of the Kurdish conflicts where the reader can compare specific reasons for the use of different periods.

A possible source of criticism for KOSIMO is its state-centrist approach – a fate that is shared by all existing databanks on political conflicts. A state-centrist point of view may underestimate personal, economic or cultural factors that affect the frequency, type and course of conflicts. If one assumes that the roots of today's conflicts lie in the forced capitalistic modernization of traditional society, the role of ethnic diversity appears rather limited when compared to the influence of the capitalistic system as a structural cause. However, KOSIMO attempts to avoid a fixation on cultural, ideological or economic premises. We regard states as the principal actors in both domestic and international conflicts because of their monopoly of (military) power and their function as the address of claims both from within the state and from the international system, for example, in the field of international or humanitarian law. We assume that conflict-behavior of states and non-governmental movements as well as the development of their conflicts is determined by three basic elements:

- the issues and objectives in dispute
- the actors' internal political system, especially their modes of conflict-management
- the international, systemic and structural constellations.

These three factors – What? Who? and Where? – are operationalized as independent variables. The instruments used during the actual conflict and the modes of conflict resolution are derived from these factors: They are – in this sense – dependent variables. Each variable can be taken by itself to describe frequencies, tendencies, concentrations, similarities, differences, long-term trends and other characteristics of a specific aspect of this complex phenomenon called 'conflict'. We also test mainstream assumptions of conflict-theory by bi-variant calculations. Some multi-variant analyses for the Middle Eastern region based on data from KOSIMO is shown in Trautner (1997).

There are three criteria to distinguish between different phases in conflicts: a change in conflict-participants, a change in the disputed issues and a change in the intensity of the conflict. The most important criterion is the change in participants with additional interests. In almost all cases, the disputed issues or values remain unchanged in the course of the conflict. The most influential criterion is the conflict's intensity. We always mark the highest level of intensity in the course of the conflict-development. For example, the Soviet military intervention in Afghanistan in 1979 was coded as war although in this period there were days and weeks without fighting. According to the above-mentioned three criteria, the Afghanistan conflict between 1979 and 1995 has entered the KOSIMO databank five times, as shown in Table 2.1.

In general, conflicts and their development over time, i.e. phases, can enter the KOSIMO data bank in the following ways:

Example 1:   Korea after the Korean War in 1953. The conflict in Korea from 1953 to 1990 has been classified as a latent conflict although incidents around the issue of national unification of the North and the

Table 2.1 The Afghanistan conflict, 1979–95

Conflict	Start	End	Intensity
Afghanistan I (civil war I)	1978	1979	Violent crisis
Afghanistan II (Soviet intervention)	1979	1988	War
Afghanistan III (civil war II)	1988	1991	War
Afghanistan IV (civil war III)	1992	1993	War
Afghanistan V (civil war IV)	1993	cont.	War

South are separate parts or partial conflicts of the basic conflict, depending on their intensity as a crisis or a severe crisis.

1947–50: latent conflict → 1950–53: war → 1953–91: latent conflict → 1986–91: crisis

Example 2:   Germany after the Second World War. The latent conflict over Germany's partition between 1945 to 1990 went through different crises (Berlin blockade 1948, upheaval of June 17, 1953, Berlin Wall 1961). Since the conflict did not constantly remain at a crisis level, the peaks of critical phases of the conflict were added as partial conflicts to the overall latent conflict.

1945–90: latent conflict → 1948–49: crisis → 1953: crisis → 1958: crisis → 1961: crisis → 1989: crisis

Example 3:   Falkland Islands/Malvinas between Great Britain and Argentina. For 200 years legitimate sovereignty over the Falkland Islands/ Malvinas has been in dispute. The conflict erupted more than once over time. The case was added to KOSIMO along distinguishable phases of negotiations and periods of intensified manifestations of sovereignty by a party. It appears as a latent conflict for those periods in which Great Britain and Argentina were still negotiating (1965–77). In 1977, the conflict escalated: Great Britain dispatched two atomic submarines into the South Atlantic Ocean in response to alleged plans by Argentina to invade the islands. Despite continued negotiations between 1977 and 1982, the situation remained tense. When negotiations broke down in February 1982, the conflict escalated into a severe crisis. On April 2, Argentina invaded the islands. The war began when British troops landed on the islands on May 21, 1982.

Over long periods of time in the nineteenth century the conflict was not pushed by either party. Though the positional differences remained unsolved, the case was neither part of negotiations nor part of any public debate. Thus, 1965, the year when Argentina brought the case before the United Nations, can be regarded as the beginning of the conflict.

1965–77: latent conflict → 1977–82: crisis → 1982: severe crisis → 1982: war → 1982–91: latent conflict.

Variables

The identification of specific features of a conflict starts with the idea that – all differences acknowledged – every conflict can be described with features which are common to all conflicts. We have selected 28 variables which describe the 661 conflicts that are the empirical basis for this book. We have grouped these 28 variables into five categories, identification, actors, context, action and management variables. The following list allows a quick overview of all variables used in the KOSIMO databank:

Databank: KOSIMO
Observations: 661
Variables: 28
Number of entries: 18,508

A: Identifying variables
   1. Number of conflict (identifying number)
   2. Name of conflict (character)
   3. Region of conflict (character)
B: Conflict parties
   4. Participants (character)
   5. External parties (character)
   6. Sum of participating parties (number)
   7. Initiator of conflict (character)
   8. Aggressor (character)
   9. Mediator (character)
C: Context variables
  10. Political system of conflict initiator (number)
  11. Political system of affected party (number)
  12. Economic and political stage of development (number)
  13. Disputed issues in conflicts (number)
D: Conflict action
  14. Beginning of conflict (year)
  15. End of conflict (year)
  16. Intensity of conflict (number)
  17. Instruments of the conflict initiator (number)
  18. Instruments used by the affected party (number)
  19. Minimum estimate of casualties (number)
  20. Maximum estimate of casualties (number)
  21. Reactions by neighboring states (number)
  22. Reactions by great powers and superpowers (number)
  23. Spheres of interest/influence of great powers (number)

E: Conflict management and resolution
 24. Modalities of conflict resolution (number)
 25. Territorial outcome (number)
 26. Military outcome (number)
 27. Political outcome (number)
 28. Treaties (character)

Description of variables

A: Identifying variables

Variable 1. Number of conflict

Each conflict is given an identifying number that indicates its position as a basic and a partial conflict.

Variable 2. Name of conflict

A conflict is usually named after the most important parties. For a better identification of different conflicts among the same parties, the issue or issues in dispute (e.g. border) or any other commonly known name is added in parentheses (e.g. Falklands for Argentina–Great Britain). In addition, different phases of the same conflict can be indicated with Roman numerals (e.g. Lebanon XIII).

Variable 3. Region of conflict

KOSIMO distinguishes eight major geographical regions around the globe: North-, Central- and South-America, Europe, Sub-Saharan Africa, Middle East and Maghreb, Asia and Australia with Oceania. In case a conflict cannot be assigned to a single region, KOSIMO locates the conflict in the region of the initiator of the conflict (see Variable 7: Initiator).

B: Conflict parties

Variable 4. Participants

The variable 'participants' includes all directly involved parties to the conflict. In theory, this number indicates the two parties to a conflict: the 'initiator' or 'aggressor' and the 'affected' or 'defendant' party. In many cases more than two parties or groups of parties are directly opposing each other. In this case, all parties are listed beginning with the initiator.

Variable 5. External parties

External participants are parties that become involved during a conflict. External parties were included in KOSIMO when their influence on one of the directly involved parties was relevant to the development of the conflict. The external party has to refrain from direct participation in the conflict, e.g. involvement in combat. A state can become an external party to a conflict through

- diplomatic, political and/or economic support
- weapons sales
- military intervention.

Variable 6. Sum of participating parties

The variable 'sum of participating parties' is the total number of both the directly involved parties to a conflict and the external parties.

Variable 7. Initiator

An initiator is the party that started a conflict by formulating a demand that is not in the interest of another party. In the pursuit of this interest or demand with verbal or physical threats, the initiator – consciously or not – provokes a latent conflict, a crisis or a severe confrontation. Still, it can be the affected party that is responsible for the escalation of a given conflict by its intolerant or aggressive reactions toward the initiator. The initiators of the decolonization conflicts are mostly liberation armies and guerillas. Thus the term 'initiator' shall not be used to indicate the moral 'right or wrong' of a party. It is a descriptive variable about those states – and not so much domestic groups – that more than other states initiated internal or international conflicts.

Variable 8. Aggressor

In terms of KOSIMO, an aggressor is the regime that is first in the use of military force. Preventive strikes may make it difficult to determine who is the actual aggressor. In these cases, it must be deliberated whether the action was appropriate *vis-à-vis* the perceived threat and whether the first striker also held demands against the attacked state. An aggressor has formulated the greatest demands and, thus, caused the greatest threat. The term aggressor also relates to the principle of collective security, and it is at the core of the United Nations security system. To be labeled 'aggressor' within the system of collective security, a state must have committed some clear-cut offenses against regional or global peace structures and international security.

Variable 9. Mediator

Mediators are intervening parties. They can be private individuals, non-governmental organizations (humanitarian organizations, church groups or the official church), delegations from regional, national and/or international organizations, UN missions or negotiation teams of one or more states (contact groups). Mediators may not be neutral to the issues involved in the conflict but they have to be impartial and equidistant with respect to the parties. A mediator's goal can be the conclusion of an immediate cease-fire or a treaty. Mediators may simply establish communication channels among parties and facilitate their dialogue or encourage a more constructive dialogue by formulating proposals or compromises for the parties. KOSIMO has listed all documented mediation efforts regardless of their outcome. Even though a mediation effort has failed to produce concrete results or a very short-lived cease-fire, it still may have eased the tensions among the disputing parties. A conclusive resolution of a conflict through mediation may have involved more than one mediation attempt by the mediator. It has to be decided case by case whether each mediation attempt is counted separately or whether they accumulate to one large-scale mediation effort.

C: Context variables

Variable 10. Political system of the conflict initiator

Variable 11. Political system of the affected party

KOSIMO categorizes all states according to their political system. This is done in view of the hypothesis that political regimes matter in conflict behavior. The political systems are differentiated by their degree of institutionalization of the rules of conflict behavior. These rules can or cannot be accepted and respected by all parties concerned. They reflect the source and distribution of power in a state. They are applicable to all systems at a given time and not limited to Western democracies. When the opposition does not question or challenge the basic distribution or allocation of power, the rules of conflict behavior are a direct reflection of the existing political forces. When the opposition challenges constitutional or fundamental principles of the state and the distribution of power, the conflict can develop in two directions. Either the parties enter negotiations or they leave the grounds of constitutional legality. Negotiations in this sense are a consensual means to refrain from the use of force. Extra-legal conflicts often involve coercive or violent means.

These reflections refer to the important question of the legitimacy of a political regime, to the question of what is considered to be right or wrong. Legitimacy is the process to get rules, norms and laws accepted by the constituency. How is this being achieved? What are the sources for legitimate rule? Although the sources of legitimacy[2] can vary enormously, in our context two principles are central, namely that of social and political self-determination and that of national integrity normally expressed in a constitution; both principles can be used quite differently and by opposing actors who claim legitimate interests. But what are legitimate interests?

Which motives for such interests are justified and which are not? What is a just war and what is the unjust use of force? Was the quarrel for independence by the Bengalis justified and was the war by the Russian Army against the Chechens a just war? Briefly, is secession legitimate and what is our reference by which we can measure the terms just and unjust?

The answer to this very important question is hardly easy to give, because it touches on moral standards and these standards are in time and space controversial and contradictory. International law – if we take this measure – states two incompatible principles of nationalism, the one referring to national sovereignty and independence and the other to self-determination. A secessionist movement can always refer to the principle of self-determination and the central authority to that of national sovereignty and national unity. Hence both opponents can justify their behavior by accepted principles.

As stated in our dynamic model, conflict development depends to a large extent on the behavior of the opponents in a conflict. In this sense seven types of behavior can be distinguished depending on their use of conflict-solving means:

1   Government and opposition are bound to non-violent actions in their dispute over conflicting interests.
2   Government and opposition resort occasionally to force or threat of force.
3   Government and opposition resort partially to the use of military means.
4   Former opposition comes to power and exercises its rule severely.
5   Governmental rule exists with suppression of counter elite opposition.
6   Governmental rule exists with oppression of opponents.
7   Groups that strive for power are using force.

It should be emphasized that these behavioral modalities of conflict resolution – seen as explaining variables – are not identical with our dependent variable of conflict behavior. This dependent variable consists of categories according to the intensity of conflict development.

Rules of conflict resolution are never meaningless mechanisms of neutral quality; they must, once accepted and adhered to, reflect the current power constellation. These rules do not have to be the known rules of Western democracies, but any rules that are valid in a given country at a given time, or any rules that at least have been adopted by the government. If the opposition follows them, we can suppose that the rules correspond to the actual power constellation. If this is not the case, a conflict situation can force the opposing groups to question the fundamental principles of the state, and we would be confronted with two different ways of conflict resolution, either consensual, that is among others through mediation, or extra-legally by means of coercion or force. At this point, we can recognize whether a political system has installed non-violent modalities of conflict resolution.

Based on these considerations, seven types of political systems can be differentiated according to their degree of legitimacy and, as a result, according to the conflict behavior of governments and oppositions:

1   Democratic legal rules are respected (Western democracies).
2   Democratic legal rules are respected by some groups (regimes in transition).
3   Democratic legal rules that serve as masquerade (facade democracies).
4   Legal rules are being established in newly evolving regimes (charismatic leadership, establishing new orders).
5   Existing rules of conflict behavior only serve the ruling elite (military dictatorships, power conflicts).
6   Existing rules of conflict behavior are adapted to a new (ideological) regime (revolutionary dictatorships, regime conflicts).
7   Existing rules not in use, or a multitude of rules, are accepted by different parties (anarchy).

We, then, can distinguish between (1) democratic, (2) transitional, (3) facade, (4) charismatic, (5) military, (6) revolutionary and (7) anarchic regimes. These seven categories of political systems are on a scale ranging from democratic systems to authoritarian and anarchic systems. The theoretical premises behind this categorization are based on concepts of institutionalization by Max Weber, Tatu Vanhanen and our dynamic phase-model. A more differentiated list of these seven types of political systems reads as follows:

TYPE 1

Political systems are democratically legitimized regimes, where rules of conflict resolution are institutionalized through a pluralistic political party system and free elections, and the governments are responsible to parliaments.

Exemplary cases: Western industrialized states

Modes of conflict resolution:
Government: parliamentary decisions, judiciary
Opposition: parliamentary opposition, judiciary, legal demonstrations, strikes, citizen movements, etc.

TYPE 2

Political systems function through democratic and parliamentary channels for conflict resolutions that are not accepted by all political groups. These regimes may be transitory and have been installed by a former colonial power. Often regime change is induced by a *coup d'état*. The upper elites control most bases of power, whereas other groups and classes remain under-represented. The national unity is usually not questioned.

Exemplary cases: Algeria (after independence 1962), Cyprus (after independence 1958/60), Uganda (1962–66), Upper Volta /Burkina Faso (1960–65)

Modes of conflict resolution:
Government: intimidation, repression, partial bans on political parties, human rights violations
Opposition: demonstrations, mass protests, terror, *coup d'état*

TYPE 3

Political systems have rules of conflict resolution, yet they do not reflect the actual power structures; regimes behind democratic facades are not or insufficiently legitimized by the people. Often the regime is characterized more or less by traditional militarized family, clan or tribe structures. When clans or tribes are in control of parts of the state territory, the central government's power diminishes. The national unity may be challenged.

Exemplary cases: Lebanon (1958–75), Peru (1980–93), Colombia (1948–93)

Modes of conflict resolution:
Government: intimidation, terror, martial law, ban on opposition parties
Opposition: Fighting among clans and internal groups, terror

TYPE 4

Political systems are found in newly independent states that were formerly ruled or influenced by external powers. New types of conflict resolution are established around a charismatic leadership. Movements of national unity give a high degree of legitimacy to the regime and cover other possible conflicts.

Exemplary cases: Egypt (after 1952: Nasser), Yugoslavia (1945–80: Tito), Indonesia (1947–57: Sukarno)

Modes of conflict resolution:
Government: ideological mobilization, populism, charismatic leadership, violence against former regime members
Opposition: marginal opposition activities

TYPE 5

Political systems are characterized by a dictatorial or totalitarian leadership. Opposition movements are suppressed or exiled and have some backing among the population. Organized elites may rival for control of central state powers. Type 5 systems are also known as military-rule regimes or traditional, absolutistic regimes.

Exemplary cases: Nicaragua (Somoza), Haiti (Duvalier), Spain (Franco)

Modes of conflict resolution:
Government: repression in all societal sectors
Opposition: acquiescence or resistance, *coups d'état*, guerilla

TYPE 6

Political systems are equally dictatorial and repressive. In contrast to Type 5 regimes, which produce power conflicts, these ideologically driven regimes produce system conflicts in order to change the basic patterns of the system. Both government and opposition pursue contrasting ideological positions. Most Eastern European states after their forceful transformation to socialist regimes belong to this category.

Exemplary cases: Rhodesia (1965–72), South Africa (1945–91), East European *Realsozialismus* (1947–89), PR China since 1949, Vietnam (1945–75)

Modes of conflict resolution:
Government: dissolution of opposition and resistance groups, monopolization of state powers by one party or elite, importance of secret services
Opposition: demonstrations, resistance through paramilitary formations

TYPE 7

Regimes lack the ability to function as a central power. The regime in power is not accepted by the vast majority of the people. Different groups are fighting for a future regime. They are backed by different parts of the populace and have effective control over larger parts of the state's territory. Street fighting, civil wars and revolutionary turmoils are indicators for this 'non-system'.

Exemplary cases: Lebanon (1975–88), Ethiopia (1974–91), Angola (1974–88), Somalia since 1988, Liberia (1991–95)

Modes of conflict resolution:
(former or nominal) government: propaganda, military force, police

opposition (groups): demonstrations, paramilitary forces, guerilla, gang, clan fighting

These seven types of political systems can be aggregated into four general categories. By this grouping we want to accentuate the major differences between democratic and authoritarian regimes in conflict situations rather than observing the differences among each of the seven more specific types. It is statistically difficult on the basis of our databank to compare in a meaningful way traditional authoritarian (Type 5) and ideological authoritarian (Type 6) systems with regard to their differences in conflict behavior. By a grouping as suggested below, it is possible to discern some general differences between democratic and authoritarian systems in conflict situations. The categories for transitory and dissolved systems (Types 2, 3, 4 and 7) can be regarded as intermediate or residual categories:

1   democratic regimes
2,3,4   transitory regimes
5,6   authoritarian totalitarian regimes
7   anarchic 'systems'

Variable 12. Economic and political stage of development

All states can be categorized by their economic and political stage of development. The purpose of such a categorization in the field of conflict research is to analyze the possible impact of a state's economic and political development on its behavior in conflict situations. Whereas Variables 10 and 11 differentiate among political systems regardless of economic or regional characteristics, this variable is closer to our everyday perception of a state's 'system' as it is presented in the media. The categorization given in Table 2.2 is used, e.g., by the World Bank. We have added the category of Eastern European states after 1989.

Variable 13. Disputed issues in conflicts

Including a residual category, we have grouped the number of possibly disputed issues in a conflict in eight categories. It is possible that two parties dispute over different issues. Here we have listed only those issues that were named by the initiator of the conflict. In our coding a maximum of three issues can be selected.
  Issues in dispute:

- territory, borders, sea borders
- decolonization, national independence
- ethnic, religious or regional autonomy

Table 2.2 Categories of development stages

Categories of economic-political stage of development	Description
OECD states	Industrialized states of the Northern/ Western hemisphere with market economies and pluralistic regimes
Industrialized states in developing regions	Australia, New Zealand, South Africa
Socialist and communist bloc states	Former USSR, eastern satellite states, PR China, Mongolia (1949–)
Eastern European democracies	Former Eastern bloc states (1989–) in transformation process toward market economy and democracy
Socialist states in developing regions	North Korea, Vietnam, Cuba
Newly industrialized economies (NIEs)	South-east Asian market economies
Developing economies	Third World states with underdeveloped market economies and weak or authoritarian political systems

- ideology, system
- internal power
- international power
- resources
- others.

These eight categories can be aggregated into three groups that characterize the conflict by the objectives in dispute:

    2,5,6   international power
    3,4   national power
    1,7,8   material or territorial issues.

Likewise, another grouping is possible. It emphasizes the international or internal nature of the conflict:

    1,2,6,7   international conflict
    3,4,5   internal conflict.

D: Conflict action

Variable 14. Beginning of conflict

Variable 15. End of conflict

Different sources may give different names and time periods to a conflict. First of all, it is important that the sources refer to the same object. It makes a difference if one includes a first attempt of intimidation, a proper crisis, a severe crisis or wars in a list of conflicts (see Brecher *et al.* 1988). The duration of a conflict depends on how a conflict is split into parts or partial conflicts. For example, the Korean conflict can be defined either as a violent conflict that lasted from 1950 to 1953 or as an ongoing conflict since 1945. Thus, 'one' conflict can be divided into several parts or partial conflicts around one issue by differentiating between levels of intensity and participants. KOSIMO follows the rule that the beginning of a conflict is the point when the initiator or aggressor formulates demands and pushes them with certain instruments.

The end of a conflict is usually the point when certain demands are dropped or when a war has come to a decisive end. The end of a conflict and a conflict's political solution do not have to be identical; a war can end with a simple cease-fire (USSR–Japan since 1945). But when a war ends without dropping the initial demands, the conflict – in terms of KOSIMO – will continue as a conflict.

Long-lasting and complicated conflicts were 'split into parts' or partial conflicts by the following rule: the time period of a partial conflict is limited by the change of participating actors, by the change of issues in dispute and by a significant change of instruments.

In most cases, the issues in a basic conflict did not change significantly; thus, the parts of a single basic conflict such as the India–Pakistan conflict over Kashmir are separated by the different levels of the conflict's intensity over the past fifty years. In some conflicts, the actors changed in the course of a conflict which led to a new partition of the basic conflict; e.g. KOSIMO regards the Iraqi invasion in Kuwait and the subsequent second Gulf War as two separate follow-up conflicts of one basic conflict.

Variable 16. Intensity of conflict

The KOSIMO databank contains both non-violent and violent conflicts. This feature is – as far as we know – unique in the field of empirical conflict research. The inclusion of non-violent conflicts has two major advantages over conventional lists of (violent) conflicts.

All violent conflicts evolve from non-violent crises. Also, most violent conflicts do not end in sudden peace, but are followed by periods of shaky consolidation and a sense of ongoing crisis. A well-known example is the violent phase of the Somalia conflict. The violence in 1992–93 was preceded by a long-lasting crisis, likewise, after the military UN intervention and the end of the major fighting there is still today the risk that tensions among local clans may again escalate into violence. KOSIMO traces the non-violent roots of violent conflicts and checks whether the end of fighting was indeed the end of the conflict.

All violent conflicts are an expression of failure at an earlier, non-violent stage of the conflict. The focus on failure, that is the conventional approach to empirical conflict research, hinders us in the recognition and analysis of the successful, that is peaceful, cases of crisis management. Since all states at all times remain potentially violent actors (even the Vatican has an armed 'Swiss guard'), a better knowledge about the frequencies and regions of both non-violent and violent conflict offers a wholly different perspective on the world of conflicts than a purely 'violent world-view' can do.

Coding of variable 16:

1   latent conflict; completely non-violent
2   crisis; non-violent
3   severe crisis; sporadic, irregular use of force, 'war-in-sight' crisis
4   war; systematic, collective use of force by regular troops.

Each level of intensity can be associated with either a single conflict that has existed only on this level, or it can be the level of intensity of a certain phase of a longer conflict with other levels of intensity and/or changing actors. Note that we split conflicts when new or other direct parties become involved, when the issues have changed or when the level of intensity has changed from violent to non-violent and vice versa.

These levels can be aggregated:

1, 2   non-violent conflict
3, 4   violent conflict.

KOSIMO indicates the year of the beginning and end of a conflict. Thus, conflicts are not divided into periods shorter than one year. In many cases, a conflict escalates from a crisis to war and back again within less than a year. For our purposes, it is not necessary fully to desegregate such a conflict. For example, the First World War could be broken down into three events: (a) shooting of the Austrian crown prince in Sarajevo, (b) two months of diplomatic activities, (c) 'military operations'. KOSIMO lists the phase of 'diplomatic activities' as a severe crisis (intensity 3) and the beginning of large-scale military operations as war (intensity 4).

Variable 17. Instruments of the conflict initiator

Variable 18. Instruments used by the affected party

All parties in a conflict use certain instruments in the pursuit of their interests. In most cases parties use more than one instrument at a time or in a sequence of events to respond to the conflict. Whatever instruments are chosen can tell a lot about the future course of the conflict. Thus, instruments can be classified according to their escalating or de-escalating effect on a conflict. Also, different instruments can be used in internal or international conflicts. Finally, instruments can be classified by their impact on the other party. Comparable to the choice of responses at the hands of the Security Council which are prescribed in Chapters VI and VII of the UN Charter, conflict parties can act more or less 'adequately' or 'inadequately' in the pursuit of their interests or in response to perceived threats and fears.

KOSIMO has a very extensive listing of possible instruments. Each instrument can be used with a positive, de-escalating or negative, escalating intention. For example, positive economic instruments in a conflict are trade agreements, lowering of tariffs or granting a most-favored-nation status. Negative economic intentions can be effected through higher tariffs, embargoes and sanctions, freezing of foreign assets, etc. Internal instruments can be used either by the government or the opposition. The government can talk with opposition leaders, free political prisoners or compromise on opposition demands. Likewise it can suppress opposition movements by legal or coercive means. The opposition can pursue their interest through, for example, demonstrations, forceful or passive resistance, or *coups d'état*.

Possible instruments that can be used positively or negatively in a conflict are:

- bilateral diplomacy
- multilateral diplomacy
- information; propaganda
- economic instruments
- military instruments
- secret agencies and services
- informal, subversive instruments
- alliances
- regional or universal integration or isolation
- internal instruments.

Variable 19. Minimum estimate of casualties

Variable 20. Maximum estimate of casualties

The number of victims in conflicts given in the media vary considerably. In many international wars such as the Iran–Iraq war, the number of victims is distorted or concealed for military and propaganda reasons; in many civil wars or protracted internal conflicts, e.g. the massacre of 1994 in Rwanda or the decades of war in Angola, it is technically impossible to estimate any exact number of victims. Also, it becomes more and more difficult to draw the line between civilian and military victims. Therefore, KOSIMO has listed the lowest and highest numbers available. In cases of doubt or unreliability of sources, no entries were made. Therefore, the sum totals in KOSIMO are an uncertain approximation to the real number of victims of wars since 1945.

Variables 21, 22 and 23. International constellations

One of the basic assumptions of KOSIMO is that the course and outcome of conflicts is determined by three factors: the domestic conditions for each party, the issues in dispute and the external or international constellations. Three variables were formulated to operationalize the external or international constellations: Variable 21 'Reactions by neighboring states', Variable 22 'Reactions by great powers' and Variable 23 'Spheres of interest/influence of a great power.

Variable 21. Reactions by neighboring states

Neighboring states in our understanding are not parties directly involved in the conflict. They may become external parties to the conflict through diplomatic, economic or military interventions. Figure 2.3 shows possible relations among direct and external conflict parties.

Based on Figure 2.3, KOSIMO has twelve categories of possible behavioral relations among neighboring states and directly involved conflict parties.

1 No activities or influence by other smaller or equal (in power, size and population) states.
2 Internal, non-governmental groups (x,y) of one state (K) are being supported or suppressed by internal non-governmental groups (z,w) of another state (L).
3 Internal, non-governmental groups (x,y) of one state (K) are being supported by another state/government (L) by subversion or interventions.
4 Internal non-governmental groups (q,p) in one state (M) are supported by other states/governments (K,L).
5 A state/government (L) supports another state/government (K) against its internal, non-governmental groups (x,y).
6 A political, non-violent conflict between two states/governments (K,L) without external interference.
7 A political, non-violent conflict between two states/governments (K,L) with external interference.

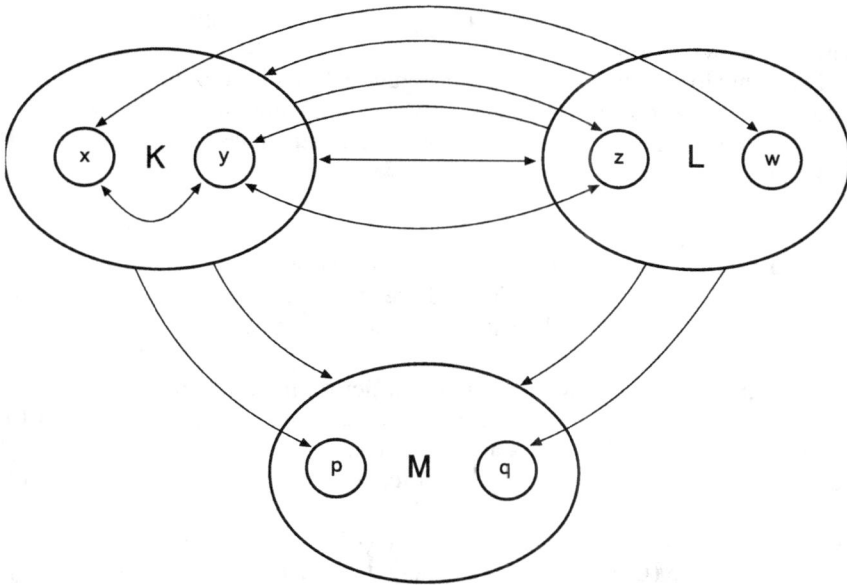

Figure 2.3 Relations among direct and external parties to a conflict.

8 A military, violent conflict between two states (K,L) without external intervention.
9 A military, violent conflict between two states (K,L) against an internal, non-governmental group (z in L).
10 A military, violent conflict between two states (K,L) with external, political interference, e.g. a down-sizing of the conflict from center to periphery or containment by North–South or East–West dimensions of the conflict.
11 A military, violent conflict between two states (K,L) with external, military intervention.
12 Other.

Variable 22. Reactions by great powers

The involvement or engagement of superpowers and dominant states or their neglect of a conflict can greatly influence the course of a dispute. For the period between 1945 and 1995 we consider the US and the USSR as superpowers and the PR China (between 1971 and 1986), France and Great Britain (between 1945 and 1956) as great powers. The time periods do not reflect the power of the state itself, but its willingness to use this power in order to influence the outcome of conflicts in other regions of the world. The superpowers and great powers can interfere in conflicts of or between smaller powers or their internal, non-governmental groups in a variety of ways as shown in Figure 2.4.

The behavioral relations shown in Figure 2.4 can be grouped into twenty categories. Superpowers or great powers (A,B) are named below – for reasons of simplicity – as 'great powers', other states (K,L) are named 'smaller powers'.

1 Two great powers (A,B) remain neutral and inactive toward each other and in their relations with other conflict parties.
2 Two great powers (A,B) mediate together between two states/ governments (K,L) or their internal, non-governmental groups (x,y;z,w).
3 Two great powers (A,B) together call upon the conflict parties (K,L,x,y,w, or z) to resolve their conflict by peaceful means.
4 One great power (A or B) calls upon the parties (K,L,x,y,w, or z) to resolve their conflict by peaceful means.
5 Two great powers (A,B) together dictate a settlement at the expense of two states (K,L).
6 A great power uses a smaller power (K) to gain influence in another smaller state (L) (e.g. wars at the height of the Cold War as a conflict by proxy).
7 A great power (A) supports one state (K) that is in conflict with another state (L).

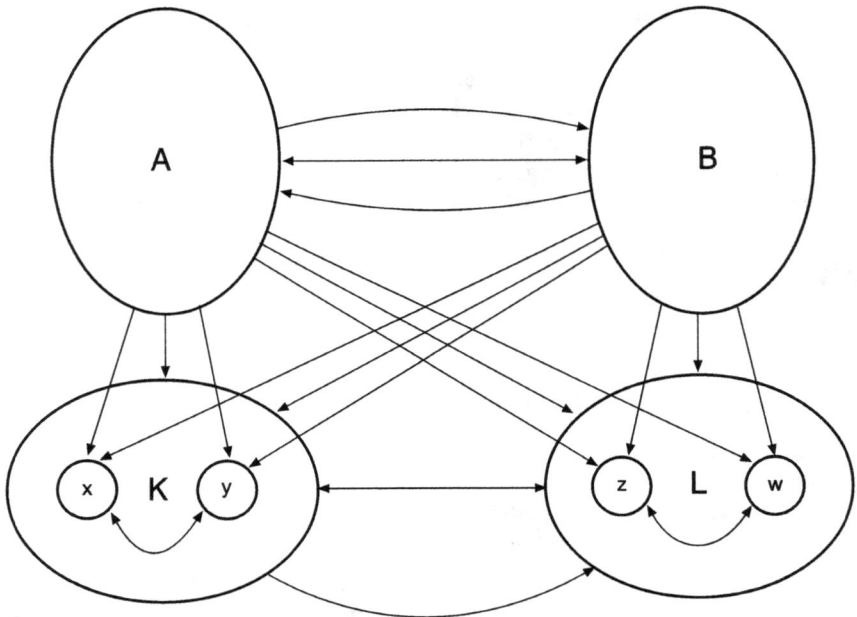

Figure 2.4 Relations among direct parties to a conflict and the great powers and superpowers.

8 A great power (A) supports an internal, non-governmental group (x) against another group (y).

9 A great power (A) supports a smaller state (K) against an internal, non-governmental group (x).

10 A great power (A) supports an internal, non-governmental group (x) against state/government (K).

11 A smaller power (K) supports a great power (A) against an internal, non-governmental group (in A).

12 Two great powers (A,B) together support different internal, non-governmental groups (x,y) in another state (K).

13 Two great powers (A//B) are confronted in a non-violent conflict (Cold War constellation).

14 Two great powers (A//B) are ideologically confronted in a non-violent conflict within or via a smaller state (K or L).

15 Two great powers (A//B) are economically confronted in a non-violent conflict within or via a smaller state.

16 A great power (A) in a political conflict with a smaller power (K).

17 A great power (A) in a military conflict with a smaller power (K), e.g. a colonial war.

18 Two great powers (A, B) in a military conflict with a smaller state (K), e.g. imperial wars.

19 Two great powers (A//B) in a military conflict (e.g. 'classic' European wars before 1945).

20 Other.

Variable 23. Spheres of interest/influence of great powers

Hegemonic states of the eighteenth and nineteenth centuries, imperialistic and colonizing states of the late nineteenth and mid-twentieth centuries and the two superpowers of the Cold War era had more or less defined spheres of interest. These spheres were based upon power, geostrategic, historic or ideological interests. They were often formulated in foreign policy doctrines (Monroe, Truman, Breshnev doctrines etc.). The spheres of interest are commonly legitimized as a crucial part of national security. Within a sphere of its interest a hegemonic state tries to influence, manipulate or control the society, economics or politics of this region. Spheres of interest are usually not challenged by other great powers for fear of a costly, direct confrontation.

One thesis in the field of conflict research holds that very little conflict occurs within declared spheres of interest but rather at the threshold or in contested or overlapping regions. Also, in areas where greater powers have no vital interests, regional conflicts often become protracted and difficult to resolve. With Variable 23 we can test the validity of these assumptions and estimate the impact of spheres of influence on the frequency and intensity of conflicts.

Coding of Variable 23:

1   Conflict is within a sphere of interest,
2   Conflict is outside a sphere of interest,
3   Conflict is in overlapping regions of spheres of interest.

E: *Conflict management and resolution*

Variable 24. Modalities of conflict resolution

KOSIMO differentiates between the resolution process in the course of a conflict and various kinds of settlement, result or outcome of a conflict. The resolution of a conflict is the process that leads to an outcome. For example, when a conflict is resolved by a military victory of one party over another, the outcome may be the annexation of the conquered territory. When a conflict is resolved by a mediator, the outcome may be a political treaty of friendship and security. The variable 'outcome' is discussed further below. Both variables 'resolution' and 'outcome' do not indicate that a certain conflict is once and forever settled. However, our hypothesis claims that consensually resolved conflicts with fair outcomes tend to last longer than coerced settlements.

The possible ways of resolving a conflict are grouped into eleven categories. The resolutions are either voluntary and consensual, authoritative, dictated or decided by military actions. In each case a mediator can become a part of the resolution process. Still, many conflicts remain unresolved. A party either stops pursuing particular claims or renounces them or, in a military confrontation, withdraws its troops.

The satisfactory termination of a conflict depends on the perception of the outcome by the parties involved. This, of course, can be interpreted in different ways. Basically, there are seven possibilities to end a conflict:

1   A solution can be reached by negotiation between the parties involved with or without the help of a third party. Such solutions must be reached with the consent of all the participating parties without reservation.
2   A peaceful settlement can also be reached by an authoritative decision, i.e. by the decision of a court, a conference, a resolution, etc. and can de-escalate a conflict for a certain period of time.
3   Results can be reached by inequitable negotiations, where the dominating powers dictate the conditions; the results are to the detriment of the party concerned.
4   Active retreat or voluntary withdrawal is another form of ending a conflict when a party does not see any chance of gains in a conflict.
5   In a stalemate situation where parties are of equal strength, most of the time there are no decisions and the ending is open. Cease-fires are often the result of a military stalemate.

6   The ending of a conflict can be reached by threats of one party against another.
7   A war is the last resort for the ending of a conflict. This kind of ending is the most coercive one in the range of the seven possible modalities.

These seven modalities of ending a conflict are categorized by the degree of consent or discontent and by the degree of force. It is important, in our opinion, to differentiate between different degrees of free consent and acceptance of an agreement:

- agreement on all issues by all actors without reservation
- agreement on all issues by all actors with reservations
- agreement on all issues by some actors without reservations
- agreement on all issues by some actors with reservations
- agreement on some issues by all actors without reservations
- agreement on some issues by all actors with reservations
- agreement on some issues by some actors without reservations
- agreement on some issues by some actors with reservations.

Bearing this in mind, we are now able to define a solution in more precise terms: A solution deserves this label only when all parties agree on all issues without reservations within given circumstances. A conflict is successfully resolved – ideally speaking – when all relevant parties have negotiated voluntarily and agreed consensually on all issues in dispute without reservations. Altogether, we have coded the following eleven modalities of the endings of conflicts:

1   consensual resolution
2   consensual resolution with mediation
3   authoritative resolution, e.g. with arbitration or court decisions
4   'negotiated resolution' dictated by third party
5   'non-resolution', passive resolution or continuation of conflict
6   withdrawal of troops
7   perseverance or success of one party by means of threat pressure and risk-taking
8   unresolved, violent conflict without mediation attempts
9   unresolved, violent conflict with mediation attempts
10   forceful, violent resolution without mediation attempts
11   forceful, violent resolution with mediation attempts.

These categories can be further reduced:

1,2	consensual resolution
3,4,6	authoritative resolution
7,8,9,10,11	coercive or violent ending.

Variables 25, 26, 27.   Outcomes, results and settlements

The outcome of a conflict is not the solution as defined above. In most cases the parties fail to reach such an ideal settlement. Most settlements exclude one or more parties or issues in the conflict or they attach conditions to the agreement that may question its fulfillment in the future.

We differentiate between territorial, military and political outcomes of a conflict. This differentiation allows for a separate analysis of material, i.e. territorial and military as well as the political outcomes. We suppose that territorial and military settlements are unstable unless they are accompanied by a political settlement. The variable 'outcome' is always coded from the perspective of the initiator of the conflict.

Variable 25.   Territorial outcome

Disputes about territories, sea boundaries and the delineation of frontiers easily escalate into violent conflicts. A state's territory belongs to the core of its national security concerns; a strong response to threats from within (separation, autonomy) or without (annexation, occupation) is highly probable. KOSIMO has grouped possible territorial outcomes into five categories:

T1   separation of territory
T2   territorial loss
T3   annexation, unification, incorporation of territory
T4   denouncement of territorial claims
T5   status quo, initiator upholds territorial claims.

Variable 26.   Military outcome

A focus on military outcomes of violent conflicts can clarify how many and what kind of military actions were successful. In which conflicts did violence pay off? How many wars were won or lost? How many ended in stalemates or troop withdrawals? What are the most likely endings of violent conflicts? KOSIMO has grouped all possible military outcomes into five categories:

M1   stalemate, cease-fire, indecisive outcome
M2   victory of initiator
M3   defeat of initiator
M4   continuation of fighting
M5   withdrawal of troops.

Variable 27.   Political outcome

Political outcomes of conflicts are, in general, a result of negotiations. They reflect the intention of the parties to settle their conflict for a longer period of time, permanently or not at all. Negotiations are successful only when they lead to a consensual agreement that includes all parties and issues without further reservations.

Two political aspects of a conflict can be distinguished: political issues can refer to the demands for a particular good, or they can refer to political matters in a more restricted meaning of the word, i.e., those which are associated with power. As to the former, we can ask whether the political goal has been

- achieved by the initiator
- not achieved by the initiator.

We can furthermore ask

- whether a compromise was possible or
- whether the demand remains on the agenda and the dispute continues.

As to the latter, we can ask what does a particular solution or outcome mean to the polity, i.e. to the government, the opposition or to foreign governments that might have become involved. A government or an opposition can become strengthened or weakened, stabilized or de-stabilized or even suppressed; a foreign government can expand or reduce its influence as a consequence of an outcome. In terms of power six outcomes are possible:

1. the government is strengthened
2. the government is weakened
3. a foreign power strengthened its influence
4. a foreign power lost its influence
5. the opposition is strengthened
6. the opposition is weakened.

These political outcomes then, can take the following forms:

Negotiated outcomes:
P1   no agreement reached, status quo ante
P2   some issues are still in dispute
P3   compromise, partial success
P4   conclusion of a consensual agreement.

Structural and positional outcomes:
P5   change of regime
P6   emergence of two different independent regimes
P7   fall of regime
P8   recognition and strengthening of opposition
P9   suppression of opposition

P10　admission or inclusion of opposition into the government
P11　denouncement of claims
P12　increased influence of an external power
P13　decreased influence of an external power.

Variable 28. Treaties

KOSIMO lists formal, judicial changes in a descriptive character variable. Formal peace treaties, cease-fire agreements, declarations of independence, communiqués, court decisions and declarations are common documents at the end of international or internationalized conflicts, whereas constitutional revisions, amendments, internal cease-fires, changes in governments or regimes, proclamations and referenda mark the outcome of internal conflicts between a government and opposition movements. Civil wars can be ended by declarations of conciliation and reconstruction.

International treaties and constitutional changes by themselves do not guarantee the durability of an agreement. Many agreements prove to be unstable, especially when some parties or issues had been excluded from the negotiations. Many territorial disputes are settled by the conclusion of a multilateral treaty, especially maritime disputes. A lack of documentation of an agreement should not lead to the conclusion that such an unwritten agreement was less stable.

Sources

The purpose of KOSIMO was to become an up-to-date databank of internal and international as well as violent and non-violent conflicts. The research team did not work on each conflict from scratch, but relied for most conflicts on published material from American (esp. Singer and Small 1972 and Butterworth 1976) and European (Kende 1971, Gantzel and Meyer-Stamer 1986) conflicts researchers. In addition, all conflicts have been studied and verbally described by our research team in two publications (F. R. Pfetsch (ed.): *Konflikte seit 1945*. 5 vol. Freiburg 1991; F. R. Pfetsch (ed.): *Globales Konfliktpanorama 1945–1995*. Münster 1996). Table 2.3 shows major works on quantitative conflict research that have been used as a basis for KOSIMO.[3]

Table 2.3 Major works on quantitative conflict research

Authors	Year of publication	Focus	Time period	Frequency of cases
Blechmann and Kaplan	1978	US use of military force	1946–1975	215
Brecher *et al.*	1988	International crises	1929–1979	278
Butterworth	1976	Interstate security conflicts	1945–1974	310
Coplin and Rochester	1972	Disputes	1920–1968	121
Cukwurah	1967	Boundary disputes	–	–
Deitchman	1964	Military engagements	1945–1964	46
Dingemann	1983	Armed conflicts	1945–1982	71
Frei	1975	International conflicts	1960–1974	65
Gantzel and Meyer–Stamer	1986	Wars	1945–1986	159
Gantzel and Schwinghammer	1994	Wars	1945–1992	184
Gödecke *et al.*	1983	Wars, *coups d'état*	1945–1983	–
Haas	1968	Conflicts	1945–1965	108
Haas	1983	Conflicts	1945–1981	282
Haas, Butterworth, Nye	1972	Disputes	1945–1977	146
Holsti	1966	International conflicts	1929–1965	77
Holsti	1977	International conflicts	1919–1975	86
Holsti	1983	International conflicts	1929–1979	94
Jütte and Grosse-Jütte	1981	International conflicts	1946–1976	246
Kaplan	1981	USSR use of military force	1956–1979	19
Kende	1982	Wars	1945–1982	148
Leiss and Bloomfield	1967	Local conflicts	1945–1964	52
Levine	1971	Mediation in conflicts	1816–1960	388
Levy	1985	General wars	1585–1945	10
Luard	1988	Principal wars	1945–1986	128
Luard	1988	Frontier wars	1866–1986	88
Luard	1988	Ideological civil wars	1918–1986	38
Luard	1988	Colonial wars	1918–1986	27
Moaz	1982	Interstate disputes	1821–1976	164
Northedge and Donelan	1971	International disputes	1945–1970	50
Pfetsch and Billing (KOSIMO)	1994	Conflicts	1945–1990	546
Pfetsch and Rohloff (KOSIMO)	1997	Conflicts	1945–1995	661
Richardson	1960	Deadly quarrels	1819–1949	–
Ruloff	1987	Wars	1792–1983	150
Small and Singer	1982	Civil and interstate wars	1816–1980	224
Siverson and Tennefoss	1982	Interstate conflicts	1815–1965	256
Sorokin	1937	Wars	1100–1925	862
Wainhouse	1966	Global organization Peace activities	1946–1965	21
Wood	1968	Conflicts	1898–1967	127
Wright	1965	Civil and international wars	1482–1940	278
Zacher	1979	International conflicts	1945–1977	116

3 Global trends

States, non-state actors and conflict

States

States are the main actors in international relations. We therefore begin with a list of states in five global regions that exist or have existed in the period from 1945 to 1995. All regional countings in this book are based on this grouping. However, the basis of our databank on conflicts is not identical with this list of states, since not all states have experienced political conflicts according to our definition. Thus, the KOSIMO project operates with states as potential actors in conflicts and with states as actual actors in conflicts. In the common language of mass media the name of a state often stands for a conflict. This is not our understanding and usage of the term. A state becomes an actor in a conflict only through its government. In a conflict situation there are always at least two actors. Therefore, a government or state, however repressive, enters a conflict only with the emergence of an identifiable opponent. For example, contemporary Iraq as a state is not war prone *per se*; only the actions of the Iraqi government *vis-à-vis* other groups or states make Iraq a conflict state. The dataset on states has, therefore, a rather descriptive use as compared with the second dataset on actual conflicts which will be presented further below.

A special note should be made on non-governmental, internal and opposition groups. These groups make up the larger part of all opponents to governments in internal conflicts. They are rarely engaged in international conflicts. Yet, despite their high frequency in conflict involvement they are difficult to group and analyze in quantitative studies. Further studies should be undertaken to analyze this dataset of opposition and resistance groups more systematically.

New states

Since 1945 the world has witnessed a quadrupling of the number of states. In 1945 fifty-one states signed the Charter of the United Nations. By the end of 1995, 185 states have become members of the United Nations. The average growth rate of the UN for the period 1945–95 is more than two new members per year. The admissions of new members to the UN occurred in three waves. The first small wave lasted from 1945 to 1949. The new members were largely former colonies of Britain and France in South and South-east Asia. A second wave followed between 1955 and 1965, including the former colonies of Great Britain, France and Belgium in Africa. Between 1950 and 1955, the superpower confrontation in the Security Council blocked the adoption of further states. Then, in 1955, fifteen states were admitted in a package deal. At the peak of the decolonization period during the year 1960, seventeen states were admitted to the UN. The breakdown of the Soviet Union and the former Yugoslavia initiated a third wave of applicants between 1989 and 1992. Between these three waves, the decolonization of the Portuguese overseas possessions and the granting of independence to smaller territories often placed under the Trusteeship Council of the UN led to further applications. Yet, the number of UN members is not identical with the number of states in the world. In 1945, the axis-powers Germany, Japan and Italy had remained outside the UN-system and joined the UN later. By 1995, Kiribati, Nauru, Western Sahara (DARS), Switzerland, Tonga, Tuvalu and the Holy See have not applied for UN membership. The Republic of China (ROC, Taiwan) lost its membership status to the People's Republic of China in 1971. New UN members are shown in Table 3.2.

Dissolved state

Within the fifty years since the Second World War, eleven states have ceased to exist. Four cessations were caused by unifications:

1 Zanzibar (merged with Tanganyika in 1964 to become Tanzania).
2 Republic of Vietnam (unified with the Democratic Republic of Vietnam 1975).
3 German Democratic Republic (unified with the Federal Republic of Germany 1990).
4 People's Republic Yemen (unified with the Arab Republic Yemen 1990).

Four states ceased to exist due to division or decomposition:

5 United Arab Republic (Egypt and Syria 1958–1961).
6 USSR (1917–1991; succeeded by the Russian Federation).
7 Yugoslavia (1919–1991; succeeded by the Federal Republic of Yugoslavia, i.e. Serbia and Montenegro).
8 Czechoslovakia (1919–1993; succeeded by the Czech and Slovak Republics).

Table 3.1 States that exist or have existed* in five global regions

Europe	Middle East/ Maghreb	Asia/Oceania	Sub-Saharan Africa	North America	Central America	South America
Albania	Afghanistan	Australia	Angola	Canada	Antigua and Barbuda	Argentina
Andorra	Algeria	Bangladesh	Benin	USA	Bahamas	Bolivia
Austria	Armenia	Bhutan	Botswana		Barbados	Brazil
Belgium	Azerbaijan	Brunei	Burkina Faso/Upper Volta		Belize	Chile
Belarus	Bahrain	Cambodia	Burundi		Costa Rica	Colombia
Bosnia-Herzegovina	DARS (Western Sahara)	China PR	Cameroon		Cuba	Ecuador
Bulgaria	Egypt	*East Timor*	Cape Verde		Dominica	Guyana
Croatia	Iran	*(1974–1975)**	Central African Republic		Dominican Republic	Paraguay
CSR; Czech Republic	Iraq	Fiji	Chad		El Salvador	Peru
Cyprus	Israel	India	Comoro Islands		Grenada	Surinam
Denmark	Jordan	Indonesia	Congo		Guatemala	Uruguay
Estonia	Kazakhstan	Japan	Djibouti		Haiti	Venezuela
Finland	Kirgistan	Kiribati	Equatorial Guinea		Honduras	
France	Kuwait	Korea (PRK)	Eritrea		Jamaica	
FRG	Lebanon	Korea (ROK)	Ethiopia		Mexico	
Georgia	Libya	Laos	Gabon		Nicaragua	
Greece	Morocco	Malaya/Malaysia	Gambia		Panama	
Hungary	Oman	Maldives	Ghana		St Kitts and Nevis	
Iceland	Qatar	Marshall Islands	Guinea		St Lucia	
Ireland	Saudi Arabia	Micronesia	Guinea-Bissau		St Vincent and Grenadines	
Italy	Syria	Mongolia	Ivory Coast		Trinidad and Tobago	
Latvia	Tajikistan	Myanmar/Burma	Kenya			
Liechtenstein	Tunisia	Nauru	Lesotho			
Lithuania	Turkey	Nepal	Liberia			
Luxembourg	Turkmenistan	New Zealand	Malagasy Republic			
Macedonian Republic	United Arab Emirates, UAE	Pakistan	Malawi			
Malta	*United Arab Republic*	Palau	Mali			
Moldavia	*(1958–61)**	Papua New Guinea	Mauritania			
			Mauritius			

Monaco
Netherlands
Norway
Poland
Portugal
Romania
Russia
San Marino
Slovakia
Slovenia
Spain
Sweden
Switzerland
UK
Ukraine
USSR*
Vatican
Yugoslavia (until 1990)*
Yugoslavia since 1990: Serbia/Montenegro

Uzbekistan
Yemen People's Republic*
Yemen (since 1990)

Philippines
Solomon Islands
Samoa, West
Singapore
Sri Lanka
Taiwan (ROC)
Thailand
Tonga
Tuvalu
Vanuatu
Vietnam (DRV)
Vietnam (RVN)*

Mozambique
Namibia
Niger
Nigeria
Rhodesia*
Rwanda
São Tomé and Principe
Senegal
Seychelles
Sierra Leone
Somalia
South Africa
Sudan
Swaziland
Tanzania
Togo
Uganda
Zaire/Congo
Zambia
Zanzibar*
Zimbabwe

| 49 | 30 | 40 | 50 | 2 | 21 | 12 |

Table 3.2 New members of the UN[1]

Afghanistan: 19 Nov. 1946	Egypt: 24 Oct. 1945
Albania: 14 Dec. 1955	El Salvador: 24 Oct. 1945
Algeria: 8 Oct. 1962	Equatorial Guinea: 12 Nov. 1968
Andorra: 28 July 1993	Eritrea: 28 May 1993
Angola: 1 Dec. 1976	Estonia: 17 Sep. 1991
Antigua and Barbuda: 11 Nov. 1981	Ethiopia: 13 Nov. 1945
Argentina: 24 Oct. 1945	Fiji: 13 Oct. 1970
Armenia: 2 Mar. 1992	Finland: 14 Dec. 1955
Australia: 1 Nov. 1945	France: 24 Oct. 1945
Austria: 14 Dec. 1955	Gabon: 20 Sep. 1960
Azerbaijan: 9 Mar. 1992	Gambia: 21 Sep. 1965
Bahamas: 18 Sep. 1973	Georgia: 31 July 1992
Bahrain: 21 Sep. 1971	Germany: 18 Sep. 1973
Bangladesh: 17 Sep. 1974	Ghana: 8 Mar. 1957
Barbados: 9 Dec. 1966	Greece: 25 Oct. 1945
Belarus: 24 Oct. 1945	Grenada: 17 Sep. 1974
Belgium: 27 Dec. 1945	Guatemala: 21 Nov. 1945
Belize: 25 Sep. 1981	Guinea: 12 Dec. 1958
Benin: 20 Sep. 1960	Guinea-Bissau: 17 Sep. 1974
Bhutan: 21 Sep. 1971	Guyana: 20 Sep. 1966
Bolivia: 14 Nov. 1945	Haiti: 24 Oct. 1945
Bosnia and Herzegovina: 22 May 1992	Honduras: 17 Dec. 1945
Botswana: 17 Oct. 1966	Hungary: 14 Dec. 1955
Brazil: 24 Oct. 1945	Iceland: 19 Nov. 1946
Brunei Darussalam: 21 Sep. 1984	India: 30 Oct. 1945
Bulgaria: 14 Dec. 1955	Indonesia: 28 Sep. 1950
Burkina Faso: 20 Sep. 1960	Iran, Islamic Republic of: 24 Oct. 1945
Burundi: 18 Sep. 1962	Iraq: 21 Dec. 1945
Cambodia: 14 Dec. 1955	Ireland: 14 Dec. 1955
Cameroon: 20 Sep. 1960	Israel: 11 May 1949
Canada: 9 Nov. 1945	Italy: 14 Dec. 1955
Cape Verde: 16 Sep. 1975	Jamaica: 18 Sep. 1962
Central African Republic: 20 Sep. 1960	Japan: 18 Dec. 1956
Chad: 20 Sep. 1960	Jordan: 14 Dec. 1955
Chile: 24 Oct. 1945	Kazakhstan: 2 Mar. 1992
China: 24 Oct. 1945	Kenya: 16 Dec. 1963
Colombia: 5 Nov. 1945	Kuwait: 14 May 1963
Comoros: 12 Nov. 1975	Kyrgyzstan: 2 Mar. 1992
Congo: 20 Sep. 1960	Lao People's Dem. Rep.: 14 Dec. 1955
Costa Rica: 2 Nov. 1945	Latvia: 17 Sep. 1991
Côte d'Ivoire: 20 Sep. 1960	Lebanon: 24 Oct. 1945
Croatia: 22 May 1992	Lesotho: 17 Oct. 1966
Cuba: 24 Oct. 1945	Liberia: 2 Nov. 1945
Cyprus: 20 Sep. 1960	Libyan Arab Jamahiriya: 14 Dec. 1955
Czech Republic: 19 Jan. 1993	Liechtenstein: 18 Sep. 1990
Dem. People's R. Korea: 17 Sep. 1991	Lithuania: 17 Sep. 1991
Dem. Rep. of the Congo: 20 Sep. 1960	Luxembourg: 24 Oct. 1945
Denmark: 24 Oct. 1945	Macedonia: 8 Apr. 1993
Djibouti: 20 Sep. 1977	Madagascar: 20 Sep. 1960
Dominica: 18 Dec. 1978	Malawi: 1 Dec. 1964
Dominican Republic: 24 Oct. 1945	Malaysia: 17 Sep. 1957
Ecuador: 21 Dec. 1945	Maldives: 21 Sep. 1965

Mali: 28 Sep. 1960
Malta: 1 Dec. 1964
Marshall Islands: 17 Sep. 1991
Mauritania: 7 Oct. 1961
Mauritius: 24 Apr. 1968
Mexico: 7 Nov. 1945
Micronesia, Fed. States of: 17 Sep. 1991
Monaco: 28 May 1993
Mongolia: 27 Oct. 1961
Morocco: 12 Nov. 1956
Mozambique: 16 Sep. 1975
Myanmar: 19 Apr. 1948
Namibia: 23 Apr. 1990
Nepal: 14 Dec. 1955
Netherlands: 10 Dec. 1945
New Zealand: 24 Oct. 1945
Nicaragua: 24 Oct. 1945
Niger: 20 Sep. 1960
Nigeria: 7 Oct. 1960
Norway: 27 Nov. 1945
Oman: 7 Oct. 1971
Pakistan: 30 Sep. 1947
Palau: 15 Dec. 1994
Panama: 13 Nov. 1945
Papua New Guinea: 10 Oct. 1975
Paraguay: 24 Oct. 1945
Peru: 31 Oct. 1945
Philippines: 24 Oct. 1945
Poland: 24 Oct. 1945
Portugal: 14 Dec. 1955
Qatar: 21 Sep. 1971
Republic of Korea: 17 Sep. 1991
Republic of Moldova: 2 Mar. 1992
Romania: 14 Dec. 1955
Russian Federation: 24 Oct. 1945
Rwanda: 18 Sep. 1962
Saint Kitts and Nevis: 23 Sep. 1983
Saint Lucia: 18 Sep. 1979
St Vincent/Grenadines: 16 Sep. 1980
Samoa: 15 Dec. 1976
San Marino: 2 Mar. 1992

São Tomé and Principe: 16 Sep. 1975
Saudi Arabia: 24 Oct. 1945
Senegal: 28 Sep. 1960
Seychelles: 21 Sep. 1976
Sierra Leone: 27 Sep. 1961
Singapore: 21 Sep. 1965
Slovakia: 19 Jan. 1993
Slovenia: 22 May 1992
Solomon Islands: 19 Sep. 1978
Somalia: 20 Sep. 1960
South Africa: 7 Nov. 1945
Spain: 14 Dec. 1955
Sri Lanka: 14 Dec. 1955
Sudan: 12 Nov. 1956
Surinam: 4 Dec. 1975
Swaziland: 24 Sep. 1968
Sweden: 19 Nov. 1946
Syrian Arab Republic: 24 Oct. 1945
Tajikistan: 2 Mar. 1992
Thailand: 16 Dec. 1946
Togo: 20 Sep. 1960
Trinidad and Tobago: 18 Sep. 1962
Tunisia: 12 Nov. 1956
Turkey: 24 Oct. 1945
Turkmenistan: 2 Mar. 1992
Uganda: 25 Oct. 1962
Ukraine: 24 Oct. 1945
United Arab Emirates: 9 Dec. 1971
United Kingdom of Great Britain and
Northern Ireland: 24 Oct. 1945
Utd. Rep. of Tanzania: 14 Dec. 1961
United States of America: 24 Oct. 1945
Uruguay: 18 Dec. 1945
Uzbekistan: 2 Mar. 1992
Vanuatu: 15 Sep. 1981
Venezuela: 15 Nov. 1945
Vietnam: 20 Sep. 1977
Yemen: 30 Sep. 1947
Yugoslavia: 24 Oct. 1945
Zambia: 1 Dec. 1964
Zimbabwe: 25 Aug. 1980

One state was forcefully annexed or incorporated by another state:

9   East Timor (indep. 1975; annexed by Indonesia 1976).

Korea was liberated from Japanese occupation in 1945. It has been divided since the Korean War in 1950. For the period 1945–50, it was occupied by Allied forces.

Hyderabad (indep. 1947; annexed by India 1948) and Sikkim (indep. 1918; annexed by India 1975) were not explicitly recognized by the international community as independent states, although there is little evidence that they were not independent states before the annexations by India. The former Portuguese colony Goa was invaded by Indian forces before it could claim independence. The attempt by Iraqi forces in 1990 to occupy and annex Kuwait (indep. 1961) failed and Kuwait was liberated by UN forces in 1991.

Partial or complete destabilization or decomposition of states can be observed in Somalia, Liberia, Burundi, Rwanda, Nigeria and Zaire. Chad and Sudan are states that maintain central control with the help of external parties, but have no effective control over larger regions.

States that exist nominally but have lost temporary or permanent control and function due to periods of civil war include Afghanistan (1980–cont.), Angola (1975–cont.), Cambodia (1979–cont.), Colombia (1982–cont.), Iraq (Kurdish regions 1991–cont.), Lebanon (1975–cont.), Mozambique (1980–cont.), Tajikistan (1991–cont.), Turkey (Kurdish regions 1991–cont.) and Vietnam (1954–1975).

Peaceful states

Out of 204 states (that exist or have existed), forty-three states have never experienced internal or international conflicts as a directly involved party. These states are listed in Table 3.3.

Forty-three states without any political conflicts – violent or non-violent – make up a little less than one-quarter of the world's states today. This is a remarkably high result regarding the often assumed conflictive nature of states. Almost one-quarter of all states since 1945 seem to have existed in circumstances that allowed for early and satisfactory negotiations and compromises for political questions and problems. They are scattered over all continents. Only the Middle Eastern and Maghreb regions have a very low number of conflict-free states.

The most obvious common feature of this group of states is their small territory. Most of these states are composed of islands, they have very small populations, small economies and few natural resources. Exceptions are found in Asia, the trading state Singapore, in Europe, the wealthy states of Luxembourg, Switzerland and the EU member Ireland as well as the young state Slovenia; in Africa, the Madagasy Republic and the Central African Republic diverge from the common mini-state feature of conflict-free states.

With regard to the political systems of conflict-free states, most states are either Western-type democracies or transitory regimes tending toward democracy. There are five traditional authoritarian political systems that have not participated directly in political conflicts: Bhutan, the Maldives, Tonga, the Central African Republic and the Comoros. Eleven states experienced changes in their political regime. In other words, about 80 percent of all conflict-free states have had stable political systems.

Table 3.3 States without direct conflict participations

States	Region
Andorra	Europe
Antigua and Barbuda	Central America
Bahamas	Central America
Barbados	Central America
Belarus	Europe
Bhutan	Asia/Oceania
Cape Verde	Sub-Saharan Africa
Central African Republic	Sub-Saharan Africa
Comoro Islands	Sub-Saharan Africa
Dominica	Central America
Fiji	Asia/Oceania
Gambia	Sub-Saharan Africa
Ireland	Europe
Jamaica	Central America
Kirgistan	Middle East/Maghreb
Kiribati	Asia/Oceania
Luxembourg	Europe
Malagasy Republic	Sub-Saharan Africa
Maldives	Asia/Oceania
Marshall Islands	Asia/Oceania
Micronesia	Asia/Oceania
Monaco	Europe
Nauru	Asia/Oceania
Palau	Asia/Oceania
Samoa, West	Asia/Oceania
San Marino	Europe
São Tomé and Principe	Sub-Saharan Africa
Seychelles	Sub-Saharan Africa
Singapore	Asia/Oceania
Slovenia	Europe
Solomon Islands	Asia/Oceania
St Kitts and Nevis	Central America
St Lucia	Central America
St Vincent and Grenadines	Central America
Swaziland	Sub-Saharan Africa
Switzerland	Europe
Tanganyika	Sub-Saharan Africa
Tonga	Asia/Oceania
Trinidad and Tobago	Central America
Turkmenistan	Middle East/Maghreb
Tuvalu	Asia/Oceania
Vatican	Europe
Zanzibar	Sub-Saharan Africa

States with non-violent conflicts

Table 3.4 shows all states with non-violent conflict participations. The list of states is differentiated by the internal and international character of the conflict as well as by the regional location of the state.

The remarkable aspect of Table 3.4 is the predominance of European states. Out of twenty-five states with non-violent conflicts, sixteen are located in Europe. Adding the forty-three states with no conflict involvements and twenty-five states that have experienced only non-violent conflicts, we identify sixty-eight states since 1945 without violent conflict participations. In other words, roughly one-third of the world's states have never experienced violence in political conflicts. Two-thirds of all states since 1945 have experienced politically motivated violence at least once. Depending on the reader's personal optimistic or pessimistic *Weltanschau-*

Table 3.4 States with non-violent direct conflict participations

State	Region	Frequency of direct participation as initiating or affected party	Frequency of internal conflicts	Frequency of international conflicts
Austria	Europe	1	0	1
Belize	Central America	1	0	1
Brazil	South America	2	1	1
CSR; Czech Rep.	Europe	3	0	3
Denmark	Europe	3	0	3
Estonia	Europe	1	0	1
Finland	Europe	2	0	2
FRG	Europe	5	0	5
Iceland	Europe	6	0	6
Japan	Asia/Oceania	2	0	2
Kazakhstan	Middle East/Maghreb	1	0	1
Latvia	Europe	1	1	0
Lesotho	Sub-Saharan Africa	1	0	1
Liechtenstein	Europe	2	0	2
Lithuania	Europe	1	0	1
Macedonia	Europe	1	0	1
Malta	Europe	1	0	1
Mauritius	Sub-Saharan Africa	2	0	2
Mongolia	Asia/Oceania	1	0	1
Namibia	Sub-Saharan Africa	1	0	1
Norway	Europe	4	0	4
Slovakia	Europe	3	0	3
Sweden	Europe	3	0	3
Ukraine	Europe	2	1	1
Uruguay	South America	1	0	1

ung this result can be hailed or condemned. Since most states without violent conflict participation are Western-type democracies the quest for further democratization of the world's states is certainly one conclusion that could be drawn. On the other hand, many of these states have little economic weight, and are small in territory, natural resources or population. Therefore, it seems that there is a proportionate relation between political weight and the number of violent conflict participations. Economically powerful and non-violent states, such as Japan or Germany, could be interpreted – so far – as exceptions to this trend when their restraints on foreign policymaking are taken into consideration.

States and violent conflicts

Next, we present the list of states with violent conflict participations. Since 1945, 134 states out of 204 states have at least once experienced a violent political conflict. Out of this group of states, eleven have experienced only internal violent conflicts: Papua New Guinea, Sri Lanka, Dominican Republic, Surinam, Georgia, Tajikistan, Uzbekistan, Djibouti, Sierra Leone, Yugoslavia (until 1990) and Zimbabwe (since 1979).

Thirty-nine states have experienced *only* international violent conflicts, as shown in Table 3.5.

Eighty-four states have gone through both, violent internal and international conflicts. Table 3.6 shows all states with violent internal and international conflicts.

Table 3.7 shows a ranking of states with the highest frequency in each conflict category. Except for internal and violent conflicts, the five permanent members of the UN Security Council can be found among the top five states in all conflict categories. The permanent members of the UNSC are the most frequent participants in overall conflicts, in non-violent conflicts, in international conflicts and as external parties to conflicts. In the category of internal conflicts, Indonesia, Ethiopia, Iraq and the Dominican Republic top the list. With regards to violent conflict participations, the USSR and the US rank relatively low (10th, 16th). India and Iraq take their place next to Great Britain, the PR China and France among the most frequent parties in violent conflicts.

As a conclusion drawn from Table 3.7, it can be said that very few, roughly ten to twenty states are responsible or active in most of the world's conflicts. Most states in the world since 1945 have experienced few or no conflicts. As a second observation, it can be said that the high frequency of old democracies, such as the US, the UK and France, is a consequence of their global role as former colonial powers and permanent members of the UN Security Council. Here, the Janus-faced feature of democracies becomes apparent. Although it is true that democracies do not fight each other, it seems that this theorem of democratic peace does not extend to relations of democratic states with non-democratic regimes.

Table 3.5 States with *only* international violent conflicts

State	Region
Australia	Asia/Oceania
Bahrain	Middle East/Maghreb
Belgium	Europe
Benin	Sub-Saharan Africa
Botswana	Sub-Saharan Africa
Brunei	Asia/Oceania
Bulgaria	Europe
Burkina Faso/Upper Volta	Sub-Saharan Africa
Cameroon	Sub-Saharan Africa
Chile	South America
Croatia	Europe
East Timor	Asia/Oceania
Ecuador	Central America
Equatorial Guinea	Sub-Saharan Africa
Eritrea	Sub-Saharan Africa
Gabon	Sub-Saharan Africa
Grenada	Central America
Guinea	Sub-Saharan Africa
Guinea-Bissau	Sub-Saharan Africa
Guyana	South America
Honduras	Central America
Italy	Europe
Ivory Coast	Sub-Saharan Africa
Korea (PRK)	Asia/Oceania
Korea (ROK)	Asia/Oceania
Kuwait	Middle East/Maghreb
Libya	Middle East/Maghreb
Malawi	Sub-Saharan Africa
Malaysia	Asia/Oceania
Moldavia	Europe
Netherlands	Europe
New Zealand	Asia/Oceania
Oman	Middle East/Maghreb
Qatar	Middle East/Maghreb
Taiwan (ROC)	Asia/Oceania
Uganda	Sub-Saharan Africa
United Arab Emirates	Middle East/Maghreb
USA	North America
Yemen PR	Middle East/Maghreb

Besides the permanent members of the UN Security Council, three states from the Middle East rank high on the list of conflict participations, namely Israel, Syria and Egypt. Ethiopia, Iraq and India are other states with equally high frequencies of overall and violent conflict participations. They have or had the status of regional powers.

Table 3.6 States with internal *and* international violent conflict participation

States	Region	Violent conflicts	Non-violent conflicts	Internal conflicts	International conflicts
Afghanistan	Middle East/Maghreb	7	2	4	5
Algeria	Middle East/Maghreb	6	3	3	6
Angola	Sub-Saharan Africa	3	1	3	1
Argentina	South America	3	11	2	12
Armenia	Middle East/Maghreb	2	1	1	2
Azerbaijan	Middle East/Maghreb	2	2	1	3
Bangladesh	Asia/Oceania	2	1	2	1
Bolivia	South America	2	3	2	3
Bosnia-Herzegovina	Europe	4	0	3	1
Burundi	Sub-Saharan Africa	3	0	2	1
Cambodia	Asia/Oceania	6	4	3	7
Chad	Sub-Saharan Africa	7	2	7	2
China PR	Asia/Oceania	20	14	7	27
Colombia	South America	6	3	6	3
Congo	Sub-Saharan Africa	3	0	1	2
Costa Rica	South America	3	0	2	1
CSSR	Europe	1	4	2	3
Cuba	Central America	4	8	1	11
Cyprus	Europe	2	2	3	1
DARS (Western Sahara)	Middle East/Maghreb	3	1	3	1
Egypt	Middle East/Maghreb	15	9	2	22
El Salvador	Central America	2	2	1	3
Ethiopia	Sub-Saharan Africa	14	6	9	11
France	Europe	17	22	1	38
GDR	Europe	1	5	2	4
Ghana	Sub-Saharan Africa	2	7	1	8
Greece	Europe	4	6	2	8

Table 3.6 Continued

States	Region	Violent conflicts	Non-violent conflicts	Internal conflicts	International conflicts
Guatemala	Central America	4	5	2	7
Haiti	Central America	2	5	4	3
Hungary	Europe	2	4	1	5
India	Asia/Oceania	19	9	8	20
Indonesia	Asia/Oceania	13	1	10	4
Iran	Middle East/Maghreb	13	6	6	13
Iraq	Middle East/Maghreb	17	8	9	17
Israel	Middle East/Maghreb	16	4	5	15
Jordan	Middle East/Maghreb	8	5	2	11
Kenya	Sub-Saharan Africa	7	4	1	10
Laos	Asia/Oceania	5	2	2	5
Lebanon	Middle East/Maghreb	12	2	6	8
Liberia	Sub-Saharan Africa	1	1	1	1
Mali	Sub-Saharan Africa	5	1	2	4
Morocco	Middle East/Maghreb	7	6	3	10
Mauritania	Sub-Saharan Africa	3	3	1	5
Mexico	Central America	1	2	1	2
Mozambique	Sub-Saharan Africa	6	0	4	2
Myanmar/Burma	Asia/Oceania	3	1	1	3
Nepal	Asia/Oceania	2	3	3	2
Nicaragua	Central America	5	4	4	5
Niger	Sub-Saharan Africa	2	2	1	3
Nigeria	Sub-Saharan Africa	2	4	2	4
Pakistan	Asia/Oceania	12	6	4	14
Panama	Central America	2	2	1	3
Paraguay	South America	1	2	2	1
Peru	South America	4	5	3	6

Country	Region				
Philippines	Asia/Oceania	4	1	4	1
Poland	Europe	2	2	1	3
Portugal	Europe	8	3	3	8
Rhodesia	Sub-Saharan Africa	11	1	6	6
Romania	Europe	1	3	1	3
Russia	Europe	4	5	3	6
Rwanda	Sub-Saharan Africa	5	0	3	2
Saudi Arabia	Middle East/Maghreb	6	3	1	8
Senegal	Sub-Saharan Africa	2	1	1	2
Somalia	Sub-Saharan Africa	7	1	1	7
South Africa	Sub-Saharan Africa	8	6	4	10
Spain	Europe	3	6	3	6
Sudan	Sub-Saharan Africa	10	2	4	8
Syria	Middle East/Maghreb	16	6	7	15
Tanzania	Sub-Saharan Africa	4	2	2	4
Thailand	Asia/Oceania	5	4	2	7
Togo	Sub-Saharan Africa	1	5	1	5
Tunisia	Middle East/Maghreb	7	4	1	10
Turkey	Middle East/Maghreb	3	7	2	8
UK	Europe	26	39	4	61
USSR	Europe	14	37	13	38
Vanuatu	Asia/Oceania	1	3	1	3
Venezuela	South America	2	3	1	4
Vietnam (DRV)	Asia/Oceania	11	2	2	11
Vietnam (RVN)	Asia/Oceania	8	0	1	7
Yemen (since 1990)	Middle East/Maghreb	3	0	1	2
Yemen AR (North Yemen)	Middle East/Maghreb	6	1	1	6
Yugoslavia (since 1990)	Europe	1	1	1	1
Zaire	Sub-Saharan Africa	11	3	7	7
Zambia	Sub-Saharan Africa	7	3	1	9

Table 3.7 Ranking of states by conflict participations

Top 20 participants in conflicts	Top 20 participants in violent conflicts	Top 20 participants in non-violent conflicts	Top 20 participants in international conflicts	Top 20 participants in internal conflicts	Top 20 states as external/indirect participants in conflicts
UK 64	UK 25	UK 39	UK 60	USSR 13	USA 116
USSR 51	India 19	USSR 38	USA 45	Indonesia 11	USSR 84
USA 45	China PR 17	USA 34	France 38	Ethiopia 9	France 36
France 41	France 16	France 25	USSR 38	Iraq 9	UK 29
China PR 34	Iraq 16	China PR 17	China PR 28	Dom. Rep. 8	China PR 26
India 26	Israel 16	Argentina 11	Egypt 22	India 8	Iran 23
Iraq 24	Syria 16	Chile 10	India 18	Chad 7	Cuba 18
Egypt 24	Egypt 15	Iraq 10	Iraq 17	Syria 7	Egypt 18
Syria 22	Ethiopia 15	Egypt 9	Israel 15	Zaire 7	Saudi Arabia 17
Ethiopia 21	Lebanon 13	India 9	Syria 15	Colombia 6	Libya 16
Israel 20	USSR 13	Cuba 8	Pakistan 14	Iran 6	Syria 14
Iran 19	Indonesia 12	Iran 8	Iran 13	Lebanon 6	Iraq 11
Pakistan 18	Pakistan 12	Ghana 7	Argentina 12	Rhod. (–79) 6	Turkey 11
Argentina 14	Iran 11	Greece 7	Ethiopia 12	China PR 5	India 10
Indonesia 14	Rhod. (–79) 11	Turkey 7	Chile 11	Israel 5	Russia 9
Lebanon 14	USA 11	Dom. Rep. 6	Cuba 11	Sri Lanka 5	Algeria 7
South Africa 14	Zaire 11	Ethiopia 6	Jordan 11	Afghanistan 5	Australia 7
Zaire 14	DR Vietnam 9	Iceland 6	DR Vietnam 11	Georgia 4	FRG 7
Jordan 13	Sudan 9	Morocco 6	Morocco 10	Haiti 4	Pakistan 7
Morocco 13	Jordan 8	Pakistan 6	Kenya 9	Mozambique 4	Israel 6

The ratio of violent conflicts per state and per region

Every state can potentially use violence through its military forces in conflict situations. The higher the number of states, the higher the potential for violent conflict. An extreme interpretation of a closely linked relation between violent conflicts and states has been formulated by Krippendorff: 'States are by their very nature likely to engage in violent conflicts and warfare' (1985).

A comparison of the number of states, the number of states that resort to violence and the number of violent conflicts per region serves also as a test of another fundamental thesis: democratic states with constructive and peaceful internal and external conflict management capacities reduce the potential for violent conflict ('OECD-peace', 'democratic peace'). In other words, democracies do not use violence among themselves in the pursuit of national interests. Since democratic political systems are the predominant regime in Europe and North America, it is here where we expect the lowest levels of violence in conflict behavior. Tables 3.8 and 3.9 list the ratios of violence per region.

Since 1945 or since their independence, 90 percent of all states in the Middle East and Maghreb region have at least once participated in violent conflicts. In Europe the 'violence-ratio' is comparatively low (45 percent). Out of thirty-four states on the whole American continent (including the maritime states), twenty states were engaged at least once in a violent conflict (57 percent). Out of forty states in South-, East-, Southeast-Asia, Australia and Oceania, twenty-four states have experienced violent conflict (60 percent). Sub-Saharan Africa has a ratio of 76 percent. The violence ratio worldwide is 64 percent (Table 3.8, rows 1 and 3).

Table 3.8 Ratio of states using violence per region

Region	[1] Number of states in this region	[2] Number of states in this region with conflict participations	[3] Number of states in this region with violent conflict participations	[4] Ratio [2]:[1]	[5] Ratio [3]:[1]
Europe	49	40	22	82%	45%
North America	2	2	1	100%	50%
Central America	21	12	11	57%	41%
South America	12	11	8	91%	66%
Middle East/ Maghreb	30	28	27	93%	90%
Asia, Oceania	40	26	24	65%	60%
Sub-Saharan Africa	50	41	38	82%	76%
Total	204	160	131	78%	64%

Table 3.9 Ratio of violent conflicts per region

Region	[6] Sum total of violent conflicts in this region	[7] Sum total of violent internal conflicts in this region	[8] Ratio [6]:[1]	[9] Ratio [7]:[1]
Europe	29	20	59%	41%
North America	0	0	–	–
Central America	24	12	114%	57%
South America	21	17	175%	142%
Middle East/Maghreb	120	56	400%	187%
Asia, Oceania	90	46	225%	115%
Sub-Saharan Africa	103	54	206%	108%
Total	387	205	190%	100%

Eighty-two percent of the European states have had internal or international conflicts. Only half of these conflicts were violent. In the Maghreb, Gulf and Middle East region – as in Europe – a high number of states have experienced conflicts (93 percent). Yet in contrast to European states, almost all Middle Eastern states have resorted at least once to violence (90 percent) (Table 3.8, rows 1, 2 and 3).

The conflict ratio of a region can be calculated by a comparison of the number of conflicts in the region and the number of states (row 1 in Table 3.8 and row 6 in Table 3.9). Over the past fifty years a total of 204 states have initiated 387 violent conflicts. In other words, statistically, each state on average has initiated two conflicts between 1945 and 1995 or since its independence. Differentiated by regions, European states account for twenty-nine violent conflicts in Europe. Compared with the number of European states (forty-nine), the regional conflict ratio is 59 percent. In contrast, the Maghreb, Gulf and Middle East region consists of thirty states that account for 120 violent conflicts in this region. In other words, on the average each state has been responsible for four violent conflicts (conflict ratio 400 percent). North America has experienced no violent conflicts at all, although the US has participated in violent conflicts elsewhere. The African, Asian and Latin American states have on average initiated two conflicts in their respective regions.

Finally, when comparing the number of states in a region with the number of internal violent conflicts (Table 3.9, row 7), the number of states worldwide and the number of internal violent conflicts is about equal (204 states and 205 internal violent conflicts). Again, Europe has the lowest ratio of internal violent conflicts when compared with the number of states in this region: 41 percent. The Arab world has the highest ratio with 187 percent. The African, Asian and Latin American ratio is a little above the global ratio with 100 percent.

Non-state actors: conflicts with sub-governmental opposition groups

Out of a total of 661 conflicts worldwide since 1945, 385 conflicts (58 percent) have involved an internal opposition or non-governmental group in conflict with a government or state. The remaining 276 conflicts were carried out directly among two or more states. In many of the 385 conflicts involving opposition groups, more than one opposition group and more than one state were engaged. KOSIMO has identified a multitude of types of opposition groups ranging from protesting farmers and fishermen to organized state-like armies, such as Angola's UNITA. An exhaustive overview and categorization of opposition groups has yet to be undertaken. We have listed only those opposition groups that could be identified as an organized group. Spontaneous groupings with no internal structure or an inner organization were not included in the sample.

During the decades of decolonization many of the opposition groups belonged to the category of 'liberation groups or armies'. Since the 1980s an increasing number of religious movements and radical factions of autonomist or secessionist movements have been observed. With the end of the Cold War and the collapse of the Soviet Union, many human and civil rights movements sought a direct confrontation with the government or state. The level of intensity for conflicts that involved opposition groups was rather high (Table 3.10). More than half of these conflicts showed spontaneous, irregular or unorganized violence. One-quarter of all conflicts involving opposition groups escalated into wars. Only 23 percent of all conflicts with opposition groups remained on a non-violent level of intensity. This result shows that those conflicts between governments, states and opposition groups that cannot be resolved within the legal or constitutional framework have a high chance of escalating into violent conflicts. Note that KOSIMO has neither included conflicts that were carried out within a country's legal or constitutional framework nor conflicts that were settled internationally according to the provisions of international law or directly by the International Court of Justice in The Hague.

Conflicts with opposition groups are predominantly internal conflicts where dissatisfied, underrepresented or suppressed groups voice their

Table 3.10 Conflicts involving opposition groups by intensity

Intensity	Total numbers	% of 385
Latent conflict	26	7
Crisis	62	16
Total non-violent conflicts	88	23
Violent crisis	203	53
War	94	24
Total violent conflicts	297	76
Total	385	100

Table 3.11 Conflicts involving opposition groups by intensity and type (national/
international)

Intensity	National	National % (n=263)	International	International % (n=122)
Latent conflict	14	5	12	10
Crisis	44	17	18	15
Total non-violent conflicts	58	22	30	25
Violent crisis	143	54	60	49
War	62	24	32	26
Total violent conflicts	205	78	92	75
Total	263	68 (n=385)	122	32 (n=385)

opposition through demonstrations, turmoil, strikes, sabotage or violence. Guerilla wars are the most violent form of internal opposition to a ruling elite. Angola, Mozambique, Nicaragua, El Salvador and many other states have suffered for decades from wars between the guerilla and the state. Table 3.11 differentiates among internal and international conflicts according to their level of intensity.

Two-thirds of all conflicts with opposition groups were internal conflicts. When this result is differentiated by the degree of violence, we find that almost four-fifths of all internal conflicts with opposition groups were violent crises or wars. The distribution of violent and non-violent conflicts for internal conflicts is comparable to the distribution for international conflicts. Three-quarters of all international conflicts with opposition groups have escalated into violent confrontations. The high degree of violent conflicts in international conflicts can be traced to the group of complex and protracted conflicts. Many of these began as internal conflicts, e.g. over decolonization. In the course of their development, the conflicts became internationalized through outside interventions or the involvement of neighboring states. The decolonization of Rhodesia and the civil war against the Smith regime or the former apartheid system in South Africa that involved neighboring states at times are examples.

What are the issues in conflicts with opposition groups? Most conflicts involved clashes over access to and representation in the national power center. The next most frequent issues were conflicts over ideology, system conflicts and conflicts over ethnic, religious or regional autonomy. Conflicts over decolonization or national independence were not as frequent as one might expect. This is a reflection of the overall low number of decolonization and independence conflicts in comparison to all conflicts that have occurred worldwide since 1945 (Table 3.12).

Conflicts over territory, borders, international power positions and resources played a minor role in conflicts with opposition groups. Yet, the increasing

Table 3.12 Issues in conflicts with opposition groups

Issues	Frequencies (multiple choice)
Territory, borders	42
National independence, decolonization	84
Ethnic, religious and regional autonomy	118
Ideology, system conflict	119
Internal power conflict	166
International power conflict	43
Resources	35
Other	12

scarcity of renewable resources in developing countries might cause an increasing number of internal conflicts over resources. These conflicts, for the most part, will remain below the state level, i.e. the states will not become a directly involved party or the states have lost control over parts of their territory due to civil unrest or violence and will not interfere. Scarce resources are not only a direct cause of conflicts over their access or distribution but also a cause for indirect conflicts. Migration of people is one consequence of increasing deforestation, desertification and water scarcity. Yet, for the most part migrants are not welcome in neighboring territories where the energy and food situation is but slightly better. The current conceptualizations of conflict databanks with a strong link to states do not grasp many of the new sub-governmental forms of violence in developing countries.

Table 3.13 lists states according to the number of conflicts in which opposition groups were also involved. The number of conflicts where more

Table 3.13 List of states in conflict with opposition groups

Conflict parties	Frequency of conflicts with or against opposition groups
Great Britain	25
India	19
USSR	18
France	14
Indonesia	12
Lebanon	11
Democratic Republic of Vietnam	11
Israel	10
USA	9
Portugal	8
Chad	7
Ethiopia	7
Republic of Vietnam	6
Iraq	6

than one opposition group was involved – regardless of which side of the conflict – makes up one-third of all conflicts coded in KOSIMO. Great Britain, India and France are on top of the list of states in conflict with opposition groups. Note that this listing does not reflect the duration and intensity of each conflict.

Basic conflicts

Certain conflicts arise again and again over the same issue with the same opposing parties. We, therefore, differentiated between 'basic' and 'partial' conflicts. The term 'basic conflicts' describes underlying, fundamental or genuine conflicts which touch on overarching disputed issues and which lead to several interrelated partial or singular conflicts among identifiable actors.

The terms 'basic conflicts' and 'partial or singular conflicts' stand for two views on conflicts. Whereas the term 'partial or singular conflict' comprises events that lead to a specific crisis or conflict that can be labeled and recognized as such (for example the Suez crisis or Cuban Missile crisis), the term 'basic conflicts' captures a greater picture.

In the conflict between the USA and Cuba, basic issues are ideology and geostrategic position. These basic issues can become manifest in different incidents and on different concrete objects. Each of these partial conflicts has been coded with its particular level of intensity. In most cases, parties and issues remain the same throughout the duration of the basic conflict. In some cases additional issues or parties enter the conflict for a certain period of time.

Altogether, we counted 287 basic conflicts from 1945 to 1995; 661 singular or partial conflicts are attributed to these 287 basic conflicts. More than half of the 287 basic conflicts erupted only once (in this sense, they are identical with one partial or singular conflict). The other half of the basic conflicts erupted at least twice. In some cases, a basic conflict escalated into many subsequent crises and several wars. Consider, for example, the conflicts around India's independence and territorial questions, the conflicts between Israel and the Arab world, the conflicts over Yemen's independence, separation and unification or the conflicts of Kurdish opposition groups against several Middle Eastern governments. On average, each basic conflict escalated twice in its history. Table 3.14 lists all 287 basic conflicts.

Most of the new basic conflicts began in the immediate post-War period or in the 1960s. The 1970s and 1980s show average rates of less than five new basic conflicts per year (see bold line in Figure 3.1 below). This descending trend is sharply interrupted in 1989 with the collapse of communist regimes, the dissolution of the USSR and the ending of the Cold War. In three years, more than 25 new basic conflicts have escalated. Since 1992, the descending trend of the earlier two decades seems to be continuing.

The decreasing number of new basic conflicts per year up to the end of the Cold War can be interpreted as an indicator of an overall more stable and

Table 3.14 All basic conflicts

Basic conflicts	Duration in years
Afghanistan (civil war)	1978–cont.
Afghanistan–Pakistan	1947–1986
Albania (foreign policy crises)	1946–1949; 1960–1991
Albania (mass flights)	1989–1991
Algeria (independence)	1945–1946; 1954–1962
Algeria (internal crises)	1988–cont.
Angola (Cabinda)	1991–cont.
Angola (independence, civil war)	1961–1994
Antarctis	1956–1959
Argentina (Montoneros)	1969–1977
Argentina–United Kingdom (Falklands)	1955–1982
Argentina–Uruguay (Rio de la Plata)	1969–1973
Argentina–Chile	1958–1994
Armenia–Azerbaijan (Nagorny-Karabakh)	1987–cont.
Austria (state-treaty)	1945–1955
Bahrain–Qatar (sea-borders)	1957–cont.
Bangladesh (India, Pakistan)	1966–1971
Bangladesh (minorities)	1971–cont.
Benin–Niger (border)	1963–1965
Bolivia (internal crises)	1946–1952; 1967
Bolivia–Chile (borders)	1962–cont.
Botswana, Lesotho, Swaziland	1950–1968
Brazil (constitution)	1986
Brazil–Paraguay (Parana)	1962–1985
British Guyana (independence)	1953–1966
Brunei (uproar)	1962
Burkina Faso–Mali	1974–1975; 1985
Burma/Myanmar (minorities)	1948–cont.
Burma–China (borders)	1948–1961
Cambodia	1958–1975
Cambodia (border)	1956–1970
Cameroon (independence, Bakassi)	1955–1967; 1981–1987; 1993–cont.
Canada (secession attempt by Quebec)	1990–cont.
Canada–France (St Pierre and Miquelon)	1975–1992
Canada–US (Gulf of Maine)	1981–1984
Chad (independence, civil war)	1966–cont.
Chad–Nigeria (islands in Chad Sea)	1983
Chile–USSR (Russian wives)	1948–1949
China (Tachen islands)	1955
China (Tibet)	1950–cont.
China (internal crises)	1945–1949; 1969; 1989
China–India (borders)	1954–1993
China–Kazakhstan	1990–1993
China–Laos	1975–1993
China–Taiwan	1947–cont.
China–United Kingdom (Hong Kong)	1983–1984; 1990–cont.
China–USSR	1960–1991
China–Vietnam (Spratly)	1974–cont.
Colombia (Violencia I)	1948
Colombia–Venezuela (Monjes Islands)	1952–cont.

Table 3.14 Continued

Basic conflicts	Duration in years
Congo (regime crisis)	1993–cont.
Costa Rica	1948–1949
CSSR, CSFR (opposition)	1948; 1953; 1968; 1989–1993
Cuba–Dominican Republic	1956
Cuba–US	1956–cont.
Cyprus (independence, internal conflicts)	1954–cont.
Denmark–United Kingdom (fishery conflict)	1961–1964
Djibouti (Afars-Issas I)	1963–1994
Dominican Republic (crises)	1947; 1949; 1951; 1959–1963; 1965
Eastern Europe (human rights)	1949–1953
Egypt (Islamists)	1988–cont.
Egypt–Israel	1951–1973
Egypt–Libya	1977
Egypt–Sudan (Wadi Halfa)	1958–1959
El Salvador (civil war)	1981–1992
Equatorial Guinea–Spain (flag removal)	1969
Eritrea (independence)	1946–1952; 1961–1993
Eritrea–Yemen (Hanish Islands)	1995–cont.
Ethiopia ('red terror')	1974–1978
Ethiopia (Gadaduma)	1947–1970
Ethiopia–Sudan (ELF)	1964–1965
Federal Republic Germany (Arab–German tensions)	1965–1972
Federal Republic Germany–France (Saarland status)	1950–1957
France (Corsica)	1975–cont.
France (New Caledonia)	1984–1991
France (Tahiti)	1987; 1995
France–Egypt (status of foreigners)	1949–1950
France–Malagasy Republic (Glorieuses Islands)	1973–1990
France–Syria, Lebanon (Levant)	1945–1946
France–United Kingdom (Minquiers and Ecrehouse)	1951–1953
Gabon–Congo (soccer revolt)	1962
Gabon–Equatorial Guinea (Corisco Bay Islands)	1972
GDR–Denmark (border)	1969–1988
GDR–FRG (division)	1945–1990
Georgia (Gamsachurdia)	1989–cont.
Georgia (minorities)	1989–cont.
Ghana (francophone Africa)	1965–1966
Ghana (Konkomba)	1994–cont.
Ghana–Guinea (hostages)	1966
Ghana–Togo	1960; 1965; 1993–1994
Ghana–Upper Volta (border)	1964–1966
Greece (civil war)	1944–1949; 1967–1975
Greece–Albania	1948–1949
Greece–Macedonia (name)	1991–1995
Guatemala I (internal conflicts)	1954; 1960–1972; 1980–cont.

Guatemala–Belize I (UK)	1960–1977; 1981–cont.
Guatemala–Mexico	1958–1961
Guinea-Bissau–Portugal (independence)	1963–1974
Guinea–Ivory Coast	1966–1967; 1970–1974
Haiti (internal conflicts)	1956–1959
Haiti–Dominican Republic	1949–1950
Honduras–El Salvador	1969–1992
Honduras–Nicaragua (border I)	1957–1961
Honduras–US (Swan Island)	1945–1991
Hungary (communism)	1946–1949; 1956; 1983–1990
Hungary–Slovakia (Gabchikowo power plant)	1989–1994
Iceland (US troops)	1956
Iceland–Norway (fishery zones)	1993–cont.
Iceland–United Kingdom (fishery conflict I)	1952–1956; 1958–1961; 1971–1973; 1975–1976
India (independence, internal conflicts)	1942–1972
India (Kashmir, Rann of Kutch)	1947–cont.
India IX (Goa I)	1950–1961
India XIX (Assam, Bodoland)	1983–1984; 1987–cont.
India XVIII (Khalistan/Punjab)	1981–cont.
India XX (Ayodhya)	1984–cont.
India–Nepal	1989–1990
India–South Africa (Apartheid)	1946–1959
Indochina	1945–cont.
Indonesia (Darul Islam separation attempt)	1947–1991
Indonesia (East Timor)	1974–cont.
Indonesia (independence)	1945–1949
Indonesia (PRRI rebels in Sumatra)	1955–1958
Indonesia (South Moluccas)	1950–1965
Indonesia (Ulama movement in Aceh I)	1953–1961; 1990–cont.
Indonesia (uproar in southern Sulawesi)	1950–1965
Indonesia (West Irian)	1950–cont.
Iran (nationalization)	1951–1953
Iran (revolution, opposition)	1978–cont.
Iran (Rushdie affair)	1989–cont.
Iran–Iraq (Schatt-al-Arab)	1969–1975; 1980–cont.
Iran–Saudi Arabia	1987–cont.
Iran–UAE (islands)	1970–1971; 1979–cont.
Iran–United Kingdom (Bahrain independence)	1970–1971
Iran–USSR (Azerbaijan)	1945–1946
Iraq–Egypt–Syria (Baghdad Pact)	1955–1995
Iraq–Jordan (Arab Federation)	1958
Iraq–Kuwait	1961–1963; 1973; 1975; 1990–1994
Israel (independence)	1946–1973
Israel–Lebanon	1974–cont.
Italy (South Tyrol)	1960–1992
Japan–USSR/Russia (Kurils)	1945–cont.
Jordan (internal conflicts)	1956–1957; 1970–1971
Jordan–Arab states (West Bank)	1949–1950
Jordan–Israel (Jordan water)	1959–1994
Kenya (independence, Mau Mau)	1952
Kenya (Rift Valley)	1991–1995

Table 3.14 Continued

Basic conflicts	Duration in years
Kenya–Somalia (Northern Frontier District)	1963
Kenya–Somalia (Shifta)	1963–1967
Korea I	1947–cont.
Kurds (Iran, Iraq, Turkey)	1945–cont.
Laos (internal conflicts)	1953–1961; 1963–1975
Laos–Thailand (border)	1975–1992
Laos–Thailand–US (Nam Tha crisis)	1962
Lebanon (internal conflicts)	1958–cont.
Liberia (civil war)	1989–1995
Libya (Cyrenaica)	1949–1951
Libya–Chad	1973–1994
Libya–Malta	1973–1986
Libya–US	1973–1989; 1991–cont.
Liechtenstein–Czech Republic–Slovakia (real estate)	1990–cont.
Liechtenstein–Guatemala	1955
Malagasy Republic (independence)	1947–1960
Malawi (independence)	1959–1964
Malawi–Zambia (East Province)	1981–1986
Malaya (independence)	1948–1977
Mali/Niger (Tuareg)	1961–1964; 1990–cont.
Mali–Mauritania (border)	1960–1963
Mali–Senegal (federation)	1960
Mauritania (independence I)	1957–1970
Mauritania–Senegal (tensions)	1989–1990
Mauritius–Malagasy Republic–France (Tromelin)	1976–cont.
Mauritius–United Kingdom (Diego Garcia)	1980–cont.
Mexico (Chiapas)	1994–cont.
Mongolia (status)	1945–1950
Morocco (independence)	1944–1958
Morocco (Western Sahara I)	1956–cont.
Morocco–Algeria (Tindouf)	1963–1970
Morocco–Spain (territories)	1957–cont.
Mozambique (independence)	1964–1975; 1978–1994
Namibia (independence)	1946–1994
Nepal (independence)	1950–cont.
Netherlands–Belgium (border)	1957–1959
Netherlands–FRG (border)	1949–1963
New Zealand–US	1984–1990
Nicaragua (internal conflicts)	1955–1994
Nicaragua–Colombia (San Andres Archipelago)	1979–cont.
Niger–Ghana (Subversion)	1964–1965
Nigeria (Biafra secession)	1967–1970
Nigeria (Ogoni)	1993–cont.
North Korea–IAEA	1991–1994
North Korea–US (*Pueblo* incident)	1968
Northern Ireland	1968–cont.
Oman (Imam–Sultan conflict)	1954–1971

Oman–UAE (territory)	1977–1988
Pakistan (Belushistan)	1973–1976
Pakistan (civil war in Karachi)	1977–cont.
Pakistan–Afghanistan (Bajaur)	1961
Panama (channel conflicts)	1959; 1964–1967; 1970–1979; 1989–1990
Papua New Guinea (internal conflicts)	1975–1977; 1988–cont.
Paraguay (internal conflicts)	1947; 1958–1961
Peru (APRA-uproar 3.10.48)	1948
Peru (Guerilla)	1965–1966; 1980–cont.
Peru–Colombia (Torre Asyl)	1948–1954
Peru–Ecuador (Amazonas)	1942–1960; 1981; 1995–cont.
Philippines (Aquino–Marcos)	1984–1986
Philippines (Luzon, HUK)	1945–1954
Philippines (Moros in Mindanao and Sulu)	1970–cont.
Philippines (uproar of 'National Front')	1968–cont.
Poland (communism)	1945–1947; 1956; 1980–1990
Poland–GDR (Stettin bay)	1977–1989
Portugal (democratization)	1973–1983
Portugal–Guinea (invasion Conacrys)	1970
Portugal–Zambia (economic sanctions)	1971
Puerto Rico–US (status)	1950–1952; 1962–1993
Qatar–Saudi Arabia (border)	1990–cont.
Rhodesia (independence, civil war)	1961–1979
Romania (internal conflicts)	1989–cont.
Russia (Chechnya)	1991–cont.
Russia (oil exploitation in the Caspian Sea)	1994–cont.
Russian Federation (attempt at *coup d'état*)	1992–1993
Russian Federation (Ingushia–North Ossetia)	1991–cont.
Russian Federation (Tartastan)	1992–1994
Rwanda–Burundi	1958–cont.
Saudi Arabia (occupation of mosque)	1979
Saudi Arabia–Abu Dhabi (Buraimi)	1949–1975
Saudi Arabia–Kuwait (islands)	1965–cont.
Senegal (Casamance)	1982–cont.
Sierra Leone (civil war)	1991–cont.
Somalia (civil war)	1988–cont.
Somalia–Ethiopia	1950–cont.
South Africa (internal conflicts)	1960; 1976–1994
Spain (Basque autonomy)	1960–cont.
Spain (internal conflicts)	1945–1950; 1975–1982
Spain–United Kingdom (Gibraltar)	1964–cont.
Sri Lanka (Ceylon) (Tamils I)	1956–1958; 1971; 1983–cont.
Sudan (independence; civil war)	1946–cont.
Surinam (internal conflicts)	1986–cont.
Sweden–Denmark (Hesseloe)	1978–1984
Sweden–USSR (Baltic Sea)	1969–1988
Syria (conflicts with Arab states)	1949; 1961; 1982
Tajikistan (civil war)	1990–cont.
Tanzania–Malawi (border)	1967
Thailand (internal conflicts)	1965–1980; 1991–1992
Thailand–Cambodia (border)	1953–1991
Togo (independence, internal conflicts)	1947–1957; 1991–1994

Table 3.14 Continued

Basic conflicts	Duration in years
Tunisia (independence; internal conflicts)	1950–1970; 1978–1987
Tunisia–Libya	1976–1988
Turkey (Russian claims)	1945–1947
Turkey–Greece	1964–cont.
Turkey–Russia (Bosporus)	1992–cont.
Turkey–Syria (border, water)	1955–1957; 1990–cont.
UAR–Jordan	1959–1965
Uganda (Obote)	1981–1986
Uganda–Kenya (territorial claims)	1976–1977; 1987–1989
Uganda–Tanzania (borders)	1972; 1978–1979
Ukraine–Russian Federation (fleet, atomic weapons)	1991–1994
United Kingdom–Argentina–Chile (Palmer)	1956–1958
United Kingdom–Norway (fishery dispute)	1948–1951
Uruguay (Tupamaros)	1964–1972
US–Grenada	1983
US–Peru, Ecuador (tuna fish)	1969–1974
USSR (*coup d'état*)	1991
USSR (minorities)	1979–cont.
USSR–Finland	1948; 1961
USSR–Norway (Svalbard)	1945–1991
USSR–Romania (tensions)	1964–1968
USSR–Sweden (Catalina affair)	1952
USSR–US (confrontations, crises)	1951–1960
USSR–Yugoslavia	1948–1956
Uzbekistan (student uprisings)	1992
Vanuatu (independence)	1980–1981
Vanuatu–Australia	1987
Venezuela (Guerilla)	1960–1969
Venezuela–British Guyana (Essequibo)	1960–1970; 1982–cont.
Yemen (independence, division, unification)	1948–cont.
Yemen–Oman, Saudi Arabia (borders)	1963–1979; 1981–cont.
Yugoslavia (status Kosovo, Sandschak)	1988–cont.
Yugoslavia, Serbia, Croatia, Bosnia	1991–1995
Yugoslavia–Italy (Trieste)	1945
Zaire (independence, internal conflicts)	1960–1967; 1977–1978; 1991–cont.
Zaire–Belgium	1989
Zaire–PR Congo (claims of invasion attempts)	1969–1970
Zaire–Zambia I (Lake Mweru)	1980–1987
Zambia–Rhodesia (border)	1965–1987
Zanzibar (massacre)	1963–1964; 1993–cont.
Zimbabwe (borders, internal conflicts)	1982–1983

less confused world compared with the period immediately after the Second World War or during the period of decolonization in the 1960s. Those issues that are still in dispute today will remain the source of future conflicts. Yet, there seem to be fewer and fewer genuinely new sources of conflict. Ongoing protracted conflicts in Algeria, Afghanistan, parts of the Philippines and in India and Indonesia, other centers of protracted conflicts, such as those in Namibia, Mozambique, Vietnam, Cambodia, Guatemala, El Salvador and Nicaragua are likely to have been settled for some time. Relatively new complex or protracted conflicts, such as the wars in former Yugoslavia, in Georgia, Tajikistan and Chechnia were ended or limited in scope by the intervention of the international community or by one of the superpowers.

Conflicts in sub-Saharan Africa, such as those in the Great Lake area, in and around Sudan and Chad and the conflicts in Somalia and its Egyptian borders lie outside the immediate spheres of interest of the superpowers or the five permanent members of the UN Security Council. There is little hope for decisive de-escalating action by the international community to settle these conflicts.

Figure 3.1 shows the new, ended and ongoing basic conflicts in one picture. The line of ended basic conflicts follows the line of new basic conflicts to a certain degree. In part, short-lived basic conflicts are responsible for this concurrence. For example the peak of new basic conflicts in 1989 is followed by a peak of ended conflicts in 1991. Here, the short and successful Eastern European revolutions become visible. Yet, most peaks and lows do not have a valid sequential connection. The line of ongoing basic conflicts indicates a constant level of forty to fifty conflicts per year since the early 1950s. The decrease in new basic conflicts in the 1970s has no effect on the frequency of ongoing conflicts. The number of ended conflicts per year remains overall lower than the number of new basic conflicts. In other words, there is an increasing number of protracted conflicts in the world. The international community is less confronted with genuinely new, but with increasingly long-standing conflicts.

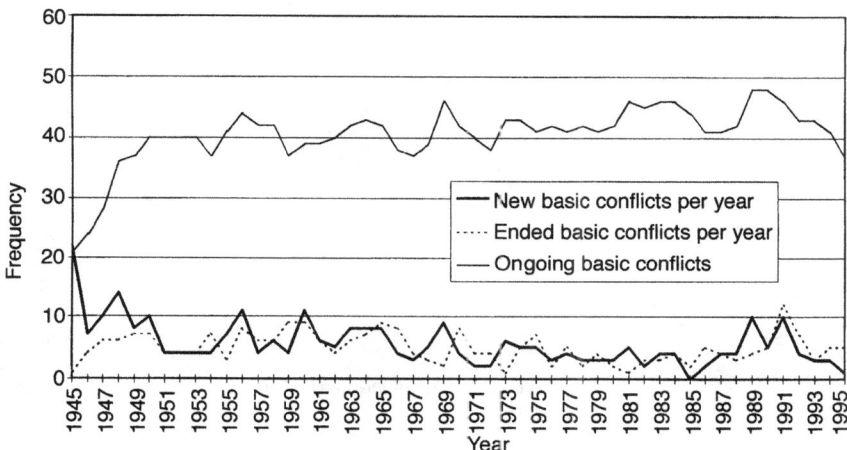

Figure 3.1 Ongoing basic conflicts.

Figure 3.1 does not discern different regions nor violent from non-violent basic conflicts. Figure 3.2 shows the regional distribution of violent and non-violent basic conflicts for the entire fifty-year period from 1945 to 1995. There are three tendencies: first, the American continent has the overall lowest frequency of both violent and non-violent basic conflicts.[2] Second, Europe as a region accounts for fifty-seven basic conflicts, which is equal to the overall regional average of basic conflicts; it is the only world region where more basic conflicts have been carried out with non-violent means than vice versa. Third, the Middle Eastern region, Asia, Oceania and sub-Saharan Africa have by two-thirds more violent basic conflicts than non-violent conflicts. Sub-Saharan Africa has the highest number of basic conflicts overall, followed closely by Asia and the Middle Eastern regions.

As an extension of the analysis of basic conflicts, we examine the group of non-violent basic conflicts. Whereas many basic conflicts have had both violent and non-violent partial conflicts, some basic conflicts remained non-violent throughout all their phases. For example the Cuban–US disputes were overall non-violent, yet the Bay of Pigs invasion escalated into a military confrontation. Thus, this basic conflict does not qualify as a completely non-violent basic conflict.

Altogether, 108 basic conflicts were resolved without a resort to arms. Table 3.15 shows a profile of these 108 basic conflicts. Note that the basis of this figure is the number of 145 partial conflicts which are attributed to the 108 non-violent basic conflicts. Of 108 non-violent basic conflicts, 94 basic conflicts remained singular episodes. Fourteen basic conflicts were subdivided into two or more partial conflicts. In other words, 87 percent of all non-violent basic conflicts were conflicts that escalated only once and had no follow-up or consequential conflicts in later years.

The overwhelming majority of non-violent basic conflicts are of an international nature. Of all internal basic conflicts, only 8 percent were

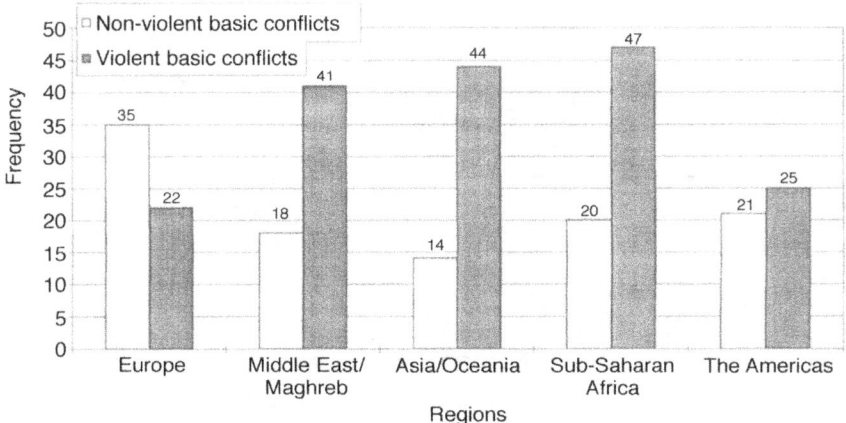

Figure 3.2 Violent and non-violent basic conflicts by regions.

Table 3.15 Profile of non-violent basic conflicts

		Frequency	% of non-violent basic conflicts	Total (%)
Type of conflict	Number of non-violent basic conflicts (*n*=108) expressed in the number of attributed partial conflicts (n=145):	145	100	
	International non-violent conflicts	134	92	
	Internal non-violent conflicts	11	8	100
Issue*	(1) Conflicts over territory, borders, sea-borders	42	30	
	(2) Conflicts over decolonization, national independence	12	9	
	(3) Conflicts over ethnic, religious or regional autonomy	1	1	
	(4) Conflicts over ideology, system	11	8	
	(5) Conflicts over internal power	9	6	
	(6) Conflicts over international power	26	19	
	(7) Conflicts over resources	31	22	
	(8) Other	7	5	100
Region	Europe	52	36	
	America	25	17	
	North America	3	2	
	Central America	9	6	
	South America	13	9	
	Sub-Saharan Africa	23	16	
	Asia, Oceania	23	16	
	Middle East/Maghreb	22	15	100

Note:
* Multiple choice.

resolved entirely by non-violent means. In all other internal basic conflicts, violence played a decisive role at least once. A look at the issues around which the non-violent basic conflicts were centered shows issues (1), (6) and (7) to have the highest frequencies. This is in part due to the international nature of most non-violent conflicts. Territorial disputes are international conflicts by definition. Still, among the three international categories 'issues of dispute', namely territorial disputes, disputes involving international power and access to resources, the issue 'territory, borders and sea borders' seems to qualify best for non-violent conflict situations. In other words, the chances of an overall non-violent conflict situation arising are better in international conflicts involving territorial and border problems. In contrast, internal conflicts involving minority issues and internal power struggles qualify least for non-violent pursuit of interests by the conflicting parties. As regards the regional distribution of non-violent basic conflicts, Europe clearly leads the group. Thirty-six percent of all non-violent basic conflicts arose in Europe, whereas the other regions have similar percentage rates around 17 percent.

In Table 3.16, all non-violent basic conflicts are listed with their attributed partial conflicts, their region and international or internal character as well as mediating parties in the conflict.

In Table 3.16, four conflicts are somewhat special: the conflicts of Germany's partition, the fishery conflicts between the United Kingdom and Iceland, the Greece–Turkey disputes about the Aegean Sea borders and the direct confrontations between the USSR and the US concerning mostly air-space violations. All four basic conflicts escalated more than four times as partial conflicts within the past fifty years, yet they never escalated into a military confrontation. They had a strong potential for violent escalation regarding the issues involved; resources, geostrategic hegemony and the drive for unification of partitioned states.

On the other hand, the restraints to use military force were equally strong. As regards the two disputes between the United Kingdom and Iceland and Greece and Turkey, all conflict parties belonged to the North Atlantic Treaty Organization, an alliance with strong enough influence on its members to restrain them from the use of force. In the other two cases involving the partition of Germany and air-space violations at the iron curtain, an escalation might have led to a military escalation between the superpowers. Except for the border conflicts between Ghana and Togo, all other non-violent basic conflicts have escalated only once or twice.

As a tentative thesis derived from the analysis of non-violent basic conflicts, we might state that conflicts that have escalated more than twice concerning the same issue have a very high potential to turn into violent conflicts. The constraints to remain non-violent, even when highly contested issues are involved, have to be very strong, for example a common military alliance or an unacceptable or existential risk. Also, the thesis of a stable OECD peace, that is non-violent behavior of democracies among themselves, can be confirmed in the positive. Most non-violent basic conflicts have occurred between democracies. Nevertheless, conflict constellations involving authoritarian political systems have equally well managed to keep their conflicts below violent escalations.

Partial conflicts

The group of partial conflicts comprises 661 conflicts that make up the group of 287 basic conflicts. Every basic conflict is composed of one or more, on average two, partial conflicts. Counting partial conflicts regardless of their attributed basic conflicts allows for a closer look at specific characteristics of each conflict and the conflict's development over time.

As it is useful to look at basic conflicts for a broad, basic picture of conflict potentials, it is equally necessary to understand each escalation as an

Table 3.16 Non-violent basic conflicts and their attributed partial conflicts

Name	Start	End	Region
Albania (mass flights)	1989	1991	Europe
Albania–United Kingdom (Corfu)	1946	1949	Europe
Albania–USSR (tensions)	1960	1991	Europe
Angola (secession of Cabinda)	1991	cont.	Sub-Saharan Africa
Antarctic	1956	1959	South America
Argentina–Uruguay (Rio de la Plata)	1969	1973	South America
Austria (state treaty)	1945	1955	Europe
Bolivia–Chile (Lauca-river)	1962	1964	South America
Bolivia–Peru–Chile (Tacna and Arica)	1964	cont.	South America
Botswana, Lesotho, Swaziland	1960	1968	Sub-Saharan Africa
Brazil (constitution)	1986	1986	South America
Brazil–Paraguay (Parana)	1962	1985	South America
Bulgaria (air traffic incident)	1955	1955	Europe
Canada (secession attempt by Québec)	1990	cont.	North America
Canada–France (St Pierre and Miquelon)	1975	1992	North America
Canada–US (Gulf of Maine)	1981	1984	North America
Chad–Nigeria (islands in Chad Sea)	1983	1983	Sub-Saharan Africa
Chile–USSR (Russian wives)	1948	1949	South America
China–Kazakhstan	1990	1993	Asia, Oceania
China–Laos	1975	1993	Asia, Oceania
China–United Kingdom (Hong Kong)	1983	1984	Asia, Oceania
China–United Kingdom (status Hong Kong)	1990	cont.	Asia, Oceania
Colombia–Venezuela (Monjes Islands)	1952	cont.	South America
Cuba–Dominican Republic	1956	1956	Central America
Denmark–United Kingdom (fishery conflict)	1961	1964	Europe
Eastern Europe (human rights)	1949	1950	Europe
Eastern Europe (US interference)	1952	1953	Europe
Egypt–Sudan (Wadi Halfa)	1958	1959	Middle East/Maghreb
Equatorial Guinea–Spain (flag removal)	1969	1969	Sub-Saharan Africa
Eritrea–Yemen (Hanish Islands)	1995	cont.	Middle East/Maghreb
Ethiopia–Kenya (Gadaduma II)	1963	1970	Sub-Saharan Africa
Ethiopia–United Kingdom (Gadaduma I)	1947	1963	Sub-Saharan Africa
Federal Republic of Germany (Arab–German tensions)	1965	1972	Middle East/Maghreb
Federal Republic of Germany–France (Saarland status)	1950	1957	Europe
France (Corsica)	1975	cont.	Europe
France (New Caledonia I)	1984	1985	Asia, Oceania
France (New Caledonia II)	1985	1988	Asia, Oceania
France (New Caledonia III)	1988	1991	Asia, Oceania
France (Tahiti: uprisings after atomic tests)	1995	1995	Asia, Oceania
France (Tahiti: uprisings)	1987	1987	Asia, Oceania
France–Egypt (status of foreigners)	1949	1950	Middle East/Maghreb
France–Malagasy Republic (Glorieuses islands)	1973	1990	Sub-Saharan Africa
France–United Kingdom (Minquiers and Ecrehouse)	1951	1953	Europe
GDR (17 June 1953)	1953	1953	Europe
GDR (democratization)	1989	1990	Europe
GDR–Denmark (border)	1969	1988	Europe
GDR–FRG (Berlin I, blockade)	1948	1949	Europe
GDR–FRG (Berlin II, status)	1958	1959	Europe
GDR–FRG (Berlin III, wall)	1961	1961	Europe

Table 3.16 Continued

Name	Start	End	Region
GDR–FRG (partition)	1945	1990	Europe
Ghana (francophone Africa)	1965	1966	Sub-Saharan Africa
Ghana–Guinea (hostages)	1966	1966	Sub-Saharan Africa
Ghana–Togo (territorial claims I)	1965	1965	Sub-Saharan Africa
Ghana–Togo (Volta Region I)	1960	1960	Sub-Saharan Africa
Ghana–Upper Volta (border)	1964	1966	Sub-Saharan Africa
Greece–Albania	1948	1949	Europe
Greece–Macedonia (name)	1991	1995	Europe
Greece–Turkey (Aegean Sea I)	1973	1976	Europe
Greece–Turkey (Aegean Sea II)	1987	1987	Europe
Greece–Turkey (Aegean Sea III)	1987	cont.	Europe
Guatemala–Mexico	1961	1961	Central America
Guatemala–Mexico (Shrimp boat)	1958	1959	Central America
Haiti–Dominican Republic	1949	1950	Central America
Honduras–US (Swan Island)	1945	1991	Central America
Hungary (C-47 plane shooting)	1951	1954	Europe
Hungary–Slovakia (power plant Gabchikowo)	1989	1994	Europe
Iceland (US troops)	1956	1956	Europe
Iceland–Norway (fishery zones)	1993	cont.	Europe
Iceland–United Kingdom (fishery conflict I)	1952	1956	Europe
Iceland–United Kingdom (fishery conflict II)	1958	1961	Europe
Iceland–United Kingdom (fishery conflict III)	1971	1973	Europe
Iceland–United Kingdom (fishery conflict IV)	1975	1976	Europe
India–Nepal	1989	1990	Asia, Oceania
India–South Africa (apartheid)	1946	1959	Sub-Saharan Africa
Iran (oil nationalization, change of government)	1951	1953	Middle East/Maghreb
Iran (Rushdie affair II)	1992	cont.	Middle East/Maghreb
Iran–United Kingdom (Bahrain independence)	1970	1971	Middle East/Maghreb
Iran–United Kingdom (Rushdie affair I)	1989	1991	Europe
Iraq–Egypt, Syria (Baghdad Pact)	1955	1959	Middle East/Maghreb
Iraq–Jordan (Arab Federation)	1958	1958	Middle East/Maghreb
Italy (South Tyrol)	1960	1992	Europe
Japan–USSR/Russia (Kurils)	1945	cont.	Asia, Oceania
Jordan–Arab states (expansion West Bank)	1949	1950	Middle East/Maghreb
Laos–Thailand (border)	1975	1992	Asia, Oceania
Laos–Thailand–US (Nam Tha crisis)	1962	1962	Asia, Oceania
Libya (Cyrenaica)	1949	1951	Middle East/Maghreb
Libya–Chad	1973	1994	Sub-Saharan Africa
Libya–Malta	1973	1986	Middle East/Maghreb
Liechtenstein–Czech Republic–Slovakia (real estate)	1990	cont.	Europe
Liechtenstein–Guatemala	1955	1955	Central America
Malawi–Zambia (eastern province)	1981	1986	Sub-Saharan Africa
Mali–Senegal (federation)	1960	1960	Sub-Saharan Africa
Mauritania (independence I)	1957	1961	Middle East/Maghreb
Mauritius–Malagasy Republic–France (Tromelin)	1976	cont.	Sub-Saharan Africa
Mauritius–United Kingdom (Diego Garcia)	1980	cont.	Sub-Saharan Africa

Mongolia (status)	1945	1950	Asia, Oceania
Morocco–Mauritania	1961	1970	Middle East/Maghreb
Netherlands–Belgium (border)	1957	1959	Europe
Netherlands–FRG (border)	1949	1963	Europe
New Zealand–US	1984	1990	Asia, Oceania
Nicaragua–Colombia (San Andres Archipelago)	1979	cont.	Central America
Niger–Ghana (subversion)	1964	1965	Sub-Saharan Africa
North Korea–IAEA	1991	1994	Asia, Oceania
North Korea–US (*Pueblo* incident)	1968	1968	Asia, Oceania
Oman–UAE (territory)	1977	1981	Middle East/Maghreb
Peru–Colombia (Torre Asyl)	1948	1954	South America
Poland–GDR (Stettin bay)	1977	1989	Europe
Portugal (democratization)	1973	1983	Europe
Portugal–Zambia (economic sanctions)	1971	1971	Sub-Saharan Africa
Puerto Rico–US (status I)	1950	1952	Central America
Puerto Rico–US (status II)	1962	1993	Central America
Qatar–Saudi Arabia (border)	1990	cont.	Middle East/Maghreb
Russia (oil exploitation in the Caspian Sea)	1994	cont.	Middle East/Maghreb
Russian Federation (Tartastan)	1992	1994	Europe
Saudi Arabia–Kuwait (islands)	1965	cont.	Middle East/Maghreb
Spain–United Kingdom (Gibraltar)	1964	cont.	Europe
Sweden–Denmark (Hesseloe)	1978	1984	Europe
Sweden–USSR (Baltic Sea)	1969	1988	Europe
Tanzania–Malawi (border)	1967	1967	Sub-Saharan Africa
Togo–Ghana (border)	1993	1994	Sub-Saharan Africa
Tunisia–Libya	1976	1988	Middle East/Maghreb
Turkey (Russian claims)	1945	1947	Middle East/Maghreb
Turkey–Greece	1964	1965	Europe
Turkey–Russia (Bosporus)	1992	cont.	Middle East/Maghreb
UAR–Jordan	1959	1965	Middle East/Maghreb
Ukraine–Russian Federation (fleet, atomic weapons)	1991	1994	Europe
United Kingdom–Argentina–Chile (Palmer)	1956	1958	South America
United Kingdom–Norway (fishery dispute)	1948	1951	Europe
US–Peru, Ecuador (tuna fish)	1969	1974	South America
US–USSR (downing of RB-47)	1960	1960	Asia, Oceania
US–USSR (U2-plane shooting)	1960	1960	Asia, Oceania
USSR–Finland I	1948	1948	Europe
USSR–Finland II (crisis)	1961	1961	Europe
USSR–Norway (Svalbard)	1945	1991	Europe
USSR–Romania (tensions)	1964	1968	Europe
USSR–Sweden (Catalina affair)	1952	1952	Europe
USSR–US (air traffic incident)	1954	1954	Asia, Oceania
USSR–US (Chinese Sea, piracy)	1954	1954	Asia, Oceania
USSR–US (Soviet airspace)	1958	1958	Asia, Oceania
USSR–Yugoslavia	1948	1956	Europe
Vanuatu–Australia	1987	1987	Asia, Oceania
Venezuela–British Guyana (Essequibo I)	1960	1970	South America
Venezuela–Guyana (Essequibo II)	1982	cont.	South America
Yugoslavia–Italy (Trieste)	1945	1954	Europe
Zaire–Belgium	1989	1989	Sub-Saharan Africa

entity in itself. The partial conflicts within one basic conflict share similarities. Yet they may cause different external reactions or interventions, involve new mediators or alter political systems and regimes by the conflict parties. In this sense, basic conflicts are a broad look at things, whereas the analysis of partial conflicts can reveal more detailed arguments for and against the existing theses on causes, structures and dynamics of conflicts.

As a first step, the frequencies per year of ongoing basic conflicts are being compared with the frequencies per year of (the attributed) ongoing partial conflicts (Figure 3.3). The line of ongoing conflicts is based on the cumulative differences between new conflicts and ended conflicts per year. This line tries to show the differentiation of basic conflicts into partial conflicts. If each conflict escalated only once and was settled immediately, satisfactorily and permanently, the two lines would be congruent. The growing gap between the lines indicates an increasing differentiation of a constant number of ongoing basic conflicts into an increasing number of ongoing partial conflicts. In other words, as we have suspected above, the number of protracted conflicts is growing.

As early as in the 1960s, the average number of escalations per basic conflict has been two; by 1990 the average number of escalations per basic conflict had reached its peak with three partial conflicts per basic conflict. Since 1992 there seems to be a decreasing trend in the numbers of both basic and partial conflicts.

The line of ongoing partial conflicts shows constant growth by roughly ten conflicts per decade. Thus, we cannot observe specific periods of low or intense conflict activity. There are no cycles or periodical peaks of overall global conflict density or activity. There are certain periods of increased growth rates of ongoing conflicts, such as immediately after the Second World War, in the mid-1960s and in 1981 and 1989. A period of decreased

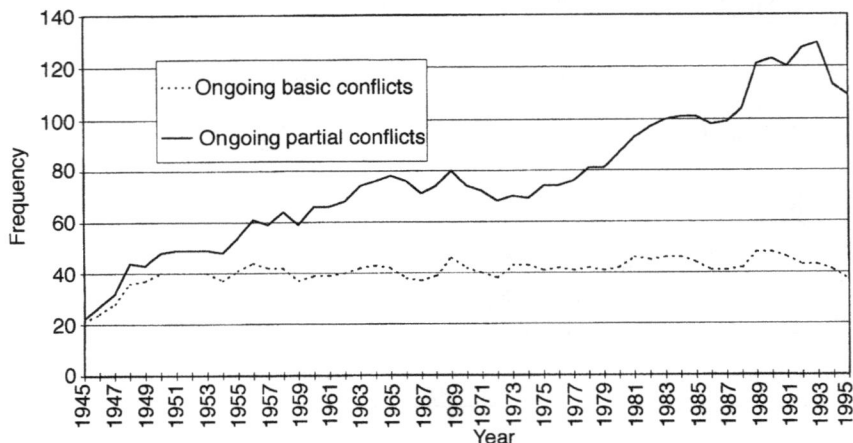

Figure 3.3 Ongoing basic and partial conflicts.

global conflict activity lies in the years between 1969 and 1973, the years both of superpower *détente* before the oil shock and after a reasonably successful decade of decolonization in Africa. The next decrease in global conflict activity lies between 1985–87, the years of a new superpower *détente* after the neo-conservative regime changes in the West and after the end of the Brezhnev system. The third decrease in global conflict activity began in 1992, the sharpest decrease ever since 1945. Obviously, the consequences of the end of the Cold War seem to be largely responsible for this decrease. Today, superpower rivalry has been reduced mainly to the question of NATO expansion; the UN Security Council became a semi-functioning body and the political regime changes in Eastern Europe, which were the cause for the largest increase in political conflict activity in 1989 and 1990, surpassed their critical phase in 1991 when violent escalations were most probable.

Figure 3.4 focuses on violent partial conflicts. Whereas the trends discussed above refer to the sum of violent and non-violent conflicts, the lines in Figure 3.4 indicate global conflict activities along the criterion of the use of violence. The term 'violent conflict' stands for both severe crises with irregular or sporadic military force as well as wars with the use of organized and regular military forces.

In general, the line of ongoing violent conflicts follows the line of all ongoing conflicts. In reference to the line of ongoing violent conflicts, two peaks are conspicuous; the period of decolonization in the 1960s and the period between 1987 and 1993. Within these two periods there is a significant increase in violent conflicts. Within the period 1987–92, the world experienced the sharpest rise in global violence by political conflicts since 1945. In reference to the second line in the figure, 'new violent

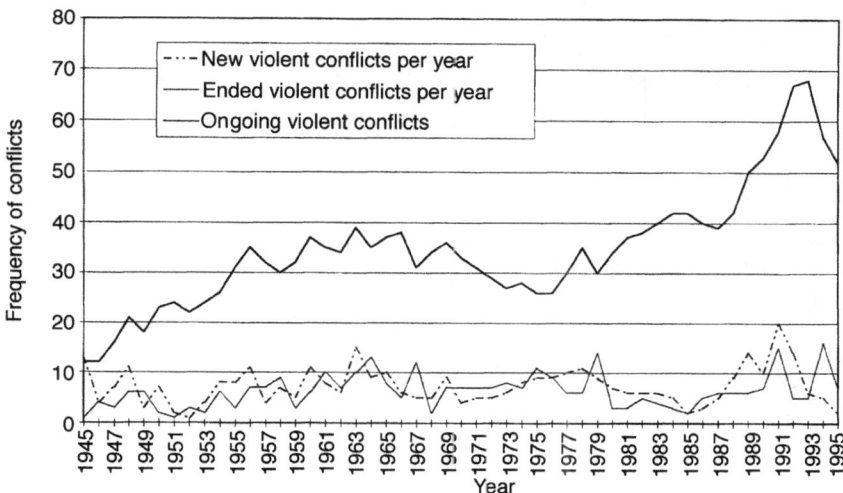

Figure 3.4 Ongoing violent conflicts.

conflicts', the rise in violent conflicts begins as early as 1985 and has its peak in 1991. Between 1980 and 1993 the frequency of ended violent conflicts is almost constantly lower than the frequency of new violent conflicts. There seem to be three aspects responsible for the all-time peak of 68 ongoing violent conflicts in 1992: a fairly large number of older, protracted conflicts, a large number of new violent conflicts since 1985 and a stagnation in the number of ended violent conflicts since 1980. This statistical observation reflects mainly the breakdown of the Eastern European communist regimes and the dissolution of the USSR and Yugoslavia. For the period immediately at and after the end of the Cold War, the Cold War peace hypothesis (e.g. Mearsheimer) can be verified. Yet in the long run, the high level of ongoing violent conflicts of the early 1990s may decrease again to Cold War frequencies.

The period between 1969 and 1979 shows a moderate decline in global violence. Despite a slowly increasing number of new violent conflicts, there were still more endings of violent political conflicts than beginnings. The only longer period with a decline in new violent conflict lies between the years 1978 and 1985. This decline may be caused by the reinforced superpower confrontation in the wake of the Soviet invasion of Afghanistan. This decline in violence may also be interpreted as a peace dividend from larger attention given to the Third World by the industrialized states. The US engagement in the Middle East peace process and the high ranking of developmental issues on the international agenda in general may have been causes for the decline in global violence.

Figure 3.5 shows the lines of both violent and non-violent conflicts in one figure. The sum of both lines per year gives the number of all ongoing conflicts per year. While violent conflicts decrease or only moderately

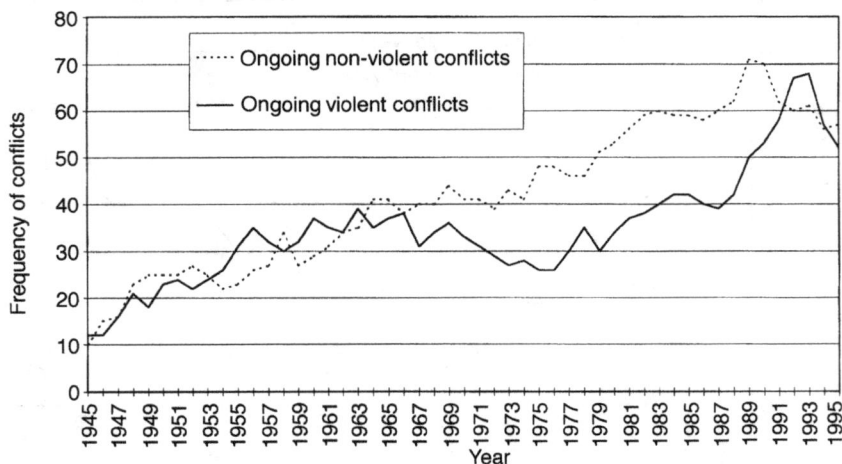

Figure 3.5 Non-violent and violent conflicts.

increase between the mid-1960s and the mid-1980s, the rate of non-violent conflicts per year keeps growing rather constantly. Between the mid-1970s and the mid-1980s the number of non-violent conflicts is on average one-third higher than the number of violent conflicts per year. This result supports the thesis that with growing global complexity and inter-dependence, the overall number of conflicts is growing, too. Yet the number of violent conflicts is growing more slowly than the number of non-violent political conflicts. Against this background, the extremely violent period between 1989 and 1992 has to be interpreted as an exception to the general trend.

Figure 3.6 shows a widening gap since the early 1960s between a decreasing number of violent and an increasing number of non-violent international conflicts. The average rate of ongoing violent international conflicts has been below ten per year since the early 1970s. In 1995, only three violent international conflicts can be observed. A comparison of the line of non-violent international conflicts with the line of overall conflicts shows there are comparable peaks in the mid-1960s, and in the early and late 1980s.

The aspirations for international security expressed in the United Nations Charter in 1945 became true in this respect; fifty years after the Second World War and thirty years after the end of the conflictive decolonization period there are hardly any ongoing violent international conflicts left. Almost all international conflicts, a relatively constant number of forty to sixty conflicts per year, are being settled by non-violent means. Furthermore, the official end of global superpower rivalry in 1989 and the shaping of a multi-polar or multi-regional world has (so far) not led to a destabilization of the overall international security situation.

The lines of internal conflicts per year since 1945 deviate significantly from those of international conflicts (Figure 3.7). The line of internal

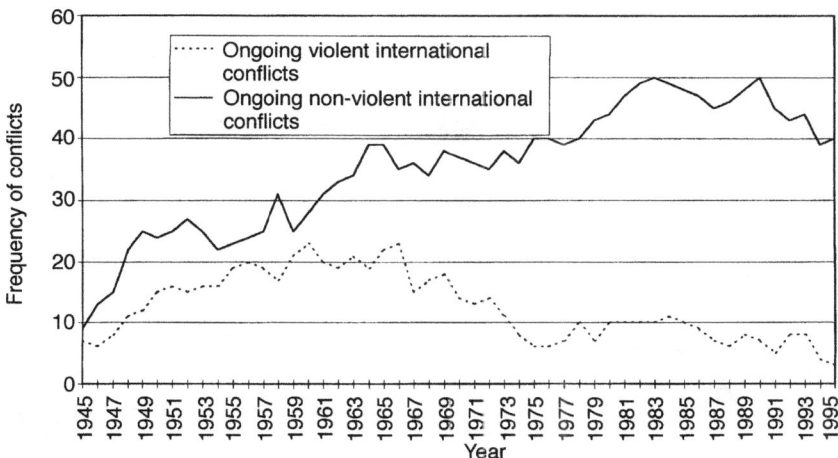

Figure 3.6 Violent and non-violent international conflicts.

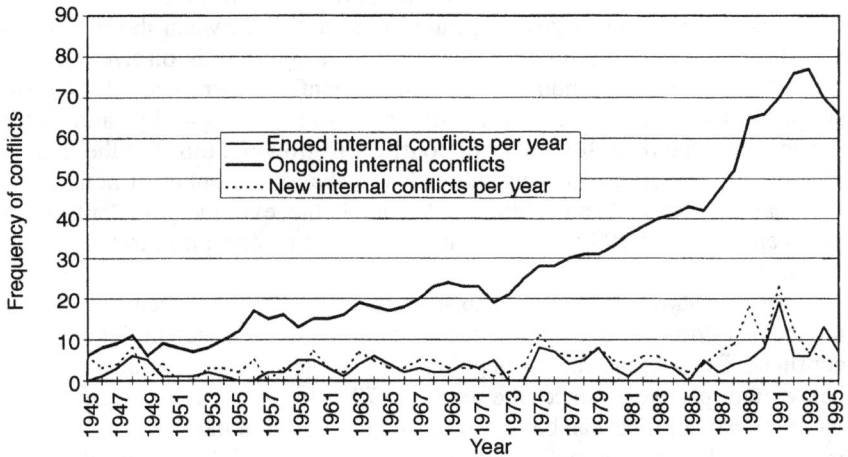

Figure 3.7 Internal conflicts.

conflicts increases from 1945 to 1992. Only since 1992 has there been a slight decrease in the number of ongoing internal conflicts per year. Still, in 1995 the level of yearly ongoing internal conflicts is at sixty-five conflicts; this is three times as high as the yearly conflict frequency during the period of decolonization in the 1960s.

The main reason for this increase in internal conflicts may be the mostly lower frequencies of ended versus beginning internal conflicts. Except for the years 1987–90, there is no period with extraordinarily high frequencies of new conflicts. It seems that the high frequencies of internal conflicts today are based on a slow but steady process over five decades of internal conflict accumulation.

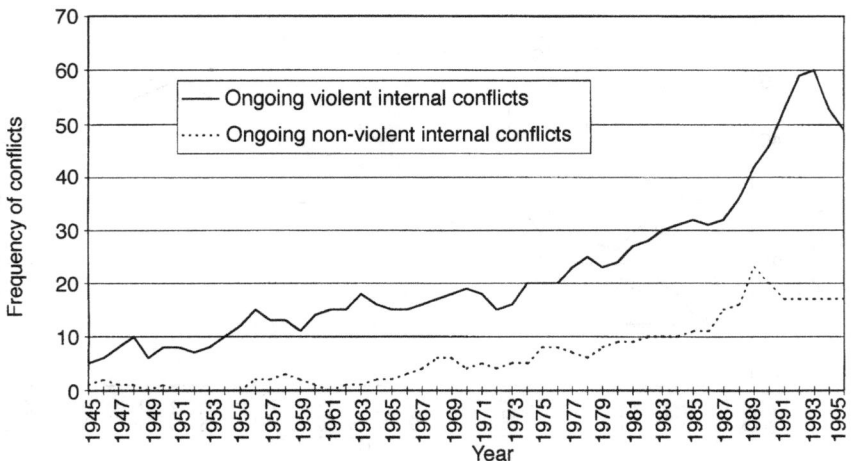

Figure 3.8 Non-violent and violent internal conflicts.

Separating violent and non-violent internal conflicts gives a similar picture (Figure 3.8). Both lines rise at comparable growth rates per year. Non-violent conflicts make up roughly one-third of all internal conflicts; two-thirds of all internal conflicts are partly or totally violent conflicts.

Figure 3.9 examines the relation between violent internal and international conflicts. Since 1969, the gap between international and internal violent conflicts has been widening. In 1995 almost all political violence was caused by internal conflicts whereas almost all international conflicts were resolved by peaceful means.

What are the possible interpretations of these results? Many theses in the study field of International Relations mark the end of the Cold War in 1989 as the beginning of a new era of internal conflicts. After high hopes based on the role of a revitalized UN system in this new era, a profound disillusion about the ongoing inefficacy of the UN replaced the hopes for this so-called New World Order. The UN is a body primarily concerned with violations against International Law. Empirically, the trend of increased violence caused by internal conflicts began as early as three decades ago. Since the late 1960s political violence has been less and less caused by international conflicts. The claim that the UN Security Council was ineffective due to the Cold War constellation and veto threats by the superpowers misses the point somewhat. The post-Cold War period proves that despite the diminished threat of superpower vetoes, the UN system is still unable to react adequately to political violence caused by internal conflicts, i.e. in the Yugoslavian, Rwandan and Burundi wars. An effective UN Security Council today, if it should be politically realistic, must be authorized to order coercive responses to internal political violence. Internal conflicts like international conflicts must be resolved at the negotiation table; yet, to get there, a symmetry of military means and instruments must be established and maintained. The

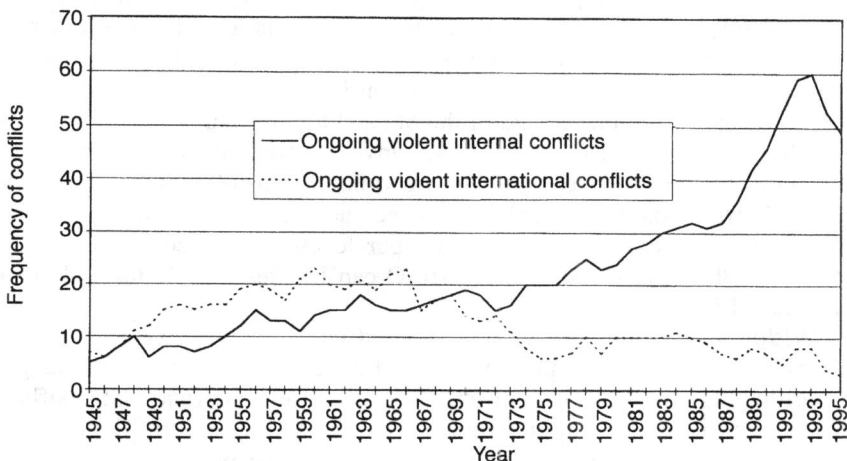

Figure 3.9 Violent internal and international conflicts.

Kurdish Resolution (1992) and the Somalian intervention (1993) were first steps in this direction. The ongoing codification of Human, Political, Social, Economic and Cultural Rights is slowly eroding the UN Charter provision on the principle of non-intervention in internal affairs of member states (Art. 2/ 7). Still, the UN is a state-based organization that by definition protects and conserves the interests of its member states. An illustrative example is the contemporary complaint about the insufficient respect for Human Rights in the People's Republic of China and in Iran. Yet the UN as an international organization is not likely to act against this violation of International Law as long as other permanent members in the UN Security Council are coping with violent internal conflicts of their own, such as the United Kingdom in Northern Ireland or France in Corsica. The sovereign right to handle one's internal affairs without external intervention is quite often defended by both democratic and authoritarian states.

Conflicts by intensity

Conflicts are carried out at various levels of intensity in different phases. KOSIMO has categorized all 661 conflicts from 1945 to 1995 into four levels of intensity (see definitions):

1   latent conflict
2   crisis
3   severe, violent crisis
4   war.

Within the dynamic development of a conflict, the levels of intensity can change. Some conflicts remain latent throughout the entire period in which opposing interests are put forward by the parties. Other conflicts escalate immediately into wars without remaining on a crisis level for any length of time. Still other conflicts change back and forth between light and violent crises. Each change in the intensity of a conflict marks (among other criteria, i.e. a change of actors) the end of the old and the beginning of a new partial conflict. Latent conflicts and crises involve predominantly non-violent instruments. Severe crises and wars are violent forms of conflicts. Thus, the general differentiation in this book between non-violent and violent conflicts is based on an aggregation of these four levels of intensity. Given these premises, the 661 conflicts in KOSIMO can be presented in the following Tables 3.17–19.

Within the group of non-violent conflicts, there is overall an even distribution between latent conflicts and crises. This distribution changes according to the type of conflict; there are many international conflicts that remain at a latent stage, whereas internal conflicts occur predominantly on a crisis level; there seems to be no regional variation to this tendency except for South America, which has a comparatively

Table 3.17 Conflicts by type and intensity

	All conflicts	%	Internal conflicts	%	International conflicts	%
Latent conflict	141	21	14	5	127	32
Crisis	145	22	44	17	101	25
Severe crisis	271	41	143	54	128	32
War	104	16	62	24	42	11
Total	661	100	263	100	398	100

high frequency of international latent conflicts concerning disputed borders and territories.

Within the group of violent conflicts, there is a clear tendency toward severe crises. Wars – in our definition – remain the exception. Regardless of the type of conflict and the region where violent conflicts occur, the number of severe crises is two to three times higher than the number of wars in the respective category. Both severe crises and wars dominate in internal conflicts. Measured by their frequency, severe crises are frequent in the Middle East, Maghreb and in sub-Saharan Africa. Europe has the lowest number both for severe crises and for wars.

War

The study of war is at the core of conflict research. Therefore we open a special chapter on this most extreme form of conflict. Although we have chosen a much broader approach toward conflicts that includes latent conflicts, crises and violent crises, wars remain the most destructive form of violence with the most far-reaching consequences on both the conflict parties and the people affected by the fighting. War countings differ substantially and cover very broad definitions like that of Kende (1978) with organized mass conflict, to Singer and Small (1972) with at least a thousand war-related deaths. Accordingly, Kende's list is much longer than Singer's. For comparative purposes we decided on a more restricted definition, i.e. taking into consideration duration, strength of both sides, war-related deaths and people involved.

A war is, then, a strategically organized mass conflict involving physical threat or force of some duration and intensity. The fighting parties must comprise organized governmental (or quasi-governmental) forces on at least one side; in addition, both parties must show for a certain period of time almost equal strength. This condition distinguishes a war from military actions among unequal opponents which usually end after a short period.

KOSIMO has identified 104 conflicts which fit this definition. According to the categories used in KOSIMO, these wars can be aggregated as shown in Table 3.20.

Table 3.18 Conflicts by regions and intensity, 1945–95

	Europe	%	Sub-Saharan Africa	%	Asia/ Oceania	%	Maghreb/ Middle East	%	America	%
Latent conflict	37	36	21	14	23	16	26	16	34	33
Crisis	38	37	22	15	35	24	28	17	22	22
Severe crisis	21	20	74	51	58	40	85	51	33	32
War	7	7	28	19	28	19	28	17	13	13
Total	103	100	145	100	144	100	167	100	102	100

Table 3.19 Conflicts in America by intensity

	North America	%	Central America	%	South America	%
Latent conflict	3	100	14	26	17	37
Crisis	0	0	15	28	7	15
Severe crisis	0	0	17	32	16	35
War	0	0	7	13	6	13
Total	3	100	53	100	46	100

The regional distribution of wars shows an even frequency of twenty-eight wars for sub-Saharan Africa, Asia/Oceania and the Middle East/Maghreb regions. Fewer wars were fought in Europe and the Central American sub-region. Note that severe, violent crises are not included in this counting. Central and South America have high levels of violent conflicts, but they are below the threshold of our rather 'strict' war definition. Despite the fact that until the late 1960s the number of yearly ongoing international violent conflicts per year was higher than the number of yearly ongoing internal violent conflicts, 60 percent of all wars were fought within a country and only 40 percent of all wars since 1945 were international wars.

With regard to the trend of increasing internal violent conflicts, it could be concluded that international wars were a phenomenon of the past. The economic globalization of the world seems to prefer trade wars over resources rather than military conquests. On the other hand, the civil wars and power conflicts in Zaire (Congo) and Congo (Brazzaville) in 1997 showed that economic interests may still fuel military conflicts. Competition over scarce or important resources fueled by ethno-political instrumentalization on the local level may become a future source of violent international conflicts. Thus, it may be premature to welcome the end of international violent conflicts especially for the developing countries. The breakup of the former Yugoslavia has shown that even in states close to the 'OECD peace zone', brutal internationalized warfare can prevail over civil traditions, and the conflict may threaten the security of an entire region.

Figure 3.10 shows the frequencies of yearly ongoing wars since 1945. Overall, there is an increasing trend until 1992–93. Thereafter, the number of wars has dropped sharply to the level of the late 1960s and – again – the late 1970s. The two periods with the largest growth rates are between 1961 and 1971 as well as between 1981 and 1991. The former period can be characterized as the decolonization period. Though the formal decolonization process was finished, many wars were fought in unstable developing countries. The second growth period can be interpreted within the background of intensified superpower confrontations. The peak around 1990 and 1993 is a consequence of the breakup of the Soviet system. The wars in Georgia, Tajikistan, Chechnya, Azerbaijan/Armenia, as well as the

Table 3.20 Profile of wars, 1945–95

Total	All wars	104	%	Total (%)
Region	Europe	7	6	
	Sub-Saharan Africa	28	24	
	Asia/Oceania	28	24	
	Middle East/Maghreb	28	24	
	America	13	11	
	North America	0	–	
	Central America	7	6	
	South America	6	5	100
Type	Internal wars	62	60	
	International wars	42	40	100
Treaty	No treaty	32	30	
	Formal conclusion	72	70	100
Basic conflicts	The last partial conflict within a basic conflict is coded as 'war'	25	24	
Resolution	By mediation	4	4	
	By threat/passive withdrawal	1	1	
	By active withdrawal	1	1	
	By continued threat/pressure	5	5	
	Unresolved wars	43	41	
	By military means	50	48	100
Military outcome*	Indecisive outcome, stalemate, cease-fire	32	31	
	Victory for initiator	25	25	
	Defeat for initiator	22	22	
	Continuation of fighting	17	16	
	Withdrawal	6	6	100
Territorial outcome*	Separation of territory	6	18	
	Loss of territory	2	6	
	Annexation, unification or incorporation of territory	9	27	
	Denouncement of territorial claims	4	11	
	Status quo ante, continued territorial claims	13	38	100
Political outcome*	Consensual agreement	23	26	
	Compromise agreement	13	15	
	None or partial agreement	51	59	100
Issues*	Territory, borders, sea borders	22	12	
	Decolonization, national independence	20	11	
	Ethnic, religious, regional autonomy	26	14	
	Ideology, system conflict	31	16	
	Internal power conflict	53	28	
	International power conflict	21	11	
	Resources	12	6	
	Other	3	2	100

Note
* Multiple choice.

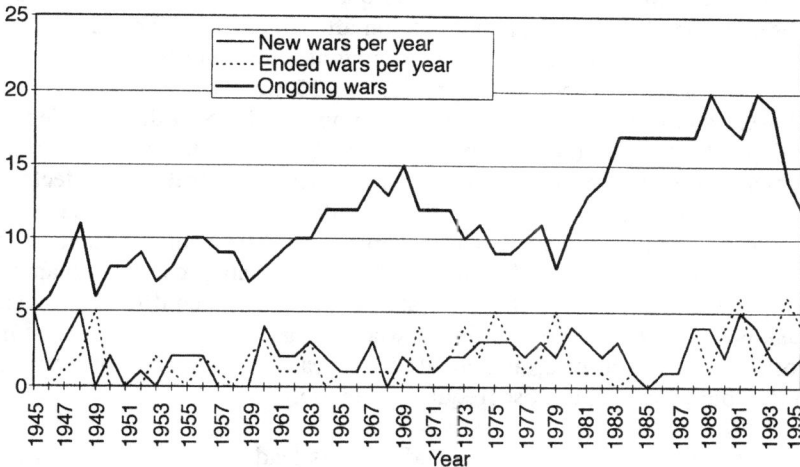

Figure 3.10 Ongoing wars.

violent breakup of the former Yugoslavia, have contributed to this all-time high of ongoing wars since 1945.

Justifiable and unjustifiable wars

There are wars fought for justifiable issues and wars fought for unjustifiable issues. What is just or unjust depends on time and space. In international law, the use of military means in order to attain political goals has been internationally outlawed only since 1928. But this did not prevent the Second World War and others which followed. Today justifiable issues are values recognized by international law, i.e. by the United Nations Charter (independence from colonial domination, self-determination, human rights). Unjustifiable issues can be aggression against another country, annexation of foreign territories, expulsion of a group of people, 'ethnic cleansing', etc. This distinction is not identical with just or unjust wars since this would imply that the use of force is justified by international law.

Single and multiple wars

We can distinguish between single wars and multiple wars. Single wars are wars which occur once on a specific issue and in a given territory; multiple wars continue either over the same issue or another more or less related issue within the same territory and lead to another war. The continuation of a war on a specific issue and/or the succession of wars on different issues may have a variety of causes and these causes have to do with the modalities of the ending of the preceding war. Hence, by studying the causes of a war we must look also at the modalities of their endings.

As to the question about continuing quarrels after the ending of a war, we observe that 79 wars had a continuation after they ended. This means that in more than three-quarters of the wars fought after 1945 the conflict did not end with a war. A look at the remaining 25 wars without further conflict phases show that twelve were ongoing in 1995; others ended with independence and a consecutive peace treaty such as the 1962 Evian treaty which terminated the Algerian war for independence or the 1963 declaration of independence for Kenya, 1949 for Indonesia or 1960 for Madagascar. Some of these wars ended with an armistice agreement (Guatemala 1995, Cambodia 1975, Laos 1973, Israel 1974). These data prove on a quantitative basis our hypothesis, i.e. that wars are not the end of a conflict. However, the task is to analyze the formalities of war endings, since we assume that many formal conclusions or arrangements do not carry the full consent required for a durable peace. The most frequent wars are:

- wars of independence which afterwards lead to civil wars and the fight for power within the new independent state
- ethnic wars which, simultaneously or successively, lead to ethnic wars either among the same ethnic group or among different ethnic groups
- wars of international power connected with wars of national power, i.e. struggle for international hegemony and for central political dominance.

There are various links between successive wars as a chain effect from one war to another:

- Exhaustion hypothesis: a war could end because resources are exhausted and/or needed for another war, e.g. Iraqi troops withdrawn from the Iranian front to the Kurdish front after the first Gulf war.
- Consolidation effect: a war can create a situation which then gives rise to another war, e.g. the many wars for independence posed, once they were ended, the problem of creating a new political order which was in most of the cases contested by rival groups.
- Internal-rivalry effect: in a multi-ethnic state the power positions are questioned by the various ethnic groups who in succession are fighting for participation in the national polity. One ethnic group is motivated by the activities of another group.
- Compensation effect: there can be a compensatory chain effect from an internal to an external war; a government could initiate an external war in order to distract attention from internal difficulties.
- Proxy effect: finally, there can be a chain effect from the external environment to internal rivalry in that two dominant powers impose rivalry upon a third country.

More wars were multiple wars than single wars. The 33 single wars counted only once in our war list (Table 3.21), i.e. wars without continuation on the same or related issues, indicate that the goals were achieved. This is the case of wars of independence (Morocco, Madagascar, Malaysia, Kenya, Algeria, Mozambique, Slovenia, Croatia), of ethnic wars (Biafra, Rwanda), and of civil wars (i.e. Yemen). Many international wars on borders and territories were resolved either by an agreement or by a stalemate (Suez, Malaya–Indonesia, Uganda–Tanzania, Ecuador–Peru, Iraq–Kuwait). There was one case of clear violation of international law, namely Iraq's invasion of Kuwait, which was then liberated by UN troops and restored in 1994. Other cases of violation of international law after 1945 are the wars in the former Yugoslavia. It has to be seen whether the ethnic, territorial and human losses will trigger further conflicts.

The 65 multiple wars are of interest since they indicate that a solution was not found by going to war and the cause of a war was a war. That is, the termination of a war of independence did not solve the following problem of installing a legitimate government (Sudan, Israel, Indonesia, Burundi, Angola, India, China, Chad, Zaire, Indochina, Bosnia, Chechnya); inter-ethnic wars did not solve the problem of self-determination of the minority groups (Lebanon, Somalia, Ethiopia, Sri Lanka, four Bosnian wars); international wars did not solve the issue of national sovereignty (Iraq, South Africa, Afghanistan, Yemen, Argentina). Very often international wars were fought in order to reach a national goal within one country or in another (Falklands, South Africa, Afghanistan, Iraq, Argentina, Yemen).

Issues in wars

We distinguished among seven issues in conflicts: autonomy, colonialism, ideology, international and national power, resources and territory. In the context of wars these issues are not independent from each other; most often there is a strong correlation between international types of issues and internal types of issues. Since most wars have been fought over more than one issue (up to three issues were coded), the counts in our databank are higher than the number of actual wars. In more than half of all wars, there was an intensive struggle over access to or the representation of national power positions. The second most frequent issues in wars are ideological conflicts and conflicts over the political system. These issues were observed in roughly one-third of all wars since 1945. Wars over territories, borders, national independence, decolonization and international power conflicts were identified in one-fifth of all conflicts respectively. Resources as an issue in wars is a comparatively rare phenomenon. In only 12 percent of all wars were resources clearly identified as an issue in dispute.

Outcomes of wars

The analysis of the military outcomes of wars does not encourage potential aggressors. In only about a quarter of all wars has the initiator of a war gained

Table 3.21 Chronological listing of wars, 1945–95

Start	End	Name
1942	1948	India II (partition)
1944	1956	Morocco (independence)
1945	1949	Indonesia (independence)
1945	1949	China (civil war)
1945	1954	1st Indochina War
1946	1949	Greece (civil war II)
1947	1960	Madagascar (independence)
1947	1949	India III (Kashmir I)
1947	1947	Paraguay (*coup d'état*)
1948	1953	Colombia (Violencia I)
1948	1948	Yemen, Arab. Rep. (civil war I)
1948	cont	Burma/Myanmar (minorities)
1948	1960	Malaya (independence)
1948	1949	Israel I (Palestine War)
1950	1965	Indonesia (South Moluccas)
1950	1953	Korea II (Korean War)
1952	1956	Kenya (independence, Mau Mau)
1954	1962	Algeria II (independence)
1954	1959	China (Tibet II)
1955	1973	2nd Indochina War (1st part)
1955	1963	Sudan (Autonomy For The South)
1956	1959	Cuba (Revolution)
1956	1957	Egypt (Suez War: France, Great Britain, Israel)
1960	1972	Guatemala II
1960	1961	Vietnam (civil war)
1960	1963	Zaire (Catanga secession)
1960	1960	Zaire–Belgium (Belgian Intervention)
1961	1970	Iraq (Kurds II)
1961	1974	Angola (Independence I)
1962	1968	Yemen, Arab Rep. (civil war II)
1962	1963	China–India (War)
1963	1972	Sudan (civil war)
1963	1975	Laos II (civil war)
1963	1966	Malaya–Indonesia (Sarawak/Sabah)
1964	1975	Mozambique (independence)
1964	1973	2nd Indochina War ('Vietnam War')
1965	1970	India XVI (Kashmir IV)
1966	1975	Chad I
1967	1970	Nigeria (Biafra Secession)
1967	1991	Eritrea III (civil war)
1967	1967	Egypt–Israel (6-Day War)
1969	1977	Argentina (Montoneros)
1969	1970	Honduras–El Salvador (Soccer War I)
1970	1975	Cambodia II
1971	1971	India XVII (Bangladesh III)
1972	1979	Rhodesia (civil war)
1972	1973	Burundi (genocide)
1973	1976	2nd Indochina War (armistice)
1973	1973	Israel IV (Yom Kippur)
1974	1991	Ethiopia (Tigray)
1974	1975	Indonesia (East Timor)
1974	1974	Cyprus (Turkish Invasion)
1975	1976	Lebanon II

1975	1976	Angola (civil war)
1975	1979	Chad II
1976	cont.	Indonesia (East Timor III)
1976	1978	Somalia–Ethiopia (Ogaden)
1976	1989	Angola (civil war)
1977	1979	Nicaragua I (revolution)
1977	1978	3rd Indochina War (1st part)
1978	1991	3rd Indochina War (2nd part)
1978	1991	Mozambique (Renamo)
1978	1979	Uganda–Tanzania (border)
1979	1988	Afghanistan III (Soviet Invasion Dec. 79)
1979	1979	China–Vietnam (War)
1980	1980	Chad III
1980	cont.	Peru (Shining Path)
1980	cont.	Guatemala III
1980	1988	Iran–Iraq I (Gulf War)
1981	1990	Nicaragua II (Contras)
1981	1991	El Salvador (civil war)
1981	1981	Ecuador–Peru (Amazonas III)
1982	1984	Lebanon VI
1982	1982	Argentina–Great Britain (Falklands IV)
1983	1990	Chad V
1983	1988	Sudan (SPLA-Rebellion)
1983	1987	Sri Lanka (Tamils II)
1984	1989	Lebanon VII
1986	1986	Yemen People's Rep. (Aden civil war)
1987	1995	Sri Lanka (Tamils III)
1988	1990	Lebanon (militia)
1988	1991	Afghanistan IV (civil war)
1988	1988	Burundi (Hutu)
1988	1991	Somalia (civil war)
1989	cont.	Turkey (Kurds)
1989	1990	Lebanon VIII
1989	1995	Liberia (civil war)
1989	cont.	Sudan (civil war)
1990	1991	Iraq–Kuwait (annexation/reconquest)
1990	1994	Rwanda (civil war)
1991	cont.	Sierra Leone (civil war)
1991	cont.	Somalia (civil war)
1991	1994	Armenia–Azerbaijan
1991	1995	Croatia (Croatia//Croatian Serbs+Fed. Army: East Slavonia)
1992	1993	Afghanistan (civil war)
1992	1994	Bosnia (Bosnian Government//Bosnian Croats)
1992	1994	Bosnia (Croatian Serbs+Separatists+Bosnian Serbs/ Bosnian Government)
1992	1993	Tajikistan
1993	cont.	Afghanistan (civil war)
1993	cont.	Burundi (civil war)
1994	1994	Yemen (civil war)
1994	cont.	Russia (Chechnya)
1995	1995	Bosnia (Krajina/West Slavonia)
1995	cont.	Sri Lanka (civil war)

Notes
cont. = continued; I, II, etc. = partial conflicts within a basic conflict.

from the outcome. Except for some cases in which the initiator withdrew military forces, the outcome of military endeavors is discouraging for aggressors. One-third of the wars ended in stalemates and cease-fires, another quarter of cases were lost to the affected party and in about 17 percent of the cases, the fighting continued into 1995. The territorial outcome for those wars in which territorial matters were at stake is also discouraging. Only in very rare cases did an aggressor gain territory. The political outcome reflects the difficult and complex nature of wars and their resolution. More than half of all wars were settled with no or only partial agreements on the issues. In a quarter of the wars, a consensual agreement or an agreement was reached by the parties.

Duration of conflicts

The duration of a conflict can depend on various factors. The most apparent factor is the unwillingness of the disputants to reach negotiated compromises. Conflict parties of equal strength and with long-lasting resources of power may also fight prolonged conflicts. The neglect of a conflict by neighboring states and the superpowers may equally prolong a conflict. Conflicts at the periphery tend to last longer than conflicts in the center of regions or states because of negligence, less attention and less of a need for powerful centers to resolve the conflict. Other arguments in the theories of International Relations about the duration of conflicts refer to the degree of complexity of a conflict. The more complex a conflict becomes, the more difficult it is to come to quick resolutions and settlements. The higher the number of issues, parties and antagonisms, the more protracted a conflict becomes. Indivisible issues such as ethnicity, beliefs, culture, history and personality make it more difficult to come to speedy de-escalations and agreements.

Therefore, the analysis of the duration of conflicts may be a useful test for the above suppositions. As in the other chapters, we group the conflicts into the categories of violent and non-violent as well as internal and international conflicts. The duration itself is measured in years. Figure 3.11 shows the duration and frequency of both violent and non-violent conflicts.

The frequency of violent conflicts is overall higher than the frequency of non-violent conflicts between the time intervals of 'less than a year' and eight years. Conflicts that lasted longer than eight years were more often non-violent conflicts. In reference to conflicts that lasted one year or less, the frequency of violent conflicts is one-third to one-fourth higher than the frequency of non-violent conflicts. For durations longer than three to four years, violent and non-violent conflicts are about equally frequent. In short, violent conflicts find quicker endings than non-violent conflicts. This finding does not quite support those by Jones, Bremer and Singer (1996: 163) who cautiously state: 'the duration of disputes appears to be positively associated with the level of hostility reached [...]'.

On the other hand, there are as many violent long-lasting conflicts as there are non-violent, long-lasting conflicts. Also, long-lasting conflicts have a

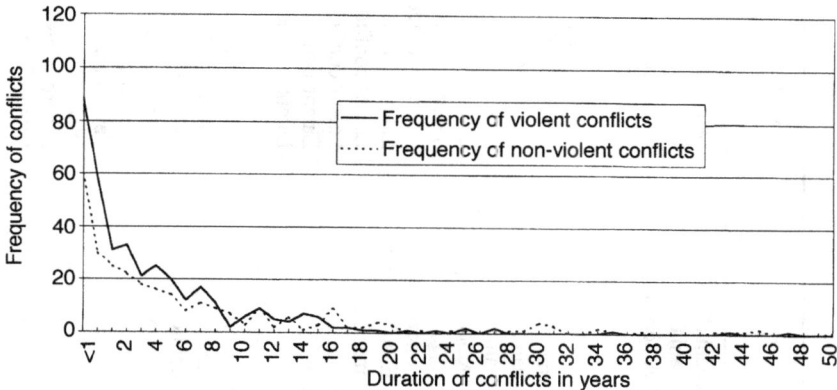

Figure 3.11 Duration and frequency of violent and non-violent conflicts.

predominantly international character, since they are fought mostly over territories and borders. The longest international conflicts – close to fifty years – in our survey are Japan–USSR/Russia (Kuril Islands), USSR–Norway (Spitzbergen) and GDR–FRG (separation). Table 3.22 lists conflicts that lasted ten years and longer, including their region and intensity.

It can be inferred from the analysis of the duration of different types of conflicts, that most conflicts are settled within less than a year. Very few conflicts last longer than eight or ten years. The differentiation between violent and non-violent conflicts did not alter this general tendency in any significant way. Violent conflicts seem to last slightly longer than non-violent conflicts. The above-mentioned factors which may be responsible for a conflict's duration can cautiously be verified. It seems that international disputes get more attention, or the parties seem to have greater national interests or greater external and internal pressures to settle these conflicts. In contrast, internal and non-violent conflicts seem to end more often in delay, deferment, stalemates or non-negotiated settlements, such as perseverance, threat and suppressive use of force of the government over internal opposition, e.g. the Indonesian suppression of opposition groups in East Timor, or the terror of the 'Shining Path' against the people and government of Peru.

Regions of conflict

The classification of states by regions can be useful for the empirical analysis of political conflicts when regions have cultural or civilizational similarities or affinities. We can identify regions of generally low and high conflict activity or violent and non-violent regions. In a diachronic view regional waves or peaks of violence can be differentiated from calmer periods. Yet, the analytical value of regional groupings should not be overestimated.

Table 3.22 Conflicts ranked by duration

Duration in years	Name	Start	End	Region	Intensity
51	Japan–USSR/Russia (Kurils)	1945	cont.	Asia/Oceania	Latent conflict
48	Burma/Myanmar (minorities)	1948	cont.	Asia/Oceania	War
46	Honduras–US (Swan Island)	1945	1991	Central America	Latent conflict
46	USSR–Norway (Spitzbergen)	1945	1991	Europe	Latent conflict
45	GDR–FRG (division)	1945	1990	Europe	Latent conflict
44	Indonesia (Darul Islam separation attempt)	1947	1991	Asia/Oceania	Severe crisis
44	Colombia–Venezuela (Monjes Islands)	1952	cont.	South America	Latent conflict
43	Korea III (partition)	1953	cont.	Asia/Oceania	Latent conflict
38	Thailand–Cambodia I (border)	1953	1991	Asia/Oceania	Crisis
36	Cuba–US (Guantanamo)	1960	cont.	Central America	Latent conflict
36	Spain (Basque autonomy)	1960	cont.	Europe	Severe crisis
35	US–Cuba (bilateral relations)	1961	cont.	Central America	Latent conflict
35	Morocco–Spain (Ceuta and Melilla)	1961	cont.	Middle East/Maghreb	Latent conflict
32	Bolivia–Peru–Chile (Tacna and Arica)	1964	cont.	South America	Latent conflict
32	Italy (South Tirol)	1960	1992	Europe	Latent conflict
32	Spain–United Kingdom (Gibraltar)	1964	cont.	Europe	Latent conflict
31	Albania–USSR (tensions)	1960	1991	Europe	Latent conflict
31	China–USSR (tensions)	1960	1991	Asia/Oceania	Crisis
31	Puerto Rico–US (status II)	1962	1993	Central America	Latent conflict
31	Saudi Arabia–Kuwait (islands)	1965	cont.	Middle East/Maghreb	Latent conflict
30	China–India (border)	1963	1993	Asia/Oceania	Latent conflict
29	Bahrain–Qatar I (sea borders)	1967	cont.	Middle East/Maghreb	Latent conflict
28	Northern Ireland	1968	cont.	Europe	Severe crisis
28	Philippines (uproar of 'National Front')	1968	cont.	Asia/Oceania	Severe crisis
26	Eritrea III (civil war)	1967	1993	Sub-Saharan Africa	War
26	Philippines (Moros in Mindanao and Sulu)	1970	cont.	Asia/Oceania	Severe crisis
26	Saudi Arabia–Abu Dhabi (Buraimi I)	1949	1975	Middle East/Maghreb	Crisis
25	Bangladesh (Chittagong Hill Tracts)	1971	cont.	Asia/Oceania	Crisis

No.	Conflict	Begin	End	Region	Status
24	Namibia II (SWAPO)	1966	1990	Sub-Saharan Africa	Severe crisis
23	Brazil–Paraguay (Parana)	1962	1985	South America	Latent conflict
22	Zambia–Rhodesia (border)	1965	1987	Sub-Saharan Africa	Severe crisis
21	France (Corsica)	1975	cont.	Europe	Latent conflict
21	Libya–Chad	1973	1994	Sub-Saharan Africa	Crisis
21	Cyprus V	1975	cont.	Europe	Latent conflict
20	Indonesia (East Timor III)	1976	1976	Asia/Oceania	War
20	Cameroon–Nigeria (Bakassi peninsula III)	1961	1981	Sub-Saharan Africa	Latent conflict
20	Morocco (Western Sahara I)	1956	1956	Middle East/Maghreb	Latent conflict
20	Mauritius–Malagasy Republic–France (Tromelin)	1976	cont.	Sub-Saharan Africa	Latent conflict
20	Namibia I	1946	1966	Sub-Saharan Africa	Latent conflict
19	GDR–Denmark (border)	1969	1988	Europe	Latent conflict
19	Pakistan (civil War in Karachi)	1977	cont.	Asia/Oceania	Severe crisis
19	Sweden–USSR (Baltic Sea)	1969	1988	Europe	Latent conflict
18	China–Laos	1975	1993	Asia/Oceania	Latent conflict
18	Peru–Ecuador (Amazonas I)	1942	1960	South America	Latent conflict
18	Indochina Ib	1955	1973	Asia/Oceania	War
18	South Africa (ANC, PAC)	1976	1994	Sub-Saharan Africa	Severe crisis
17	Argentina–United Kingdom (Falklands I)	1965	1982	South America	Latent conflict
17	Ethiopia (Tigray)	1974	1991	Sub-Saharan Africa	War
17	France–Malagasy Republic (Glorieuses Islands)	1973	1990	Sub-Saharan Africa	Latent conflict
17	Guatemala–Belize I (UK)	1960	1977	Central America	Crisis
17	Iran–UAE III (islands)	1979	cont.	Middle East/Maghreb	Latent conflict
17	Jordan–Israel (Jordan water III)	1977	1994	Middle East/Maghreb	Latent conflict
17	Canada–France (St Pierre and Miquelon)	1975	1992	North America	Latent conflict
17	Laos–Thailand (border)	1975	1992	Asia/Oceania	Crisis
17	Namibia–South Africa (Walfish bay)	1977	1994	Sub-Saharan Africa	Latent conflict
17	Nicaragua–Colombia (San Andres Archipelago)	1979	cont.	Central America	Latent conflict
17	Oman (Imam–Sultan conflict)	1954	1971	Middle East/Maghreb	Severe crisis
16	Afghanistan–Pakistan (Pashtunistan I)	1947	1963	Middle East/Maghreb	Severe crisis
16	Ethiopia–United Kingdom (Gadaduma I)	1947	1963	Sub-Saharan Africa	Latent conflict
16	Guatemala III	1980	cont.	Central America	War

Table 3.22 Continued

Duration in years	Name	Start	End	Region	Intensity
16	Yemen PR–Oman (Dhofar uproar)	1963	1979	Middle East/Maghreb	Severe crisis
16	Libya–US I	1973	1989	Middle East/Maghreb	Severe crisis
16	Malaysia–Philippines	1961	1977	Asia/Oceania	Latent conflict
16	Mauritius–United Kingdom (Diego Garcia)	1980	cont.	Sub-Saharan Africa	Latent conflict
16	Mozambique (civil war; RENAMO)	1978	1994	Sub-Saharan Africa	War
16	Peru (Illuminated path)	1980	cont.	South America	War
16	Angola (civil war II)	1976	1991	Sub-Saharan Africa	War
15	Guatemala–Belize III	1981	cont.	Central America	Latent conflict
15	India VIII (Kashmir II)	1949	1964	Asia/Oceania	Severe crisis
15	India XVIII (Khalistan/Punjab)	1981	cont.	Asia/Oceania	Severe crisis
15	Indonesia (uproar in southern Sulawesi)	1950	1965	Asia/Oceania	Severe crisis
15	Indonesia (South Moluccas)	1950	1965	Asia/Oceania	War
15	Yemen–United Kingdom (Aden I)	1948	1963	Middle East/Maghreb	Severe crisis
15	Thailand (communism)	1965	1980	Asia/Oceania	Severe crisis
14	Argentina–United Kingdom (Falklands III)	1982	cont.	South America	Latent conflict
14	Argentina–Chile (Beagle I)	1958	1972	South America	Crisis
14	Ethiopia (Oromo)	1977	1991	Sub-Saharan Africa	Severe crisis
14	Djibouti (Afars–Issas I)	1963	1977	Sub-Saharan Africa	Latent conflict
14	India X (Nagas)	1950	1964	Asia/Oceania	Severe crisis
14	Indonesia (West Irian IV)	1982	cont.	Asia/Oceania	Crisis
14	Cambodia (border)	1956	1970	Asia/Oceania	Severe crisis
14	Netherlands–FRG (border)	1949	1963	Europe	Latent conflict
14	Senegal (Casamance)	1982	cont.	Sub-Saharan Africa	Severe crisis
14	Venezuela–Guyana (Essequibo II)	1982	cont.	South America	Latent conflict
13	Angola (independence)	1961	1974	Sub-Saharan Africa	War
13	British Guyana (independence)	1953	1966	South America	Severe crisis
13	India–South Africa (apartheid)	1946	1959	Sub-Saharan Africa	Latent conflict
13	Indochina IIIb	1978	1991	Asia/Oceania	War

13	Indonesia (West Irian III)	1969	1982	Asia/Oceania	Severe crisis
13	Libya–Malta	1973	1986	Middle East/Maghreb	Latent conflict
13	Malagasy Republic (independence)	1947	1960	Sub-Saharan Africa	War
12	Bangladesh (Chakma, Marma)	1975	1987	Asia/Oceania	Severe crisis
12	Burma–China (border)	1948	1960	Asia/Oceania	Latent conflict
12	Burma (Chinese troops)	1949	1961	Asia/Oceania	Severe crisis
12	China–Vietnam (Spratly III)	1975	1987	Asia/Oceania	Latent conflict
12	China–Vietnam (border, emigrants, ideology)	1979	1991	Asia/Oceania	Crisis
12	El Salvador–Honduras (border)	1980	1992	Central America	Latent conflict
12	Guatemala II	1960	1972	Central America	War
12	India VII (Indus channel)	1948	1960	Asia/Oceania	Latent conflict
12	India XX (Ayodhya)	1984	cont.	Asia/Oceania	Severe crisis
12	Iraq (Shi'ites II)	1979	1991	Middle East/Maghreb	Crisis
12	Cameroon (independence)	1955	1967	Sub-Saharan Africa	Severe crisis
12	Laos II (civil war)	1963	1975	Asia/Oceania	War
12	Malaya (independence)	1948	1960	Asia/Oceania	War
12	Morocco (independence)	1944	1956	Middle East/Maghreb	War
12	Morocco (Western Sahara III)	1979	1991	Middle East/Maghreb	Severe crisis
12	Poland–GDR (Stettin bay)	1977	1989	Europe	Latent conflict
12	Tunisia–Libya	1976	1988	Middle East/Maghreb	Latent conflict
12	USSR (Volga Germans)	1979	1991	Europe	Latent conflict
11	Angola (border)	1963	1974	Sub-Saharan Africa	Severe crisis
11	Somalia–Ethiopia (border)	1950	1961	Sub-Saharan Africa	Severe crisis
11	El Salvador (civil war)	1981	1992	Central America	War
11	El Salvador–Honduras (soccer war II (aftermath))	1969	1980	Central America	Latent conflict
11	Guinea-Bissau–Portugal (independence)	1963	1974	Sub-Saharan Africa	Severe crisis
11	India IX (Goa I)	1950	1961	Asia/Oceania	Crisis
11	Yemen PR–Oman (border)	1981	1992	Middle East/Maghreb	Crisis
11	Colombia (Guerilla IV)	1985	cont.	South America	Severe crisis
11	Mozambique (independence)	1964	1975	Sub-Saharan Africa	War
10	Ethiopia (Ogaden, WSLF)	1978	1988	Sub-Saharan Africa	Severe crisis

Table 3.22 Continued

Duration in years	Name	Start	End	Region	Intensity
10	Indonesia (West Irian I)	1950	1960	Asia/Oceania	Crisis
10	Iraq (Shi'ites I)	1968	1978	Middle East/Maghreb	Latent conflict
10	Israel III (border)	1957	1967	Middle East/Maghreb	Severe crisis
10	Austria (state treaty)	1945	1955	Europe	Latent conflict
10	Poland (democratization)	1980	1990	Europe	Crisis
10	Portugal (democratization)	1973	1983	Europe	Crisis
10	Togo (independence)	1947	1957	Sub-Saharan Africa	Latent conflict
10	Venezuela–British Guyana (Essequibo I)	1960	1970	South America	Crisis

When differentiating states by geographic, cultural or civilizational characteristics, we are disregarding bonds, features, similarities or inter-dependencies that might exist on different levels among states which might also have an effect on the conflict behavior of states or regional conflict frequencies.

One common thesis in conflict research states that the occurrence of international conflicts is more likely among neighboring, regional or geographically closer states than among states that lie far apart. This is obviously true except for the conflict relations of the superpowers and the former colonial powers. The latter pursue their national interests worldwide, the former often show military responsibility for their discharged former colonies in times of crisis. Still, we can observe a cluster of conflicts in one region although these conflicts have no causal or synchronic relations with each other. For example, an economically induced political crisis in one state, ethnically motivated conflicts in another state and a third conflict for power among competing elites in yet another state may make up a conflict region.

Also, there can be 'islands of peace' in otherwise highly conflictive regions. Costa Rica in the Central American region or Botswana in the Southern African region are examples of states that have not been affected by the frequently violent conflicts of their surrounding neighbor states.

Figures 3.12–3.22 show the frequencies of certain types of conflicts in our five global regions: Europe, Middle East/Maghreb, sub-Saharan Africa, Asia/Oceania and America. Figure 3.12 is concerned with the regional distribution of violent and non-violent conflicts. Between 1945 and 1995, the Middle East/Maghreb region and sub-Saharan Africa were the most violent regions, whereas Europe and America were the two regions with the lowest frequencies of violent conflicts. As regards the frequencies of non-violent conflicts per region, Europe leads the list, whereas the other four global regions show approximately equal numbers of non-violent conflicts. For the overall number of conflicts per region, the Middle East/Maghreb region accounts for the most conflicts, followed by sub-Saharan Africa, Asia/Oceania, Europe and America. A look at the relation between violent and non-violent conflicts per region shows Europe with the biggest difference in favor of non-violent conflicts. Less than half of all conflicts in Europe escalated into violent conflicts. In contrast, in the Middle East/Maghreb and the sub-Saharan African regions, on average more than every second conflict escalated into a violent conflict.

Figure 3.13 shows the regional distribution of international and internal conflicts. The exact location of an international conflict is either the place where the conflict actually occurs or the region in which the initiating state is located. Because of the overall higher number of international conflicts over internal conflicts between 1945 and 1995, all regions have higher frequencies of international conflicts than internal conflicts – although the trend has been to more internal conflicts than international conflicts since the

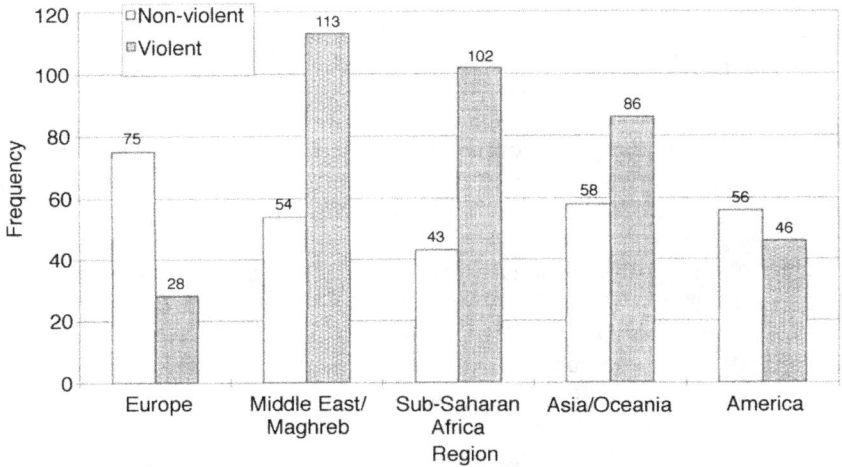

Figure 3.12 Regional distribution of violent and non-violent conflicts.

1970s. The highest difference concerning this relation is in the Middle East/
Maghreb region, the lowest in Europe. In absolute numbers, the Middle East/
Maghreb region has the highest number of international conflicts, Asia/
Oceania has the highest number of internal conflicts. There seems to be no
significant difference in the number of internal conflicts per region.
Although America has a relatively low number of internal conflicts, the
range lies between thirty-nine and sixty-three internal conflicts per region
between 1945 and 1995.

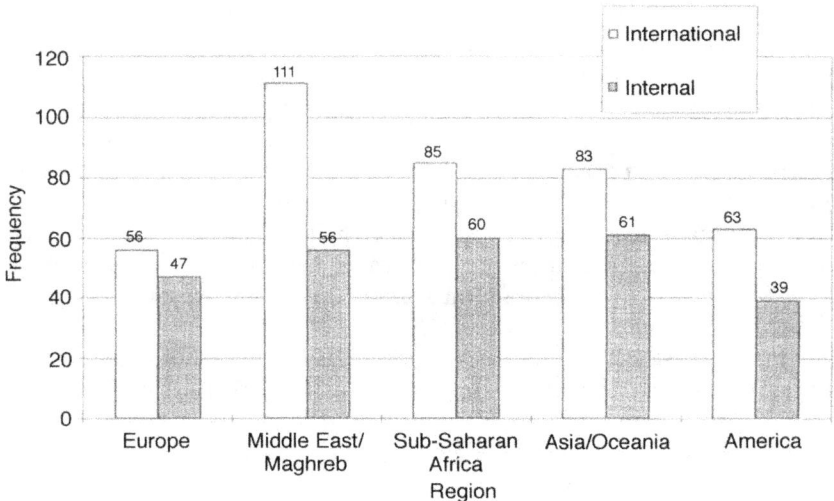

Figure 3.13 Regional distribution of internal and international conflicts.

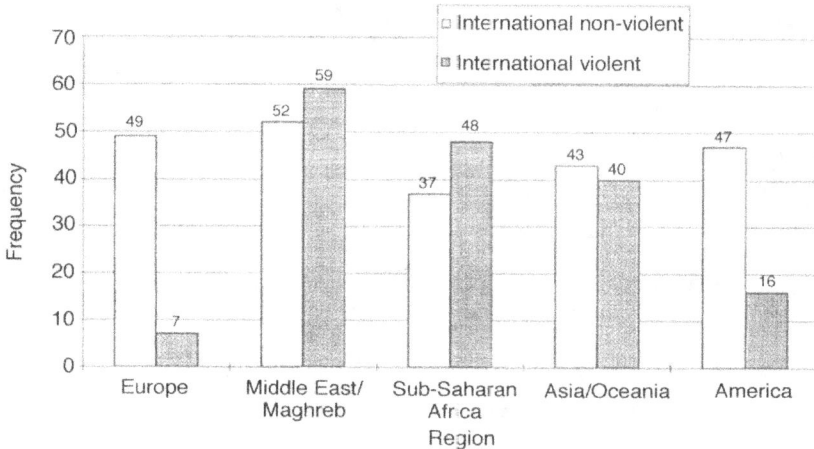

Figure 3.14 Violent and non-violent international conflicts by regions.

Figure 3.14 differentiates between regions by violent and non-violent international conflict frequencies. All five regions have high frequencies of non-violent international conflicts. The range lies between thirty-seven and fifty-two non-violent international conflicts per region since 1945. The significant regional differences are to be found in the distribution of violent international conflicts. Whereas Europe experienced only seven and the American continent sixteen international conflicts that escalated into a violent crisis, the Middle East/Maghreb region accounts for fifty-nine or roughly a quarter of all violent international conflicts. The other two regions, Asia/Oceania and sub-Saharan Africa, had similar rates of forty and forty-eight violent international conflicts between 1945 and 1995. In other words, Europe and the American continent account for only twenty-three violent international conflicts, whereas in Asia, the Middle East and Africa a total of 147 violent international conflicts were carried out. This equals 86 percent out of a total of 170 violent international conflicts since 1945. These results underline the assumptions on democratic peace, since most democratic political systems can be found in Europe and on the American continent.

Looking at internal conflicts and their violent or non-violent escalation (Figure 3.15), we find a similar distribution of conflicts as above. Again, Europe and the American continent have the highest number of non-violent internal conflicts. This underlines the thesis that democracies have higher capacities for internal conflict management due to accepted and participatory rules in conflict behavior. On the other hand, the Middle East/Maghreb, Asia/Oceania and sub-Saharan Africa show the highest rates in internal violent conflicts, between forty-six and fifty-four violent internal conflicts. These regions also have the lowest rates of non-violent internal conflicts. It must be added here that there is certainly a high number of non-violent

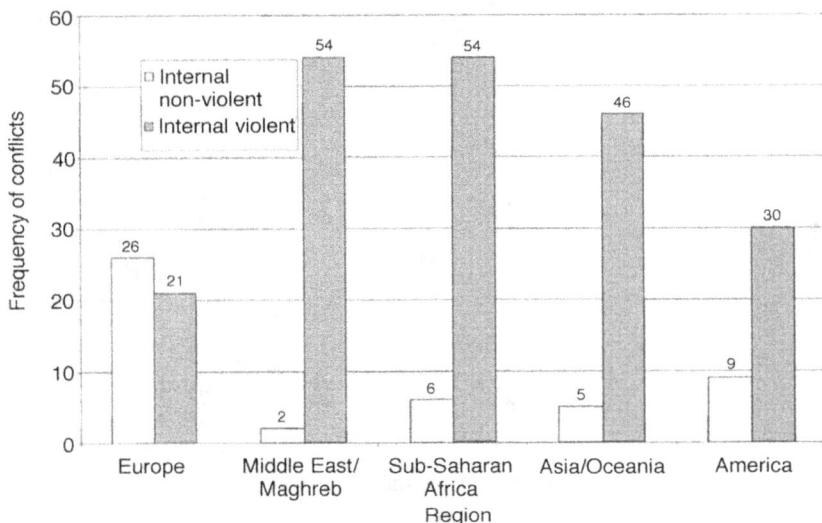

Figure 3.15 Violent and non-violent internal conflicts by regions.

internal conflicts in the Middle East/Maghreb, Asia, Oceania and in sub-Saharan Africa. Yet for lack of information on our part, these were not included in the KOSIMO databank. Therefore, Figure 3.15 is only partially representative for the actual distribution of internal conflicts due to a lack of complete information.

Regional conflict profiles

So far, the regional analysis of conflicts referred to absolute frequencies within the time period 1945–95. Now, the regional analysis refers to ongoing conflicts within the fifty-year time period. We analyze the diachronic developments of certain types of conflicts in each of the five global regions.

Europe

Figure 3.16 shows the new, ended and ongoing conflicts in Europe over a fifty-year period. There are three periods with an increased conflict activity, the beginning of the Cold War 1947 to 1952, the late 1970s and the period at the end of the Cold War, 1987 to 1993. At the end of the last peak, in 1993–95, the level of conflict frequency remained as high as at the peak of the late 1970s. The years between 1953 and 1970, that is during the height of the Cold War, and for a long time during the years of *détente*, the frequency of ongoing conflicts remained comparatively low. With respect to the lines of new and ended conflicts, two related peaks are significant in 1989 and 1991

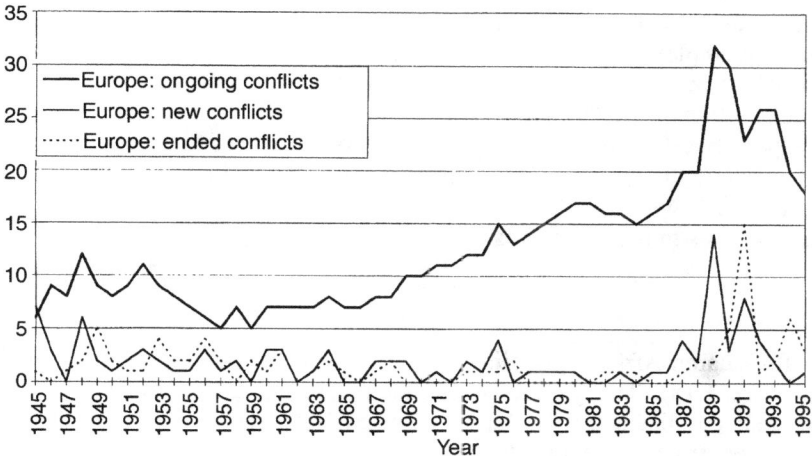

Figure 3.16 New, ended and ongoing conflicts in Europe.

respectively. Despite a continuously growing number of ongoing conflicts since the mid 1950s in Europe, the sharp increase at the end of the Cold War has had no long-term effects. It seems likely that the line will level out at twenty ongoing conflicts per year in the future.

Middle East/Maghreb

The line of new, ended and on-going conflicts for the Middle East and the Maghreb region follows the global trend rather closely (Figure 3.17). The number of on-going conflicts increases in two steps, firstly during the period of decolonization in the 1960s and in the 1980s after a cooling-off among the

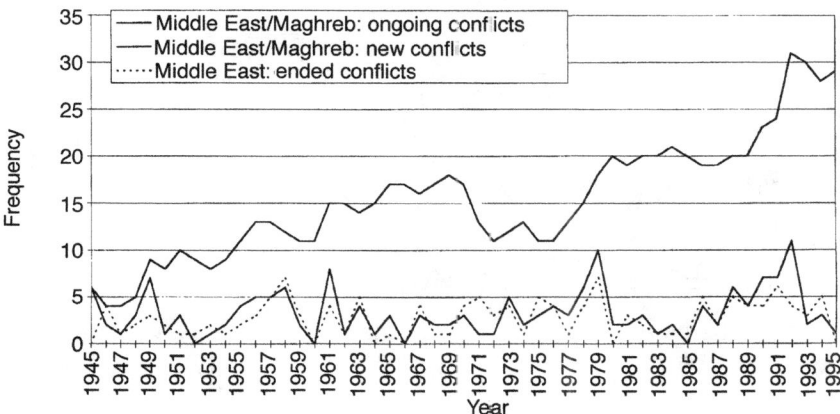

Figure 3.17 New, ended and ongoing conflicts in the Middle East/Maghreb region.

superpowers until the end of the Cold War. Besides local conflicts, like the Algerian independence or Morocco's annexation of the Western Sahara, more complex and protracted conflicts, like the Israeli–Arab conflicts, the conflicts in and around the southern and eastern Arab peninsula as well as the conflicts in and around the Gulf states of Iraq and Iran are mainly responsible for the steady growth of ongoing conflicts in this region. Regarding the line of new conflicts, there are sharp increases in certain years, in 1949, 1958, 1961, 1979 and 1991–92. The line of ended conflicts shows no significant increase or decrease.

Sub-Saharan Africa

Sub-Saharan Africa's ongoing conflicts follow by and large the global trend (Figure 3.18). The period of decolonization caused an initial increase in overall conflict activity. During the next two decades this level stabilized between fifteen and twenty ongoing conflicts each year. A second sharp increase in ongoing conflicts began in 1989 when the number of ongoing conflicts rose to thirty-two conflicts; this is more than a third compared with the peaks of the decolonization period. By 1995, a high level of roughly twenty ongoing conflicts per year seems to be a future trend.

Asia/Oceania

The Asian region has shown a consistently high level of conflicts since the 1950s (Figure 3.19). In other world regions we observed a moderate decline in conflict frequencies during the 1970s. In Asia/Oceania, this global decrease began ten years earlier in 1960 with a decline from twenty-five to about eighteen conflicts per year. A second increase began in 1983–87 which

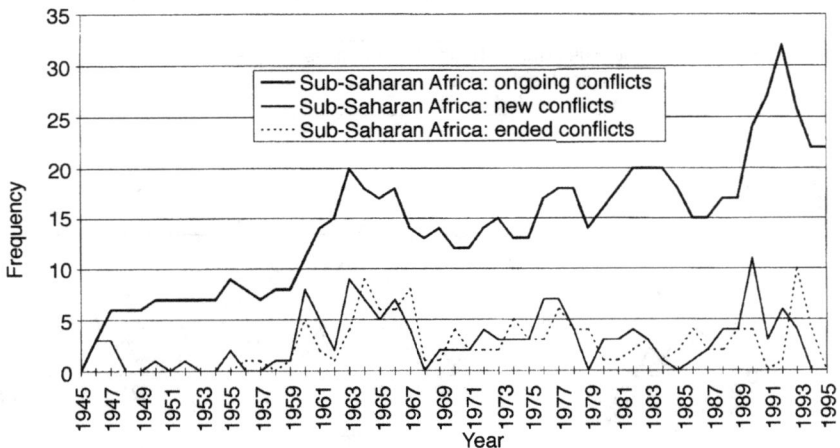

Figure 3.18 New, ended and ongoing conflicts in Sub-Saharan Africa.

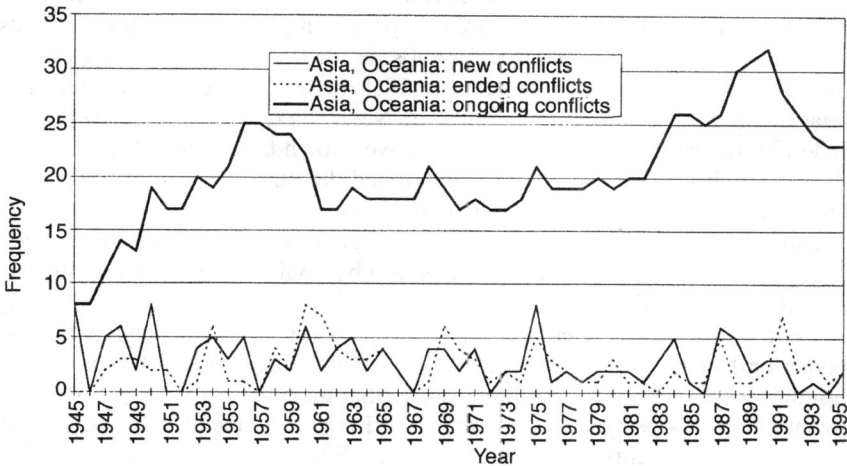

Figure 3.19 New, ended and ongoing conflicts in Asia/Oceania.

was followed by a peak in 1990 with thirty-two conflicts. Thereafter, there seems to be a future level of twenty-two conflicts per year. A look at the statistical reasons for the increase in ongoing conflicts in the 1980s shows that the Asian region did not produce many new conflicts per year, but fewer conflicts have ended per year. In earlier decades this difference between new and ended conflicts was smaller.

America

North America has experienced three conflicts since 1945 that qualified as political conflicts by KOSIMO criteria. The most prominent of these is the separation movement of the Canadian province of Quebec. The longest conflict lasted between Canada and France over the islands St Pierre and Miquelon from 1975 until 1992. A second territorial dispute was carried out between Canada and the US over the exact borders at the Gulf of Maine. The latter two conflicts have been settled through negotiations. The Quebecois conflict remains a latent conflict despite a referendum in 1995.

The low number of conflicts on the North American continent is the unique exception in comparison with all other world regions. The low number of states seems to support the thesis that the number of conflicts rises with the number of states in a region. Also, the theorem of inter- and inner-democratic peace can be verified for this region. Thirdly, the theorem of peace induced by economic wealth has some explanatory powers for North America as a peace zone. On the other hand, it should not be forgotten that the urban areas in North America are a region with highly explosive issues and great potential for violent conflict escalations.

Among these potentials for conflict are the deep-rooted racial conflicts in the 1950s and 1960s, periodic violent uproars in ghetto-like neighborhoods of Los Angeles in the 1980s and 1990s as well as gang- and drug-related violence on the Mexican borders and elsewhere. Recently, the terrorist attacks on the World Trade Center in New York, and home-grown anti-federal terrorist acts by militia groups have shown the inner vulnerability of the US. In this respect, it must be mentioned that the 250 million Americans are a legally armed people, a fact that can easily help to create volatile situations. All other states on earth are organized on the basis of a much stricter state monopoly on arms; states torn by civil wars may be regarded as an exception to this rule.

Central and South America stand in sharp economic, political and conflict–behavioral contrast to the North. A look at the frequencies of Central and South American ongoing conflicts shows that there are on average sixteen to twenty conflicts per year for the whole of Latin America. These frequencies are distributed evenly between Central and South America. Figures 3.20–1 show respectively, the frequencies for the period between 1945 and 1995 for both Central and South America. Whereas Central America experienced its height of conflict activities in the 1980s, South America's period of high conflict frequencies was in the 1960s. Still, both regions have had relatively high frequencies through the fifty-year period since the Second World War. The exception to this observation are the immediate years after the Second World War. During these years there were only two to four ongoing conflicts per year in Central and South America.

The main findings of the comparison of world regions according to their conflict activities are summarized in Table 3.23. It shows the overall regional distribution of conflicts by non-violent and violent, internal and international conflicts and their combinations in absolute numbers and percentages for the fifty years from 1945 to 1995.

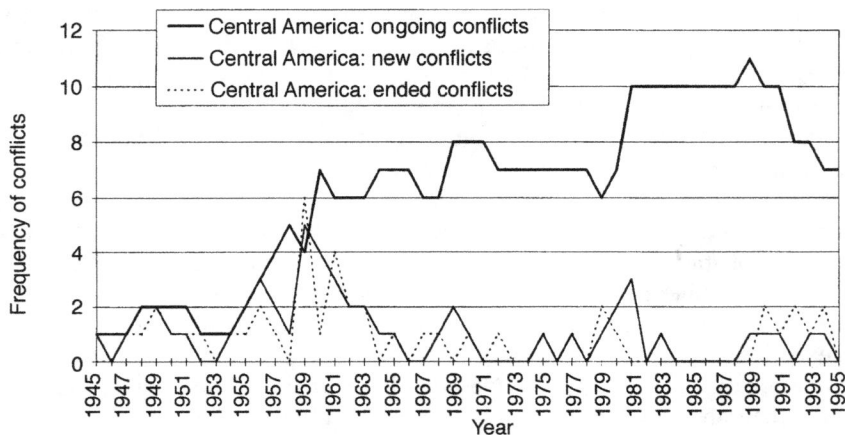

Figure 3.20 Ongoing conflicts in Central America.

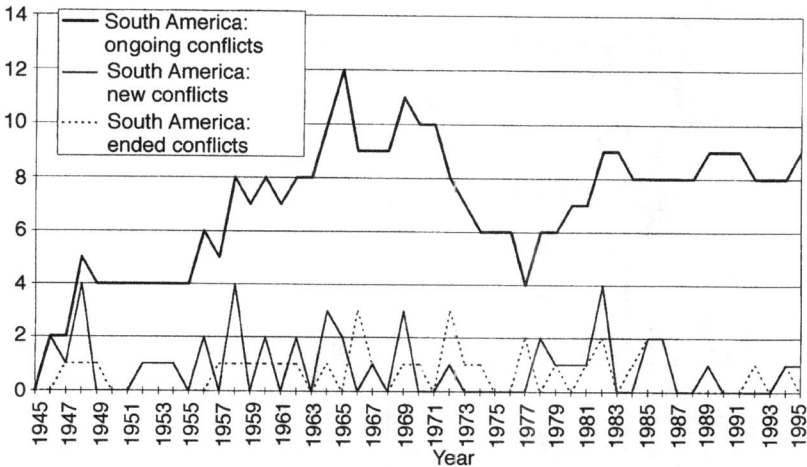

Figure 3.21 Ongoing conflicts in South America.

The main findings on the regional occurrence of conflicts are:

- The Middle East and Maghreb region with thirty states accounts for 113 violent conflicts; this is by far the world's most violent region.
- Europe has forty-nine states which statistically fought 28 violent conflicts. It is thus by far the least violent region apart from North America.
- On the American continent there were about as many conflicts as in Europe. Yet the proportion of violent conflicts is slightly higher in America. With regard to the population of the Americas and Europe, it can be maintained that the Americas comprise the more peaceful region. When only the number of states are taken into consideration, Europe takes the lead in peaceful internal and international relations.
- Sub-Saharan Africa has experienced almost as many conflicts as the Middle East region.
- Both Asia and sub-Saharan Africa have more internal conflicts than the Middle Eastern region which has more international conflicts.
- In all regions, there is a trend toward decreasing numbers of international conflicts and increasing numbers of internal conflicts.
- The regional lines of frequencies for international and internal conflicts have different crossing points. The global trend for internal conflicts to become the dominant type of conflict is different in every region. In Europe, the crossing point was in 1987, in sub-Saharan Africa in 1975 and again in 1987, in Asia in 1969, in Central America from 1989 until 1992 and in South America in 1988. In the Middle East international conflicts remain slightly more frequent than internal conflicts.

Table 3.23 Summary of the regional distribution of conflicts

	All conflicts	Non-violent	Violent	% of all conflicts in this region	Inter-national	% of all conflicts in this region	Internal	% of all conflicts in this region
Europe	103	75	28	27	56	54	47	46
Middle East/Maghreb	167	54	113	68	111	66	56	34
Sub-Saharan Africa	145	43	102	70	85	59	60	41
Asia/Oceania	144	58	86	60	83	58	61	42
America	102	56	46	45	63	62	39	38
North America	3	3	0	0	2	67	1	33
Central America	53	29	24	45	36	68	17	32
South America	46	24	22	48	25	54	21	46
Total	661	286	375		398		263	

	Inter-national non-violent	% of all international conflicts in this region	Inter-national violent	% of all international conflicts in this region	Internal non-violent	% of all internal conflicts in this region	Internal violent	% of all internal conflicts in this region
Europe	49	88	7	13	26	55	21	45
Middle East/Maghreb	52	47	59	53	2	4	54	96
Sub-Saharan Africa	37	44	48	56	6	10	54	90
Asia/Oceania	43	52	40	48	15	8	46	75
America	47	75	16	25	9	23	30	77
North America	2	100	0	0	1	100	0	0
Central America	24	67	12	33	5	29	12	71
South America	21	84	4	16	3	14	18	86
Total	228		170		58		205	

Issues of conflicts

So far, we have been concerned with (a) states as principal actors in conflicts, (b) basic conflicts that are at the roots of all ongoing conflicts, (c) partial conflicts which reflect the ongoing escalations and de-escalations of basic conflicts and (d) the regional distribution of the 661 conflicts that were entered into the KOSIMO databank.

Our analysis of issues and objectives in conflicts is concerned with a structural rather than actor-oriented component of conflicts. According to our KOSIMO definition on pages 47–8, issues and objectives are an important component of conflicts in addition to being the instruments to carry out the conflict and the modes of conflict resolution and settlement.

In general, technical or material issues and objects are more suitable for non-violent, negotiated conflict resolutions due to their divisibility. Compromises can be reached by re-grouping issues, by establishing new linkages among formerly unrelated objectives – in short – by creating promising win–win constellations among the disputants instead of win–lose and zero-sum constellations. Common objectives in conflicts of the latter type are territorial questions, disputes over access or exploitation of resources such as oil, minerals, or staple crops or fish.

Objectives which are difficult to manage with regard to non-violent conflict resolution and negotiated settlements are historical antagonisms among the parties, previous escalations of a basic conflict, and person- and group-oriented values such as religion, ethnicity, language, political autonomy, separation and the denial of political participation.

The following figures refer to the accumulated numbers of objectives and issues in conflicts over fifty years. Conflicts are fought in most cases over more than one objective. Therefore, KOSIMO assigned a multiple coding for this variable. The maximum number of issues in one conflict has been limited up to the three most important issues. Due to the multiple choice coding procedure, the numbers below have to be interpreted in relation to each other rather than as absolute numbers.

The analysis of issues in conflicts will first focus on the overall frequencies according to different types of conflicts. Then, we will look at the yearly accumulated frequencies of issues in conflicts.

In Figure 3.22 the frequencies of issues in different types of conflicts are marked on the *y*-axis. The different types of conflicts are marked on the *x*-axis. In the first group, 'all conflicts', the frequencies of eight different issues in 661 conflicts are shown. This is the overall global distribution of issues in conflicts between 1945 and 1995. Note that up to three issues were identified for each conflict (the frequencies are tendencies and must be interpreted within the respective sample). The most disputed issues are territories and borders. Conflicts over the defense of or access to national power positions make up the second most frequent group of issues in conflicts. A third distinct group of issues are ideologically motivated system conflicts. The other four

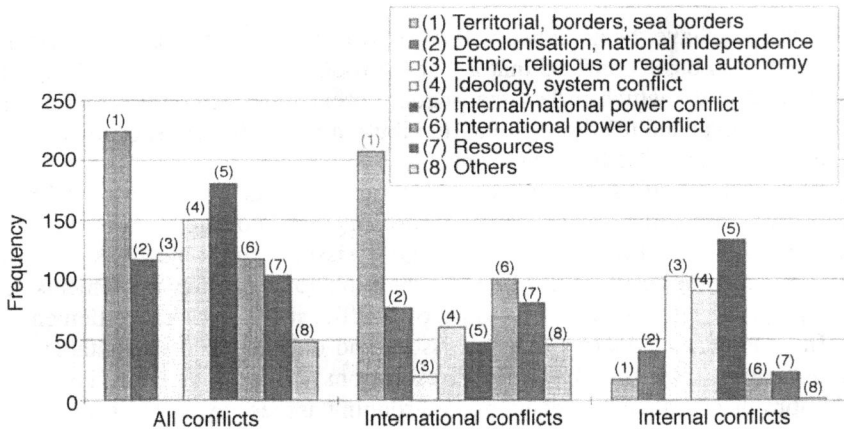

Figure 3.22 Frequencies of issues, international and internal conflicts.

groups of issues, namely conflicts over decolonization and national independence, ethnic, religious and regional conflicts for autonomy, international power conflicts and conflict over resources are almost evenly distributed.

The frequency distribution of the eight issues are dependent on the types of conflicts. In international conflicts territorial and border disputes are by far the most common issue. Disputes over international power positions, resources and national independence also have fairly high frequencies; still, each of the latter make up less than half of the frequency of territorial and border disputes. In regard to internal conflicts, the reciprocal trend becomes apparent. Ethnic, religious and regional autonomy, ideological system conflicts and defense of or access to national power positions are the most common issues. There is a strong auto-correlation in the analysis of objectives in international and internal conflicts. It goes without saying that it is more common for internal conflicts to be fought over ethnic autonomy than it is for international conflicts. Our purpose here is to demonstrate the existence of very different objectives in these two types of conflicts. Figure 3.23 differentiates the issues in conflicts according to the criterion of violent or non-violent conflicts.

In non-violent conflicts, territorial and border disputes are by far the most common issues. All other issues are distributed almost evenly and in smaller frequencies. This result specifies the first observation in Figure 3.23. Although territorial and border disputes are the most common type, these conflicts are, by and large, carried out non-violently. In contrast, internal conflicts over national power positions are the second most common objective in conflicts overall. They are also, by and large, violent. In the group of non-violent conflicts, conflicts over national power positions have

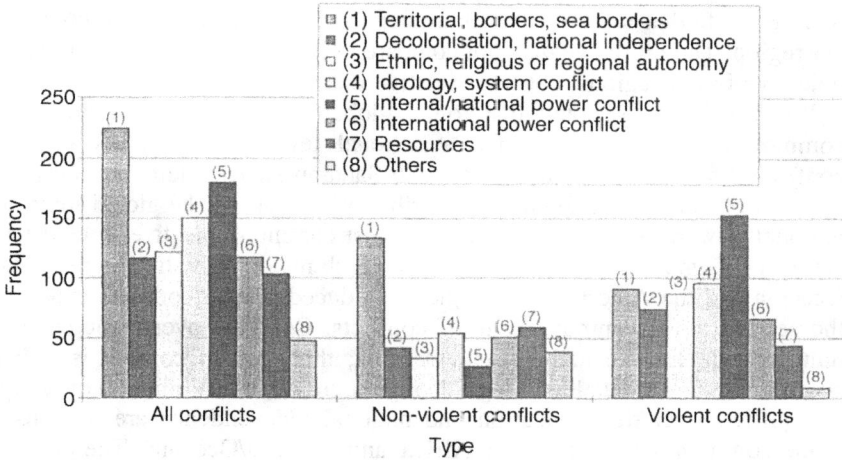

Figure 3.23 Issues in violent and non-violent conflicts.

the lowest frequency. International power conflicts and conflicts over resources have a comparatively low level of violence. They are, next to territorial conflicts, the second most common group of non-violent conflicts. Conflicts over decolonization, national independence, ethnic, religious or regional autonomy and ideological system conflicts escalate in more than one out of two cases into violent conflicts.

As shown under 'Regions of conflict' (pages 47–8), regions have different profiles of conflict-behavior. Figure 3.24 shows the frequencies of eight

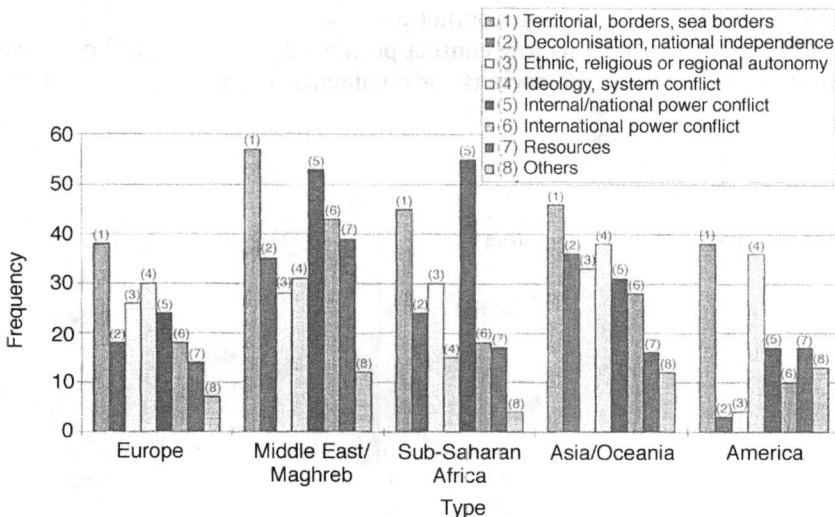

Figure 3.24 Regional distribution of conflicts in five global regions.

different objectives in conflicts over the past fifty years differentiated by five regions. Note that the frequencies are dependent on the number of conflicts per region. Therefore, we may not compare the absolute frequencies for each objective in the regions, but their relative distribution.

We have already noted that, on a global scale, territory is the most common issue in conflicts. On a regional level, this tendency can be confirmed for all regions except for sub-Saharan Africa. Here, conflicts for national power top the frequency distribution of issues. The global trend of national power conflicts as the second most common objective in conflicts can be confirmed for the Middle East/Maghreb region only. In Europe, Asia, Oceania and the Americas, ideologically induced system conflicts make up the second most common group of conflicts. Conflicts over resources are quite rare in Europe and in Asia/Oceania; this type of conflict is rather common in the Middle East/Maghreb region, mostly concerning oil or water.

Conflicts over decolonization and national independence are obviously more common in sub-Saharan Africa and in Asia/Oceania. The overall frequency of conflicts over decolonization and national independence is high in Asia/Oceania. The decolonization process was clearly more disruptive in this region than in Africa. The rather high number of conflicts over national independence in Europe is derived from the conflicts caused by the breakdown of the Soviet Empire and Yugoslavia from 1988 until 1992–95. Conflicts over ethnic, religious and regional autonomy are evenly distributed over the five global regions except for the American continents. Apart from the Quebec dispute, separation disputes are a rather unknown phenomenon. Figure 3.25 focuses on the distribution of frequencies of issues on the American continents. The majority of conflicts in the Americas occurred in Central and South America. Looking at the issues in each conflict, we find little difference in the overall conflict profiles.

North America, with its low conflict profile, has no ideological or power conflicts. In contrast, the socialist or communist inspired uprisings of the

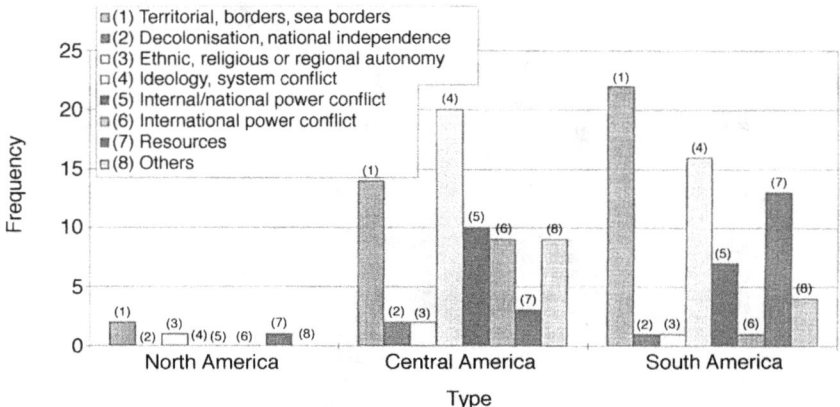

Figure 3.25 Issues in conflicts in the Americas.

1960s and the 1970s are reflected in the high frequencies of system conflicts in Latin America. In the Central American region conflicts over ideological issues and system conflicts played a more dominant role than in South America. Here, territorial and border issues played an important role in many conflicts. In South America, more conflicts were fought over resources than in Central America. Note the low frequencies of regional, ethnic or religious autonomy in all of Latin America.

In the second part of the analysis of issues in conflicts, we are interested in their distribution over time. In the earlier figures, we looked at the number of issues as sum totals of fifty years of conflict. Now, we look at the yearly frequencies of ongoing conflicts with certain issues in dispute. Again, up to three issues were coded with each conflict; the sum total of frequencies shown below are therefore not identical with the number of all conflicts.

Figure 3.26 shows the distribution of conflicts over territory and borders. Rather surprisingly, the frequency in this grouping has remained on a high level since the 1960s. Territory and borders are still the single most common issue in political conflicts. The Convention of the Law on the Sea of 1982 has caused many new uncertainties about the borders of fishery and exploitation zones in the off-shore regions. Despite these high frequencies, the number of cases that escalated into violent conflicts has been steadily decreasing. After a comparatively high level of violent conflicts over territories and borders in the 1960s, the 1970s showed almost no violent conflicts over these issues. The end of the Cold War and the breakdown of the Soviet Union caused some territorial and border conflicts to escalate. This sudden increase had its peak with ten violent conflicts in 1993. Since then, the low level of the previous decades has been maintained and may indicate a future trend.

In contrast to territorial and border conflicts among states, the issue of decolonization and the struggle for national independence was to a much

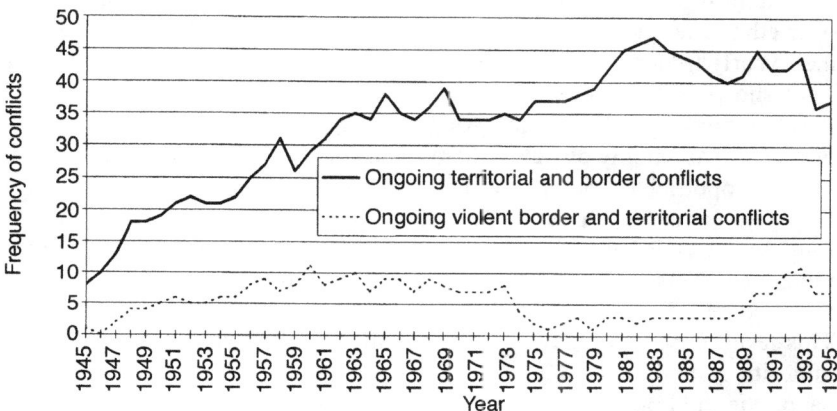

Figure 3.26 Ongoing territorial border conflicts.

lesser degree an issue in conflicts. Yet, decolonization and national independence were certainly topics and issues that moved and mobilized more people into political participation, especially in Africa, the Middle East/Maghreb and Asia/Oceania than any other issue in this century. More than two-thirds of today's states gained their independence after 1945. Therefore, the analysis of this issue in conflicts will be more extensive, including a selected list of all violent conflicts over decolonization and national independence after 1945.

Table 3.24 reflects a stable level of ten to twenty conflicts over decolonization or national independence since 1945. In most figures so far, the 1970s were a period with lower levels of conflicts. This is not true for these issues. Although the peaks since 1945 were in 1965 and in 1989–92 with twenty conflicts in each year, the 1950s, 1970s and 1980s showed no significant decrease. Comparing the frequencies of violent and non-violent conflicts of this type, we find that the proportion of violent conflicts is about three out of four conflicts per year. In total, seventy-six conflicts over decolonization and national independence escalated into violent conflicts. Forty-two conflicts remained on a non-violent intensity level. The internal conflicts over national independence of minority groups escalated by 90 percent into violent conflicts (thirty-one conflicts out of forty). The ratio for international types of conflicts over the same issues is at about 50 percent (forty-three conflicts out of seventy-six).

In recent years the formerly typical violent international conflicts over decolonization were replaced by internal conflicts within states about the granting of national independence to separationist groups. The period of decolonization is over. Today's issues concern in many cases minority rights in the territories of the former Soviet Union and elsewhere. Compared with other issues in conflicts, conflicts over decolonization and national independence seem to last longer.

As a third group of possible objectives and issues in conflicts, the conflicts over ethnic, religious and regional autonomy show a distinct distribution in their yearly frequencies since 1945 (Figure 3.27). The period from 1945 until 1971 shows a slow increase, the period from 1971 until 1990 a sharper one. After the peak in 1990 with forty ongoing conflicts involving ethnic, religious or regional autonomy disputes, there seems to be a steady, but slow decrease.

The proportion of violent conflicts to all conflicts in this grouping over the fifty-year period is three out of four conflicts. This proportion remained roughly the same over the fifty-year period. We could not observe any non-violent conflicts in this category for the time period before 1959. In 1995, the violence ratio has declined to about 60 percent of all conflicts in this group. This result confirms today's perception that we are living in a period where minority rights are gaining more attention than ever before. On the other hand, the findings show that this is not a recent trend, but a long-term tendency that can be traced back to the mid-1970s. The overlying superpower conflict might have diverted public attention from this increase

Table 3.24 Violent conflicts over decolonization and national independence (chronological order)

Name of conflict	Start	End	Duration in years	Region	International/national
India I (independence)	1942	1947	5	Asia/Oceania	International
India II (partition)	1942	1948	6	Asia/Oceania	Internal
Morocco (independence)	1944	1956	12	Middle East/Maghreb	International
Algeria (independence I)	1945	1946	1	Middle East/Maghreb	International
France–Syria, Lebanon (Levant)	1945	1946	1	Middle East/Maghreb	International
Iran (Kurds I)	1945	1946	1	Middle East/Maghreb	Internal
Indonesia (independence)	1945	1949	4	Asia/Oceania	International
Indochina Ia	1945	1954	9	Asia/Oceania	International
Israel I (independence)	1946	1948	2	Middle East/Maghreb	International
India IV (Kashmir I)	1947	1949	2	Asia/Oceania	Internal
Malagasy Republic (independence)	1947	1960	13	Sub-Saharan Africa	International
India VI (Mahe)	1948	1954	6	Asia/Oceania	International
Malaya (independence)	1948	1960	12	Asia/Oceania	International
Yemen–United Kingdom (Aden I)	1948	1963	15	Middle East/Maghreb	International
Tunisia (independence)	1950	1956	6	Middle East/Maghreb	International
Egypt (1st Suez crisis)	1951	1954	3	Middle East/Maghreb	International
Kenya (independence, Mau Mau)	1952	1956	4	Sub-Saharan Africa	International
British Guyana (independence)	1953	1966	13	South America	International
Cyprus I (independence)	1954	1960	6	Europe	Internal
Algeria (independence II)	1954	1962	8	Middle East/Maghreb	International
Cameroon (independence)	1955	1967	12	Sub-Saharan Africa	International
Egypt (Suez War)	1956	1957	1	Middle East/Maghreb	International
Morocco (French troops)	1956	1958	2	Middle East/Maghreb	International
Yemen–United Kingdom (Aden II)	1956	1958	2	Middle East/Maghreb	International
India XI (Rann of Kutch I)	1956	1964	8	Asia/Oceania	International
Tunisia–France (Algerian border)	1957	1957	0	Middle East/Maghreb	International
Morocco–Spain (attempted expansion)	1957	1958	1	Middle East/Maghreb	International

Table 3.24 Continued

Name of conflict	Start	End	Duration in years	Region	International/national
Malawi (independence)	1959	1964	5	Sub-Saharan Africa	International
India XII (Goa II)	1961	1961	0	Asia/Oceania	International
Tunisia (Biserta)	1961	1963	2	Middle East/Maghreb	International
Eritrea II (declaration of independence)	1961	1967	6	Sub-Saharan Africa	Internal
Angola (independence)	1961	1974	13	Sub-Saharan Africa	International
Brunei (uproar)	1962	1962	0	Asia/Oceania	International
Malaya–Indonesia (Sarawak/Sabah)	1963	1966	3	Asia/Oceania	International
Guinea-Bissau–Portugal (independence)	1963	1974	11	Sub-Saharan Africa	International
Yemen PR–Oman (Dhofar uproar)	1963	1979	16	Middle East/Maghreb	International
Mozambique (independence)	1964	1975	11	Sub-Saharan Africa	International
India XIV (Kashmir III)	1965	1965	0	Asia/Oceania	International
Rhodesia (UDI)	1965	1966	1	Sub-Saharan Africa	Internal
Yemen PR (independence)	1965	1967	2	Middle East/Maghreb	International
India XVI (Kashmir IV)	1965	1970	5	Asia/Oceania	International
Zambia–Rhodesia (border)	1965	1987	22	Sub-Saharan Africa	International
Mozambique (border)	1966	1974	8	Sub-Saharan Africa	International
Namibia II (SWAPO)	1966	1990	24	Sub-Saharan Africa	Internal
Northern Ireland	1968	cont.	28	Europe	Internal
Indonesia (West Irian III)	1969	1982	13	Asia/Oceania	Internal
Philippines (Moros in Mindanao and Sulu)	1970	cont.	26	Asia/Oceania	Internal
India XVII (Bangladesh III)	1971	1971	0	Asia/Oceania	International
Namibia (Caprivi)	1971	1971	0	Sub-Saharan Africa	International
Pakistan (Bangladesh II)	1971	1971	0	Asia/Oceania	Internal
Rhodesia (civil war)	1972	1979	7	Sub-Saharan Africa	Internal
Rhodesia–Zambia (closure of border)	1973	1973	0	Sub-Saharan Africa	International
Indonesia East Timor (civil war I)	1974	1975	1	Asia/Oceania	Internal
Indonesia–FRETILIN (East Timor II)	1975	1976	1	Asia/Oceania	Internal

	1975	1979	4	Sub-Saharan Africa	International
Rhodesia–Mozambique (attempt at destabilization)					
Indonesia (East Timor III)	1976	cont.	20	Asia/Oceania	Internal
Morocco (Western Sahara II)	1976	1979	3	Middle East/Maghreb	Internal
Rhodesia (Chimoio Tembue attacks)	1977	1978	1	Sub-Saharan Africa	Internal
Morocco (Western Sahara III)	1979	1991	12	Middle East/Maghreb	Internal
Vanuatu (attempt at secession)	1980	1980	0	Asia/Oceania	Internal
India XVIII (Khalistan/Punjab)	1981	cont.	15	Asia/Oceania	Internal
Turkey (Kurds I)	1984	1989	5	Middle East/Maghreb	Internal
USSR (Nagorny-Karabakh I)	1987	1991	4	Europe	Internal
Israel V (Intifada)	1987	1993	6	Middle East/Maghreb	Internal
India XXII (Kashmir V)	1988	cont.	8	Asia/Oceania	International
Yugoslavia (Serbia: Kosovo)	1988	cont.	8	Europe	Internal
Georgia (Abchasia)	1989	cont.	7	Europe	Internal
USSR (Uzbekistan)	1989	1989	0	Europe	Internal
USSR (Nachizewan)	1989	1991	2	Europe	Internal
Indonesia (GAM movement in Aceh II)	1990	cont.	6	Asia/Oceania	Internal
Russia (Chechnya)	1991	cont.	5	Europe	Internal
Russian Federation (Ingushia–North Ossetia)	1991	cont.	5	Europe	Internal
Armenia–Azerbaijan (Nagorny-Karabakh II)	1991	1994	3	Middle East/Maghreb	International
Morocco (Western Sahara IV)	1992	cont.	4	Middle East/Maghreb	Internal

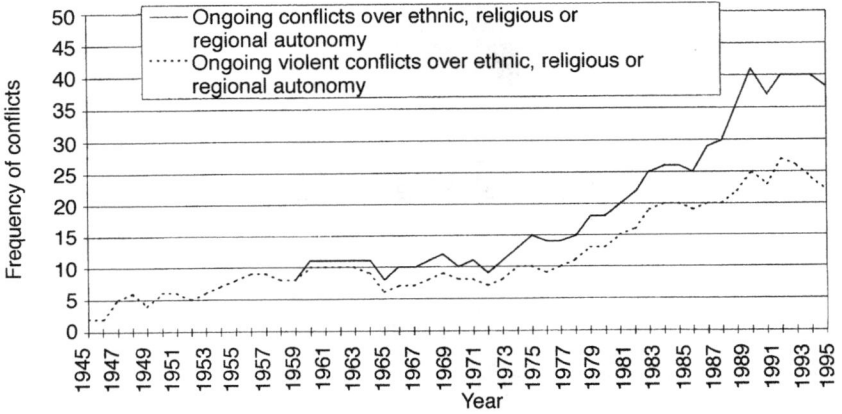

Figure 3.27 Ongoing conflicts over ethnic, religious and regional autonomy.

in minority conflicts. The superpowers and the former colonial powers had in many instances a greater interest in the stabilization of authoritarian regimes that seemed to guarantee a certain system and block loyalty. Minority issues were a lesser concern then. Today, the oppression of the Ogoni people in Nigeria is but one example of a long-lasting minority conflict that only recently gained public attention because of a diversion of interest of both the major states and a globalized media audience.

Conflicts over ideological issues and system conflicts have played a significant role throughout the past fifty years (Figure 3.28). On average about twenty to twenty-five conflicts of this type were observed as ongoing conflicts each year. The ideological East–West conflicts have been replaced by other dichotomies such as Islamic versus secular regimes. Overall, the

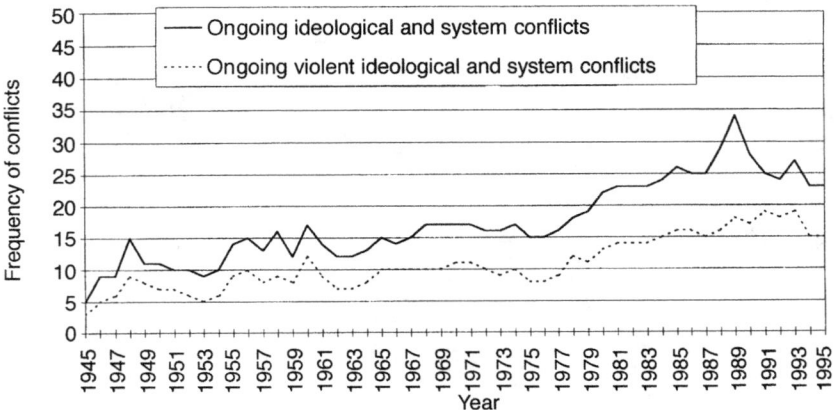

Figure 3.28 Ongoing ideological and system conflicts.

number of conflicts over the issue of which political system should be established was on the rise between 1945 and 1990. In 1995 the level was still as high as in the mid-1980s. The proportion of violent conflicts among all system conflicts is two to three out of four conflicts per year. In 1995, we counted seventeen ongoing violent conflicts over the political set-up in states.

Figure 3.29 shows the distribution of conflicts over defense of or access to internal, national power positions. Almost all of these conflicts have escalated into violent conflicts. The lines follow the global trend for all internal conflicts: a moderate increase until the early 1980s, and an accelerated increase until the early 1990s. Between 1993 and 1995, the line drops by one-third to twenty-five ongoing internal conflicts for power positions. Note that at the immediate end of the Cold War, after the crumbling of the Berlin Wall and the non-intervention of the USSR in 1989 and 1990, we observe a drop in the frequency of internal power conflicts. Not until 1990–91 did this frequency rise by almost twenty conflicts. It can be concluded from this that the velvet revolutions in the Eastern European states did not cause political conflicts in the KOSIMO sense of the word until the newly established political systems were in turn challenged by (new) minorities and other dissatisfied or neglected groups. The conflict in Russia with Chechnya or the Hungarian minority conflict with the Romanian government are illustrative examples of this phenomenon.

Overall, internal power conflicts must be regarded as a relatively new phenomenon. Most such conflicts did not start before the 1980s. If *coups d'état* were included in this picture, it would, of course, be different. Yet, *coups d'état* do not fulfill the criterion of a 'conflict of some scope, duration and intensity'; they are by and large sudden uprisings by a dissatisfied military; the actual power set-up of a state, as in Bolivia's many coups, is rarely altered by coups. Table 3.25 gives the chronology of attempted and successful *coups d'état* from 1945 until 1995. These coups are not included

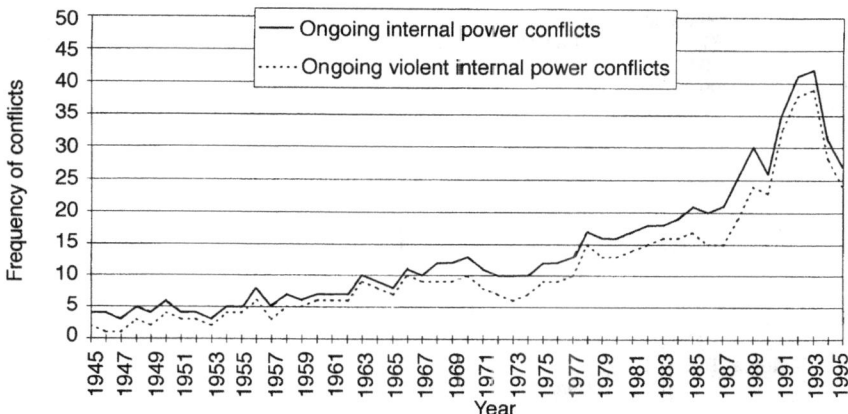

Figure 3.29 Internal power conflicts.

Table 3.25 Coups d'état, 1945–95 (ordered by regions)

State	Date	Type, initiator	Affected	Victims
Europe				
Albania	28.09.82	Attempted *coup d'état*	Government	Uncertain
Bulgaria	Apr. 65	Attempted *coup d'état*	Government	Uncertain
France	1958	Attempted *coup d'état*	President de Gaulle	Uncertain
France	1961	Attempted *coup d'état*	President de Gaulle	Uncertain
Greece	21.04.67	*Coup d'état* (army)	Government	Uncertain
Greece	13.12.67	Attempted *coup d'état*	Government	Uncertain
Greece	May 73	Attempted *coup d'état*	Government	Uncertain
Greece	29.07.73	*Coup d'état*	Government	No victims
Greece	25.11.73	*Coup d'état*	Government	Uncertain
Greece	02.06.81	Attempted *coup d'état*	Government	Uncertain
Portugal	05.04.74	*Coup d'état* (army)	Government	Uncertain
Portugal	11.03.75	Attempted *coup d'état*	Government	Uncertain
Spain	23.02.81	Attempted *coup d'état*	Government	No victims
Turkey	27.04.60	*Coup d'état* (army)	Government	No victims
Turkey	12.03.71	*Coup d'état* (army)	Government	No victims
Turkey	12.09.80	*Coup d'état* (army)	Government	No victims
USSR	19–22.08.91	Attempted *coup d'état*	Government	No victims
Cyprus	15.07.74	*Coup d'état*	Makarios	Uncertain
Asia/Oceania				
Bangladesh	02.10.78	Attempted *coup d'état*	Government	Uncertain
Bangladesh	30.05.81	Attempted *coup d'état*	President Rahman	Victims*
Bangladesh	23.03.82	*Coup d'état* (army)	Government	Uncertain
Bangladesh	03.11.75	*Coup d'état*		Uncertain
Burma	03.03.62			Uncertain
Burma	1966			Uncertain
Burma	1972			Uncertain
Burma	1976			Uncertain
Burma	18.09.88			Uncertain
Fiji	14.05.87	*Coup d'état* (Rabuka)	Government	Uncertain
Indonesia	30.09.65	Attempted *coup d'état*	Government	6 victims
Indonesia	01.10.65	*Coup d'état*	Government	700,000
Cambodia	18.03.70	*Coup d'état* (Lon Nol)	Government	Uncertain
Cambodia	27.06.78	Attempted *coup d'état*	Government	Uncertain
Cambodia	07.01.79	*Coup d'état* (intervention)	Government	Uncertain
Laos	09.08.60	*Coup d'état* (Kong Lé)	Government	Uncertain
Laos	31.01–04.02.65	Attempted *coup d'état*	Government	Uncertain
Malaysia	09.11.84	Attempted *coup d'état*	Government	Uncertain
Maldives	03.11.88	Attempted *coup d'état*	Government	12 victims
Nepal	15.12.60	*Coup d'état* (king)	Government	Uncertain
East Timor	09.08.75	*Coup d'état* (UDT)	Government	2,000 victims
Papua New Guinea	15.03.90	Attempted *coup d'état*	Government	No victims
Philippines	25.02.86	*Coup d'état*	President Marcos	Uncertain
Philippines	06.07.86	Attempted *coup d'état*	Government	Uncertain
Philippines	09.07.87	Attempted *coup d'état*	Government	Uncertain
Philippines	28.08.87	Attempted *coup d'état*	Government	Uncertain
Philippines	30.11–07.12.89	Attempted *coup d'état*	President Aquino	Uncertain
South Korea	16.05.61			Uncertain
South Vietnam	01.11–02.11.63	*Coup d'état* (army)	President Diem	Uncertain
South Vietnam	30.01.64	*Coup d'état* (army)	Government	Uncertain

South Vietnam	30.04.75	*Coup d'état*/intervention	Government	Uncertain
Thailand	25.03.77	Attempted *coup d'état*	Government	Uncertain
Thailand	20.10.77	*Coup d'état*	Government	No victims
Thailand	01.04.81	Attempted *coup d'état*	Government	Uncertain
Thailand	09.09.85	Attempted *coup d'état*	Government	Uncertain
Thailand	23.02.91	Military *coup d'état*	Government	No victims
Central America				
Dominican Rep.	16.01–18.01.62	*Coup d'état* (army)	President Balaguer	No victims
Dominican Rep.	23.09.63	*Coup d'état* (army)	President Juan Bosch	Uncertain
Dominican Rep.	24.04.65	Attempted *coup d'état*	Cabral Junta	Victims*
Dominican Rep.	27.04.81	Attempted *coup d'état*	Government	Uncertain
Dominican Rep.	19.12.81	Attempted *coup d'état*	Government	Uncertain
El Salvador	14.12.48	*Coup d'état* (Major)	Government	Uncertain
El Salvador	26.10.60	*Coup d'état* (army)	President Lemus	No victims
El Salvador	25.01.61	*Coup d'état* (Major)	Lemus government	Uncertain
El Salvador	1972			Uncertain
El Salvador	25.03.72	Attempted *coup d'état*	President Molina	100 victims
El Salvador	15.10.79	*Coup d'état*	President Romero	Uncertain
Grenada	12.03.79	*Coup d'état*	Government	No victims
Grenada	05.11.79	Attempted *coup d'état*	Government	Uncertain
Grenada	19.06.80	Attempted *coup d'état*	Government	Uncertain
Grenada	14.10—19.10.83	*Coup d'état*	Government	8 victims
Guatemala	30.03.63	*Coup d'état* (army)	President Fuentes	Uncertain
Guatemala	23.03.82	*Coup d'état* (army)	Government	Uncertain
Guatemala	08.08.83	*Coup d'état* (Mejla)	Rios Montt government	Uncertain
Guatemala	1984			Uncertain
Guatemala	11.05.88	Attempted *coup d'état*	Government	Uncertain
Haiti	14.06.57	*Coup d'état* (army)	President Fignole	Victims*
Haiti	14.02.79	Attempted *coup d'état*		Uncertain
Haiti	02.11.84	Attempted *coup d'état*	Government	Uncertain
Haiti	07.02.86	*Coup d'état*	President Duvalier	Victims*
Haiti	20.06.88	*Coup d'état* (army)	President Manigat	Uncertain
Haiti	17.09.88	*Coup d'état* (President's guard)		Uncertain
Haiti	18.09.88	*Coup d'état* (army)		Uncertain
Haiti	02.04.89	Attempted *coup d'état*	Government	Uncertain
Haiti	07.01.91	Attempted *coup d'état*	Aristide government	ca. 20
Haiti	02.10.91	*Coup d'état* military	Aristide government	Uncertain
Honduras	21.10.56	Pressure (army)	Government	No victims
Honduras	03.10.63	*Coup d'état* (army)	Government	Victims*
Honduras	04.12.72	*Coup d'état* (army)	Government	Uncertain
Honduras	22.04.75	Displacement (army)	President Lopes	No victims
Honduras	07.08—09.08.78	*Coup d'état*	Government	Uncertain
Jamaica	23.06.80	Attempted *coup d'état*	Government	Uncertain
Nicaragua	26.05.47	*Coup d'état* (army)	President Arguello	Uncertain
Panama	20.11.49	*Coup d'état* (Police)		Uncertain
Panama	10.05.51	Loss of power	President Arias	Uncertain
Panama	11.10.68	*Coup d'état*	President Arias	Uncertain
Panama	1969	*Coup d'état*		Uncertain
Panama	16.12.69	Attempted *coup d'état*	Government	Uncertain

Table 3.25 Continued

State	Date	Type, initiator	Affected	Victims
Panama	16.03.88	Attempted *coup d'état*	Government	Uncertain
South America				
Argentina	1945	*Coup d'état* (army)	Government	Uncertain
Argentina	19.09.55	*Coup d'état* (army)	President Perón	Uncertain
Argentina	09.06–10.06.56	Attempted *coup d'état*	Government	39–252 victims*
Argentina	28.03.62	*Coup d'état* (army)	President Frondizi	Uncertain
Argentina	25.09.62	*Coup d'état* (Colorados)	Government	15 victims
Argentina	02.04–05.04.63	Attempted *coup d'état*	Government	350 victims
Argentina	27.06.66	*Coup d'état* (army)	Government	Uncertain
Argentina	24.03.76	*Coup d'état* (army)	Government	Uncertain
Argentina	30.09.79	Attempted *coup d'état*	Government	Uncertain
Argentina	15.04–19.04.87	Attempted *coup d'état*	Government	Uncertain
Bolivia	16.05.51	*Coup d'état* (army)	Government	No victims
Bolivia	16.05.61	*Coup d'état* (army)	Government	No victims
Bolivia	05.11.64	*Coup d'état* (Ortuna)	President Estenssoro	No victims
Bolivia	26.09.69	*Coup d'état* (army)	President Salinas	No victims
Bolivia	07.10.70	*Coup d'état* (Torres)	General Gandia	Uncertain
Bolivia	22.08.71	*Coup d'état* (army)	President Torres	Victims*
Bolivia	05.06.74	Attempted *coup d'état*	President Banzer	Uncertain
Bolivia	07.11.74	Attempted *coup d'état*	President Banzer	Uncertain
Bolivia	21.07.78	*Coup d'état*	Government	Uncertain
Bolivia	07–08.08.78	*Coup d'état* (army)	President Banzer	No victims
Bolivia	24.11.78	*Coup d'état* (army)	President Asbun	No victims
Bolivia	17.07.79	*Coup d'état* (army)	President Guevara	Uncertain
Bolivia	01.11.79	*Coup d'état* (army)	Government	No victims
Bolivia	17.07.80	*Coup d'état* (army)	Government	Uncertain
Bolivia	12.05.81	Attempted *coup d'état*	Government	Uncertain
Bolivia	24.05.81	Attempted *coup d'état*	Government	Uncertain
Bolivia	27.06.81	Attempted *coup d'état*	Government	Uncertain
Bolivia	04.08.81	*Coup d'état* (army)	President	Uncertain
Brazil	11.11.55	*Coup d'état* (army)	President Luz	Uncertain
Brazil	31.03.64	*Coup d'état* (army)	President Goulart	No victims
Chile	13.08–25.09.73	*Coup d'état* (army)	President Allende	ca. 4000
Colombia	13.06.53	*Coup d'état* (army)	Government	Victims*
Ecuador	23.08.47	*Coup d'état* (army)	President Ibarra	No victims
Ecuador	11.07.63	*Coup d'état* (army)	Government	No victims
Ecuador	31.03.66	*Coup d'état* (army)	Government	Uncertain
Ecuador	16.02.72	*Coup d'état* (R. Lara)	President Ibarra	Uncertain
Ecuador	01.09.75	Attempted *coup d'état*	President Lara	Uncertain
Ecuador	11.01.76	*Coup d'état* (Burbano)	President Lara	Uncertain
Paraguay	30.01.49	*Coup d'état* (army)	Government	Uncertain
Paraguay	26.02.49	*Coup d'état* (army)	President Rolon	Uncertain
Paraguay	1954	*Coup d'état* (army)	President Chaves	Uncertain
Paraguay	03.02.89	*Coup d'état* (army)	President Stroessner	100–300
Peru	02.11.48	*Coup d'état*	President Bustamante	No victims
Peru	18.07.62	*Coup d'état* (army)	Government	No victims
Peru	03.03.63	*Coup d'état* (army)	President Perez	No victims
Peru	03.10.68	*Coup d'état* (army)	President Terry	Uncertain
Peru	29.08.75	*Coup d'état* (Bermúdez)	Government	No victims
Peru	09.05.89	Attempted *coup d'état*	Government	Uncertain

Surinam	25.02–15.03.80	*Coup d'état* (Officers)	Government	Uncertain
Surinam	15.03.81	Attempted *coup d'état*	Government	Uncertain
Surinam	04.02.82	*Coup d'état* (Bouterse)	Government	Uncertain
Surinam	11.03.82	Attempted *coup d'état*	President Bouterse	Uncertain
Surinam	28.07.86	Attempted *coup d'état*	Government	Uncertain
Uruguay	07.02–30.03.73	*Coup d'état* (army)	Government	Uncertain
Uruguay	27.06.73	Pressure (army)	President Bordaberry	Uncertain
Venezuela	19.10.45	Upheaval	Government	Victims*
Venezuela	23.09.48	*Coup d'état* (army)	President Gallegos	Uncertain
Venezuela	23.01.58	*Coup d'état* (army)	President Jimenez	Uncertain
Sub-Saharan Africa				
Angola	27.05.77	Attempted *coup d'état*	Government	Uncertain
Benin	28.10.63			Uncertain
Benin	17.12.67	*Coup d'état*	Government	No victims
Benin	10.12.69	*Coup d'état* (army)	Government	Uncertain
Benin	26.10.72	*Coup d'état* (army)	Government	Uncertain
Benin	18.10.75	Attempted *coup d'état*	Government	Uncertain
Botswana	10.02.88	Attempted *coup d'état*	Government	Uncertain
Burkina Faso	27.05.84	Attempted *coup d'état*	Government	Uncertain
Burkina Faso	15.10.87	*Coup d'état* (army)	President Sankara	Victims*
Burundi	19.10.65	Attempted *coup d'état*	Government	Uncertain
Burundi	08.07.66	*Coup d'état* (crowne prince)	Government	No victims
Burundi	29.11.66	*Coup d'état*	King Ntare V.	Uncertain
Burundi	29.04.72	Attempted *coup d'état*	Government	Massacre
Burundi	01.11.76	*Coup d'état* (army)	Government	No victims
Burundi	03.09.87	*Coup d'état* (army)	Government	Uncertain
Cameroon	06.04.84	Attempted *coup d'état*	Government	Uncertain
Central African Rep.	01.01.66	*Coup d'état* (army)	Government	3 victims
Central African Rep.	12.04.69	Attempted *coup d'état*	Government	Uncertain
Central African Rep.	21.09.79	*Coup d'état* (Ex-President)	Bokassa	Uncertain
Central African Rep.	01.09.81	*Coup d'état* (army)	Government	Uncertain
Central African Rep.	03.03.82	Attempted *coup d'état*	Government	Uncertain
Central African Rep.	26.11.83	Attempted *coup d'état*	Government	Uncertain
Chad	16.09.63			Uncertain
Chad	13.04.75	*Coup d'état* (army)	Government	Uncertain
Chad	01.04.77	Attempted *coup d'état*	Government	Uncertain
Chad	07.06.82	*Coup d'état* (Habre)	Queddei government	Uncertain
Comoro	05.06.77	Attempted *coup d'état*	Government	Uncertain
Comoro	13.05.78	*Coup d'état*	Government	Uncertain
Comoro	06.04.85	Attempted *coup d'état*	Government	Uncertain
Comoro	10.12.87	Attempted *coup d'état*	Government	Uncertain
Congo	12.07.63	*Coup d'état* (army)	President Youlou	No victims
Congo	25.11.65	*Coup d'état* (Mobutu)	Government	No victims
Congo	28.06.66	Attempted *coup d'état*	Government	Uncertain
Congo	16.08–04/05.09.68	*Coup d'état*	Government	No victims
Congo	22.02.72	Attempted *coup d'état*		Uncertain
Congo	18.03.77	Attempted *coup d'état*	Government	Uncertain
Congo	15.08.78	Attempted *coup d'état*	Government	Uncertain

Table 3.25 Continued

State	Date	Type, initiator	Affected	Victims
Congo	06.02.79			Uncertain
Congo	July 87	Attempted *coup d'état*	Government	Uncertain
Dahomey	22.12.65	*Coup d'état* (army)	Government	No victims
Dahomey	02.01.66	*Coup d'état* (army)	Government	Uncertain
Djibouti	09.01.91	Attempted *coup d'état*		Uncertain
Equatorial-Guinea	05.08.79	*Coup d'état*	Government	Uncertain
Equatorial-Guinea	28.04.81	Attempted *coup d'état*	Government	Uncertain
Equatorial-Guinea	10.05–13.05.83	Attempted *coup d'état*	Government	Uncertain
Equatorial-Guinea	19.07.86	Attempted *coup d'état*	Government	Uncertain
Ethiopia	20.02.74	*Coup d'état* (army)	Government	Uncertain
Ethiopia	12.09.74	*Coup d'état* (army)	Haile Selassie	Uncertain
Ethiopia	24.11.74			Uncertain
Ethiopia	03.02.77	Attempted *coup d'état*	Government	Uncertain
Ethiopia	07.04.85	Attempted *coup d'état*	Government	Uncertain
Ethiopia	16.05.89	Attempted *coup d'état*	Government	Uncertain
Gabon	18.02.64	*Coup d'état*		Uncertain
Gambia	30.07.81	Attempted *coup d'état*	Government	Victims*
Ghana	24.02.66	*Coup d'état* (army)	Nkrumah	Uncertain
Ghana	13.01.72	*Coup d'état* (army)	Government	Uncertain
Ghana	05.07.78	*Coup d'état* (Akuffo)	Government	Uncertain
Ghana	04.06.79	*Coup d'état*	Government	Uncertain
Ghana	31.12.81	*Coup d'état* (Rawlings)	President Limann	Uncertain
Ghana	23.11.82	Attempted *coup d'état*	Government	Uncertain
Ghana	27.02.83	Attempted *coup d'état*	Government	Uncertain
Ghana	19.06.83	Attempted *coup d'état*	Government	Uncertain
Ghana	23.03.84	Attempted *coup d'état*	Government	Uncertain
Guinea	03.04.84	*Coup d'état* (army)	Government	Uncertain
Guinea	04.07.85	Attempted *coup d'état*	Government	Uncertain
Guinea-Bissau	15.11.78	Attempted intervention	Government	Uncertain
Guinea-Bissau	14.11.80	*Coup d'état*	Government	Uncertain
Kenya	01.08.82	Attempted *coup d'état*	Government	Victims*
Lesotho	30.01.70	*Coup d'état* (prime-minister)	King	Uncertain
Lesotho	07.01.74	Attempted *coup d'état*	Government	Uncertain
Lesotho	20.01.86	*Coup d'état* (army)	Government	Uncertain
Liberia	12.04.80	*Coup d'état* (army)	Government	Uncertain
Liberia	21.11.83	Attempted *coup d'état*	Government	Uncertain
Liberia	19.08.84	Attempted *coup d'état*	Government	Uncertain
Liberia	12.09.85	Attempted *coup d'état*	Government	Uncertain
Liberia	Aug. 86	*Coup d'état* (rumors)	Government	Uncertain
Madagascar	25.06.72	*Coup d'état* (army)	Government	Uncertain
Madagascar	05.02.75			Uncertain
Madagascar	11.02.75	*Coup d'état* (military)	Government	Victims*
Mali	19.11.68	*Coup d'état* (liberation-committee)	Government	Uncertain
Mali	26.03.91	Military *coup d'état*	Traoré government	ca. 200
Mauritania	10.07.78	*Coup d'état*	Government	Uncertain
Mauritania	18.04.79			Uncertain
Mauritania	16.03.81	Attempted *coup d'état*	Government	Uncertain
Mauritania	07.02.82	Attempted *coup d'état*	Government	Uncertain

Mauritania	12.12.84	*Coup d'état* (Taya)	Haidalla government	No victims
Mauritania	22.10.87	Attempted *coup d'état*	Government	Uncertain
Mozambique	20.12.75	Attempted *coup d'état*	Government	Uncertain
Niger	15.04.74	*Coup d'état* (army)	Government	Uncertain
Niger	15.03.76	Attempted *coup d'état*	Government	Uncertain
Niger	05.10.83	Attempted *coup d'état*	Government	Uncertain
Nigeria	15.01.66			Uncertain
Nigeria	16.01.66			Uncertain
Nigeria	05.02.66	*Coup d'état* (army)	Government	Uncertain
Nigeria	01.08.66	*Coup d'état*	Government	Uncertain
Nigeria	23.08.67			Uncertain
Nigeria	29.07.75	*Coup d'état* (army)	President Gowon	Uncertain
Nigeria	13.02.76	Attempted *coup d'état*	Government	Uncertain
Nigeria	31.12.83	*Coup d'état* (Buhari)	Government	Uncertain
Nigeria	27.08.85	*Coup d'état*	Government	No victims
Nigeria	20.12.85	Attempted *coup d'état*	Government	Uncertain
Nigeria	23.04.90	Attempted *coup d'état*	Government	Victims*
Rwanda	05.07.73	*Coup d'état* (army)	Government	Uncertain
Rwanda	05.05.80	Attempted *coup d'état*	Government	Uncertain
Sao Tomé and Principe	10.07.77	Attempted *coup d'état*	Government	Uncertain
Sao Tomé and Principe	28.09.79	Attempted *coup d'état*	Government	Uncertain
Sao Tomé and Principe	07.03.88	Attempted *coup d'état*	Government	Uncertain
Seychelles	04.06.77	*Coup d'état*	Government	Uncertain
Seychelles	30.04.78	Attempted *coup d'état*	Government	Uncertain
Seychelles	26.11.81	Attempted *coup d'état*	Government	Uncertain
Seychelles	17.08.82	*Coup d'état* (army)	Government	Uncertain
Seychelles	02.12.83	Attempted *coup d'état*	Government	Uncertain
Sierra Leone	21.03–23.03.67	*Coup d'état* (National Reform Council)	Government	Uncertain
Sierra Leone	18.04.68	*Coup d'état* (army)	Government	No victims
Sierra Leone	23.03.87	Attempted *coup d'état*	Government	Uncertain
Somalia	21.10.69	*Coup d'état* (military)	Government	No victims
Somalia	09.04.78	Attempted *coup d'état*	Government	Uncertain
South Africa	16.07.83	Attempted *coup d'état*	Government	Uncertain
South Africa	10.02.91	Attempted *coup d'état*		Uncertain
South Africa	30.12.87	*Coup d'état* (Holomisa)	Government	No victims
Sudan	17.11.58			Uncertain
Sudan	31.10.64	*Coup d'état*	Abboud regime	Victims*
Sudan	29.12.66	Attempted *coup d'état*	Government	Uncertain
Sudan	25.05.69			Uncertain
Sudan	19.07.71	Attempted *coup d'état*		Uncertain
Sudan	22.07.71			Uncertain
Sudan	05.09.75	Attempted *coup d'état*	Government	Uncertain
Sudan	02.07.76	Attempted *coup d'état*	Government	Victims*
Sudan	16.03.81	Attempted *coup d'état*	Government	Uncertain
Sudan	21.09.85	Attempted *coup d'état*	Government	Uncertain
Sudan	18.06.89	Attempted *coup d'état*	Government	Uncertain
Sudan	30.06.89	*Coup d'état* (army)	Government	Uncertain
Sudan	23.04.90	Attempted *coup d'état*	General	No victims
Swaziland	02.04.84	Attempted *coup d'état*	Government	Uncertain
Togo	13.01.63	*Coup d'état*	President Olympio	Uncertain
Togo	21.11.66	Attempted *coup d'état*	Government	Uncertain
Togo	13.01.67	*Coup d'état* (army)	Government	Uncertain
Togo	23.09.86	Attempted *coup d'état*	Government	Uncertain
Togo	02.10.91	Attempted *coup d'état*	Provisional government	Uncertain
Uganda	25.01.71	*Coup d'état* (Amin)	Obote government	Uncertain

Table 3.25 Continued

State	Date	Type, initiator	Affected	Victims
Uganda	24.03.74	Attempted *coup d'état*	Government	Uncertain
Uganda	20.04.79	*Coup d'état* (Benaisa)	Lule government	Uncertain
Uganda	10.05.80			Uncertain
Uganda	27.07.85	*Coup d'état* (army)	President Obote	Uncertain
Uganda	29.01.86	*Coup d'état*	Government	Uncertain
Uganda	07.10.86	Attempted *coup d'état*	Government	Uncertain
Upper Volta	03.01.66	*Coup d'état* (army)	Yameogo government	Uncertain
Upper Volta	08.02.74	*Coup d'état* (army)	Government	Uncertain
Upper Volta	25.11.80	*Coup d'état* (army)	Government	Uncertain
Upper Volta	07.11.82	*Coup d'état*	Government	3 victims
Upper Volta	07.03.83	Attempted *coup d'état*	Government	Uncertain
Upper Volta	05.08.83	*Coup d'état* (Sankara)	Government	Uncertain
Upper Volta	09.08.83	Attempted *coup d'état*	Sankara government	Uncertain
Zaire	25.11.65			Uncertain
Zanzibar	12.01.64	*Coup d'état*	Sultanate	Victims*
Zanzibar	12.07.80	Attempted *coup d'état*	Government	Uncertain

Middle East/Maghreb

State	Date	Type, initiator	Affected	Victims
Afghanistan	17.07.73	*Coup d'état* (Daud)	Monarch	Uncertain
Afghanistan	09.12.76	Attempted *coup d'état*	Government	Uncertain
Afghanistan	27.04.78	*Coup d'état* (army)	Government	Victims*
Afghanistan	17.08.78	Attempted *coup d'état*	Government	Uncertain
Afghanistan	14.09.79	Attempted *coup d'état*	Taraki	Uncertain
Afghanistan	27.12.79	*Coup d'état* (Karmal/ DUSSR)	Government	Victims*
Afghanistan	06.03.90	Attempted *coup d'état*	Government	Uncertain
Egypt	23.07.52	*Coup d'état*	Government (Nasser)	Uncertain
Egypt	18.07.74	Attempted *coup d'état*		Uncertain
Iran	16.08.53	*Coup d'état* (army, Mossadegh)	Government	Uncertain
Iran	1963	Attempted *coup d'état*	Government	Uncertain
Iran	16.01.79	*Coup d'état*/revolution (Khomeini)	Shah Reza	Uncertain
Iraq	14.07.58	*Coup d'état* (Kassem)	Government	Uncertain
Iraq	March 1959	Attempted *coup d'état*	Government	Uncertain
Iraq	07.10.59	Attempted *coup d'état* (Hussein)	Government	Uncertain
Iraq	08.02.63	*Coup d'état* (Arif)	President Kassem	Victims*
Iraq	25.05.63	Dissolution	Pro-Nasser Movement	Victims*
Iraq	13.11.63	*Coup d'état*	Baath party	Uncertain
Iraq	17.09.65	Attempted *coup d'état*	Government	Uncertain
Iraq	05.12.65	Attempted *coup d'état*	Government	Uncertain
Iraq	Jun. 66	Attempted *coup d'état*	Government	Uncertain
Iraq	30.06.66	Attempted *coup d'état*	Government	Uncertain
Iraq	17.07.68	*Coup d'état* (Nayef, Daoud)	Government	Uncertain
Iraq	01.07.73	Attempted *coup d'état*	Government	Uncertain
Iraq	28.07.79	Attempted *coup d'état*	Government	Uncertain
Iraq	Jan. 89	*Coup d'état* (rumors)	Government	Uncertain
Jordan	20.05.63	Attempted *coup d'état*	Government	Uncertain
Jordan	03.11.68	Attempted *coup d'état*	Government	Uncertain
Libya	01.09.69	*Coup d'état* (al-Gaddafi)	Monarchy	Uncertain
Libya	17.08.75	Attempted *coup d'état*	Government	Uncertain
Libya	08.05.84	Attempted *coup d'état*	Government	Uncertain
Libya	Apr. 85	Attempted *coup d'état*	Gaddafi government	Victims*
Morocco	10.07.71	Attempted *coup d'état*		Uncertain

Morocco	16.08.72	Attempted *coup d'état*		Uncertain
Oman	23.07.70	*Coup d'état* (Kabus)	Sultan	Uncertain
Pakistan	05.07.77	*Coup d'état* (army)	Government	Uncertain
Qatar	22.02.72	*Coup d'état* (crown prince)	Emir	Uncertain
Saudi Arabia	02.11.64	Change of government (Faisal)	King Saud	Uncertain
Syria	29.03.49	*Coup d'état* (as-Saim)	Government	Uncertain
Syria	18.08.49	*Coup d'état* (Hinnawi)	as-Saim government	Victims*
Syria	19.12.49	*Coup d'état* (Hinnawi)	Government	Uncertain
Syria	25.11.51	*Coup d'état*		Uncertain
Syria	25.02.54	Military coup	Government	Uncertain
Syria	28.09.61	*Coup d'état*	Government/Nasser	Uncertain
Syria	28.03.62	*Coup d'état* (army)	Daualibi government	Uncertain
Syria	05.04.62	Attempted *coup d'état*	Government	Uncertain
Syria	14.01.63	Attempted *coup d'état*	Government	No victims
Syria	08.03.63	*Coup d'état* (Baath party)	Government	Uncertain
Syria	08.05.63	Dissolution	Pro-Nasser Movement	Victims*
Syria	18.07.63	Attempted *coup d'état*	Pro-Nasser Movement	Victims*
Syria	Jun. 64	*Coup d'état* (army)	Government	Uncertain
Syria	23.02.66	*Coup d'état* (Jadid)		Uncertain
Syria	06.09.66	Attempted *coup d'état*	Government	Uncertain
Syria	Jul. 68	Attempted *coup d'état*	Government	Uncertain
Syria	13.11.70	*Coup d'état*	Rightist groups	Uncertain
Tunisia	Dec. 67	Attempted *coup d'état*	Government	Uncertain
Yemen PR	Jul. 77	Attempted *coup d'état*	Government	Uncertain
Yemen PR	13.01.86	*Coup d'état* (Ismail)	Government	Uncertain
Yemen AR	17.02.48	Attempted *coup d'état*	Imam Jahja	Victims*
Yemen AR	27.09.62	*Coup d'état* (army, as-Sallal)	Imam	Uncertain
Yemen AR	04.11.67	*Coup d'état* (al-Irjani)	as-Sallal government	Uncertain
Yemen AR	21.05.68	*Coup d'état*	Imam al-Bado	Uncertain
Yemen AR	13.06.74	*Coup d'état* (Al-Hamadi)	Government	Uncertain
Yemen AR	15.10.78	Attempted *coup d'état*	Government	Uncertain

Note
* Victims known of but numbers unconfirmed

in the 661 conflicts analyzed in this book, but are a separate listing. This long list of more than 370 attempted or realized *coups d'état* reveals the lack of legal regulations for succession or change of governments in many countries – foremost in sub-Saharan Africa and Latin America.

In sharp contrast to the increasing number of internal power conflicts, the number of international, geo-strategic power conflicts is relatively low and the long-term tendency seems toward a decreasing trend (Figure 3.30). The frequencies are between ten and fifteen ongoing international power conflicts each year. The peaks in this line are in the late 1960s; the end of the Cold War has had no influence on the frequency of this type of conflict. The proportion of violent conflicts with regard to all international power conflicts is low. Not more than one out of three conflicts escalated into a violent conflict. This rather non-violent character of international conflicts can be explained in part by the greater international implications and reactions triggered by power and geo-strategic conflicts. An illustrative example is the conflict over the Spratly Islands in the South China Sea. The

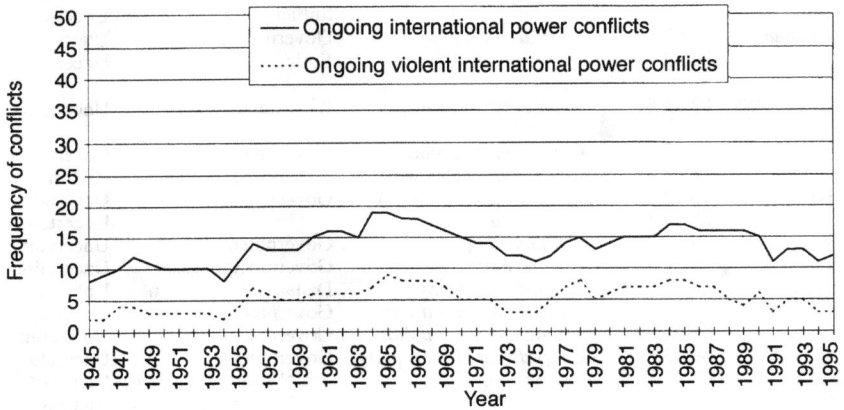

Figure 3.30 International power conflicts.

oil resources in the seabed are highly contested by at least six regional states. After the withdrawal of Soviet troops from Vietnam and American troops from the Philippines, the South China Sea was open for geo-strategic maneuverings by Vietnam, China and others. Yet, none of the contestants for these oil resources seemed prepared to risk a violent escalation. In contrast, a miscalculated attempt at a geo-strategic improvement of one's position was Iraq's annexation of Kuwait in 1990.

The seventh possible issue in conflicts coded by KOSIMO is resources (Figure 3.31). In contrast to scenarios that predict the forceful exploitation of resources on a global, imperialistic scale, the empirical evidence – so far – can only in part verify these assumptions. Conflicts over resources play an increasing role within the set of all conflicts, yet compared with other issues in conflicts, the

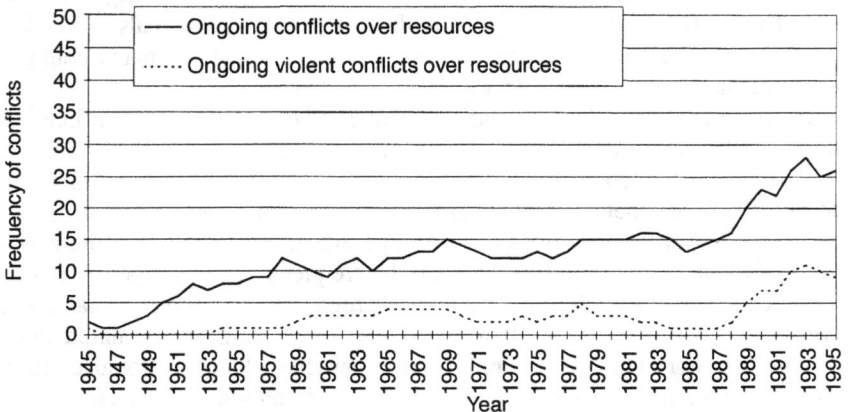

Figure 3.31 Ongoing conflicts over resources.

issue of control over or access to resources is not a dominant factor. In 1995, we counted twenty-five ongoing conflicts of this type. In contrast to the global trends of most of the other conflict categories, the frequency of conflicts over resources has not been decreasing since the end of the Cold War, but was still on the rise in 1995. Also, throughout the 1950s until the late 1980s the number of violent conflicts over resources was insignificant; since 1989 this frequency of violent conflicts over resources has been on the rise. In 1993, KOSIMO listed ten violent conflicts of this type. Since conflicts over resources are the only ones that are on the rise in the 1990s, they should be given greater attention in the future. Rather than 'classic' conflicts over oil, conflicts over access to water and fertile soil may be future sources of conflicts. Conflicts over resources may also have the potential to revise the otherwise inspiring global trend of non-violence among states in international conflicts since the late 1980s (see page 148). Disputes over the control of rivers that run through two or more states, such as the Jordan, the Euphrates or Nile rivers, are already the source of intense rivalries. Fertile soil, over- or underpopulation and subsequent migrations in sub-Saharan Africa, such as in Rwanda or Mali and Niger, are equally explosive sources of new international violent conflicts.

As explained earlier, the seven possible issues in conflicts can be aggregated into two groupings: international and internal types of issues. Territorial and border conflicts (1), conflicts over decolonization and national independence (2), international power conflicts (6) and conflicts over resources (7) can be grouped as international types of issues. Conflicts over ethnic, religious and regional autonomy (3), ideological and system conflicts (4) as well as internal, national power conflicts (5) can be grouped as internal types of issues in conflicts. In Figures 3.32 and 3.33, these lines are shown in one figure.

Figure 3.32 shows the internal types of issues in conflicts. Note that the multiple coding of the variables does not allow for absolute, but only interpretations of the relative frequencies. All lines show a comparable and

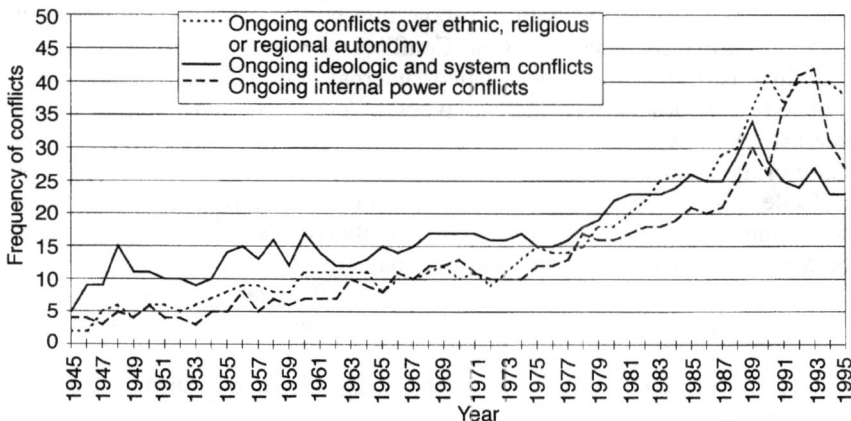

Figure 3.32 Issues in ongoing internal types of conflicts.

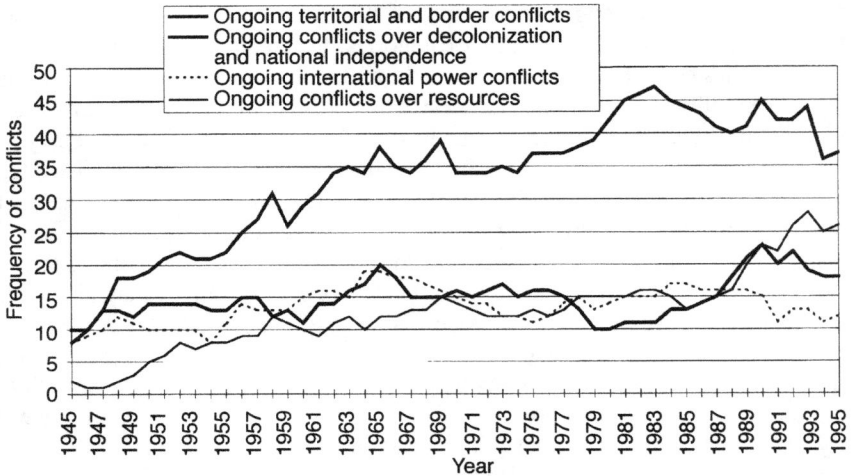

Figure 3.33 Issues in ongoing international types of conflicts.

accelerating increase in frequencies until the end of the Cold War. Since then, all internal types of objectives have been on the decrease. Yet a continuation of this trend cannot be predicted from these short-term tendencies. Ethnic, religious and regional autonomy conflicts will most likely be the dominant issue in internal conflicts in the near future. Ideological system conflicts will be by comparison less frequent.

Figure 3.33 shows the combined lines for international issues in conflicts. The four possible objectives show different tendencies. Whereas territorial and border issues are by far the most frequent issue in international conflicts, the frequency of this objective is slowly decreasing. International and geo-strategic power conflicts are also a constant, but less significant issue in international conflicts. By comparison with territorial and border conflicts, they make up only half of that frequency per year. Conflicts over resources are on a constant rise. In this, they follow the trend of internal conflicts. Although they are grouped as issues in international types of conflicts (there are, of course, internal conflicts over resources, e.g. conflicts over the resources in Catanga/Zaire or the copper mines in the Bougainville conflict in Papua New Guinea).

Table 3.26 summarizes the numeric findings on regional conflict activities according to the issues in dispute. Note that there is an auto-correlation between the high number of international types of conflicts and the high number of territorial and border issues as well as between the number of internal conflicts and the number of internal power conflicts as issues.

- Territories and borders were the most disputed issues in political conflicts between 1945 and 1995.

Table 3.26 Issues in conflicts*

Types	(1) Territory, borders, sea borders	(2) Decolonization, national independence	(3) Ethnic, religious or regional autonomy	(4) Ideology, system conflict	(5) Internal power conflict	(6) International power conflict	(7) Resources
All conflicts	224	116	121	150	180	117	103
Non-violent conflicts	133	42	34	54	27	51	59
Violent conflicts	91	74	87	96	153	66	44
International conflicts	207	76	19	60	47	100	80
International non-violent conflicts	130	33	8	29	13	49	53
International violent conflicts	77	43	11	31	34	51	27
Internal conflicts	17	40	102	90	133	17	23
Internal non-violent conflicts	3	9	26	25	14	2	6
Internal violent conflicts	14	31	76	65	119	15	17
Regions							
Europe	38	18	26	30	24	18	14
Middle East/Maghreb	57	35	28	31	53	43	39
Sub-Saharan Africa	45	24	30	15	55	18	17
Asia/Oceania	46	36	33	38	31	28	16
America	38	3	4	36	17	10	17
North America	2	0	1	0	0	0	1
Central America	14	2	2	20	10	9	3
South America	22	1	1	16	7	1	13

Note
* Multiple choice.

- From a regional perspective, only in sub-Saharan Africa did the number of internal power conflicts exceed the number of territorial and border conflicts.
- On average, conflicts over resources are carried out at a low level of intensity; conflicts over ideology and internal power positions generally show more violence.

Victims of violent conflicts

The coding of structural and actor-related data on conflicts is one undertaking, the counting of conflict-related casualties such as material losses, refugees and victims, is quite another. The statistical treatment of battle deaths is a risky undertaking. On the one hand, the bitter individual tragedies behind the abstract numbers cannot and should not be subsumed or hidden. On the other hand, there is no comparison without the aggregation of numbers into comparable units. The decision to include data on conflict-related casualties into a statistical analysis must, therefore, be made with the expressed acknowledgment about the artificial, distorting and minimizing effects that such an abstracting approach brings along. Given the above premise, the counting of conflict-related victims becomes no easier. Several obstacles make it difficult to present 'exact' numbers (see also pages 51–2).

First, at least since the Japanese–Russian War of 1904 and the First World War, civilians have been the most affected party in modern military conflicts. Therefore it must first be decided whether one counts either one group or both groups. KOSIMO has listed data on the overall number of people killed in conflicts, unrelated to their civilian or military status.

Secondly, with the advance of guerrilla warfare, warlordism, marauding gang wars and other new forms of violence, it becomes increasingly difficult to know whether all casualties that were reported are conflict-related deaths. In many cases, famine caused by cut supply lines, devastated farmland or forced migration and other 'side-effects' of conflicts may indirectly kill people. Again, KOSIMO has not made a clear-cut differentiation between – in this sense – direct and indirect numbers of casualties.

Thirdly, numbers of casualties are sensitive information. They trigger public reactions and influence opinions on the justification of military actions on either side of a conflict. Therefore, in many cases the numbers of victims are either kept secret or they have been changed for the better or worse. Also, in many cases, even when neutral observers are present in conflicts, as during the Rwandan massacre in 1994, it is technically or logistically impossible to estimate an exact number of deaths. Different sources may report different numbers of casualties on the same day in the media. Therefore, KOSIMO has introduced two categories: minimum and maximum estimates of conflict-related deaths. Table 3.27 shows in chronological order the names of the conflicts by their year of beginning and ending and the minimum and maximum numbers of deaths. The list

Table 3.27 Estimates of victims in violent conflicts (chronological order)

Name	Start	End	Conflict-related deaths Maximum estimate	Minimum estimate
India I (independence)	1942	1947	800,000	Not available
Greece (civil war I)	1944	1945	16,000	16,000
Algeria (independence I)	1945	1946	45,000	1,500
China (civil war)	1945	1949	2,000,000	1,000,000
Indonesia (independence)	1945	1949	100,000	5,000
Indochina I (part 1)	1945	1954	600,000	95,000
Greece (civil war II)	1946	1949	160,000	44,000
Paraguay (*coup d'état*)	1947	1947	28,000	28,000
India IV (Kashmir I)	1947	1949	10,000	1,500
Malagasy Republic (independence)	1947	1960	80,000	5,000
Burma/Myanmar (minorities)	1948	cont.	60,000	40,000
India V (Hyderabad)	1948	1948	10,000	2,000
Israel II (Palestine war)	1948	1949	20,000	8,000
Colombia (Violencia I)	1948	1953	300,000	80,000
Malaya (independence)	1948	1960	13,000	12,500
India VIII (Kashmir II)	1949	1964	10,000	2,000
Korea II (Korean War)	1950	1953	2,000,000	1,500,000
Indonesia (South Moluccas)	1950	1965	10,000	5,000
Kenya (independence, Mau Mau)	1952	1956	10,745	10,000
China (Tibet II)	1954	1959	65,000	65,000
Algeria (independence II)	1954	1962	190,000	100,000
Egypt (Suez war)	1956	1957	10,000	3,230
Hungary (revolt)	1956	1957	32,000	10,000
Rwanda–Burundi (independence)	1958	1964	20,000	100
Iraq (Kurds I)	1961	1970	50,000	25,500
Angola (independence)	1961	1974	90,000	60,000
Yemen AR (civil war II)	1962	1968	100,000	100,000
Rwanda (Bugesera invasion)	1963	1964	14,000	14,000
Sudan (civil war I)	1963	1972	500,000	100,000
Guinea-Bissau–Portugal (independence)	1963	1974	15,000	2,000
Laos II (civil war)	1963	1975	100,000	100,000
Zaire (civil war)	1964	1965	100,000	20,000
Indochina II (Vietnam War)	1964	1973	2,000,000	1,215,992
Mozambique (independence)	1964	1975	30,000	25,000
Dominican Republic II (intervention)	1965	1965	10,000	3,000
India XIV (Kashmir III)	1965	1965	20,000	20,000
Mozambique (border)	1966	1974	30,000	1,000
Namibia II (SWAPO)	1966	1990	40,000	40,000
Egypt–Israel (6-day War)	1967	1967	25,000	19,600
Nigeria (Biafra secession)	1967	1970	2,000,000	1,000,000
Eritrea III (civil war)	1967	1993	2,000,000	36,000
Philippines (uproar of 'National Front')	1968	cont.	12,000	10,000
Indonesia (West Irian III)	1969	cont.	100,000	50,000

Table 3.27 Continued

Name	Start	End	Conflict-related deaths Maximum estimate	Minimum estimate
Argentina (Montoneros)	1969	1977	10,000	10,000
Philippines (Moros in Mindanao and Sulu)	1970	cont.	100,000	100,000
Cambodia II	1970	1975	1,000,000	150,000
India XVII (Bangladesh III)	1971	1971	1,000,000	300,000
Burundi I (genocide)	1972	1973	200,000	100,000
Rhodesia (civil war)	1972	1979	20,000	12,000
Israel IV (Yom Kippur War)	1973	1973	25,000	16,401
Indochina II (cease-fire)	1973	1976	100,000	100,000
Iraq (Kurds II)	1974	1975	20,000	2,000
Ethiopia ('red terror')	1974	1978	2,000,000	Not available
Ethiopia (Tigray)	1974	1991	25,000	25,000
Indonesia–FRETILIN (East Timor I)	1975	1976	200,000	100,000
Bangladesh (Chakma, Marma)	1975	1987	200,000	200,000
Indonesia (East Timor III)	1976	cont.	250,000	100,000
Somalia–Ethiopia (Ogaden II)	1976	1978	21,000	9,000
Morocco (Western Sahara II)	1976	1979	10,000	7,000
Iraq (Kurds III)	1976	1990	200,000	182,000
Angola (civil war II)	1976	1991	150,000	150,000
South Africa (ANC, PAC)	1976	1994	15,000	15,000
Nicaragua I (revolution)	1977	1979	40,000	10,000
Indochina III (part 2)	1978	1991	150,000	25,000
Mozambique (civil war; RENAMO)	1978	1994	400,000	100,000
China–Vietnam (war)	1979	1979	70,000	20,000
Iran (Islamic revolution II)	1979	1981	20,000	4,000
Afghanistan II (Soviet intervention)	1979	1988	1,200,000	14,454
Morocco (Western Sahara III)	1979	1991	10,000	10,000
Peru (Illuminated path)	1980	cont.	17,000	12,000
Iran–Iraq I (Gulf War)	1980	1988	450,000	400,000
India XVIII (Khalistan/Punjab)	1981	cont.	18,000	10,000
Nicaragua II (Contras)	1981	1990	40,000	20,000
El Salvador (civil war)	1981	1992	65,000	30,000
Syria (February uproar in Hama)	1982	1982	20,000	20,000
Israel–Lebanon III	1982	1985	50,000	7,200
Sri Lanka (Tamils II)	1983	1987	25,000	1,000
Yemen PR (Aden civil war)	1986	1986	13,000	10,000
Sri Lanka (Tamils III)	1987	1995	100,000	30,000
India XXII (Kashmir V)	1988	cont.	20,000	15,000
Burundi II (Hutu)	1988	1988	50,000	5,000
Somalia (civil war I)	1988	1991	50,000	15,000
Sudan (civil war III)	1989	cont.	1,300,000	Not available
Liberia (civil war)	1989	1995	200,000	200,000

Indonesia (GAM movement in Aceh II)	1990	cont.	20,000	2,000
South Africa (ANC Inkatha)	1990	cont.	12,000	12,000
Iraq–Kuwait VI (US intervention)	1990	1991	100,000	100
Rwanda (civil war)	1990	1994	1,000,000	500,000
Sierra Leone (civil war)	1991	cont.	50,000	50,000
Somalia (civil war II)	1991	cont.	300,000	300,000
Armenia–Azerbaijan (Nagorny-Karabakh II)	1991	1994	15,000	15,000
Iraq–Kuwait VII	1991	1994	200,000	Not available
Zaire (regime crisis)	1991	1994	10,000	500
Algeria (Islamists vs. secularists II)	1992	cont.	30,000	10,000
Tajikistan (civil war II)	1992	1993	20,000	20,000
Angola (civil war III)	1992	1994	500,000	500,000
Bosnia–Herzegovina (Serbs–Croats)	1992	1994	200,000	200,000
Burundi III (civil war)	1993	cont.	100,000	100,000
Yemen (Seventy-Day War)	1994	1994	15,000	10,000
Sub-total (estimates)	1945	1995	26,251,745	10,132,577

includes only conflicts with estimates of at least 10,000 reported deaths. The reasons for this limitation are the unreliability and great variances of these numbers by 'smaller' conflicts. Also, we want to avoid the impression of being able to present a complete death register – a task which no one seriously could undertake for 385 violent conflicts.

Between 1945 and 1995, at least ten million and possibly as many as almost thirty million people have died from direct or war-related violence. Note that our sample includes only wars with at least 10,000 war-related deaths. Also, in many cases the figures could not be confirmed or verified. The total figure of war-related deaths after the end of the Second World War is probably way above thirty million.

4 Conflict structures

In Chapters 2 and 3, we presented the concept and methods of the KOSIMO project and analyzed global findings and trends by states, conflicts, duration, regions, issues and number of victims.

In this chapter we try to capture structural and behavioral elements of the conflicts between 1945 and 1995. First, we focus on relations between conflict frequencies and political systems of states. This aspect serves as a further test for the democratic peace theorem. Second, we group states and conflicts according to their economic stage of development (North–South dimensions of conflicts) and, for the Cold War period, their place in the political and military alliances (East–West dimensions). A third focus will be on conflicts within certain groups of states, i.e. South–South conflicts, conflicts within the Eastern bloc states and within the Western alliance. Fourth, we analyze the behavior of neighboring or proxy states as well as the behavior of superpowers toward a certain conflict. Last, we glance at post-Cold War trends in global conflicts.

Political systems of states

The term political 'system' refers to states. Therefore, non-state actors do not fall under this category although they may be organized and act as political entities, and they have been responsible for a substantial part of the world's conflicts since 1945. Their role is examined in Chapter 3 under 'Non-state actors'.

The four basic categories of political systems of states, democracy, transitory regimes, authoritarian regimes and anarchic regimes are aggregated sets from seven sub-categories (see Chapter 1).

1 Western-type democracies.
2 'Transitory regimes' as a category of political systems include
   - states close to fully accepted democratic rules of conflict execution
   - transitory regimes trying to establish basic democratic rules and
   - ideologically inspired ones, systems which for a short period are popular or legitimate after a revolution or a fundamental change of systems.

3 'Authoritarian systems' as a category of political systems are aggregated from
   • 'traditional authoritarian systems', e.g. clan-rule and
   • 'ideologically inspired authoritarian systems', e.g. rigid communist rule.
4 An extra-categorical type is comprised of anarchic systems, which have lost central control over the essential state functions.

Figure 4.1 shows the four categories of political systems together with non-sovereign, subnational opposition groups (x-axis). Each category is differentiated by four aspects (y-axis): System frequency (1), 'all conflicts' (2), 'non-violent conflicts' (3) and 'violent conflicts' (4).

A look at the first group of columns in Figure 4.1, 'system frequency' shows that this counting gives us the number of states for each category. For the period 1945–95, we counted 71 democracies, 158 transitory regimes and 113 authoritarian systems. In seven cases, we found territories or states in anarchic conditions. Non-sovereign groups are not included in this sample. Altogether 349 political systems existed in 204 states between 1945 and 1995. In other words, on average, every state since 1945 has experienced two different political systems. Adding transitory and authoritarian regimes into one group, we end up with 271 non- or partially democratic states and 71 'fully' democratic states since 1945. This proportion is comparable with, e.g., the results of the Freedom House (1999) or the Stockholm International Peace Research Institute, SIPRI (1995).

Democratic regimes are still a minority among the political systems and they are still far from becoming a majority regime in the world. On the other hand, the number of transitory regimes that seem to be on the road toward

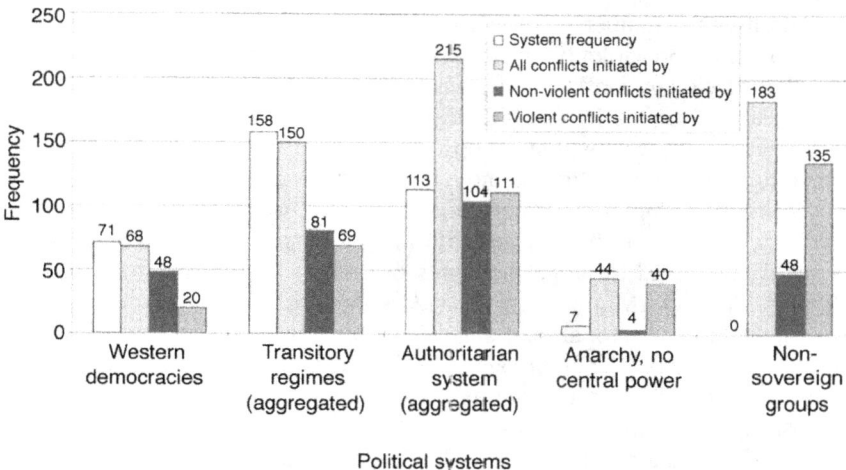

Figure 4.1 Political systems and types of conflicts.

democratization is the largest group among our regime types, larger than the number of authoritarian systems. This trend has been decisively strengthened with the end of the Cold War and the collapse of almost all communist regimes worldwide. These states are now on a more or less difficult road toward democracy and market economies. Very few of these states have experienced backsliding into authoritarian rule such as Belarus in 1996. Even the autocratic rule of Slobodan Milosevic in Serbia had to give in to large-scale demonstrations calling for democratization and acknowledgment of municipal election results in 1996.

The second bloc of columns in Figure 4.1 shows the numbers of all conflict initiations for each category of political systems. The total number of conflict initiations by all political actors is 660.[1] Most conflicts were initiated by authoritarian systems (215 conflicts). Democracies initiated fewer conflicts (68 conflicts). Transitory regimes initiated twice as many conflicts as democracies; yet the system frequency is also twice as high. This is also true for the authoritarian states. In other words, when we consider both system frequency and number of conflict initiations by political systems, we find a ratio of one conflict for every democracy or transitory regime and two initiated conflicts for every authoritarian regime. These observations have to be grouped into violent and non-violent conflict initiations. Two-thirds of all conflicts initiated by democracies remained non-violent throughout their development. More than 50 percent of all conflict initiations by democracies in transition remained below the level of military conflicts. The proportion of violent and non-violent conflicts initiated by authoritarian systems is not much higher (52 percent). In consideration of the absolute numbers, authoritarian systems are nevertheless responsible for more than five times as many violent conflicts as democratic states.

The highest number of initiations of violent conflicts is caused by non-state actors (135 violent conflicts). This number is more than six times the number of violent conflict initiations by democratic states. This high number is in part influenced by our KOSIMO definition of conflict initiators. Non-state actors, e.g. opposition groups, separatists, guerillas, freedom fighters, liberation armies or religious movements, are considered as 'initiators' due to the logic of the conflict constellation. Those who oppose the status quo will have to initiate the conflict with the government. Using this definition, we did not intend to judge the rights or wrongs of opposition movements. Rather, the KOSIMO concept considers the state as the principal actor in internal and international relations. We assume that conflicts that grew out of opposition against state reprisals were caused by the state's behavior. But, if we label an authoritarian state as the initiator of a conflict merely because this state is authoritarian, it will leave us with the result that all authoritarian states are initiators of conflicts. In this case, the category 'authoritarian system' becomes meaningless. Table 4.1 is a conversion of the above figure into a cross-table figure.

Table 4.1 Political systems by conflict initiations

Political system of initiator	System frequency	All conflicts* initiated by (row)	Non-violent conflicts initiated by (row)	Violent conflicts initiated by (row)
Western democracies	71	68	48	20
Transitory regimes (aggregated)	158	150	81	69
Authoritarian system (aggregated)	113	215	104	111
Anarchy, no central power	7	44	4	40
Non-sovereign groups	0	183	48	135
Sum	349	660	285	375

Note
* Missing: Antarctic conflict

If the categories 'transitory regimes' and 'authoritarian system' are desegregated, then the category 'transitory regime with partially accepted democratic rules of conflict management' makes up half of all transitory regimes. They have a clearly positive ratio of non-violent over violent conflict initiations. Transitory regimes with a weak central power and fewer accepted rules of democratic conflict management make up one-fourth of all transitory regimes. Every second conflict initiated by this type of political system becomes a violent conflict. The small group of revolutionary regimes with new charismatic leaderships has a comparable profile. The two types of authoritarian regimes, traditional and ideological authoritarian political systems, also share similar profiles. They are both responsible for over one hundred conflicts in their respective category. Fifty percent of these conflicts escalated into violent conflicts.

A further aspect of political systems is their stability. By definition, stable political systems are those systems that have not experienced a regime change since 1945 or since their independence. The degree of inner stability of political systems may influence the system's capacity for effective and peaceful conflict management. The assumption is that stable systems have a higher capacity to resolve conflicts peacefully. Less stable political systems are supposed to have higher frequencies of violent conflicts. Table 4.2 supports this thesis to some degree. It shows the frequency of stable political systems since 1945 or since the state's independence (after 1945).

Western democracies have been by far the most stable political systems since 1945. In forty-seven states, democracy as a political system has prevailed over a fifty-year period. The second most stable type of political systems are traditional-authoritarian systems. Sixteen of these systems have been in effect since 1945 or since the states' independence. North Korea has

Table 4.2 Frequency of stable political systems since 1945 or independence

Type of political system	Frequency of stable political systems
Western democracies	47
Transitory regimes (aggregated)	25
Authoritarian systems (aggregated)	17

been the only remaining communist-authoritarian political system in place since 1945. Twenty-five systems remain in transitory phases on their road to democracy. Many of these states are former Soviet republics with only a short history since independence.

As a conclusion, it can be said that democracies are the most stable political regimes in the post-Second World War era. While it is true that democracies as well as stable political systems are more effective in peaceful and effective conflict management, these findings support the democratic peace theorem. On the other hand, stability by itself is not a criterion for effective and peaceful conflict management. As shown above, authoritarian systems are responsible for a large part of violent conflicts and authoritarian systems may well be stable over time. However, stability here is only defined by a system's period of existence. It goes without saying that authoritarian or totalitarian systems can be maintained for a long period of time without legitimacy and with repressive measures.

East–West conflict

East–West conflict as a term in conflict research may be confusing. On the one hand, the East–West conflict refers to the overall, fundamental and existential conflict between the two competing political and economic models of Western free-market democracy and East European communism. This conflict began – for our purposes – with the ending of cooperation among the Allied Powers in 1946–47, and it lasted until the formal ending of the Cold War period in 1990. Understood as such, the East–West conflict as a term means a specific constellation of ideological, military and economic forces that lay underneath most of the actions of states, be they conflictive or cooperative.

On the other hand, the main characteristic of the East–West conflict is that it never escalated into particular conflicts – it remained a Cold War with intermittent crises. This was certainly due to the inherent logic of mutual nuclear deterrence. Rarely did the superpowers oppose each other directly over a certain issue. In Table 4.3 we have identified forty-nine instances where the superpowers were simultaneously involved on opposite sides of a conflict.

Figure 4.2 shows a first analysis of the list in Table 4.3 of superpower confrontations during the Cold War period. Seventy-five percent of these

Table 4.3 The US and the USSR as external participants on opposite sides of a conflict

Name	Start	End	Intensity	Type
Afghanistan III (civil war II)	1988	1992	Violent	Internal
Afghanistan–Pakistan (Pashtunistan I)	1947	1963	Violent	International
Afghanistan–Pakistan (Pashtunistan III)	1978	1986	Non-violent	International
Angola (civil war II)	1976	1991	Violent	International
Angola (independence)	1961	1974	Violent	International
Antarctic	1956	1959	Non-violent	International
Austria (state treaty)	1945	1955	Non-violent	International
Bulgaria (air-traffic incident)	1955	1955	Non-violent	International
China (civil war)	1945	1949	Violent	Internal
China (Tachen Islands)	1955	1955	Violent	International
China–Taiwan (Quemoy II)	1958	1958	Violent	International
China–Vietnam (border, emigrants, ideology)	1979	1991	Violent	International
Cuba (Cuban Missile Crisis)	1962	1962	Violent	International
Egypt–Israel (6–day War)	1967	1967	Violent	International
Egypt–Libya	1977	1977	Violent	International
France–Syria, Lebanon (Levant)	1945	1946	Violent	International
GDR–FRG (Berlin I, blockade)	1948	1949	Non-violent	International
GDR–FRG (Berlin II, status)	1958	1959	Non-violent	International
GDR–FRG (Berlin III, wall)	1961	1961	Non-violent	International
GDR–FRG (partition)	1945	1990	Non-violent	International
Greece (civil war II)	1946	1949	Violent	Internal
Hungary (communism)	1946	1949	Non-violent	Internal
India XVII (Bangladesh III)	1971	1971	Violent	International
Indochina II (cease-fire)	1973	1976	Violent	International
Indochina III (part 2)	1978	1991	Violent	International
Israel IV (Yom Kippur War)	1973	1973	Violent	International
Israel–Lebanon II (Litani operation)	1978	1978	Non-violent	International
Jordan (Arab Legion)	1956	1957	Violent	Internal
Jordan (Black September)	1970	1971	Violent	Internal
Korea I	1947	1950	Violent	International
Korea II (Korean War)	1950	1953	Violent	International
Korea III (partition)	1953	cont.	Non-violent	International
Laos I	1953	1961	Violent	Internal
Libya (Cyrenaica)	1949	1951	Non-violent	International
Namibia II (SWAPO)	1966	1990	Violent	Internal
Nicaragua II (Contras)	1981	1990	Violent	Internal
Poland (communism)	1945	1947	Non-violent	Internal
Rhodesia (Nagomia attack)	1976	1976	Violent	Internal
Turkey–Syria (border)	1955	1957	Violent	International
Uganda–Tanzania (border war)	1978	1979	Violent	International
US–USSR (downing of RB-47)	1960	1960	Non-violent	International
US–USSR (U2 downing)	1960	1960	Non-violent	International
USSR–US (air-traffic incident)	1954	1954	Non-violent	International
USSR–US (Chinese Sea, piracy)	1954	1954	Non-violent	International
USSR–US (Soviet airspace)	1958	1958	Non-violent	International
Yemen PR–Yemen AR II	1978	1979	Violent	International
Yugoslavia–Italy (Trieste)	1945	1954	Non-violent	International
Zaire (civil war)	1964	1965	Violent	Internal
Zaire (Shaba II)	1977	1977	Violent	Internal

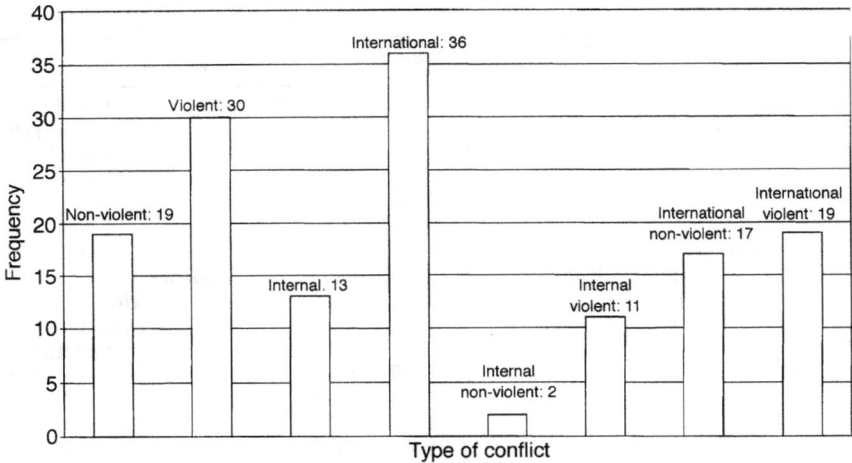

Figure 4.2 Superpower confrontations.

conflicts were international types of conflicts. Fifty percent of these international conflicts were in a violent phase at the time of the concurrent superpower involvement. The superpowers refrained from frequent direct confrontations in internal types of conflicts; only thirteen such instances were identified.

The superpowers appeared in seven conflicts as partners on the same side (Table 4.4). Note that four of these incidents occurred between 1945 and 1955 during the height of the Cold War. In recent years, the unanimous condemnation of Iraq's annexation of Kuwait in the UN Security Council and the liberation of Kuwait has been an exceptional case of active superpower cooperation.

Figure 4.3 shows the confrontational and cooperative behavior of the superpowers in certain conflicts over a fifty-year period. Whereas the

Table 4.4 The US and the USSR together on the same side of a conflict

Name	Start	End	Intensity	Type
Indonesia (Darul Islam separation attempt)	1947	1991	Violent	Internal
Indonesia (independence)	1945	1949	Violent	International
Indonesia (separation attempt II: PRRI rebels in Sumatra)	1955	1958	Violent	Internal
Iraq–Kuwait V (annexation)	1990	1991	Violent	International
Rhodesia (Operation Thrasher)	1976	1976	Violent	Internal
Saudi Arabia–Abu Dhabi (Buraimi I)	1949	1975	Non-violent	International
Sri Lanka (Ceylon) (uproar)	1971	1971	Violent	Internal

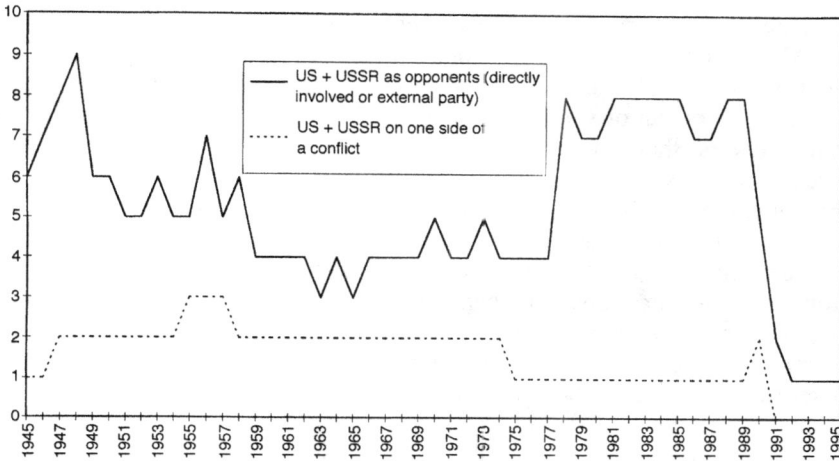

Figure 4.3 Frequency of superpower confrontation and cooperation in ongoing conflicts.

number of cases in which the superpowers have cooperated is negligible, direct confrontations were rather frequent at the beginning and at the end of the East–West conflict, i.e. 1947 and 1955; 1979 and 1991. We have observed – statistically – little superpower activity in ongoing conflicts, either confrontational or cooperative, since 1991.

A further step in the analysis of superpower behavior in ongoing conflicts is the consideration of the disputed issues. Figure 4.4 shows seven categories of issues that were identified in forty-nine conflicts. The superpowers most frequently became involved on opposite sides of a conflict when ideological issues were in dispute. Conflicts about the type of system for a weak, transitory or newly established regime obviously motivated the superpowers

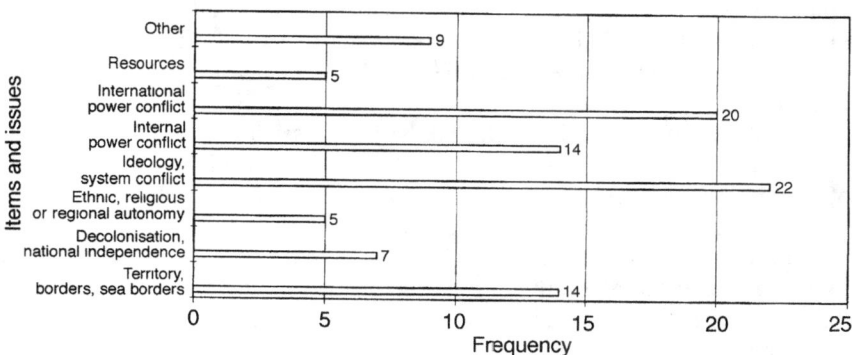

Figure 4.4 Issues in East–West conflicts.

to become actively involved in conflicts. The second most frequent issue in dispute involved international power conflicts.

When a conflict was carried out over the international or geo-strategic power position of one or more states, both superpowers rather frequently became involved on opposite sides of the conflict. In other cases, the superpowers themselves were the driving forces behind a conflict's escalation. This phenomenon was called 'war by proxy'. The superpowers remained behind the scenes and used other states, regimes or armies in the pursuit of their own geo-strategic interests.

Conflicts over territory and borders as well as internal power conflicts form the second most frequent issue in conflicts with simultaneous superpower involvement. Conflicts over resources or internal conflicts over ethnic, religious or regional autonomy very rarely arouse the superpowers' interest sufficiently to become involved.

Spheres of interest and conflict frequencies

KOSIMO has applied three criteria along which conflicts can be grouped according to their geo-strategic position *vis-à-vis* the superpowers. According to these criteria conflicts can occur outside, inside, at the edge or in overlapping zones of declared spheres of interest of the great powers. The assumption is that those conflicts at the edge or in overlapping or contested spheres of interest have a high potential to escalate into severe crises. By the same token, the responsible powers have a greater concern for the containment and management of these conflicts. Therefore, we expect most conflicts with long duration and violent escalations to occur outside the spheres of interest of the great powers. A certain number of conflicts occurred within these respective spheres (intra-bloc conflicts). But only very few conflicts erupted at the edges of these spheres. Table 4.5 shows a list of thirty-nine violent conflicts at the edges of spheres of interest for the past fifty years out of the subset of all violent conflicts.

Most of the conflicts that took place in contested or overlapping spheres of interest of the superpowers were international conflicts and lasted for a relatively short period of time (exceptions of long and severely fought violent conflicts are Indochina, Cambodia and Ethiopia). Two-thirds of all conflicts had ended by the end of the 1960s. Very few new conflicts broke out after 1980.

Except for the Greek Civil War and the US–Russian discords over the wars in former Yugoslavia, all violent conflicts that took place in contested spheres of interest were located in the Orient, i.e. the Middle East, East and Southeast Asia. In Europe, the American continent and in sub-Saharan Africa the superpowers either respected the regional or local dominance of the 'other' or used subversive and non-military means to strengthen their influence. It seems that the superpowers considered the Middle East and East and Southeast Asia as regions of such vital national interest that they provoked or accepted the outbreak of local or regional military confrontations. None of these conflicts

Table 4.5 Violent conflicts in overlapping spheres of interest (chronological order)

Name	Start	End	Type
Greece (civil war I)	1944	1945	International
China (civil war)	1945	1949	Internal
Indochina Ia	1945	1954	International
Greece (civil war II)	1946	1949	Internal
China–Taiwan	1947	1947	Internal
Korea I	1947	1950	International
Korea II (Korean War)	1950	1953	International
China–Taiwan (Quemoy I)	1954	1954	International
China (Tachen Islands)	1955	1955	International
Turkey–Syria (border)	1955	1957	International
Indochina Ib	1955	1973	International
Cambodia (border)	1956	1970	International
Israel III (border)	1957	1967	International
China–Taiwan (Quemoy II)	1958	1958	International
Jordan–Israel (Jordan water I)	1959	1967	International
Vietnam (civil war)	1960	1961	International
Iraq (Kurds I)	1961	1970	Internal
Indochina II (Vietnam War)	1964	1973	International
Thailand (communism)	1965	1980	Internal
Namibia II (SWAPO)	1966	1990	Internal
Egypt–Israel (6-day War)	1967	1967	International
Egypt–Israel (confrontations)	1967	1973	International
Thailand–Cambodia III (border)	1968	1969	International
China–USSR (Usury conflict)	1969	1969	International
Cambodia II	1970	1975	Internal
Israel IV (Yom Kippur War)	1973	1973	International
Indochina II (cease-fire)	1973	1976	International
Iraq (Kurds II)	1974	1975	Internal
Ethiopia (Tigray)	1974	1991	Internal
Angola (civil war I)	1975	1976	Internal
Somalia–Ethiopia (Ogaden II)	1976	1978	International
Indochina IIIa	1977	1978	International
Ethiopia (Oromo)	1977	1991	Internal
Indochina IIIb	1978	1991	International
China–Vietnam (war)	1979	1979	International
Iran–Iraq I (Gulf War)	1980	1988	International
Afghanistan III (civil war II)	1988	1991	Internal
Iraq–Kuwait VI (US intervention)	1990	1991	International
Bosnia–Herzegovina (Serbs–Croats)	1992	1994	Internal

escalated into direct superpower confrontations, although some conflicts such as the Korean War had a high potential for a Third World War scenario.

Military interventions by the US and the USSR

The attempt to capture the East–West conflict would not be complete without an analysis of the interventions by the superpowers in ongoing conflicts. So far we have looked only at the direct and indirect participation of the superpowers in ongoing conflicts as well as at their direct non-military confrontations during the height of the Cold War in the 1950s. The impression that we have gained from the conflict statistics of the superpowers so far is that they are by and large rather restrictive in their use of force. This impression must be corrected by the analysis of their respective number of military interventions. Tables 4.6 and 4.7 show the aggregated number of non-military and military interventions of the US and the USSR in ongoing conflicts.

KOSIMO differentiated among three different forms of interventions by a foreign power into an ongoing conflict. The first form is an intervention with non-violent political, economic and diplomatic instruments. The second form is best described as military assistance through logistic support, weapon sales and other military supportive measures short of a direct military intervention, which is the third category. The category non-military intervention subsumes the first two non-violent forms of interventions whereas the category military interventions refers to the third KOSIMO type of possible forms of interventions.

Altogether, the US intervened 104 times in ongoing conflicts. Out of these 104 conflicts, twelve cases were the type in which intervention was a direct military one. In all these cases the respective conflicts had already been escalating into violent conflicts. These violent conflicts were two-thirds international conflicts. In four cases the US intervened with military means in internal and violent conflicts. In ninety-two cases, the US intervened with political, diplomatic, economic or logistic instruments in ongoing conflicts. More than half of these conflicts were internal conflicts. In 77 percent of all non-military interventions by the US, these conflicts were violent crises or wars.

Most conflicts that triggered a direct military US intervention were either system conflicts over ideological issues or conflicts over international power and geo-strategic power positions (respectively 35 and 30 percent of all observed issues in these conflicts (multiple choice)). Internal power conflicts are a third issue that triggered US military interventions in conflicts. The US refrained from direct military interventions in conflicts when the conflict was fought over issues of decolonization and national independence or over resources. Ethnic, religious and regional autonomy as well as territory, borders and sea borders as issues of conflicts did not trigger directly military US interventions.

When a military US intervention occurred, in almost half the cases the troops intervened in territories that were located within the declared sphere of interest of the US. In contrast, non-military interventions occurred in almost half of the cases outside the spheres of interest. It is rather difficult to deduce from these figures conclusions about interventionist patterns of the US with regard to the geo-strategic location of the conflict. All that can be confirmed is that the US is reluctant to intervene with military means when its vital interests are not in question.

Table 4.6 The interventions by the US in ongoing conflicts

US interventions	Non-military interventions	% of total (n=92)	Military interventions	% of total (n=12)
In non-violent conflicts	21	23	0	0
In violent conflicts	71	77	12	100
In international conflicts	43	47	8	67
In internal conflicts	49	53	4	33
Total	92	100	12	100

US interventions by items in dispute	Non-military interventions		Military interventions	
Territory, borders, sea borders	16	10	2	9
Decolonization, national independence	14	9	0	0
Ethnic, religious or regional autonomy	10	7	1	4
Ideology, system conflict	41	27	8	35
Internal power conflict	33	22	5	22
International power conflict	24	16	7	30
Resources	8	5	0	0
Other	7	5	0	0
Total	153	100	23	100

US interventions by geostrategic location of the conflict	Non-military interventions	% of total (n=92)	Military interventions	% of total (n=12)
Within spheres of interest	36	39	5	42
Outside of spheres of interest	40	43	3	25
At iron curtain, overlapping spheres	16	17	4	33
Total	92	100	12	100

US interventions by regions	Non-military interventions	% of total (n=92)	Military interventions	% of total (n=12)
Africa	13	14	0	0
Asia	21	23	6	50
Europe	6	7	0	0
Middle East and Maghreb	25	27	3	25
Central America	15	16	3	25
South America	12	13	0	0
Total	92	100	12	100

Table 4.7 The interventions by the USSR in ongoing conflicts

USSR interventions	Non-military interventions	% of total (n=77)	Military interventions	% of total (n=5)
In non-violent conflicts	14	18	2	40
In violent conflicts	63	82	3	60
In international conflicts	47	61	1	20
In internal conflicts	30	39	4	80
Total	77	100	5	100

USSR interventions by items in dispute	Non-military interventions		Military interventions	
Territory, borders, sea borders	21	15	1	11
Decolonization, national independence	15	11	1	11
Ethnic, religious or regional autonomy	17	12	3	33
Ideology, system conflict	21	15	4	44
Internal power conflict	24	17	0	0
International power conflict	29	21	0	0
Resources	10	7	0	0
Other	4	3	0	0
Total	141	100	9	100

USSR interventions by geostrategic location of the conflict	Non-military interventions	% of total (n=77)	Military interventions	% of total (n=5)
Within spheres of interest	13	17	4	80
Outside of spheres of interest	36	47	1	20
At iron curtain, overlapping spheres	28	36	0	0
Total	77	100	5	100

USSR interventions by regions	Non-military interventions	% in total (n=77)	Military interventions	% of total (n=5)
Africa	22	29	0	0
Asia	18	23	0	0
Europe	6	8	2	40
Middle East and Maghreb	29	38	3	60
Central America	2	3	0	0
South America	0	0	0	0
Total	77	100	5	100

The USSR intervened with military means in five conflicts, two of which took place in Europe and three in the Middle East region. Four of the five military interventions were interventions into internal conflicts (which is in contrast to the US, which refrained from military interventions in internal conflicts). Also, two of the interventions took place in – until the intervention – non-violent conflicts (Hungary 1956 and Czechoslovakia 1968). Again in contrast, the US did not intervene in non-violent conflicts with military means. On the other hand, the overall number of USSR-military interventions is less than half the number of US interventions. Also, the number of non-military interventions (seventy-seven interventions) is three-quarters of the number of US non-military interventions. From these interventions, 82 percent occurred in violent conflicts and two-thirds of the same sample were international conflicts. This observation is comparable to our findings for the US interventions. As a general comparative finding, it can be confirmed that the US intervened more often in conflicts than the USSR. On the other hand, the USSR intervened more openly or bluntly in non-violent and internal conflicts. These interventions seemed – from Moscow's perspective – necessary to uphold the Soviet satellite system against internal opposition movements.

The issues in dispute in the conflicts involving USSR interventions were, foremost, ideological issues, system disputes and disputes over autonomy from Soviet dominance. Eighty percent of Soviet military interventions occurred within its declared spheres of interest as against 42 percent of the US military interventions. The relatively low number of non-military interventions in its own spheres of interest must be explained by the fact that the East European communist regimes as such – compared with the dictatorships supported by the US in Latin America – were not counted as 'interventions' in the KOSIMO dataset. From a regional perspective, the USSR intervened almost twice as often in conflicts on the African continent than the US (twenty-two versus thirteen non-military interventions). The Middle East seems to be the classic region for interventions by both the US and the USSR. The US intervened three times with military means and twenty-five times with non-military means in this region; the USSR three times with military means and twenty-nine times with non-military means.

As a general conclusion it can be said that 'the West' relied on less coercive means to guarantee bloc coherence than 'the East'. Both the superpowers carried out conflicts in territories or over issues that lay outside their immediate spheres of influence (which is a manifestation of their power and global interests). In part, this behavior is also a repetition of the balance of power concept of nineteenth-century European politics.

Intra-bloc conflict

Intra-bloc conflict is a KOSIMO category that tries to capture the international conflicts within the Western and Eastern bloc during the Cold

War. The general hypothesis for this category of conflicts is that the respective coherent forces in each bloc by and large prevented the outbreak of violent in-group conflicts. The Western side includes the OECD states, the Eastern bloc comprises the Soviet satellites in Eastern Europe as well as the Far Eastern communist regimes in China, Mongolia, Vietnam, North Korea and Cuba. For the period after 1989, i.e. the end of the Warsaw Pact and the opening of NATO toward Eastern Europe, this category has lost most of its relevance.

Table 4.8 shows a list of international in-group conflicts that were observed in the Western and Eastern camps. Figure 4.5 shows the issues in dispute for intra-bloc conflicts.

The two lists in Table 4.8 show some remarkable differences. The Western states experienced twenty international conflicts among its members. None of these conflicts escalated into a violent conflict. Almost all conflicts on the Western side emerged from territorial and border questions as well as disputes over access to or usage of resources. In most cases these disputes concerned fishery conflicts. The only conflict that has a serious potential for a future violent escalation seems to be the Turkish–Greek dispute over the Aegean Sea and the Cyprus conflict. Almost all of these conflicts were mediated by an international organization or by judicial decision or arbitration. In contrast, the international conflicts among communist states have escalated quite frequently into violent conflicts, although the overall number of conflicts is lower than the number of conflicts in the West.

From the statistical results two conclusions can be drawn. On the one hand, it seems reasonable to conclude that the coercion to coherence in the Eastern bloc was much stronger than in the West. This stronger coherency might have diminished the number of conflicts among its members. On the other hand, it can be said that democratic forms of conflict execution and settlement are, by experience, less prone to escalate into violent conflicts. Therefore, the risk to begin a conflict and to end up with a violent confrontation was much lower in the West than in the East. The chance for a conflict in the Eastern bloc to be 'managed' with military pressure or force seemed to be higher than in the West. Support for the latter interpretation is the rather high frequency of violent conflicts among communist states. Also, six of the thirteen conflicts among communist states involved ideological issues and conflicts over international power positions (Figure 4.5). These issues did not play any significant role in conflicts among OECD states. Concluding the section on East–West and intra-bloc relations, it can be said:

- Remarkably few conflicts took place within the blocs. The superpowers played a pacifying role – yet with ideologically different meanings of peace.
- At the 'iron curtain', no war started; severe crises were contained by the superpowers.

Table 4.8 International conflicts among Western and among Eastern states
(chronological order)

Name	Start	End	Intensity	Mediation by
International conflicts among OECD states				
United Kingdom–Norway (fishery dispute)	1948	1951	Non-violent	ICJ
Netherlands–FRG (border)	1949	1963	Non-violent	
Federal Republic Germany–France (Saarland status)	1950	1957	Non-violent	European Council
France–United Kingdom (Minquiers and Ecrehouse)	1951	1953	Non-violent	ICJ
Iceland–United Kingdom (fishery conflict I)	1952	1956	Non-violent	OEEC
Iceland (US troops)	1956	1956	Non-violent	NATO
Netherlands–Belgium (border)	1957	1959	Non-violent	ICJ
Iceland–United Kingdom (fishery conflict II)	1958	1961	Non-violent	UNO
Italy (South Tyrol)	1960	1992	Non-violent	UNO, European Council
Greece–Turkey (Cyprus)	1960	cont.	Non-violent	NATO, UNO
Denmark–United Kingdom (fishery conflict)	1961	1964	Non-violent	European Fishery Conference
Spain–United Kingdom (Gibraltar)	1964	cont.	Non-violent	UNO
Iceland–United Kingdom (fishery conflict III)	1971	1973	Non-violent	ICJ, UNO, NATO
Iceland–United Kingdom (fishery conflict IV)	1975	1976	Non-violent	UNO
Canada–France (St Pierre and Miquelon)	1975	1992	Non-violent	
Sweden–Denmark (Hesseloe)	1978	1984	Non-violent	
Canada–US (Gulf of Mayne)	1981	1984	Non-violent	ICJ
New Zealand–US	1984	1990	Non-violent	
Greece–Turkey (Aegean Sea III)	1987	cont.	Non-violent	NATO, US
Iceland–Norway (fishery conflict)	1993	cont.	Non-violent	Sweden
International conflicts among Eastern bloc and socialist states				
Mongolia (status)	1945	1950	Non-violent	
USSR–Yugoslavia	1948	1956	Non-violent	UNO
Poland (October uprisings)	1956	1956	Violent	
Hungary (revolt)	1956	1957	Violent	UNO
China–USSR (tensions)	1960	1991	Violent	
USSR–Romania (tensions)	1964	1968	Non-violent	
China–USSR (diplomats)	1966	1966	Non-violent	
CSSR (Prague spring)	1968	1968	Violent	
China–USSR (Ussuri conflict)	1969	1969	Violent	
China–Vietnam (Spratly III)	1975	1987	Non-violent	
Poland–GDR (Stettin bay)	1977	1989	Non-violent	
China–Vietnam (war)	1979	1979	Violent	
Vietnam–China (Spratly II)	1988	cont.	Violent	

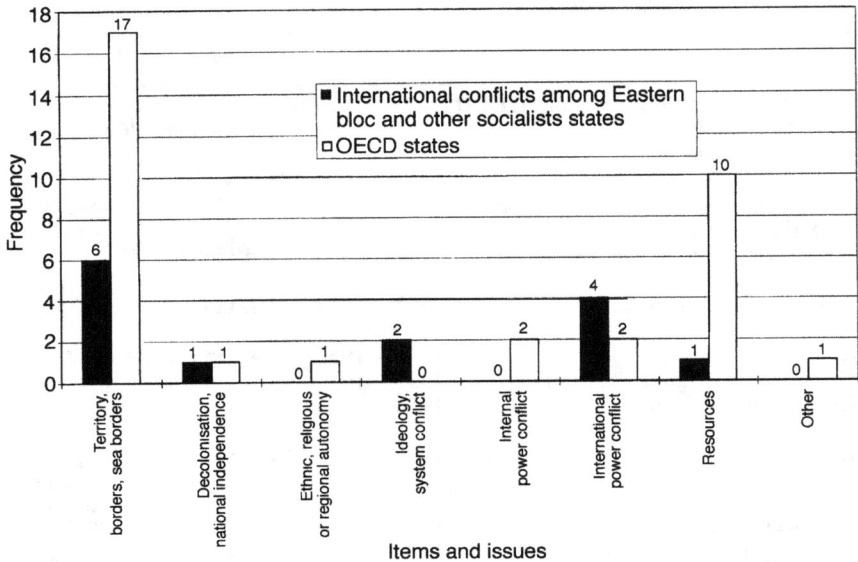

Figure 4.5 Issues in dispute in intra-bloc conflicts.

- The superpowers exerted pressure on zones outside their immediate spheres of interest in order to gain influence in these countries.

Conflicts between North and South

The process of North–South relations after 1945 went through three phases, political emancipation, economic emancipation and, lastly, cultural emancipation of countries in the southern hemisphere from their northern colonizers.

In the first phase of North–South relations the colonies were asking or fighting for independence from their colonizers. The second phase refers to what is called the 'North–South conflict'. This term stands for the structural aspects of economic emancipation. The related 'New International Economic World Order' became popular in the 1960s and referred to the widening gap between developing and developed economies. The third phase focused on cultural emancipation and the political debate was labeled 'New Information World Order'.

At the end of this century, the concept of 'North–South' is again questioned by some authors; they point to the decreasing influence of groups such as the G77, UNCTAD, UNIDO or the non-aligned movement. Also, the 'South' as a general term for an area of 'underdeveloped' countries nowadays has to be differentiated in many more sub-groups and sub-regions than was usually done in the 1970s.

Statistics cannot describe or explain such fundamental structures captured in the term 'North–South'. A quantitative approach must be limited to the observable facts of separate conflicts. It is understood that structural preconditions lie underneath each specific conflict between a country in the North and one in the South, and they co-determine their development. What should be the criterion to single out these specific 'North–South' conflicts from our total sample of 661 conflicts? KOSIMO introduced the variable of 'economic stage of development'. This qualitative, independent variable describes the economic system or stage of economic development during the period of conflict for each of the direct participants in the conflict. Non-state actors, such as opposition movements, are excluded from this variable. For our purposes, the variable can take the forms of 'developing economies' on the one hand and 'industrialized states' on the other. Between or rather beyond these poles, economic systems can take the form of 'planned economies', i.e. socialist and communist systems, as well as 'newly industrialized economies', i.e. Asian 'tigers' and transitory market democracies in Eastern Europe after 1989.

In Table 4.9, we have listed only those conflicts between industrialized states and developing economies, and we have included both conflicts that were initiated by the industrialized states and those initiated primarily by the developing economies. The list shows a surprising multitude of types of conflicts that share the criterion of economically less and fully developed conflict parties. Various issues have become an objective in 'North–South conflicts'. The former colonial powers are parties to the greater part of all 'North–South' conflicts. The only significant non-colonial actor on the side of the industrialized states in North–South conflicts is the US. The overall number of ninety-five conflicts in relation to a total of 661 observed conflicts indicates that the systemic and economic North–South differences are not a prime source of actual conflicts, but more likely a cause for phenomena best described by Johan Galtung's term: 'structural violence'. The low number of actual 'North–South' conflicts in the KOSIMO sense of the word 'conflict' on the one hand and the diverse nature of these conflicts, apart from the economic status of the participants, may lead to a revision of the usefulness of the term 'North–South' conflict in empirical conflict research. Ted Gurr (1993) in his dataset on ethno-political conflicts, for example, uses variables that are more apt to describe and analyze conflictive 'North–South' constellations and their societal impacts. Here, KOSIMO has not coded sufficient social indicators.

Table 4.10 groups North–South conflicts according to the degree of violence, the regions where they have been carried out and according to the main issues that were in dispute. Most of the conflicts with 'North–South' dimensions were fought over questions of decolonization and national independence. Almost as frequent were conflicts over territories and land and sea borders. Ideology and internal power conflicts as well as conflicts over autonomy played a minor role in 'North–South' related conflicts. Access to or the distribution of resources played a role in roughly 12 percent

Table 4.9 Conflicts between North and South

Name	Start	End	Intensity	Region
Albania–United Kingdom (Corfu)	1946	1949	Non-violent	Europe
Algeria (independence I)	1945	1946	Violent	Middle East/Maghreb
Algeria (independence II)	1954	1962	Violent	Middle East/Maghreb
Angola (independence)	1961	1974	Violent	Sub-Saharan Africa
Argentina–United Kingdom (Falklands III)	1982	cont.	Non-violent	South America
British Guyana (independence)	1953	1966	Violent	South America
Brunei (uproar)	1962	1962	Violent	Asia/Oceania
Cambodia (border)	1956	1970	Violent	Asia/Oceania
Cameroon (independence)	1955	1967	Violent	Sub-Saharan Africa
China–United Kingdom (status Hong Kong)	1990	cont.	Non-violent	Asia/Oceania
Cuba (Bay of Pigs)	1961	1961	Violent	Central America
Cuba–US	1959	1961	Non-violent	Central America
Dominican Republic II (intervention)	1965	1965	Violent	Central America
Egypt (1st Suez crisis)	1951	1954	Violent	Middle East/Maghreb
Egypt (Suez war)	1956	1957	Violent	Middle East/Maghreb
Equatorial Guinea–Spain (flag removal)	1969	1969	Non-violent	Sub-Saharan Africa
Ethiopia–United Kingdom (Gadaduma I)	1947	1963	Non-violent	Sub-Saharan Africa
France (New Caledonia I)	1984	1985	Non-violent	Asia/Oceania
France (New Caledonia II)	1985	1988	Non-violent	Asia/Oceania
France (New Caledonia III)	1988	1991	Non-violent	Asia/Oceania
France (Tahiti: uprisings)	1987	1987	Non-violent	Asia/Oceania
France–Egypt (status of foreigners)	1949	1950	Non-violent	Middle East/Maghreb
France–Malagasy Republic (Glorieuses Islands)	1973	1990	Non-violent	Sub-Saharan Africa
France–Syria, Lebanon (Levant)	1945	1946	Violent	Middle East/Maghreb
Greece (civil war I)	1944	1945	Violent	Europe
Guinea-Bissau–Portugal (independence)	1963	1974	Violent	Sub-Saharan Africa
Honduras–US (Swan Island)	1945	1991	Non-violent	Central America
India I (independence)	1942	1947	Violent	Asia/Oceania
India IX (Goa I)	1950	1961	Non-violent	Asia/Oceania
India VI (Mahe)	1948	1954	Violent	Asia/Oceania
India XII (Goa II)	1961	1961	Violent	Asia/Oceania
Indochina Ia	1945	1954	Violent	Asia/Oceania
Indochina Ib	1955	1973	Violent	Asia/Oceania
Indochina II (Vietnam War)	1964	1973	Violent	Asia/Oceania
Indonesia (independence)	1945	1949	Violent	Asia/Oceania
Indonesia (West Irian I)	1950	1960	Non-violent	Asia/Oceania
Indonesia (West Irian II)	1960	1969	Violent	Asia/Oceania
Iran (oil nationalization, change of government)	1951	1953	Non-violent	Middle East/Maghreb
Iran (Rushdie affair II)	1992	cont.	Non-violent	Middle East/Maghreb

Iran–United Kingdom (Bahrain independence)	1970	1971	Non-violent	Middle East/Maghreb
Iran–United Kingdom (Rushdie affair I)	1989	1991	Non-violent	Europe
Iraq–Kuwait VI (US intervention)	1990	1991	Violent	Middle East/Maghreb
Israel III (border)	1957	1967	Violent	Middle East/Maghreb
Kenya (independence, Mau Mau)	1952	1956	Violent	Sub-Saharan Africa
Libya (Cyrenaica)	1949	1951	Non-violent	Middle East/Maghreb
Libya–Malta	1973	1986	Non-violent	Middle East/Maghreb
Libya–US I	1973	1989	Violent	Middle East/Maghreb
Libya–US II	1991	cont.	Non-violent	Middle East/Maghreb
Liechtenstein–Guatemala	1955	1955	Non-violent	Central America
Malagasy Republic (independence)	1947	1960	Violent	Sub-Saharan Africa
Malawi (independence)	1959	1964	Violent	Sub-Saharan Africa
Malaya (independence)	1948	1960	Violent	Asia/Oceania
Malaya–Indonesia (Sarawak/Sabah)	1963	1966	Violent	Asia/Oceania
Mauritius–Malagasy Republic–France (Tromelin)	1976	cont.	Non-violent	Sub-Saharan Africa
Mauritius–United Kingdom (Diego Garcia)	1980	cont.	Non-violent	Sub-Saharan Africa
Morocco (French troops)	1956	1958	Violent	Middle East/Maghreb
Morocco (independence)	1944	1956	Violent	Middle East/Maghreb
Morocco–Spain (attempt of expansion)	1957	1958	Violent	Middle East/Maghreb
Morocco–Spain (Ceuta and Melilla)	1961	cont.	Non-violent	Middle East/Maghreb
Morocco–Spain (Ifni)	1964	1969	Non-violent	Middle East/Maghreb
Mozambique (border)	1966	1974	Violent	Sub-Saharan Africa
Mozambique (independence)	1964	1975	Violent	Sub-Saharan Africa
North Korea–IAEA	1991	1994	Non-violent	Asia/Oceania
North Korea–US (Pueblo)	1968	1968	Non-violent	Asia/Oceania
Oman (Imam–Sultan conflict)	1954	1971	Violent	Middle East/Maghreb
Panama (channel I)	1964	1967	Violent	Central America
Panama (power struggle and US intervention)	1989	1990	Violent	Central America
Portugal–Zambia (economic sanctions)	1971	1971	Non-violent	Sub-Saharan Africa
Puerto Rico–US (status I)	1950	1952	Non-violent	Central America
Rhodesia (constitution 1961)	1961	1965	Non-violent	Sub-Saharan Africa
Rwanda–Burundi (independence)	1958	1964	Violent	Sub-Saharan Africa
Saudi Arabia–Abu Dhabi (Buraimi II)	1951	1952	Violent	Middle East/Maghreb
Saudi Arabia–Abu Dhabi (Buraimi III)	1955	1955	Violent	Middle East/Maghreb
Sudan (independence I)	1946	1953	Non-violent	Middle East/Maghreb
Sudan (independence II)	1953	1955	Violent	Middle East/Maghreb
Togo (independence)	1947	1957	Non-violent	Sub-Saharan Africa
Tunisia (Biserta)	1961	1963	Violent	Middle East/Maghreb
Tunisia (independence)	1950	1956	Violent	Middle East/Maghreb
Tunisia (Remada)	1958	1958	Violent	Middle East/Maghreb

Table 4.9 Continued

Name	Start	End	Intensity	Region
Tunisia (Sakiet)	1958	1958	Violent	Middle East/Maghreb
Tunisia (weapon sales)	1957	1957	Non-violent	Middle East/Maghreb
Tunisia–France (Algerian border)	1957	1957	Violent	Middle East/Maghreb
Turkey–Syria, Iraq (water)	1990	cont.	Non-violent	Middle East/Maghreb
United Kingdom–Argentina–Chile (Palmer)	1956	1958	Non-violent	South America
US–Cambodia (Mayaguez)	1975	1975	Non-violent	Asia/Oceania
US–Grenada	1983	1983	Violent	Central America
US–Iran (hostages)	1979	1981	Violent	Middle East/Maghreb
US–Peru, Ecuador (tuna fish)	1969	1974	Non-violent	South America
Vanuatu (independence)	1980	1980	Non-violent	Asia/Oceania
Vanuatu–France	1981	1981	Non-violent	Asia/Oceania
Yemen PR (independence)	1965	1967	Violent	Middle East/Maghreb
Yemen–United Kingdom (Aden I)	1948	1963	Violent	Middle East/Maghreb
Yemen–United Kingdom (Aden II)	1956	1958	Violent	Middle East/Maghreb
Zaire–Belgium	1989	1989	Non-violent	Sub-Saharan Africa
Zaire–Belgium (Belgian intervention)	1960	1960	Violent	Sub-Saharan Africa

Table 4.10 Analysis of conflicts between countries in the North and South

Types	Frequency	%	Total (%)
All North-South conflicts	95	100	
Non-violent	42	44	
Violent	53	56	
Issues*			
Territory, borders	19	21	
Decolonization, national independence	23	25	
Ethnic, religious, regional autonomy	1	1	
Ideology, system conflict	7	7	
Internal power conflict	9	10	
International power conflict	22	24	
Resources	11	12	100
Regions			
Europe	3	3	
Sub-Saharan Africa	19	20	
Asia/Oceania	24	25	
Middle East/Maghreb	36	38	
North America	0	0	
Central America	9	9	
South America	4	4	100

Note
* Multiple choice.

of the conflicts. This relatively low frequency of conflicts over resources in 'North–South' relations needs further attention. It can be interpreted either that the economic means for the exploitation of resources by the industrialized states are so refined that they do not trigger or provoke violent conflicts, or they remain a background variable which is hidden in conflicts over territories and borders.

From a perspective of the industrialized states and the former colonial powers, one would expect most of the 'North–South' related conflicts to be in sub-Saharan Africa. In our sample, most conflicts of this kind occurred in the Middle East and Maghreb regions, whereas only nineteen 'North–South' related conflicts were observed in sub-Saharan Africa. Asia and Oceania have seen one-quarter of the world's 'North–South' related conflicts. Latin America shows the lowest numbers of 'North–South' conflicts. On the one hand, decolonization and national independence were completed long ago on the American continent, on the other hand the US exerted its influence in the region to prevent, control or contain the outbreak of internal system and power conflicts. Note that overall, half of the 'North–South' conflicts in our sample remained non-violent throughout their course. The sample of ninety-five 'North–South' conflicts represents less than 15 percent of the total sample of conflicts between 1945 and 1995 (661 conflicts). This leads us to the conclusion that 'North–South' conflicts, albeit on top of the programmatic international agenda since the 1960s, is but a minor part of actual concrete conflict. Here, the structural analysis of economic and social 'North–South' dependencies may reveal better insights than empirical conflict research can do.

Conflicts in and among developing countries

KOSIMO has identified 359 conflicts that were carried out exclusively in and among countries with developing economies. As indicated in the previous chapter, the criterion of economic development is used as a discerning, descriptive and independent variable to hint at structural factors in global conflict activity and patterns. The statistical data does not explain or indicate the causes of conflicts *per se*; rather, it is a means to group conflicts along certain criteria that have been chosen as variables to test certain hypotheses.

One of the fundamental hypotheses in the broad field of development theory is the circular linkage between under-development, political instability and high conflict and violence rates. As shown in Chapters 2 and 3, Western-type democracies have been the most stable political system since 1945. Also, this type of political system shows the lowest number of violent conflicts. In contrast, transitory regimes (by definition) as well as traditional or ideological authoritarian systems have much shorter 'life-cycles' compared with democracies. Also, they more often initiate violent internal and international conflicts. Note that democracies do not have lower conflict frequencies as such; they only have lower violent conflict frequencies. As it is not permitted to conclude a monocausal relationship from political instability to violence, it is equally false to deduce from economic stages of development certain patterns of conflict. The specific causal constellations for the outbreak of violent conflict must be analyzed in case studies or qualitative and comparative regional studies. The statistical data can merely serve as a common ground from where groups of conflicts can be singled out that seem to fit to or fulfill certain explanations about violent conflict escalations.

Nevertheless, the general trends of conflicts in and among developing countries over a fifty-year period can hint at the plausibility of theoretic assumptions and at promising orientations of case studies. Figure 4.6 shows two lines that indicate the frequency of ongoing conflicts in and among developing countries from 1945 until 1995.

At first glance the lines are similar to the overall global trends. Whereas international conflicts have been declining in frequency since the early 1970s, the number of internal conflicts has been on the rise. This growth accelerated in the years around the end of the Cold War. Since 1993 there seems to have been a decline in the number of internal conflicts.

The interpretation of the figure on the basis of pure frequencies might lead to distorted conclusions. In Chapter 2 we looked at the fourfold multiplication of the number of states since 1945. This rapid growth from fifty states then to almost 200 states and territories today took place mainly in regions with developing economies during the period of decolonization. The recognition of formal independence to many small states and islands added to an average growth rate of states by 3 percent annually. The thesis is that – in a linear function – more states produce more conflicts. Yet, Figure 4.6

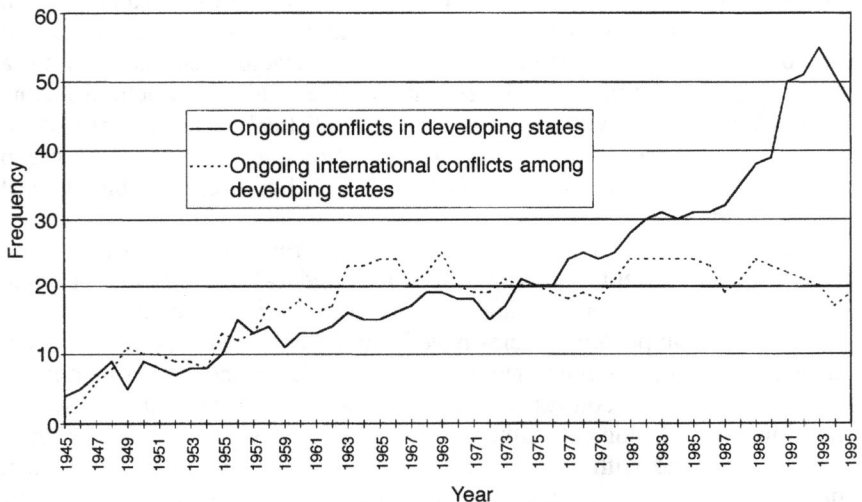

Figure 4.6 Ongoing conflicts in and among developing countries.

presents a much more moderate growth of ongoing conflicts than expected from this thesis.

The frequencies of internal conflicts in developing countries have shown a stable, slightly exponential growth rate since 1945. By the mid-1980s this growth rate accelerated and reached its peak in 1993. Since then, there seems to have been a decline in the frequency of ongoing internal conflicts in developing countries. With regard to the line of international conflicts among developing countries, the stable frequency of about twenty ongoing conflicts per year since the early 1960s indicates a certain international conflict management capacity in the Third World. In Africa, the respect or observance of colonial state borders might be an explanatory factor for low rates of international conflicts. In Asia and in the Middle East/Maghreb region, where this principle was not explicitly established, the frequency of violent territorial conflicts became higher than in Africa.

On the other hand, it must be stated clearly that the conflicts in and among developing countries have constituted about two-thirds of all conflicts since the Second World War. It is the largest group of conflicts with regard to affinities of the participants, and it is the most violent group with regard to the intensity of the conflicts. The global trend of violent conflicts points to the Southern hemisphere and the developing economies, or in the words of the German conflict researcher, Gantzel: 'The developing countries are at war against each other' (1995). Here, the high frequency of violent internal conflicts is the single most dangerous threat to world peace and international security, seen from the perspective of empirical conflict research. Table 4.11 shows aggregated absolute and relative numbers for the fifty-year period of conflict in and among developing countries to underline the above statements.

The first column of Table 4.11 lists the numbers and percentages of 359 conflicts observed in and among developing countries. The second column lists the numbers and percentages of all 661 conflicts worldwide. The third column shows for each row the proportion between conflicts in and among developing countries and all conflicts worldwide. More than half of all conflicts took place in and among developing countries (54 percent). Out of 375 violent conflicts worldwide, 240 conflicts, or 64 percent, took place in and among developing countries. With regard to internal conflicts, we find that 71 percent of all internal conflicts took place in developing countries. Conflicts in and among developing countries escalated more often into violent conflicts than conflicts with East–West or North–South dimensions. The issues in conflicts in and among developing countries are presented in Figure 4.7.

Most of the violent as well as internal conflicts were fought over access to or in defense of internal power positions followed by conflicts over ethnic, religious or regional autonomy and ideological system conflicts. On the other hand, most of the non-violent as well as international conflicts concerned territorial and border issues. The second most frequent issue in

Table 4.11 Conflicts in and among developing countries

Type of conflict	Frequency of conflicts in and among developing countries	%	Frequency of conflicts worldwide	%	Frequency of conflicts in and among developing countries in % of all conflicts worldwide of the same type
All conflicts	359	100	661	100	54
Non-violent conflicts	119	33	286	43	42
Violent conflicts	240	67	375	57	64
International conflicts	173	48	398	60	43
International non-violent conflicts	91	53	228	57	40
International violent conflicts	82	47	170	43	48
Internal conflicts	186	52	263	40	71
Internal non-violent conflicts	28	15	58	22	48
Internal violent conflicts	158	85	205	78	77

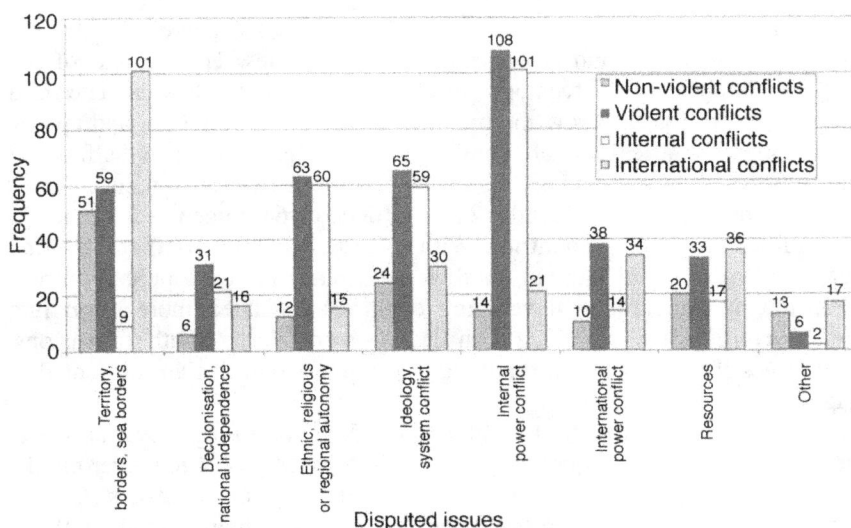

Figure 4.7 Issues in conflicts in and among developing countries.

international conflicts among developing countries is access to or distribution of resources.

Compared with the overall global frequency of issues in conflicts from 1945 to 1995, conflicts over geo-strategic and international power positions as well as conflicts over resources and national independence played a rather minor role. In general global trends concerning the distribution of issues in conflicts are confirmed by the findings for conflicts in and among developing countries.

Summarizing, we observe that

- More than half of all conflicts since 1945 have occurred in or among developing countries.
- Developing countries are fighting each other with more violent means than other countries or regions.
- The degree of violence is especially high in internal conflicts of developing countries.
- The period immediately at and after decolonization and national independence shows more international conflicts; since the early 1970s, internal conflicts in developing states have become the dominant type of conflict.

Neighbors and great powers

The analysis of East–West conflicts (pages 160–64) has already revealed some patterns of conflict behavior by the superpowers. In this section the focus is on great powers, superpowers and neighboring states as potential parties to a conflict.

The assumption is that neighboring states as well as globally acting great powers and superpowers will not remain unaffected by a conflict in their region or within their spheres of interest. The reactions toward a certain conflict can be described in three basic ways: neutral, constructive and destructive. In reality, the reactions will be mixed depending on the interests and the intensity of the conflict, the number of parties involved, the issues in dispute, historic, religious or any other cultural proximity or antagonisms and general priorities or doctrines in foreign policy.

The second thesis is that potentially affected parties such as neighboring states will mostly remain neutral or inactive toward a conflict between two other states or another state in conflict with its internal opposition. Only in a few cases will external parties become actively involved on one or both sides of the conflict. In most of these cases, the support will be de-escalating. Yet in rare instances, neighboring states do have an interest in destabilizing a neighboring regime or in the escalation of a latent conflict between two states in their region. Table 4.12 lists the reactions of neighboring states toward a conflict in their region.

In 54 percent of 661 conflicts worldwide the neighboring or regional states did not interfere in an ongoing conflict (types 1, 2, 6 and 12 in Table 4.12); they remained neutral or inactive. In 46 percent of the cases the neighboring states showed some reaction toward an ongoing conflict in their region. The external support of internal opposition groups seems to be the most frequent type of reaction whereas an external engagement in violent conflicts is much less frequent. With regard to the reactions of great powers and superpowers toward conflicts, Table 4.13 shows some more findings.

The tendency of neighboring states to remain inactive or neutral toward conflicts can also be confirmed for the reactions of great powers and superpowers toward conflicts. They remained inactive or neutral in 50 percent of all observed conflicts. In 3 percent of 661 conflicts the great

Table 4.12 Reactions by neighboring states

Type	Reaction	Frequency	% of total (661 conflicts)
1	No activities or influence by other smaller or equal (in power, size and population) states	181	27
2	Internal, non-governmental groups (x,y) of one state (K) are being supported or suppressed by internal non-governmental groups of another state (L)	19	3
3	Internal, non-governmental groups (X,Y) of one state (K) are being supported by another state/government (L) by subversion or interventions	88	13
4	Internal, non-governmental groups (q,p) in one state (M) are supported by other states/governments (K,L)	39	6
5	A state/government (L) supports another state/government (K) against its internal, non-governmental groups (x,y)	28	4
6	A political, non-violent conflict between two states/governments (K,L) without external interference	117	18
7	A political, non-violent conflict between two states/governments (K,L) with external interferences	54	8
8	A violent, military conflict between two states (K,L) without external interference	42	6
9	A violent, military conflict between two states (K,L) against an internal, non-governmental group (z in L)	0	0
10	A violent, military conflict between two states (K,L) with external, political interference, e.g. a downsizing of the conflict from center to periphery or containment by North-South or East-West dimensions of the conflict	34	5
11	A violent, military conflict between two states (K,L) with external, military interference	17	3
12	Other	42	6
Total		661	100

Table 4.13 Reactions by great powers and superpowers

Type	Reaction	Frequency	% of sum (661 conflicts)
1	Two great powers remain neutral and inactive mutually and in their relations with the conflict parties	331	50
2	Two great powers (A,B) mediate between two states/ governments (K,L) or their internal, non-governmental groups (x,y,z,w)	20	3
3	Two great powers (A,B) call upon the conflict parties (K,L,x,y,w, or z) to resolve their conflict by peaceful means	23	3
4	A great power (A or B) calls upon the parties (K,L,x,y,w, or z) to resolve their conflict by peaceful means	17	3
5	Two great powers (A,B) dictate a settlement on the expense of two states (K,L)	0	0
6	A great power uses a smaller power (K) to gain influence in another smaller state (L) (e.g. substitute wars at the height of the Cold War)	2	0
7	A great power (A) supports one state (K) that is in conflict with another state (L)	31	5
8	A great power (A) supports an internal, non-governmental group (x) against another group (y)	6	1
9	A great power (A) supports a smaller state (K) against an internal, non-governmental group (x)	71	11
10	A great power (A) supports an internal, non-governmental group (x) against a state/government (K)	33	5
11	A smaller power (K) supports a great power (A) against an internal, non-governmental group (in A)	0	0
12	Two great powers (A,B) support different internal, non-governmental groups (x,y) in another state (K)	3	0
13	Two great powers (A//B) are confronted in a non-violent conflict (Cold War constellation)	16	2
14	Two great powers (A//B) are ideologically confronted in a non-violent conflict within or via a smaller state	3	0
15	Two great powers (A//B) are economically confronted in a non-violent conflict within or via a smaller state	2	0
16	A great power (A) in a political conflict with a smaller power (K)	49	7
17	A great power (A) in a military conflict with a smaller power (K), e.g. a colonial war	17	3
18	Two great powers (A,B) in a military conflict within a smaller state (K), e.g. imperial wars	0	0
19	Two great powers (A//B) in a military conflict	0	0
20	Other	37	6
Total		661	100

powers mediated between the parties. In another 6 percent the great powers called upon the parties to resolve their conflict by peaceful means. In 32 percent of all cases, the great powers took sides with one party in the conflict.

Thus, the most likely reaction by external parties, neighbors, great powers and superpowers toward a conflict is passivity. When the external party does not remain neutral or inactive, an engagement on one side of the conflict is most likely. In relation to the high number of conflicts and the global interests of great and superpowers, the neighboring states or great powers rarely mediate between parties in a conflict. For more detailed findings on mediation, conflict management and conflict resolution, see also Chapter 5.

Post-Cold War trends

The last part of this chapter considers possible trends of conflicts after the end of the Cold War. Almost a decade after the revolutionary changes in Eastern Europe in 1989, the world experienced neither a 'New World Order' nor the 'End of History'. Instead, new social, political and foremost economic structures and dynamics on various levels seem to have emerged which are often summarized under the term 'globalization'.

For the domain of empirical conflict research, we would expect a change in the global or regional conflict patterns, trends and activities. But a direct relation between the end of the Cold War and changes in the patterns, trends and developments of conflicts cannot be found. It could well be argued that the end of the Cold War in 1989 had on the whole a small effect on the beginning of new and the ending of old conflicts. Indeed, our findings show some support for this thesis.

1   We counted only forty-nine incidents which were directly caused by and linked to the East–West conflict. This is less than 8 percent of all 661 conflicts in our sample for the same period.
2   Superpower cooperation in certain policy fields started as early as the aftermath of the Cuban Missile Crisis. The veto policy of the USSR in the United Nations Security Council ended in the late 1960s. Almost all vetoes since then have been given by the US, the UK and France concerning the Palestinian question in the Middle East.
3   The Eastern European revolutions in 1989–90 were predominantly peaceful regime changes that caused hardly any violent conflicts – except in the former Yugoslavia.
4   Finally, the Third World and the developing states, which, as we have seen, are responsible for more than half of the world's conflicts and for two-thirds of the world's violent conflicts with a growing tendency, have not been active in or affected by the end of the Cold War as such, although it is true that a 'wave of democratization' has swept through Africa and Southeast Asia around the year 1990. Yet these democratic

changes were mostly short-lived and could not overcome the fundamental structural and economic deficits, e.g. in Cambodia, Zaire (Congo) or Angola.

Therefore, it is difficult to establish a causal relation between the end of the Cold War and a change in conflict patterns in 1989. To the contrary, it can be argued that the global trends of conflict do not end or begin with the end of the Cold War, and there seems to be no peace dividend in this regard.

Another argument in the analysis of post-Cold War trends is that the Cold War produced centripetal in-group forces that prevented the outbreak of conflicts. While many regions in the world were subjected to East–West rivalry and became a potential cause for a dangerous escalation among the superpowers, other potential sources of conflict were either not perceived as such, prevented, suppressed or ignored. The outbreak of many ethno-political conflicts around the end of the Cold War can be explained by this thesis. The East–West conflict was 'freezing' conflicts that 'heated up' once the Cold War was over. Yet, pages 96–100 on global trends of ongoing basic and partial conflicts show contradictory findings to this thesis. The lines for the dominant type of conflict in the 1990s, i.e. internal, often violent conflicts over ethnic, religious or regional autonomy mostly in Third World countries and in former Soviet spheres have been on the rise since the early 1980s. It seems that the superpower tensions after the Soviet invasion of Afghanistan in 1979 and the conservative changes in Western governments caused misperceptions concerning the factual trends of conflicts. The dominant security-related topics in Europe and the US in the 1980s were not ethno-political conflicts but nuclear arms reduction talks, the Strategic Defense Initiative and NATO's installation of Pershing II missiles and Cruise missiles in Europe. The collapse of the communist system was not perceived as a possibility until it took everybody by surprise.

Therefore, it is plausible to conclude that the secessionist ethno-political, religious and regional conflicts and the conflicts over access to and participation in internally weak Third World regimes were simply ignored or not perceived as the new dominant type of conflict. The increased peacekeeping activities of the United Nations in Angola and Mozambique, in Yugoslavia, Cambodia, Somalia and elsewhere in the years from 1990 until 1993 led to the false perception in the Western media that these conflicts had just 'broken out'. The partly euphoric mood after the end of the Cold War and the collapse of communist regimes ended at the latest in 1993 when the debacle in Somalia and the stalemate in Bosnia-Herzegovina showed that this new type of conflict was little understood and that the UN community had little means to resolve these conflicts.

The collapse of the communist regimes itself was a cause for many conflicts, most of which were quickly settled. Some of these conflicts, on the other hand, became protracted conflicts that look as if they will last for some years to come. Table 4.14 shows a list of conflicts that belong to this group

Table 4.14 Conflicts around the collapse of the communist systems

No.	Name	Start	End	Intensity	Mediation
1	China (student uprisings)	1989	1989	Violent	
2	USSR (Uzbekistan)	1989	1989	Violent	
3	CSFR (democratization)	1989	1990	Non-violent	
4	GDR (democratization)	1989	1990	Non-violent	
5	Albania (mass flights)	1989	1991	Non-violent	
6	Romania (revolt)	1989	1991	Violent	
7	USSR (Belarus)	1989	1991	Non-violent	
8	USSR (Karelia)	1989	1991	Non-violent	
9	USSR (Nachizewan)	1989	1991	Violent	
10	USSR (Ukraine independence)	1989	1991	Non-violent	
11	Hungary–Slovakia (power plant Gabchikowo)	1989	1994	Non-violent	EC, ICJ
12	Georgia (Abchasia)	1989	cont.	Violent	UNO, Russia
13	Georgia (Adcharia)	1989	cont.	Non-violent	
14	Georgia (Gamsachurdia)	1989	cont.	Violent	
15	Tajikistan (civil war I)	1990	1992	Violent	
16	CSFR (division)	1990	1993	Non-violent	
17	Liechtenstein–Czech Republic–Slovakia (real estate)	1990	cont.	Non-violent	CSCE
18	Romania (minorities)	1990	cont.	Non-violent	Carter
19	USSR (attempted *coup d'état*)	1991	1991	Violent	
20	Ukraine–Russian Federation (fleet, atomic weapons)	1991	1994	Non-violent	OSCE
21	Croatia (occupation East Slavonia)	1991	1995	Violent	UNO
22	Georgia (South Ossetia)	1991	cont.	Violent	
23	Russia (Chechnya)	1991	cont.	Violent	OSCE
24	Russian Federation (Ingushia–North Ossetia)	1991	cont.	Violent	
25	Yugoslavia (Serbia: Sandchak)	1991	cont.	Non-violent	
26	Russian Federation (attempted *coup d'état*)	1992	1993	Violent	
27	Tajikistan (civil war II)	1992	1993	Violent	Afghanistan
28	Bosnia–Herzegovina (Muslims–Croats)	1992	1994	Violent	UNO
29	Bosnia–Herzegovina (Serbs–Croats)	1992	1994	Violent	EU, UNO
30	Russian Federation (Tartastan)	1992	1994	Non-violent	
31	Tajikistan (civil war III)	1992	cont.	Violent	
32	Turkey–Russia (Bosporus)	1992	cont.	Non-violent	
33	Bosnia–Herzegovina (Muslims–Muslims (Bihac))	1993	1994	Violent	
34	Cuba–US (refugees)	1993	cont.	Non-violent	
35	Russia (oil exploitation of the Caspian Sea)	1994	cont.	Non-violent	
36	Bosnia–Herzegovina (re-conquest Krajina/ West Slavonia)	1995	1995	Violent	UNO, US

Table 4.15 New conflicts involving industrialized states after 1989

Name	Start	End	Intensity
Zaire–Belgium	1989	1989	Non-violent
Panama (power struggle and US intervention)	1989	1990	Violent
Iran–United Kingdom (Rushdie affair I)	1989	1991	Non-violent
Turkey (Kurds II)	1989	cont.	Violent
Iraq–Kuwait VI (US/UN intervention)	1990	1991	Violent
South Africa (ANC–Inkatha)	1990	1994	Violent
Canada (secession attempt by Québec)	1990	cont.	Non-violent
China–United Kingdom (status Hong Kong)	1990	cont.	Non-violent
Liechtenstein–Czech Republic–Slovakia (real estate)	1990	cont.	Non-violent
Turkey–Syria, Iraq (water)	1990	cont.	Non-violent
North Korea–IAEA	1991	1994	Non-violent
Greece–Macedonia (name)	1991	1995	Non-violent
Libya–US II	1991	cont.	Non-violent
Iran (Rushdie affair II)	1992	cont.	Non-violent
Turkey–Russia (Bosporus)	1992	cont.	Non-violent
China–Taiwan (Chinese maneuvers)	1993	cont.	Non-violent
Cuba–US (refugees)	1993	cont.	Non-violent
Iceland–Norway (fishery zones)	1993	cont.	Non-violent
France (Tahiti: uprisings after atomic tests)	1995	1995	Non-violent

of conflicts that have emerged or re-emerged with the crisis and collapse of the communist systems.

In contrast to the increasing number of internal conflicts in the South and those conflicts that emerged or re-emerged with the collapse of the communist regimes, the industrialized states themselves were involved in only very few new conflicts. Table 4.15 shows that out of nineteen conflicts only four conflicts were carried out with the use of force. The bombing of Bosnian Serb positions in 1995 by NATO forces should be added to this list although NATO as such was not a party to the conflict and is therefore not listed.

In conclusion, what are the global trends of conflicts in the post-Cold War era?

- West: continuation of non-violent conflict resolution among industrialized states.
- East: settlement of most of the conflicts that emerged or re-emerged from the collapse of communist regimes, but degradation of some formerly minor ethno-political conflicts into protracted, violent conflicts (Afghanistan, Tajikistan).
- South: stabilization of a high frequency of internal and violent conflicts over access to and participation in power positions in weak states in the Third World.

5   Conflict management

An analysis of the 'phenomenon conflict' must include not only the identification of the actors, the conflicts' location in time and space, relevant structural components, national and international settings, but also the efforts to end conflicts. The term 'conflict management' is one way to describe these efforts. Management stands for the attempts to control and regulate a certain social, political or military development. It is commonly understood that the intention of an external conflict manager is not to aggravate the situation for the affected groups, i.e. intensify the use of force, but to re-direct, to re-orientate and to transform the conflict into a setting that allows for peaceful and consensual resolution of the conflict by all participating parties.

Conflict management can be negatively interpreted as a means, especially for external parties, to continue or intensify a conflict. For example, the eight-year-long first Gulf War between Iraq and Iran was managed by the international community in a way that allowed for its continuation, i.e. over years the parties remained able to mobilize military, political and human resources.

Conflict management can take various forms. In general, conflict management is conducted by the affected parties themselves. This self-management of conflicts needs a large degree of political autonomy by the responsible parties. In many non-violent conflicts, the issues are being negotiated in bilateral meetings of delegates. In non-violent internal conflicts round tables are an effective form of negotiating the issues in dispute with all affected parties. International regime building is another effective form of handling potential sources of conflict, especially those that transcend national regulation capacities such as environmental issues. The term 'global governance' best describes the global political handling of issue-oriented regimes and networks in an interdependent global communication society.

The analysis of third-party interventions and mediation in crises has matured in the past ten years and the body of literature is rapidly growing. Especially the end of the Cold War and the euphoria for a new world order has nourished the belief that proper instruments of negotiations and a humanitarian and rational approach that is freed from ideological chains will be one step toward world peace. The debacles in Somalia and Yugoslavia have shown that the high hopes that were put especially on the United Nations were misplaced. Instead, new types of conflicts, namely ethno-political conflicts in unstable, weak or corrupt Third World states top the agenda. Mediation and negotiation theory has developed a whole set of premises, criteria and scenarios for the management and de-escalation of these types of conflicts. It seems that professional mediation is one of the effective non-coercive instruments to handle escalated conflicts.[1]

Mediation

Mediation has only recently become an object of systematic empirical research. Few researchers have undertaken the effort to count and categorize mediation efforts in conflicts. Haas (1983) has observed mediation in 75 percent out of 108 conflicts from 1945 to 1965. Butterworth (1976) found mediators in 77 percent of his cases; Bercovitch (1986) analyzed seventy-nine international conflicts since 1945 and counted forty-four conflicts with a total of 257 mediation efforts. The Hamburg based 'working unit on the causes of war' (Gantzel and Schwinghammer 1995) reports 131 mediated endings of wars from 1945 to 1992. KOSIMO has found in 55 percent of its 661 conflicts attempts at mediation by one or more parties.

When, where and why does mediation occur? KOSIMO cannot answer the why question on the basis of its data, but it can offer a comparatively detailed profile of conflicts with and without mediation. This profile allows for some general conclusions about global trends in mediation. Table 5.1 lists eight types of conflicts and separates them by mediated and non-mediated types of conflicts.

Fifty-five percent of all conflicts that entered the KOSIMO databank have been mediated by one or more third parties in the course of their development. This number is the lowest result when compared with the findings of other databanks, because our sample includes not only wars or violent conflicts, but also non-violent conflicts. Yet it confirms the trend that, depending on the dataset, more than half and up to 75 percent of all conflicts are mediated at one point in their development.

A look at the 286 non-violent conflicts shows that the frequency of mediated conflicts is down to 50 percent. This finding can be interpreted in two ways. On the one hand, it is plausible to assume that in non-violent conflicts, the parties are still autonomous and capable of rational approaches and constructive resolutions to their conflict. Both parties feel solely responsible for their conflict and capable of solving the issue without external interference. Therefore, the need for a mediator is low. On the other hand, it can be argued that all violent conflicts developed from non-violent phases after constructive communication has broken down. Therefore, negotiations should be monitored or accompanied by mediators at the

Table 5.1 Mediated and non-mediated types of conflicts

Type	Frequency	%
Total conflicts	661	100
Non-mediated conflicts	297	45
Mediated conflicts	364	55
Non-violent conflicts	286	100
Non-violent non-mediated conflicts	142	50
Non-violent mediated conflicts	144	50
Violent conflicts	375	100
Violent non-mediated conflicts	155	41
Violent mediated conflicts	220	59
International conflicts	398	100
International non-mediated conflicts	138	35
International mediated conflicts	260	65
International non-violent conflicts	228	100
International non-violent non-mediated	95	42
International non-violent mediated conflicts	133	58
International violent conflicts	170	100
International violent non-mediated conflicts	43	25
International violent mediated conflicts	127	75
Internal conflicts	263	100
Internal non-mediated conflicts	159	60
Internal mediated conflicts	104	40
Internal non-violent conflicts	58	100
Internal non-violent non-mediated conflicts	47	81
Internal non-violent mediated conflicts	11	19
Internal violent conflicts	205	100
Internal violent non-mediated conflicts	112	55
Internal violent mediated conflicts	93	45

earliest stage possible. In this respect, the frequency of 50 percent non-mediated non-violent conflicts is too low.

With regard to the subset of 375 violent conflicts that entered the KOSIMO databank, the frequency of a mediated result is 59 percent. This finding supports the assumption that in violent conflicts, the parties lost some or all control over constructive conflict-management forms and were in need of third-party intervention. On the other hand, 41 percent of all violent conflicts between 1945 and 1995 were carried out without third-party mediation. One reason for this result is the fact that the most frequent type of violent conflicts, namely internal conflicts, are not subject to International

Law and the United Nations crisis mechanism. Likewise, regional organizations have very limited rights to intervene in the internal affairs of one of its member states without the member's consent. Although the trend toward international enforcement of human rights inside of member states is irreversible, the realization of this goal is still in a distant future.

The findings for the subset of 398 international conflicts reveal are much clearer. Two-thirds of all international conflicts have been mediated. A look at 170 international violent conflicts out of this group shows that the proportion of mediated conflicts rises to 75 percent of all international violent conflicts. But also the non-violent international conflicts were mediated in 58 percent of the cases.

Internal conflicts show the reverse trend. Out of 263 internal conflicts, only 40 percent were mediated conflicts. A look at non-violent internal conflicts shows that the proportion of mediated conflicts dropped to 19 percent. With regards to violent internal conflicts, the proportion of mediated conflicts is still below half of all cases (45 percent).

The general conclusion from Table 5.1 is that mediation occurs foremost in international and in violent conflicts. Non-violent and internal conflicts show lower frequencies. This can be explained by a shortage of internationally accepted instruments for the mediation of internal conflicts on the one hand. On the other hand, international violent conflicts have a much higher potential to become a threat to world peace and international security than other types of conflicts. The world's concern for this type of conflict is understandably higher – although violent international conflicts have been decreasing in number since the early 1970s and are a rather exceptional phenomenon today (see Chapter 3, 'Partial conflicts').

Are there regional differences for the frequencies of mediated conflicts? The literature on cross-cultural negotiations assumes different styles and attitudes to concepts such as 'mediation' or 'compromise'. Whereas 'compromise' in the Western concept is a positive term, it is a rather mistrusted concept in the Oriental style of negotiations. From our data we cannot deduce cultural differences with regard to acceptance of mediation. But, vice-versa, the regional frequencies of documented mediation efforts can serve as a basis for inductive speculations. Table 5.2 lists all mediation efforts by regions. In a second row, the percentage of mediations by each regional organization is included. Below we will analyze the mediators as actors in conflicts in more detail.

The overall trend in Table 5.2 shows that Europe, South America and Asia/Oceania have rather low frequencies of mediated conflicts whereas the Middle East/Maghreb, Central America and sub-Saharan Africa have higher frequencies than the global average of 55 percent. North America with two mediated conflicts out of three conflicts cannot be accepted as a representative sample.

Europe's low rate of mediated conflicts can be partially explained by the high number of democratic systems that show a high problem-solving

Table 5.2 Mediation efforts in conflicts by regions

Type of conflict	Frequency	%
All conflicts	661	100
Mediated conflicts	364	55
Conflicts in Europe	103	100
Mediated conflicts	46	45
Conflicts in Asia/Oceania	144	100
Mediated conflicts	58	40
Conflicts in sub-Saharan Africa	145	100
Mediated conflicts	94	65
Mediated by OAU	43	30
Conflicts in Middle East/Maghreb	167	100
Mediated conflicts	110	66
Mediated by Arab League	30	18
Conflicts in North America	3	100
Mediated conflicts	2	67
Mediated by OAS	0	0
Conflicts in Central America	53	100
Mediated conflicts	39	74
Mediated by OAS	24	45
Conflicts in South America	46	100
Mediated conflicts	15	33
Mediated by OAS	6	13

capacity (when linked with successful economies) compared to other political systems.

Asia/Oceania as a world region has the second-lowest rate of mediated conflicts (40 percent). A possible explanation here may be the high frequency of conflict involvement by the superpowers (US and USSR) and great powers (China, India, France and Great Britain). Great powers and superpowers have by definition the ambition to solve their problems by themselves. The chance of accepting a mediator as a third party in conflicts where great or superpowers are involved is therefore low.

The lowest rate of mediated conflicts is found in South America. Here, only fifteen conflicts have seen the activities of a mediator. As for the Asian region, the influential role of the US in the region may be partially responsible for the low mediation activities. Also, most international conflicts in South America concerned territorial problems. As the analysis of issues of conflict in Chapter 3 has shown, territorial issues are open to a variety of negotiation techniques and have rarely escalated into violent conflicts. Mediation, on the other hand, is mostly needed in protracted and complex situations where the problem-solving capacities of the actors are severely limited. If this is true, then the high number of mediated conflicts in the Central American region is more difficult to explain. Here, 74 percent of all conflicts have been mediated at least once in the course of their development. Both the UN and the OAS have been very active in solving

Central American conflicts. The conflicts in Central America are mostly multi-issue conflicts. Economic underdevelopment, ethno-political tensions, ideological system conflicts, access to resources and corrupt governments that are facing armed guerilla and liberation movements have been the causes for protracted civil wars.

The third aspect of a global analysis of mediations, after the analysis of types of conflicts and regions of conflicts, are the issues over which the conflicts have escalated. As before, we differentiate among seven issues and a residual eighth category. The focus is on the proportion of mediated conflicts within each issue subset, e.g. 62 percent of all territorial conflicts have been mediated, regardless of how many conflicts have been carried out over – among other – territorial issues. In other words, the analysis of issues in mediated conflicts is not extended to the analysis of the column percentages in Table 5.3. This is due to the multiple coding of up to three issues for each conflict (see Chapter 3, 'Issues of conflicts' – pages 129–52).

The analysis of Table 5.3 confirms by and large the profile in Table 5.2. The seven issues can be grouped into 'international issues' and 'internal issues'. Conflicts over territory, land borders and sea borders, international power conflicts, decolonization, national independence, and conflicts over resources are found in conflicts with an international dimension; whereas conflicts over ethnic, religious and regional autonomy or secession, ideological systems conflicts and internal power conflicts, are typically found in internal conflicts. Now, the highest frequencies for mediated conflicts are found for conflicts involving resources (73 percent), international power conflicts (71 percent) and conflicts over territory, land and sea borders (62 percent). From the subset of typically internal issues of

Table 5.3 Issues in mediated and non-mediated conflicts

Items*	Frequency	% of all items (n=1059*)	Non-mediated conflicts	Row %	Mediated conflicts	Row %
Territory, borders, sea borders	224	21	85	38	139	62
Decolonization, national independence	116	11	50	43	66	57
Ethnic, religious or regional autonomy	121	11	67	55	54	45
Ideology, system conflict	150	14	80	53	70	47
Internal power conflict	180	17	81	45	99	55
International power conflict	117	11	34	29	83	71
Resources	103	10	28	27	75	73
Other	48	5	20	42	28	58
Total	1059*	100				

Note
* Multiple choice.

conflicts, the category internal power shows the highest proportion of mediated conflicts (55 percent) whereas the other 'internal issues', autonomy or secession and ideological system conflicts show frequencies around or below 50 percent of all conflicts carried out over the respective issue.

Taking together these findings and the findings from Chapter 3, 'Partial conflicts', there seems to be a widening gap between global trends of conflicts and global trends of mediations. On the one hand, the frequency of internal conflicts over autonomist or secessionist issues and internal power positions are on the rise, while the number of violent international conflicts has been decreasing for decades and is negligible today. Yet, the conflicts that are most frequently approached by mediation are these international conflicts over rather material issues as compared with value and identity disputes in internal conflicts. The next focus on mediation as a means to manage conflicts is on some of the most frequent mediators, namely international organizations.

Actors in conflict management

This section looks at the mediating and peacefully intervening actors in ongoing conflicts. To be successful a mediator should be equipped with certain qualifications. Bercovitch (1986), Grewe (1981: 136f), Pfetsch *et al.* (1994) have singled out necessary qualifications of the mediator such as equidistance to the parties and issues involved, integrity and professionalism, negotiation skills such as flexibility in reactions, positions, perceptions and, last but not least, creativity in finding solutions. Beyond these more or less personal assets, a successful mediator must possess a certain amount of leverage or bargaining power, a capacity to use one or more sticks and carrots to motivate the parties to change their positions and perceptions. This can lead to win–win constellations which in turn are the necessary basis for compromises.

During mediations, very few people are directly involved. In a bilateral mediation or shuttle diplomacy, the parties are often kept separate from each other and the mediator serves as a messenger between the two. In advanced phases of negotiations a first dinner evening or a round-table talk can bring the delegates together. In initial, critical or final phases of mediation processes, the leaders of each party, e.g. the presidents of the states or the guerilla leaders have direct contact, while between these crucial moments the negotiations are continuing among delegates and specialists by each party in subordinate *ad hoc* bodies, e.g. in a committee of engineers for the delineation of a border.

The empirical analysis of mediation activities is difficult and a complete overview of all mediations impossible since one of the tools and strategies of mediation is secrecy. Therefore, only mediations that resulted in the signing of a document or ended with a public declaration can be observed by the scientific community. Among these secret or unspectacular mediations are many that were conducted privately or semi-officially by individuals that did not act in the name of an organization or state, but as private individuals. This form can allow for more flexibility in the finding of solutions than official delegations with clienteles or orders 'from above'. In ethnic, religious or other value conflicts, religious groups such as the Quakers have produced formidable mediation results of which only few are documented. The Carter Center in Atlanta, which was initiated by the former US President Jimmy Carter, entertains a network of over one hundred elder statesmen that have declared their readiness to mediate if wished to do so by a certain conflict party. Jimmy Carter himself is another active private mediator whose many informal mediations after the end of his presidency are yet to be documented. A new form of mediation which has received only scant attention from the political-science community is that conducted by the non-governmental organizations. Their focus is not so much on the arena of high politics with decisions over peace treaties but on a societal level. In former conflict or war zones such as in South Africa since 1992 or in Bosnia-Herzegovina since 1995 NGOs have mediated among segments in the population that were former 'enemies'. Peace consolidation in this respect has to be seen as a hopefully final and integral part of overall conflict management and conflict settlement with the help of third parties.

International organizations

In this book, the focus is limited to four international organizations as mediating agencies, namely the United Nations, the Organization of American States (OAS), the Organization of African Unity (OAU) and the Arab League (AL). For the European continent, the OSCE should be included in further studies. Likewise, for the Asian region, the mediating efforts of ASEAN should be objects of scientific documentation and analysis in the future. A comprehensive empirical overview of mediations has yet to be undertaken.

The United Nations is the only universal international organization. The Charter spells out the obligation of the member states within the principle of collective security to settle their conflicts by peaceful means. When conflicts escalate, the Charter provides strategies and instruments that increase in intensity and severity in proportion to the conflict's intensity. According to these provisions a conflict should, above all, be settled by the parties themselves and with peaceful means. If this becomes difficult, third-party mediation, arbitration or judicial settlement are further means to settle the issue. In case an aggressor threatens another state, the Security Council can turn to coercive measures according to Chapter VII of the Charter. Once an aggressor has been identified and a threat to peace and international security has been recognized by the Security Council, this body can impose cultural, economic and military sanctions. When all of the above measures have failed, the Security Council can use 'all necessary means' to restore peace

and international security. The Iraqi invasion into Kuwait was one of the rare
cases when the UN authorized multinational armed forces to liberate Kuwait
and to restore the status quo ante bellum.

What is the record of the United Nations after fifty years of peaceful and
violent conflicts in and among states? Table 5.4 gives a survey of the
frequencies of UN involvement in conflicts. These numbers are not
exhaustive. In innumerable cases UN observers, information bureaus,
special envoys and delegations mediated behind the scenes and promoted
peaceful conflict behavior. Here, we have listed those documented cases in
which the UN played a major or significant role – alone, parallel or in
cooperation with other mediating states or agencies. Note that 'issues' are
not absolute, but relative numbers due to the multiple coding (up to three
issues per conflict).

Table 5.4 The UN as a global mediator

		Frequency	%	Total (%)
	All conflicts mediated by the UN	192	100	
Regions	Europe	28	15	
	Middle East/Maghreb	53	28	
	Sub-Saharan Africa	46	24	
	Asia/Oceania	41	21	
	America	24	13	
	North America	0	0	
	Central America	19	79	
	South America	5	21	
Types	Non-violent conflicts	71	37	
	Violent conflicts	121	63	100
	International conflicts	143	74	
	International non-violent conflicts	65	45	
	International violent conflicts	78	55	100
	Internal conflicts	49	26	
	Internal non-violent conflicts	6	12	
	Internal violent conflicts	43	88	100
Issues*	Territory, borders, sea boundaries	68	20	
	Decolonization, national independence	55	16	
	Ethnic, religious or regional autonomy	25	7	
	Ideology, system	40	12	
	Internal power	49	14	
	International power	61	18	
	Resources	29	9	
	Others	12	4	100

Note
* Multiple choice.

The UN mediated in 192 conflicts or in 29 percent out of a total of 661 conflicts between 1945 and 1995. The preferred region for UN involvement in conflicts was the Middle East/Maghreb region with 28 percent out of all mediated conflicts. The American continent has seen comparatively little UN engagement. Four-fifths of the UN engagement on the American continent were in conflicts in Central America. When comparing the regional frequencies for UN engagements and the regional frequencies of conflicts (see Chapter 3, 'Regions of conflict'), we detect an even distribution of engagements according to the local conflict 'density'. In each region the ratio is comparable to the global ratio of roughly one engagement in three conflicts.

Obviously, the UN security mechanisms function according to other criteria than the mere geographical location of a conflict. When contrasting the engagements in non-violent and violent conflicts, two-thirds of all engagements are undertaken in violent conflicts. We can conclude that the UN monitors or mediates, besides armed conflicts, a relatively large number of non-violent crises and latent conflicts. This finding may be used against the charge that the UN is intervening too often too late in ongoing conflicts.

Seventy-four percent of the UN mediation activities were spent on international conflicts. This finding reflects the growing anachronism between the UN's international character and security instruments on the one hand and on the other the new and dominant type of conflict, namely internal ethno-politically charged power and distribution conflicts within states with weak, corrupt or dictatorial regimes. The differentiation of internal and international conflicts according to their intensity confirms the above trend.

Are there certain issues that trigger or provoke UN engagements more than other issues? The UN was most active in conflicts over territorial and border issues as well as in conflicts over international power positions. Also decolonization conflicts show high rates of UN involvement – as should be expected. The least engagement was observed when the conflict involved issues such as ethnic, religious or regional autonomy or access or distribution of resources. With regard to the internal and international nature of the issues, the trend toward a clear UN preference for international conflicts can be confirmed.

Besides the globally active United Nations Organization, several regional organizations are concerned with security matters and conflict intervention.

Organizations with primarily security and defense concerns are, e.g., the North Atlantic Treaty Organization (NATO), the US–Japan and the US–South Korea defense alliances. The military nature of these and other defense alliances limits their role as mediators with primarily de-escalating capacities. NATO's military intervention in Bosnia-Herzegovina in 1995 should be interpreted as a non-peaceful strategy of conflict management regardless of NATO's legitimization and the consequences of the military intervention for the beginning of negotiations.

Another type of international organization has its focus on economic cooperation. Economic cooperation strengthens global interdependence; and interdependence seems to be a structural component of peaceful international relations (Keohane and Nye 1977). In this sense, it is justifiable to grant a peace dividend to economic cooperation. On the other hand, economic interdependence by itself is not a sufficient condition for a peace zone or regime. Democratic, multi-party regimes with institutionalized channels of conflict resolution are equally necessary for the peaceful handling of conflicts. Examples for successful – that is peace-promoting, economic international organizations – are the European Union, the Association of Southeast Asian Nations (ASEAN), and the North American Free Trade Organization (NAFTA).

Here, we are concerned with a third type of international organization. The aim of these regional security organizations is the promotion of peaceful international relations – not so much by military or economic means, but through international multi-lateral negotiations and mediations. The regional organizations understand themselves as the responsible institution for security matters in their respective regions. For Europe, including Eastern Europe and Russia as well as North America, this is the Organization of Security and Cooperation in Europe (OSCE), for the Middle East and Maghreb region it is the Arab League (AL), for the African continent it is the Organization of African Unity (OAU), and for the American continent it is the Organization of American States (OAS). Tables 5.5–5.7 show, respectively, the frequency of mediating interventions by the OAS, the OAU and the AL.

The OAS, like the UN, clearly emphasizes the Central American region where 80 percent of its attempts to de-escalate ongoing conflicts took place. In only six cases did the OAS intervene in ongoing South American conflicts. The OAS intervened in almost every second conflict on the American continent. International conflicts were mediated by the OAS more often than internal conflicts. In contrast with the trend of the UN, the OAS intervened in every second latent conflict or non-violent crisis in Central and South America.

The OAU as a regional organization for unity, cooperation and security has mediated in every third conflict on the sub-Saharan continent. Only one-quarter of latent conflicts and crises have triggered a OAU mediation, whereas three-quarters of all violent conflicts have been treated with OAU mediation. The bias for international conflicts over mediation in internal conflicts is repeated in the case of the OAU. Seventy-one percent of all international conflicts were mediated as against 29 percent of all internal conflicts on the African continent. All of the fourteen internal conflicts in which the OAU attempted mediations were violent conflicts, and most of these violent conflicts were fights over internal power positions rather than conflicts over minority or autonomy issues.

The Arab League has the lowest level of mediation attempts in relation to the frequency of conflicts in the Middle East and Maghreb region. Only 19 percent of all conflicts have seen mediation attempts by the Arab League. A clear preference exists for international and for violent conflicts.

Table 5.5 The OAS as mediator in America

	Frequency in Central America	% of all conflicts of this type in this region (row %)	Total (%)	Frequency in South America	% of all conflicts of this type in this region (row %)	Total (%)
All conflicts mediated by the OAS	24	45		6	13	
Types						
Non-violent conflicts	14	58		3	50	
Violent conflicts	10	42	100	3	50	100
International conflicts	19	68		5	83	
International non-violent conflicts	12	63		4	80	
International violent conflicts	7	37	100	1	20	100
Internal conflicts	5	21		1	17	
Internal non-violent conflicts	2	40		0	0	
Internal violent conflicts	3	60	100	1	100	100
Issues*						
Territory, borders, sea borders	3	21		3	43	
Decolonization, national independence	0	0		0	0	
Ethnic, religious or regional autonomy	0	0		0	0	
Ideology, system	4	29		0	0	
Internal power	1	7		0	0	
International power	1	7		0	0	
Resources	2	14		3	43	
Others	3	22	100	1	14	100

Note
* Multiple choice.

Table 5.6 The OAU as mediator in sub-Saharan Africa

		Frequency of OAU mediations in sub-Saharan Africa	% of all conflicts of this type in this region (row %)	Total (%)
	All conflicts mediated by the OAU	48	33	
Types	Non-violent conflicts	12	25	
	Violent conflicts	36	75	100
	International conflicts	34	71	
	International non-violent conflicts	12	35	
	International violent conflicts	22	65	100
	Internal conflicts	14	29	
	Internal non-violent conflicts	0	0	
	Internal violent conflicts	14	100	100
Issues*	Territory, borders, sea borders	16	23	
	Decolonization, national independence	6	9	
	Ethnic, religious or regional autonomy	7	10	
	Ideology, system	2	3	
	Internal power	18	26	
	International power	11	16	
	Resources	8	12	
	Others	1	1	100

Note
* Multiple choice.

Table 5.7 The Arab League as mediator in the Middle East/Maghreb region

		Frequency	%	Total (%)
	All conflicts mediated by the Arab League	31	19	
Types	Non-violent conflicts	9	29	
	Violent conflicts	22	71	100
	International conflicts	21	68	
	International non-violent conflicts	9	43	
	International violent conflicts	12	57	100
	Internal conflicts	10	32	
	Internal non-violent conflicts	0	0	
	Internal violent conflicts	10	100	100
Issues*	Territory, borders, sea borders	10	18	
	Decolonization, national independence	2	3	
	Ethnic, religious or regional autonomy	1	2	
	Ideology, system	4	7	
	Internal power	13	22	
	International power	11	18	
	Resources	8	13	
	Others	1	2	100

Note
* Multiple choice.

Modalities of conflict resolution

So far, this chapter has covered mediation (pages 189–94) and the mediating international organizations (pages 194–98). Conflict management as defined in Chapter 5 (page 188) is understood as de-escalating action by the parties to settle the conflict either by themselves or with the help of intervening, mediating third parties. This management is a process over time that eventually will lead to a certain outcome, result, settlement or resolution of the conflict. In general, three outcomes are conceivable: negotiated, consensual agreements; resolutions by threat; resolution by force. When all parties have reached a consensual, negotiated and non-coercive agreement on all issues without reservations or conditions to the agreement, the agreement will most probably settle the conflict permanently or for a long time. If one or more of these criteria should be missing, i.e. parties, issues and no reservations or conditions, the agreement will be less stable and the conflict will not be completely, permanently and satisfactorily settled. Resolutions by threat or force cannot be counted as settlements of conflicts, but must be subsumed under the heading 'war ends – conflict continues' (see pages 107–12).

In order to aggregate data on the basis of the above conceptualization, KOSIMO has four general categories for the process of conflict resolution:

- non-violent, negotiated resolutions
- undecided or passive resolution, withdrawal of demands
- resolutions by threat or pressure
- resolutions by the use of force.

Figure 5.1 shows the distribution of conflict resolution processes according to the four categories for all 661 conflicts from 1945 to 1995. The figure also differentiates among internal and international conflicts and their forms of resolution.

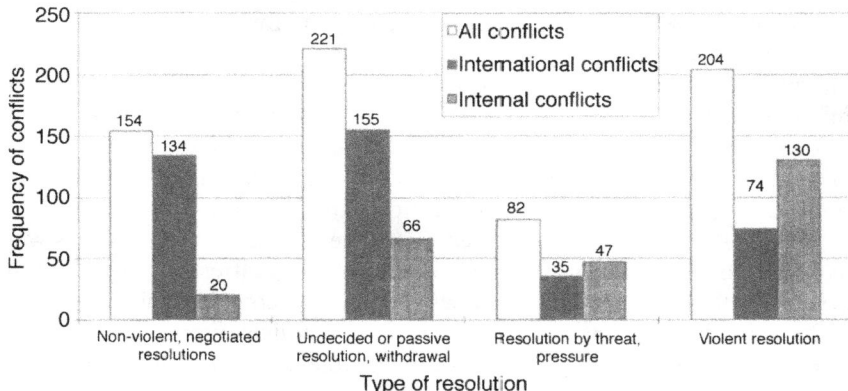

Figure 5.1 Negotiated, passive and coercive conflict resolutions.

Almost one-third of all conflicts have been resolved by violent means. In other words, not only was the conflict itself violent, but also the attempts to bring the conflict to an end. The largest group of resolutions are undecided or passive resolutions. A partial explanation for this finding is the inclusion in this category of 109 conflicts that have been ongoing since 1995. If this group is subtracted, there remain 112 unresolved conflicts. In other words, in 112 cases, or 17 percent of 661 conflicts, the parties have officially neither continued nor ended the conflict.

In 154 cases, or 24 percent of 661 conflicts, the parties were able to resolve their conflict through negotiations and consensus. Note that the conflict itself could have been carried out with the use of force. Here, we are only concerned with the forms of conflict resolution, i.e. the ending of the conflict.

A fourth group of eighty-two conflicts has been resolved by the use of threats and pressure. The rather low proportion of this type, 12 percent of 661 conflicts, can be interpreted as a tendency for parties in conflicts to come to a decision, either to come to an end or to come to no end. Mere pressure or threat by one party seems to be but a phase in the process of conflict development and resolution.

The differentiation of the findings for conflict resolutions in internal and international conflicts specifies the above general findings. International conflicts are most likely to be resolved by non-violent negotiations or they remain undecided while internal conflicts are most likely to be resolved by violent means. These findings confirm the results in Chapter 3, 'Partial conflicts' about the violent and non-violent character of internal and international conflicts; internal conflicts are not only mostly initiated and carried out by violent means. They are also most likely to be ended by violent action. International conflicts are more likely to be initiated, carried out and resolved by non-violent means.

Figure 5.2 singles out two subsets of conflicts that were carried out over certain issues, namely conflicts over decolonization and national independence as well as conflicts over ethnic, religious and regional autonomy. These subsets are then grouped by the forms of their resolution.

The number of non-violent, negotiated resolutions is – as expected from the analysis of internal conflicts – low. Out of 121 conflicts over ethnic, religious and regional autonomy, only thirteen conflicts or 11 percent were resolved by negotiations. Half of these conflicts remain undecided while 40 percent of them are resolved by the use of force. A similar trend can be observed for conflicts over decolonization and national independence.

In contrast to the above issues, conflicts over territory and borders as well as access to and the distribution of resources have a different profile. Figure 5.3 shows that in the subset of forcefully resolved conflicts only 16 percent were territorial conflicts and 21 percent were conflicts over resources. Also, threats and pressure played a subordinate role in the resolution of these conflicts. On the other hand, the figures for non-violent negotiated resolutions are 37 percent for territorial conflicts and 32 percent for

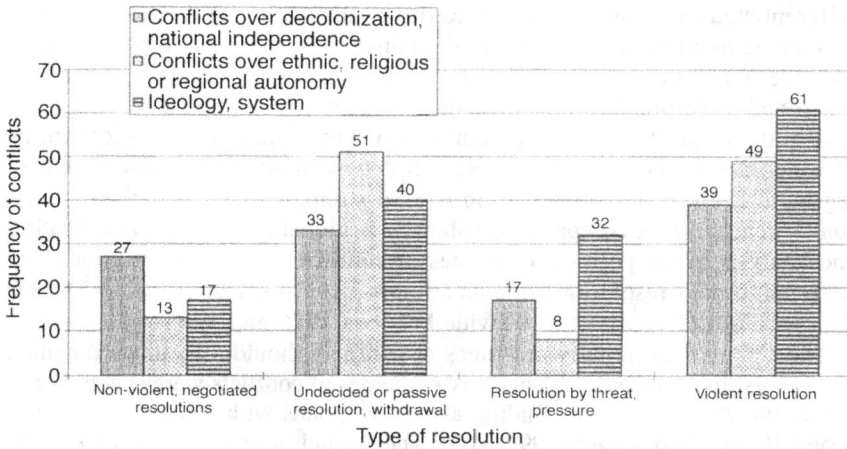

Figure 5.2 Resolution of conflicts over decolonization, national independence and ethnic, religious and regional autonomy.

conflicts over resources. In the group of territorial conflicts, the number of undecided cases is rather high with 41 percent. It seems that territorial issues do not top the agenda of states when it comes to their actual resolution.

Outcomes of conflicts

The outcome of a conflict is the status after the ending of a conflict. Outcomes can be differentiated by the territorial, military or political dimension of the conflict. Each of these dimensions can take various forms. When a conflict is still ongoing, the outcome remains open and the outcome is coded as 'continuing'. Military outcomes are differentiated by victory,

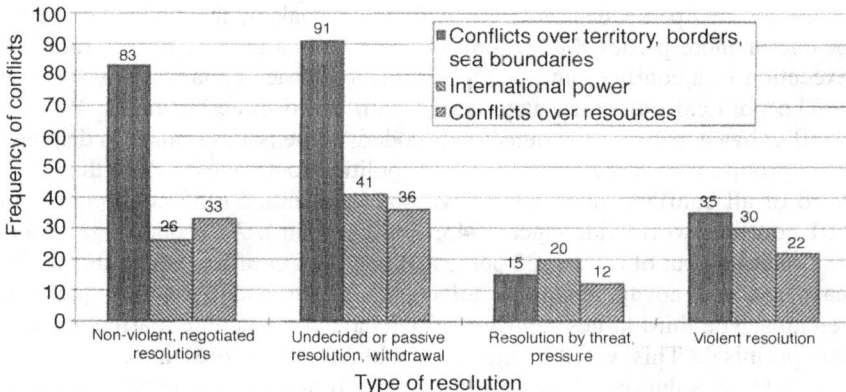

Figure 5.3 Resolutions of conflicts over territory and resources.

defeat, withdrawal, stalemate or continuation; territorial outcomes are differentiated by the gain or loss of territory, annexation or unification, status quo or renouncement of territorial claims. The political dimensions of possible outcomes of conflicts are differentiated by a strengthened or weakened government, opposition or third party, by a change, a fall or the new building of regimes and by compromise outcomes. The political forms of outcomes of conflicts have been coded with multiple choices, e.g. a regime can change, the opposition can be strengthened and the settlement can be reached as a compromise solution. A global empirical quantification and analysis of the political outcomes of conflicts and the negotiations that have led to their resolution remains a future field of research. Table 5.8 lists the outcomes of conflicts worldwide between 1945 and 1995.

The survey over military outcomes of conflicts should discourage potential aggressors. In most cases, the military outcomes of conflicts were stalemates or indecisive cease-fires. This finding also corresponds with results presented in Jones, Bremer and Singer (1996: 203). The second most likely outcome is the defeat of the initiator or the aggressor. Only in a small number of cases was the military outcome of a conflict in favor of the initiator or aggressor.

The same tendency for military outcomes is true for the territorial outcomes in those conflicts where this issue or dimension mattered. In very few cases did an initiator of a conflict succeed with territorial claims. In most cases, the status quo ante was upheld. Losses of territory as a result of a conflict are a rare exception.

When a conflict had military or territorial issues and dimensions, mediation played a role in more than half of these conflicts. Seventy-seven percent of all cease-fires were mediated, 74 percent of all troop withdrawals. When the initiator was either defeated or had territorial losses, the activities of external mediating parties dropped to 50 percent of these cases. On the other hand, these findings can lead to the conclusion that mediation has little or no effect on the eventual outcome of a conflict, since all possible outcomes have comparable mediation rates between 50 and 75 percent. This interpretation would be more in line with the general assumption in mediation theory that mediation processes are open-ended processes without set goals by the mediating agency or one or more parties. Mediation in this sense is a method to transform the execution of a conflict, but not an instrument to reach certain outcomes.

The political outcomes were coded with up to three attributes. When a conflict has not ended, the outcome is coded 'some issues remain in dispute'. This group is the largest in the subset 'political outcomes'. More than one-third of all conflicts since 1945 have not been settled (255 conflicts out of 601 conflicts worldwide since 1945, or 42 percent). A second large group, 133 conflicts out of 601, or 22 percent, consists of conflicts where the parties have reached no agreement at all on the issues and the status quo ante remains. The third largest set of conflicts have the outcome 'partial success, compromise'. This variable indicates whether the parties have reached a compromise solution which is – according to negotiation theory – a stable outcome in a win–win constellation. Nineteen percent of all outcomes

Table 5.8 Outcomes of conflicts

Type	Outcome	Total	%
Military outcomes*	Stalemate, cease-fire, indecisive outcome	106	34
	Victory of initiator	57	18
	Defeat of initiator	86	28
	Continuation of fighting	38	12
	Withdrawal of troops	23	7
	Total	310	100
Territorial outcomes	Separation/division of territory	28	12
	Territorial losses	17	7
	Annexation, unification, incorporation of territory	39	17
	Denouncement of territorial claims	33	14
	Status quo, initiator upholds territorial claims	112	49
	Total	229	100
Political outcomes for the conflict**	Status quo ante, no agreement	133	22
	Some issues remain in dispute	255	42
	Conclusion of a consensual agreement	97	16
	Compromise, partial success	116	19
	Total	601	100
Political outcomes for the actors**	Change of regime	45	14
	Emergence of new regimes	12	4
	Fall of regime	28	9
	Weakening of bargaining positions	14	4
	Strengthening of bargaining positions	32	10
	Recognition and strengthening of opposition	21	7
	Suppression of opposition	81	25
	Admission/inclusion of opposition to government	14	4
	Renouncement of claims	15	5
	Increased influence of external power	29	9
	Decreased influence of external power	28	9
	Total		100

Notes
* Some conflicts had no military or territorial outcomes; also, by the end of 1995, some conflicts were in phases that did not allow a coding with military, territorial and political outcome variables.
** Multiple choice.

qualified for this category. Only 16 percent of all possible outcomes in conflicts can be labeled 'consensual agreements'.

Political outcomes have also been categorized according to changes in the power position of the ruling regime, of the opposition movements or the external parties. The findings show a trend toward changes of regimes themselves rather than the complete fall of regimes or the emergence of new regimes as an outcome of conflicts. Opposition movements are most likely suppressed as an outcome of conflicts. In only a few cases were the opposition movements strengthened or admitted to the government. The outcomes of conflicts seem to have little or no effect on the position of external parties.

When – as an outcome of a conflict – the opposition was suppressed, the regime abdicated or changed, mediation was a less frequently used instrument of conflict management. In contrast, when an external power lost its influence in the conflict, when the initiator of a conflict denounced some of the demands, when new regimes emerged and when consensual agreements were found, mediation was observed much more frequently. As for the analysis of the factor 'mediation' above, the relevance of mediation for certain political outcomes in conflicts needs further empirical studies.

Treaties

Throughout history, most wars among peoples and states began with some kind of formal announcement, and they ended with an agreement on truce or peace. Wars were regarded as a natural and inevitable part of human history, and the formal opening and ending of wars legitimated one's actions. War as a legitimate means of politics was not outlawed before the first half of the twentieth century. The universal ban on war, except for self-defense, evidently led to the disappearance of formal declarations of war (although, in reality, the number of wars worldwide has kept growing throughout the twentieth century). The function of peace treaties has changed accordingly. Peace treaties in modern, undeclared wars acknowledge implicitly the existence of a war and they express the will of the parties to end it, however illegal and illegitimate the war is considered. Modern peace treaties often have the character of a compromise solution, since the concepts of absolute victors and losers no longer applies. Spoils have become illegal and moral guilt may be regarded as an inadequate concept for cooperation. Today, the annexation, occupation, colonization, slavery or subjugation of conquered territories and peoples are outdated concepts which, so far, have not been replaced by equally accepted codes of conduct or norms concerning the legality of the beginnings and endings of domestic conflict. Peace treaties have more and more the function to reconcile hostile parties and to open new ways of coexistence and cooperation for the future. They try to bridge the normative gap[2] between the high aspirations in the United Nations Charter which outlaws war and refers to war in the narrow and traditional context of 'aggressors' and 'self-defense' on the one hand and, on the other hand, the grim reality of 375 violent crises and wars since 1945 which by and large were neither caused by genuine aggressors nor conducted as self-defense measures. When analyzing peace treaties and other forms of formal endings of violent and non-violent conflicts, empirical conflict researchers must be aware of these additional functions that the documents have since 1945.

The main interest in the analysis of formal endings of conflicts is to find out which factors contribute to stable and lasting conflict resolutions. From negotiation and mediation theory, we know that agreements – to be effective in the future – must have a win–win character; they must be based on mutual compromises and on mutual confidence. Formal treaties may be an instrument to document this change in attitudes and behavior among former

Table 5.9 Types of treaties

International treaties	Frequency	Internal treaties	Frequency
International peace treaties	154	Constitutional changes, referenda, autonomy	57
Cease-fires, withdrawals	30		
Declarations of independence	35	Internal cease-fires	26
		Internal peace treaties	13
International arbitration, judicial decisions	13		

foes. However, we cannot conclude that formal treaties are necessary to end wars and to begin peace.

In the foreseeable future, the dominant type of conflict is likely to be internal disputes over minority issues. International peace treaties will remain relevant in internal conflicts when external mediators or guarantors become part of the peace-accord; constitutional changes, revisions, treaties about religious, regional or cultural autonomy and regime changes have become an increasingly important instrument to end periods of violence and to make a new start. The observation of 328 internal and international formal agreements to end conflicts has led to the formation of the categories shown in Table 5.9. Table 5.10 lists 154 formal agreements of the first category, i.e. international peace treaties pertaining to international conflicts (order by regions and chronology).

Table 5.11 lists major military treaties, especially cease-fires and official troop withdrawals, in international conflicts which ended the hostilities or had a significant influence on the development of the conflict (ordered by regions and chronology).

Table 5.12 lists declarations of independence or separation which became decisive for the development of conflicts and their resolution (ordered by region and chronology).

Table 5.13 presents those rulings of the International Court of Justice in The Hague or other courts and arbitrating agencies which influenced the resolution of conflicts.

Table 5.14 lists conflicts in which constitutional changes played a decisive role in the conflicts' development and resolution. Constitutional changes, i.e. promulgations, revisions, interim constitutions, etc., as well as changes in the federal constitution of states are attempts at regulating and resolving internal conflicts between opposition groups and the ruling elites.

Table 5.15 lists internal violent conflicts that were influenced by cease-fire agreements and troop withdrawals by either the government's military or the opposition forces.

Finally, Table 5.16 presents internal, mostly violent conflicts that were ended or influenced by an extraordinary treaty between the government and the opposition group – these fundamental or framework treaties include constitutional changes or cease-fires.

Table 5.10 International treaties

No	Name	Start	End	Region	Intensity	Treaties
1	Mongolia (status)	1945	1950	Asia	Crisis	China–USSR Treaty 4.2.50
2	Indochina Ia	1945	1954	Asia	War	Geneva Conference 1954
3	India VI (Mahe)	1948	1954	Asia	Violent crisis	Pact 1.11.54
4	Burma–China (border)	1948	1960	Asia	Latent conflict	Border treaty 1.10.60
5	India VII (Indus channel)	1948	1960	Asia	Latent conflict	Indus Water Treaty 60
6	Burma (Chinese troops)	1949	1961	Asia	Violent crisis	Border agreement 19.10.61
7	China (Tibet I)	1950	1951	Asia	Violent crisis	Chinese–Tibetan Treaty 1951
8	Korea III (partition)	1953	cont.	Asia	Latent conflict	Conciliation agreement 13.12.91
9	China–Burma	1956	1956	Asia	Violent crisis	Border treaty
10	India XI (Rann of Kutch I)	1956	1964	Asia	Violent crisis	Agreement on status quo 30.6.65
11	Nepal II	1959	1961	Asia	Violent crisis	Border treaty 6.10.61
12	Indonesia (West Irian II)	1960	1969	Asia	Violent crisis	Agreement 8.62, autonomy agreement 1969
13	China–USSR (tensions)	1960	1991	Asia	Crisis	Announcements by Gorbachev 28.7.1986
14	Malaysia–Philippines	1961	1977	Asia	Latent conflict	End claims by Mali government to Sabah 5.8.77
15	China–India (war)	1962	1963	Asia	War	Partial agreement on Colombo proposals 14.2.63
16	China–Pakistan–India (border)	1963	1963	Asia	Latent conflict	Provisional border agreement, Pakistan–China 2.3.63
17	Malaya–Indonesia (Sarawak/Sabah)	1963	1966	Asia	War	Agreement on normalization relations 12.8.66
18	China–India (border)	1963	1993	Asia	Latent conflict	Border agreement 7.9.93
19	India XV (Rann of Kutch II)	1965	1969	Asia	Violent crisis	Kutch Agreement 1969
20	India XVI (Kashmir IV)	1965	1970	Asia	War	Tashkent 66, Simla Agreement 1972
21	China–USSR (Ussuri conflict)	1969	1969	Asia	Violent crisis	Protocol 20.12.70
22	India XVII (Bangladesh III)	1971	1971	Asia	War	Simla Agreement 1972

No.	Parties	Start	End	Region	Conflict type	Outcome
23	Indochina II (cease-fire)	1973	1976	Asia	War	Unification 1976
24	China–Laos	1975	1993	Asia	Latent conflict	Border agreement 24.10.91 and border protocol 31.1.93
25	Indochina IIIb	1978	1991	Asia	War	Peace treaty 23.10.91
26	China–Vietnam (border, emigrants, ideology)	1979	1991	Asia	Crisis	Agreement Sept. 1991; trade and border agreement Nov. 1991
27	Vanuatu–France	1981	1981	Asia	Latent conflict	Agreement on cooperation Feb. 1995
28	China–United Kingdom (Hong Kong)	1983	1984	Asia	Latent conflict	Treaty 26.9.84
29	France (New Caledonia I)	1984	1985	Asia	Crisis	Statute for New Caledonia 4.6.85
30	France (New Caledonia II)	1985	1988	Asia	Crisis	Treaty 26.6.88
31	France (New Caledonia III)	1988	1991	Asia	Latent conflict	Matignon Agreement 26.6.88
32	India–Nepal	1989	1990	Asia	Crisis	Treaty 10.6.90
33	China–Kazakhstan	1990	1993	Asia	Latent conflict	Border agreement 26.4.94
34	North Korea–IAEA	1991	1994	Asia	Crisis	Treaty US–PR Korea 21.10.94
35	Honduras–US (Swan island)	1945	1991	Central America	Latent conflict	Agreement 23.11.71
36	Haiti–Dominican Republic	1949	1950	Central America	Crisis	Declaration 10.6.49 (non-intervention principle)
37	Dominican Republic–Cuba (sailors)	1951	1951	Central America	Crisis	Agreement on non-interference
38	Nicaragua–Costa Rica (exiled people I)	1955	1956	Central America	Violent crisis	Friendship treaty 56
39	Cuba ('Cuba crisis')	1962	1962	Central America	Violent crisis	Agreement 28.10.62
40	Panama (channel I)	1964	1967	Central America	Violent crisis	Joint declaration June 1967
41	Dominican Republic II (intervention)	1965	1965	Central America	Violent crisis	Conciliation agreement 31.8.65
42	Honduras–El Salvador (soccer war I)	1969	1970	Central America	War	Agreement 4.6.70
43	El Salvador–Honduras (soccer war II) (aftermath))	1969	1980	Central America	Latent conflict	Treaty 30.10.80
44	Panama (channel II)	1970	1979	Central America	Latent conflict	Channel Treaty 7.9.77
45	Guatemala–Belize II (UK)	1975	1975	Central America	Violent crisis	Agreement 30.11.75

Table 5.10 Continued

No	Name	Start	End	Region	Intensity	Treaties
46	Cuba–US (refugees)	1993	cont.	Central America	Crisis	Agreement 9.9.94
47	Greece (civil war I)	1944	1945	Europe	Violent crisis	Varkiza Agreement 12.2.45
48	Yugoslavia–Italy (Trieste)	1945	1954	Europe	Crisis	Memo understanding 6.10.54
49	Austria (state treaty)	1945	1955	Europe	Latent conflict	Treaty 15.5.55
50	GDR–FRG (division)	1945	1990	Europe	Latent conflict	'2+4Treaty' 1990
51	USSR–Norway (Spitzbergen)	1945	1991	Europe	Latent conflict	Provisional treaty 1978
52	USSR–Finland I	1948	1948	Europe	Crisis	Friendship treaty 6.4.48
53	GDR–FRG (Berlin I, blockade)	1948	1949	Europe	Crisis	Agreement 4.5.49
54	USSR–Yugoslavia	1948	1956	Europe	Crisis	Declaration 20.6.56
55	Netherlands–FRG (border)	1949	1963	Europe	Latent conflict	Treaty 8.4.60
56	FRG–France (Saarland status)	1950	1957	Europe	Latent conflict	Treaty 27.10.56
57	Iceland–United Kingdom (fishery conflict I)	1952	1956	Europe	Latent conflict	OEEC Agreement 14.11.56
58	Iceland (US troops)	1956	1956	Europe	Latent conflict	Agreement 26.11.56
59	Poland (October uprisings)	1956	1956	Europe	Violent crisis	Military statute 17.12.56
60	GDR–FRG (Berlin II, status)	1958	1959	Europe	Crisis	Agreement 1959
61	Iceland–United Kingdom (fishery conflict II)	1958	1961	Europe	Latent conflict	Agreement Feb. 1961
62	GDR–FRG (Berlin III, wall)	1961	1961	Europe	Crisis	Treaty 1972
63	CSSR (Prague spring)	1968	1968	Europe	Violent crisis	Secret protocol 26.8.68
64	Sweden–USSR (Baltic Sea)	1969	1988	Europe	Latent conflict	Baltic agreement 13.1.88
65	GDR–Denmark (border)	1969	1988	Europe	Latent conflict	Fishery Agreement
66	Iceland–United Kingdom (fishery conflict III)	1971	1973	Europe	Crisis	Interim agreement 31.12.73
67	Greece–Turkey (Aegean Sea I)	1973	1976	Europe	Crisis	Agreement 11.11.76
68	Cyprus IV (Turkey invasion)	1974	1974	Europe	War	Geneva Declaration 30.7.74
69	Iceland–United Kingdom (fishery conflict IV)	1975	1976	Europe	Latent conflict	Interim agreement 1.6.76

No.	Conflict	Year 1	Year 2	Region	Intensity	Outcome
70	Poland–GDR (Stettin bay)	1977	1989	Europe	Latent conflict	Agreement 22.5.89
71	Sweden–Denmark (Hesseloe)	1978	1984	Europe	Latent conflict	Agreement on sea borders
72	Hungary–Slovakia (power plant Gabchikovo)	1989	1994	Europe	Crisis	Treaty Hunslo 19.3.95
73	Ukraine–Russian Federation (fleet, atomic weapons)	1991	1994	Europe	Crisis	Agreement on cooperation Feb. 1995
74	Greece–Macedonia (name)	1991	1995	Europe	Latent conflict	Interim accord 13.9.95
75	Croatia (occupation East Slavonia)	1991	1995	Europe	War	Dayton Peace Agreement 14.12.95
76	Bosnia–Herzegovina (Muslims–Croats)	1992	1994	Europe	War	Dayton Peace Agreement 24.11.95, Paris 14.12.95
77	Iran–USSR (Azerbaijan)	1945	1946	Middle East	Violent crisis	Communiqué 5.4.46
78	Sudan (independence I)	1946	1953	Middle East	Crisis	British–Egyptian Agreement 12.2.53
79	Afghanistan–Pakistan (Pashtunistan I)	1947	1963	Middle East	Violent crisis	Teheran Accord 1963
80	Yemen–United Kingdom (Aden I)	1948	1963	Middle East	Violent crisis	Aden joins South Arab Federation 16.1.63
81	Saudi Arabia–Abu Dhabi (Buraimi II)	1951	1952	Middle East	Violent crisis	Cease-fire agreement
82	Iran (oil nationalization, change of government)	1951	1953	Middle East	Crisis	Agreement on operations
83	Egypt (1st Suez crisis)	1951	1954	Middle East	Violent crisis	Evacuation Agreement 19.10.54
84	Iraq–Egypt, Syria (Baghdad Pact)	1955	1959	Middle East	Crisis	Agreed separation 24.3.59
85	Tunisia–Egypt (Ben Yussuf)	1955	1961	Middle East	Crisis	Agreement Jan. 61
86	Egypt (Suez War)	1956	1957	Middle East	War	Law for the regulation disputes 19.7.57
87	Morocco (West Sahara I)	1956	1976	Middle East	Latent conflict	Agreement 14.11.75
88	Morocco–Spain (attempt at expansion)	1957	1958	Middle East	Violent crisis	Treaty 7.4.58
89	Mauritania (independence I)	1957	1961	Middle East	Latent conflict	Treaty on solidarity
90	Egypt–Sudan (Wadi Halfa)	1958	1959	Middle East	Crisis	Agreement 8.11.59
91	Tunisia–Algeria (Sahara)	1961	1970	Middle East	Latent conflict	Recognition borders
92	Morocco–Mauritania	1961	1970	Middle East	Latent conflict	Treaty on solidarity

Table 5.10 Continued

No	Name	Start	End	Region	Intensity	Treaties
93	Morocco–Algeria (Tindouf I)	1963	1963	Middle East	Violent crisis	Bamako Agreement 30.10.63
94	Morocco–Algeria (Tindouf II)	1963	1970	Middle East	Latent conflict	Communiqué 27.5.70
95	Yemen PR–Oman (Dhofar uproar)	1963	1979	Middle East	Violent crisis	Agreement 1976
96	Morocco–Spain (Ifni)	1964	1969	Middle East	Latent conflict	Fez Treaty 5.1.69
97	FRG (Arab–German tensions)	1965	1972	Middle East	Latent conflict	Agreement with AL (diplomatic relations) 12.3.72
98	Egypt–Israel (confrontations)	1967	1973	Middle East	Violent crisis	Camp David 26.3.79
99	Yemen PR (borders)	1968	1973	Middle East	Violent crisis	Agreement 1972
100	Iran–Iraq (Shatt-al-Arab)	1969	1975	Middle East	Violent crisis	Algiers Treaty 1975
101	Jordan–Israel (Jordan water II)	1969	1976	Middle East	Violent crisis	Compromise agreement with US mediation
102	Iran–UAE I (islands)	1970	1971	Middle East	Crisis	Iran–Emir Agreement
103	Yemen AR–Yemen PR I	1972	1972	Middle East	Violent crisis	Tripoli Treaty 28.11.72
104	Libya–Malta	1973	1986	Middle East	Latent conflict	Agreement 10.11.86
105	Egypt–Libya	1977	1977	Middle East	Violent crisis	Agreement 14.11.78
106	Jordan–Israel (Jordan water III)	1977	1994	Middle East	Latent conflict	Peace treaty 26.10.94
107	Yemen PR–Yemen AR II	1978	1979	Middle East	Violent crisis	Kuwait Peace Conference 31.3.79
108	US–Iran (hostages)	1979	1981	Middle East	Violent crisis	Algiers Treaty 1975
109	Iran–Iraq I (Gulf War)	1980	1988	Middle East	War	(UN Security Council Res. 598)
110	Yemen PR–Oman (border)	1981	1992	Middle East	Crisis	Border agreement 1990
111	Turkey–Syria, Iraq (water)	1990	cont.	Middle East	Crisis	Syria–Iraq Agreement on Euphrates
112	Iraq–Kuwait VII	1991	1994	Middle East	Violent crisis	Recognition of Kuwait by Iraq 10.11.94
113	Canada–France (St Pierre and Miquelon)	1975	1992	North America	Latent conflict	Judicial decision 1992
114	Peru–Ecuador (Amazonas I)	1942	1960	South America	Latent conflict	Rio de Janeiro Protocol
115	Peru–Colombia (Torre Asyl)	1948	1954	South America	Latent conflict	Agreement on travels 1954
116	Colombia–Venezuela (Monjes Islands)	1952	cont.	South America	Latent conflict	Agreement 1980

No.	Dispute			Region		Agreement
117	United Kingdom–Argentina–Chile (Palmer)	1956	1958	South America	Latent conflict	
118	Antarctic	1956	1959	South America	Latent conflict	Antarctic Treaty 1.12.59
119	Argentina–Chile (Palena dispute)	1958	1966	South America	Latent conflict	Judicial decision 14.12.66
120	Argentina–Chile (Beagle I)	1958	1972	South America	Crisis	'Compromiso' 1972
121	Venezuela–British Guyana (Essequibo I)	1960	1970	South America	Crisis	Trinidad Protocol 1970
122	Bolivia–Peru–Chile (Tacna and Arica)	1964	cont.	South America	Latent conflict	Bolivia–Peru Treaty 3.8.93
123	Argentina–United Kingdom (Falklands I)	1965	1982	South America	Latent conflict	Communications Agreement 1971 UA
124	Argentina–Uruguay (Rio de la Plata)	1969	1973	South America	Crisis	Border agreement 19.11.73
125	US–Peru, Ecuador (tuna fish)	1969	1974	South America	Latent conflict	Convention on the Law the Sea 18.6.74
126	Argentina–Chile (Beagle III)	1978	1979	South America	Violent crisis	Montevideo Agreement
127	Argentina–Chile (Beagle IV)	1979	1985	South America	Crisis	Peace and Friendship Treaty
128	Argentina–United Kingdom (Falklands III)	1982	cont.	South America	Latent conflict	End of limits zone 1990
129	Ecuador–Peru (Amazonas III)	1995	cont.	South America	Latent conflict	Itamaraty Peace Declaration 17.2.95
130	Ethiopia–United Kingdom (Gadaduma I)	1947	1963	Sub-Saharan Africa	Latent conflict	Agreement June 1970
131	Ethiopia (Somalis)	1960	1961	Sub-Saharan Africa	Violent crisis	Monrovia Conference 1961, Agreement 1967
132	Mali–Mauritania (border)	1960	1963	Sub-Saharan Africa	Violent crisis	Kayes Agreement 18.2.63
133	Cameroon–Nigeria (Bakassi peninsula III)	1961	1981	Sub-Saharan Africa	Latent conflict	Sea border agreement 1975
134	Gabon–Congo (soccer revolt)	1962	1962	Sub-Saharan Africa	Violent crisis	Agreement
135	Somalia–Ethiopia (Ogaden I)	1962	1964	Sub-Saharan Africa	Violent crisis	Agreement 30.3.64

Table 5.10 Continued

No	Name	Start	End	Region	Intensity	Treaties
136	Benin–Niger (border)	1963	1965	Sub-Saharan Africa	Violent crisis	Agreement 15.6.65
137	Ethiopia–Kenya (Gadaduma II)	1963	1970	Sub-Saharan Africa	Latent conflict	Agreement June 1970
138	Ethiopia–Sudan (ELF)	1964	1965	Sub-Saharan Africa	Violent crisis	Agreement 26.6.66
139	Mozambique (independence)	1964	1975	Sub-Saharan Africa	War	Lusaka Agreement 1974
140	Ghana–Togo (territorial claims I)	1965	1965	Sub-Saharan Africa	Crisis	Agreement 12.6.60
141	Kenya (Shifta attack)	1965	1967	Sub-Saharan Africa	Violent crisis	Agreement with Somalia on borders 13.9.67
142	Rwanda–Burundi (Tutsi Terror)	1966	1967	Sub-Saharan Africa	Violent crisis	Agreement March 67
143	Mozambique (border)	1966	1974	Sub-Saharan Africa	Violent crisis	Cease-fire 7.9.74
144	Equatorial Guinea–Spain (flag removal)	1969	1969	Sub-Saharan Africa	Crisis	Agreement 10.3.69
145	Guinea (invasion)	1970	1974	Sub-Saharan Africa	Crisis	Agreement 30.5.72
146	Gabon–Equatorial Guinea (Corisco bay islands)	1972	1972	Sub-Saharan Africa	Violent crisis	Agreement 13.11.72
147	Uganda–Tanzania (invasion)	1972	1972	Sub-Saharan Africa	Violent crisis	Mogadishu Agreement 7.10.72
148	Burkina Faso (Upper Volta)–Mali (border I)	1974	1975	Sub-Saharan Africa	Violent crisis	Conakry 10.7.75
149	Uganda–Kenya (territorial claims)	1976	1977	Sub-Saharan Africa	Crisis	Communiqué 8.2.78

150	Angola (civil war II)	1976	1991	Sub-Saharan Africa	War	Bicesse Agreement 31.5.91
151	Namibia–South Africa (Walfishbay)	1977	1994	Sub-Saharan Africa	Latent conflict	Free-trade zone declaration 1.3.94
152	Mozambique (civil war; RENAMO)	1978	1994	Sub-Saharan Africa	War	Nkomati Treaty 1984, peace treaty Rome 4.10.92
153	Chad–Nigeria (islands in Chad Sea)	1983	1983	Sub-Saharan Africa	Latent conflict	Agreement 2.7.83
154	Zaire–Belgium	1989	1989	Sub-Saharan Africa	Latent conflict	Treaty 16.7.89

Table 5.11 Major cease-fire and armistice agreements in international conflicts

No.	Name	Start	End	Region	Intensity	Treaties
1	Korea II (Korean War)	1950	1953	Asia	War	Cease-fire 17.7.53
2	China–India (Aksai Chin)	1954	1962	Asia	Violent crisis	One-sided cease-fire of 21.11.62
3	China (Tachen islands)	1955	1955	Asia	Violent crisis	Agreement (islands) 12.2.55
4	Indochina Ib	1955	1973	Asia	War	Cease-fire 23.1.73
5	China–Taiwan (Quemoy II)	1958	1958	Asia	Violent crisis	Cease-fire of 8.10.58
6	Indochina II (Vietnam War)	1964	1973	Asia	War	Cease-fire 23.1.73
7	India XIV (Kashmir III)	1965	1965	Asia	Violent crisis	Mutual troop withdrawals of Jan. 1966
8	Laos–Thailand (border)	1975	1992	Asia	Crisis	Cease-fire 17.2.88; friendship treaty of 20.2.92
9	Honduras–Nicaragua (border I)	1957	1957	Central America	Violent crisis	Troops withdrawal 9.5.57
10	USSR/Russia–Moldavia (independence)	1988	cont.	Europe	Crisis	Troops withdrawal 23.12.94
11	France–Syria, Lebanon (Levant)	1945	1946	Middle East	Violent crisis	Plan for troops withdrawal of 4.3.46
12	Israel II (Palestine war)	1948	1949	Middle East	War	Cease-fire 1949
13	Morocco (French troops)	1956	1958	Middle East	Violent crisis	Troops withdrawal 15.6.58
14	Tunisia (Sakiet)	1958	1958	Middle East	Violent crisis	Troops withdrawal 17.6.58
15	Tunisia (Biserta)	1961	1963	Middle East	Violent crisis	Withdrawal of French troops 15.10.63
16	Egypt–Israel (6-day War)	1967	1967	Middle East	War	Cease-fire
17	Israel IV (Yom Kippur War)	1973	1973	Middle East	War	Troops withdrawal 1974
18	Israel–Lebanon II (Litani operation)	1978	1978	Middle East	Crisis	One-sided cease-fire (ISR) of 21.3.78
19	Afghanistan II (Soviet intervention)	1979	1988	Middle East	War	Troops withdrawal USSR 14.4.88 Geneva
20	Israel–Lebanon III	1982	1985	Middle East	Violent crisis	Troops withdrawal 17.5.83
21	Bahrain–Qatar II (sea borders)	1986	1986	Middle East	Violent crisis	Troops withdrawal 1.5.86
22	Lebanon VIII	1989	1990	Middle East	War	Capitulation by Aoun 14.10.90
23	Iraq–Kuwait V (annexation)	1990	1991	Middle East	Violent crisis	Cease-fire of 6.4.91
24	Armenia–Azerbaijan (Nagorny-Karabakh II)	1991	1994	Middle East	War	Cease-fire 3.3.94

25	Armenia–Azerbaijan (Nagorny-Karabakh III)	1994	cont.	Middle East	Crisis	Cease-fire 3.3.94
26	Ecuador–Peru (Amazonas II)	1981	1981	South America	War	Troop withdrawal 1981
27	Argentina–United Kingdom (Falklands II)	1982	1982	South America	War	Cease-fire
28	Zaire–Belgium (Belgian intervention)	1960	1960	Sub-Saharan Africa	War	Withdrawal of British troops by Nov. 1960
29	Ethiopia–Somalia (Shifta)	1964	1964	Sub-Saharan Africa	Violent crisis	Cease-fire of 30.3.64
30	Burkina Faso–Mali (border II)	1985	1985	Sub-Saharan Africa	Violent crisis	Cease-fire 29.12.85

Table 5.12 Declarations of independence and separation

No.	Name	Start	end	Region	Intensity	Treaties
1	India I (independence)	1942	1947	Asia	Violent crisis	Indian Independence Act 15.8.47
2	Indonesia (independence)	1945	1949	Asia	War	Independence 1949
3	Korea I	1947	1950	Asia	Violent crisis	Declaration of independence
4	Malaya (independence)	1948	1960	Asia	War	Declaration of independence 31.8.57
5	Cambodia I	1968	1970	Asia	Crisis	Proclamation of Republic 9.10.70
6	Pakistan (Bangladesh II)	1971	1971	Asia	Violent crisis	Bangladesh independence Dec. 1971
7	Indonesia–FRETILIN (East Timor II)	1975	1976	Asia	Violent crisis	Annexation by Indonesia 17.7.76
8	Vanuatu (independence)	1980	1980	Asia	Latent conflict	Independence 30.7.80
9	Guatemala–Belize I (UK)	1960	1977	Central America	Crisis	Independence 21.9.81
10	Italy (South Tyrol)	1960	1992	Europe	Latent conflict	Partial agreement of autonomy 1969, 1971 (ratification 1988); agreement with Austria 1992
11	USSR (Ukraine independence)	1989	1991	Europe	Latent conflict	Declaration of independence 24.8.91; referendum on independence 1.12.91
12	Morocco (independence)	1944	1956	Middle East	War	Independence 5.6.56
13	Israel I (independence)	1946	1948	Middle East	Violent crisis	Proclamation of Israel 14.5.48
14	Libya (Cyrenaica)	1949	1951	Middle East	Latent conflict	Independence 24.12.51
15	Tunisia (independence)	1950	1956	Middle East	Violent crisis	Independence 20.3.56
16	Sudan (independence II)	1953	1955	Middle East	Violent crisis	Independence 17.12.55
17	Algeria (independence II)	1954	1962	Middle East	War	Evian 18.3., independence 3.7.62
18	Syria–Egypt (end of VAR)	1961	1961	Middle East	Crisis	Intl. recognition of Syria 30.9–6.10.61
19	Iraq–Kuwait I (independence)	1961	1963	Middle East	Crisis	Declaration of independence 19.6.61
20	Yemen PR (independence)	1965	1967	Middle East	Violent crisis	Independence 30.11.67
21	Iran–United Kingdom (Bahrain independence)	1970	1971	Middle East	Latent conflict	Declaration of independence 14.8.71
22	Afghanistan III (civil war II)	1988	1991	Middle East	War	Islamic Republic proclamation 28.4.92
23	British Guyana (independence)	1953	1966	South America	Violent crisis	Independence 26.5.66

No.	Name	Start	End	Region / Conflict type	Description
24	Togo (independence)	1947	1957	Sub-Saharan Africa Latent conflict	Independence 27.4.60 plebiscite 9.5.56
25	Malagasy Republic (independence)	1947	1960	Sub-Saharan Africa War	Proclamation of independence 28.6.60
26	Kenya (independence, Mau Mau)	1952	1956	Sub-Saharan Africa War	Declaration of independence Kenya 12.12.63
27	Cameroon (independence)	1955	1967	Sub-Saharan Africa Violent crisis	Proclamation of Republic Cameroon 2.6.72
28	Malawi (independence)	1959	1964	Sub-Saharan Africa Violent crisis	Independence 6.7.64
29	Mali–Senegal (federation)	1960	1960	Sub-Saharan Africa Crisis	Recognition of Mali and Senegal by US and FRG 24.9.60
30	Botswana, Lesotho, Swaziland	1960	1968	Sub-Saharan Africa Latent conflict	Independence: Les. 4.10.66 Bot. 30.9.66 Swa. 6.9.68
31	Angola (independence)	1961	1974	Sub-Saharan Africa War	Agreement of Alvor 1975
32	Zanzibar (massacre)	1963	1964	Sub-Saharan Africa Violent crisis	Proclamation of People's Republic 18.1.64
33	Guinea-Bissau–Portugal (independence)	1963	1974	Sub-Saharan Africa Violent crisis	Independence 26.8.74
34	Djibouti (Afars–Issas I)	1963	1977	Sub-Saharan Africa Latent conflict	Declaration of independence of 27.6.77
35	Angola (civil war I)	1975	1976	Sub-Saharan Africa War	Recognition of PR Angola 1976

Table 5.13 Arbitration and judicial settlements of conflicts

No.	Name	Start	end	Region	Intensity	Treaties
1	Liechtenstein–Guatemala	1955	1955	Central America	Latent conflict	ICJ decision 1955
2	Honduras–Nicaragua (border II)	1957	1961	Central America	Latent conflict	ICJ decision Nov. 60
3	El Salvador–Honduras (border)	1980	1992	Central America	Latent conflict	ICJ decision 11.9.92
4	Albania–United Kingdom (Corfu)	1946	1949	Europe	Crisis	ICJ 9.4.49, 25.12.49
5	United Kingdom–Norway (fishery dispute)	1948	1951	Europe	Latent conflict	ICJ decision 18.12.51
6	France–United Kingdom (Minquiers and Ecrehouse)	1951	1953	Europe	Latent conflict	ICJ judicial decision 17.11.53
7	Netherlands–Belgium (border)	1957	1959	Europe	Latent conflict	ICJ decision 20.6.59
8	Syria–Lebanon	1949	1949	Middle East	Crisis	Arbitration
9	Tunisia–Libya	1976	1988	Middle East	Latent conflict	ICJ decision 1982 and 1985
10	Canada–US (Gulf of Maine)	1981	1984	North America	Latent conflict	ICJ decision 1984
11	Argentina–Chile (Beagle II)	1972	1977	South America	Latent conflict	Arbitration 2.5.77
12	Chile–Argentina (Campo de Hielo)	1985	1994	South America	Latent conflict	Judicial decision Oct. 1994
13	Libya–Chad	1973	1994	Sub-Saharan Africa	Crisis	ICJ decision 3.2.94; friendship treaty 4.6.94

Table 5.14 Constitutional changes and conflict resolution

No.	Name	Start	End	Region	Intensity	Treaties
1	India II (partition)	1942	1948	Asia	War	Indian Independence Act
2	Nepal I	1950	1951	Asia	Crisis	Constitutional monarchy 1951
3	India X (Nagas)	1950	1964	Asia	Violent crisis	Proclamation of 16th federal state
4	North Vietnam (land reform)	1956	1960	Asia	Crisis	New constitution 1960
5	Nepal III	1960	1960	Asia	Violent crisis	Change of government 27.12.60
6	India XIII (Mizo)	1964	1972	Asia	Crisis	Partial autonomy 21.1.72
7	China (cultural revolution)	1969	1969	Asia	Violent crisis	Constitutional revision 1975
8	Sri Lanka (Ceylon) (uproar)	1971	1971	Asia	Violent crisis	New constitution 1972
9	Papua New Guinea (Papua)	1975	1975	Asia	Crisis	New constitution 15.8.75
10	Papua New Guinea (Bougainville I)	1975	1977	Asia	Crisis	New constitution 15.8.75
11	Philippines (Aquino–Marcos)	1984	1986	Asia	Violent crisis	New constitution 2.2.87
12	Nepal IV	1987	cont.	Asia	Crisis	Constitution of 9.11.90
13	Thailand (democratization)	1991	1992	Asia	Crisis	Constitutional revision of 10.6.92
14	Costa Rica (opposition)	1948	1948	Central America	Violent crisis	New constitution of Dec. 1948
15	Puerto Rico–US (status I)	1950	1952	Central America	Latent conflict	Constitution 25.7.52
16	Guatemala I (intervention)	1954	1954	Central America	Violent crisis	Referendum of Oct. 1954
17	Haiti I	1956	1959	Central America	Crisis	Government Duvalier 22.9.57
18	Cuba (revolution)	1956	1959	Central America	War	Interim constitution of 14.2.59
19	Dominican Republic I	1959	1962	Central America	Violent crisis	Regime change (state council) 19.1.62
20	Puerto Rico–US (status II)	1962	1993	Central America	Latent conflict	Referenda of 23.7.67 and 14.11.93
21	Nicaragua I (revolution)	1977	1979	Central America	War	New constitution
22	US–Grenada	1983	1983	Central America	Violent crisis	Interim government of 9.11.83
23	Haiti V (military government vs. President Aristide)	1991	1994	Central America	Violent crisis	Regime change Sept. 1994
24	CSSR (communism)	1948	1948	Europe	Crisis	New constitution of May 1948
25	Hungary (revolt)	1956	1957	Europe	Violent crisis	New constitution of Aug. 1949
26	Greece (democratization)	1967	1975	Europe	Crisis	Restoration of constitution

Table 5.14 Continued

No.	Name	Start	End	Region	Intensity	Treaties
27	Portugal (democratization)	1973	1983	Europe	Crisis	Constitutional reform 1982
28	Spain (democratization)	1975	1982	Europe	Crisis	Constitution of 27.12.78
29	Hungary (democratization)	1983	1990	Europe	Latent conflict	Interim constitution 18.10.89
30	USSR (perestroika)	1985	1991	Europe	Latent conflict	New constitution 1985
31	CSFR (democratization)	1989	1990	Europe	Crisis	Regime change 10.12.90
32	Romania (revolt)	1989	1991	Europe	Violent crisis	New constitution 21.11.91
33	CSFR (division)	1990	1993	Europe	Crisis	Decision on separation of 25.11.92 for 1.1.93
34	Russian Federation (Tartastan)	1992	1994	Europe	Crisis	Agreement on competencies 15.2.94
35	Algeria (independence I)	1945	1946	Middle East	Violent crisis	Algeria statute 1947
36	Lebanon II	1975	1976	Middle East	War	Constitutional draft
37	Iran (Islamic revolution I)	1978	1979	Middle East	Violent crisis	Referendum on constitution 2.12.79
38	Iran (Islamic revolution II)	1979	1981	Middle East	Violent crisis	New constitution
39	Lebanon VI	1982	1984	Middle East	War	Government 'of national unity,' of 4.4.84
40	Sudan (civil war II)	1983	1988	Middle East	War	Interim Charter 16.11.88
41	Yemen PR–Yemen AR (unification) I	1986	1990	Middle East	Latent conflict	Constitution 15/16.5.91
42	Algeria (October uprisings)	1988	1989	Middle East	Violent crisis	Constitution (referendum) 23.2.89
43	Yemen (unification) II	1991	cont.	Middle East	Violent crisis	Conciliation Agreement, 1994
44	Morocco (Western Sahara IV)	1992	cont.	Middle East	Violent crisis	UN referendum (scheduled)
45	Yemen (70-Days War)	1994	1994	Middle East	War	Constitution 28.9.94
46	Bolivia (teachers' strike)	1946	1952	South America	Violent crisis	New government of 12.4.52
47	Argentina (Montoneros)	1969	1977	South America	War	Agreement of 21.12.77
48	Argentina (consequences of Falklands defeat)	1982	1986	South America	Crisis	Constitutional changes
49	Brazil (constitution)	1986	1986	South America	Latent conflict	New constitution
50	Eritrea I (annexation)	1946	1952	Sub-Saharan Africa	Violent crisis	New constitution 12.8.52

51	Rhodesia (constitution 1961)	1961 1965	Sub-Saharan Africa	Latent conflict	New constitution
52	Chad I	1966 1975	Sub-Saharan Africa	War	Military government 13.4.75
53	Eritrea III (civil war)	1967 1993	Sub-Saharan Africa	War	Referendum for independence 25.4.93
54	South Africa (ANC, PAC)	1976 1994	Sub-Saharan Africa	Violent crisis	Interim constitution Nov. 1993; elections 9.5.94
55	Ethiopia (Oromo)	1977 1991	Sub-Saharan Africa	Violent crisis	Provisionary government EPRDF 1.6.91
56	Zaire (autonomy Shaba IV)	1991 cont.	Sub-Saharan Africa	Crisis	Provisional constitution 8.4.94
57	Burundi III (civil war)	1993 cont.	Sub-Saharan Africa	War	Government convention 10.9.94

Table 5.15 Cease-fires in internal conflicts

No.	Name	Start	end	Region	Intensity	Treaties
1	India IV (Kashmir I)	1947	1949	Asia	War	Cease-fire agreement 1.1.49
2	Laos II (civil war)	1963	1975	Asia	War	Cease-fire 1973
3	Philippines (uproar of National Front)	1968	cont.	Asia	Violent crisis	Cease-fire 1986
4	Cambodia II	1970	1975	Asia	War	Cease-fire April 1975
5	Guatemala III	1980	cont.	Central America	Violent crisis	Cease-fire 1995
6	Cyprus II (civil war)	1963	1964	Europe	Violent crisis	Cease-fire 9.8.64
7	Northern Ireland	1968	cont.	Europe	Violent crisis	Framework agreement 22.2.95
8	Georgia (Abchasia)	1989	cont.	Europe	Violent crisis	Cease-fire 4.4.94; new Constitution 26.11.94
9	Georgia (South Ossetia)	1991	cont.	Europe	Violent crisis	Cease-fire 28.6.92
10	Bosnia–Herzegovina (Serbs–Croats)	1992	1994	Europe	War	Cease-fire (Washington Agreement 1994)
11	Bosnia–Herzegovina (Muslims–Muslims (Bihac))	1993	1994	Europe	Violent crisis	Cease-fire 1.1.95
12	Jordan (Black September)	1970	1971	Middle East	Violent crisis	Cease-fire Syria–Jordan 27.9.71
13	Iraq (Kurds II)	1974	1975	Middle East	Violent crisis	Cease-fire 26.8.74
14	Lebanon III	1976	1976	Middle East	Violent crisis	Cease-fire 29.7.76
15	Lebanon V	1979	1982	Middle East	Violent crisis	Cease-fire
16	Morocco (Western Sahara III)	1979	1991	Middle East	Violent crisis	Cease-fire 6.9.91
17	Sudan (SPLA split-up)	1991	1994	Middle East	Violent crisis	Washington Agreement 21.10.93
18	Tajikistan (civil war II)	1992	1993	Middle East	War	Cease-fire of 17.9.94
19	Israel–Lebanon IV (Hizbollah vs. government)	1993	cont.	Middle East	Violent crisis	Cease-fire 93
20	Colombia (Guerilla III)	1978	1984	South America	Violent crisis	Cease-fire 84, amnesty 82
21	Sudan (autonomy for Southern region)	1955	1963	Sub-Saharan Africa	War	Cease-fire 1972; agreement of autonomy Agreement 14.10.79
22	Zaire (Shaba II)	1977	1977	Sub-Saharan Africa	Violent crisis	Agreement 30.7.78; 14.10.79
23	Zaire (Shaba III)	1978	1978	Sub-Saharan Africa	Violent crisis	Cease-fire 28.11.80
24	Chad III	1980	1980	Sub-Saharan Africa	War	Cease-fire 8.7.93
25	Senegal (Casamance)	1982	cont.	Sub-Saharan Africa	Violent crisis	Cease-fire 27.9.95 (fragile)
26	Angola (secession Cabinda)	1991	cont.	Sub-Saharan Africa	crisis	

Table 5.16 General treaties in internal conflicts

No.	Name	Start	End	Region	Intensity	Treaties
2	Laos I	1953	1961	Asia	Violent crisis	Geneva Agreement on Laos
3	Indonesia (Ulama movement in Aceh I)	1953	1961	Asia	Violent crisis	Special status for Aceh
4	China (Tibet III)	1959	1965	Asia	Violent crisis	Agreement of autonomy 9.9.65
8	India XIX (Ass I)	1983	1984	Asia	Violent crisis	Agreement 25.6.86
9	Sri Lanka (Tamils II)	1983	1987	Asia	War	Peace treaty 29.7.87
10	Sri Lanka (Tamils III)	1987	1995	Asia	War	India–Sri Lanka Agreement 87; change of regime Aug.–Nov. 1994
11	Costa Rica (exiled people)	1948	1949	Central America	Violent crisis	Friendship treaty 21.2.49
12	Nicaragua II (Contras)	1981	1990	Central America	War	Peace agreement 1990
13	El Salvador (civil war)	1981	1992	Central America	War	Peace agreement 16.1.92
14	Nicaragua III (Recontras)	1990	1994	Central America	Violent crisis	Peace treaty 16.4.94
15	Mexico (Chiapas)	1994	cont.	Central America	Violent crisis	Peace agreement 2.3.94 (fragile)
16	Hungary (communism)	1946	1949	Europe	Crisis	Military statute 27.5.57
17	Cyprus I (independence)	1954	1960	Europe	Violent crisis	Treaties of Zurich and London 1959
18	Cyprus III (crisis)	1967	1967	Europe	Crisis	Agreement 4.12.67
19	Poland (democratization)	1980	1990	Europe	Crisis	Round table negotiations April 89
20	USSR (Estonia, Latvia, Lithuania)	1986	1991	Europe	Crisis	Independence of Baltic states 6.9.91
21	GDR (democratization)	1989	1990	Europe	Crisis	Treaty July 1990
23	Georgia (Gamsachurdia)	1989	cont.	Europe	Violent crisis	Russia–Georgia peace treaty 3.2.94
24	USSR (attempt at *coup d'état*)	1991	1991	Europe	Violent crisis	Agreement of Alma-Ata 21.12.91
25	Bosnia–Herzegovina (re-conquest Krajina/Westslavonia)	1995	1995	Europe	War	Dayton Peace Agreement 24.11.95, Paris 14.12.95
26	Iraq (Kurds I)	1961	1970	Middle East	War	Agreement 11.3.70
27	Yemen AR (civil war II)	1962	1968	Middle East	War	Khartoum 31.8.67; constitution 28.12.70
28	Sudan (civil war I)	1963	1972	Middle East	War	Addis Ababa 27.2.72; constitution 14.4.73
29	Morocco (Western Sahara II)	1976	1979	Middle East	Violent crisis	Treaty Morocco–Polisario 5.8.79
30	Lebanon VII	1984	1989	Middle East	War	Agreement of Taif 22.10.89
31	Israel V (Intifada)	1987	1993	Middle East	Violent crisis	Oslo 11.9.93; Cairo 4.5.94
32	Lebanon (Shi'ite militia)	1988	1990	Middle East	War	Agreement 5.11.90
34	Lebanon IX (Fatah-militia)	1990	cont.	Middle East	Violent crisis	Informal agreement PLO–Lebanon

Table 5.16 Continued

No.	Name	Start	End	Region	Intensity	Treaties
35	Iraq (Kurds IV)	1991	cont.	Middle East	Violent crisis	Peace treaty 24.11.94
36	Afghanistan IV (civil war III)	1992	1993	Middle East	War	Agreement Mecca 7.3.93, Jalabad 7.5.93
37	Colombia (Violencia II)	1954	1957	South America	Violent crisis	Agreement 1957
38	Surinam ('jungle war')	1986	1992	South America	Violent crisis	Peace Agreement of Kourou 21.7.89
39	Zaire (Katanga secession (Shaba))	1960	1963	Sub-Saharan Africa	War	Kitona Agreement 21.12.61
40	Namibia II (SWAPO)	1966	1990	Sub-Saharan Africa	Violent crisis	Agreement of Brazzaville 1988
41	Rhodesia (civil war)	1972	1979	Sub-Saharan Africa	War	Lancaster House Agreement 1979
42	Chad II	1975	1979	Sub-Saharan Africa	War	Peace agreement 23.3.79
43	Ethiopia (Ogaden, WSLF)	1978	1988	Sub-Saharan Africa	Violent crisis	Peace agreement April 1988
44	Liberia (civil war)	1989	1995	Sub-Saharan Africa	War	Cotonou Agreement 25.7.93; Agreement of Accra 21.12.94; Agreement Abuja 19.8.95
45	Rwanda (civil war)	1990	1994	Sub-Saharan Africa	War	Arusha Agreement V. 4.8.93; cease-fire since 19.7.94
46	Niger (Tuareg II)	1990	1995	Sub-Saharan Africa	Violent crisis	Peace treaty 24.4.95
47	Mali (Tuareg III)	1990	cont.	Sub-Saharan Africa	Violent crisis	National pact 11.4.92; Peace agreement 11.11.94
48	Djibouti (Afar-Issas II)	1991	1994	Sub-Saharan Africa	Violent crisis	Peace agreement 26.12.94
49	Angola (civil war III)	1992	1994	Sub-Saharan Africa	Violent crisis	Peace treaty of Lusaka 20.11.94
50	Chad (autonomy Southern provinces)	1992	cont.	Sub-Saharan Africa	Violent crisis	Peace agreement 10.8.94
51	Congo (regime crisis)	1993	1995	Sub-Saharan Africa	Violent crisis	Peace Pact 24.12.95

6 Empirical findings
Summary and outlook

Our analysis of 661 peaceful and violent political conflicts in and among states has revealed major global trends and patterns since 1945. This chapter summarizes the results according to descriptive findings, generated hypotheses, validated theories and, finally, the challenges for conflict research.

Descriptive findings

General conflict trends

- The period after 1945 has witnessed more conflicts than any other period before. Yet, the number of new violent conflicts per year did not at all increase at the same rate that can be expected from the number of newly independent states per year.
- The overall number of new basic conflicts is decreasing.
- Between 1945 and 1992, the number of new conflicts was on average higher than the number of conflicts that have been resolved. Thus, the overall number of conflicts was rising.
- Since 1992, there has been a slight decrease in the number of ongoing conflicts per year. This is caused by a relative decline of new conflicts.
- The duration of conflicts is, on average, less than one year. Few conflicts last longer than eight or ten years.

Regional profile

- Most conflicts occurred in the Middle East, followed by sub-Saharan Africa and Asia.
- Relative to the number of states in a region, the Middle East and South America showed the highest frequencies of conflicts per state.
- North America and Europe show the lowest frequencies for violent conflicts.
- More than half of the conflicts occurred exclusively in or among developing countries with a high level of violence especially in internal conflicts.

- We identified 104 wars in the period between 1945 and 1995, most of them in sub-Saharan Africa, Asia and in the Middle East and Maghreb.
- More than two-thirds of all wars are multiple wars, i.e. wars that have escalated before.
- Between 1945 and 1995, between at least ten million (low estimate) and up to thirty million (high estimate) people lost their lives from direct or war-related violence.
- Domestic conflicts are bloodier than international conflicts.
- International conflicts remain abundant, but violent international conflicts are the exception. Since 1969, internal wars have become the dominant type of violent conflict. Since 1988, the overall number of non-violent and violent internal conflicts has become higher than this sum for international conflicts.

States and their political regime

- States remain the principal actors in international relations and in domestic conflicts. States remain the targets of complaint by non-state actors and the agent which has to comply with internal constitutional and international norms, rules and procedures.
- Very few states have participated in violent conflicts. The five permanent members of the Security Council rank highest in conflict participations.
- The number of potential actors in conflicts in and among states has quadrupled since 1945. In relation to the number of new conflicts for the same period, the increase in conflicts is rather moderate.
- Yet, in an increasing number of states, governments are losing central control over parts of their territory or their people. The partial or permanent re-privatization of violence is a new phenomenon which needs further systematic empirical inquiry.
- Authoritarian systems have been engaged more often in violent conflicts than democracies.
- Since 1945, democracies have fought no wars among themselves.
- Democracies have fewer internal conflicts than authoritarian regimes.

Issues in conflicts

- With the shift from international conflicts to domestic conflicts, we observe a shift of issues in conflicts. Internal conflicts are fought mostly over ethnic, religious or regional autonomy and over access to and the distribution of central power positions. Territorial conflicts remain the most frequent issue overall. In contrast to ethnic and power conflicts, territorial conflicts are by and large resolved by peaceful means.
- Conflicts that are carried out only over resources – compared with territorial, regional and power conflicts – are a rather rare phenomenon. Resources seem to be a background variable in many conflicts.

Conflict management

- International and regional security arrangements and organizations were founded after the Second World War to handle international violent conflicts caused by genuine aggressors like Hitler. Since then, the nature of political conflicts has changed completely. Still, without international organizations, violent conflicts would be more frequent and intensive, and would last longer.
- The drastic changes since 1945 in the number of actors and the dominant types of conflicts have been a challenge to international conflict management capacities. The principle of non-intervention in the internal affairs of states remains often an obstacle to effective early-warning and management activities. Our quantitative-empirical analysis of the actions of international and regional organizations has revealed an overall low turnout of successfully managed conflicts.
- Non-governmental organizations have gained importance in the fields of conflict management, mediation, preventive action and post-conflict peace consolidation.

Generating hypotheses

An important purpose of quantitative conflict research is the generation and testing of hypotheses. Here, we present central hypotheses from our studies and other, related works. Many of the following theses have been validated with KOSIMO data, other theses need further study.

General theses

- Democracies among themselves do not go to war ('OECD peace').
- Conflicts are more difficult to solve, when there are many differing economic, social, ethnic, religious, cultural, political variables (Pfetsch 1990: 104).
- Conflicts with more than one disputed issue have a higher frequency of violent escalations than single-issue conflicts (Billing 1992: 160).
- Conflicts are more difficult to resolve, the more aspects of national sovereignty are at stake (Pfetsch 1990: 104–5), i.e. territory/boundaries, national independence, leadership, demographic aspects, nationalities, ethnicities, security interests or welfare interests and resources.
- Domestic conflicts are more difficult to solve than international conflicts (Pfetsch 1990: 16).
- Ideological conflicts are more difficult to solve than other types of conflict (Pfetsch 1990: 105; Trautner 1997). Conflicts have a higher frequency of violence when opposing ideological positions are in dispute (Billing 1992: 164).
- International wars seem to have become a phenomenon of the past.

Instead, the privatization of violence or – using Holsti's term – 'wars of the third kind' are on the increase.

- The post-Cold War trends seem to indicate the continuation of non-violent resolution of conflicts among Western states, the settlement of most of the conflicts that emerged from the collapse of communist regimes, but degradation of some formerly minor ethno-political conflicts. In the South, we still observe a high frequency of internal and violent conflicts.

Actors in conflicts

- A conflict will escalate with an increase in the number of parties to the conflict (Billing 1992: 174).
- Conflicts that are rooted in the past and have engaged the parties for a long time are more difficult to solve than those which do not have such a burdened history (Trautner 1997).
- Conflicts are more difficult to solve, when there is nothing or little to win for all parties (Pfetsch 1990: 106). Conflict resolution requires an outcome that has something for everyone (Zartman 1985: 242).
- Conflicts have a higher chance of being solved, the more efforts are undertaken in due time at a propitious moment (Zartman 1985: 232; Pfetsch 1990: 106).

Political systems

- Conflicts initiated by democracies have a lower frequency of violent escalations than those initiated by other political systems due to a broader political participation of the people in democracies (Billing 1992: 159).
- Conflicts tend to escalate into violent conflicts when different political systems are parties to the conflict (Billing 1992: 165).
- Conflicts tend to escalate into violent conflicts when their political-economic status is different (Billing 1992: 166).
- Diplomatic or logistic support by neighboring states to the conflict parties leads to escalations. Neutral or containing behavior of neighboring states tends to de-escalate conflicts (Billing 1992: 168).
- Diplomatic or logistic support by a superpower leads to the escalation of a conflict, since the party has better access to resources for the continued pursuit of its interests. Neutral or containing behavior of the superpowers tends to de-escalate a conflict (Billing 1992: 170).
- Conflicts within the spheres of interest of the superpowers were contained by them. Conflicts outside of these spheres escalate more often (Billing 1992: 173).

Conflict resolution

- We may still be far away from a new conflict resolution culture; this would imply a change in foreign policy behavior of many states and a more influential role for international organizations. Still, there are signs of a civilizing process from within many societies and from above by the effects of a nascent global governance.
- The differentiation and codification of human, political, economic, social and cultural rights by the UN has helped their international acceptance and enforcement.
- A conflict must be 'ripe for resolution' (Zartman 1985: 232, 236). Thus, conflicts are likely to escalate to the point of a military stalemate or mutual exhaustion of the parties (Billing 1992: 175).
- If both parties find themselves in a stalemate, they are likely to negotiate an agreement (Zartman 1995: 334).
- Partial solutions may prevent an overall solution. Parties may agree on minor issues as long as they are not forced to agree on the basic conflict (Trautner 1997).
- A positive outcome is more likely in low-intensity conflicts (Frei 1976). Yet, this hypothesis is highly contradictory. It also can be said that the higher the intensity of a conflict and the higher the expected losses by the parties the more likely the parties will wish to resolve the conflict (Jackson 1972: 123).
- Conflicts are more difficult to solve, the fewer the institutionalized rules for the management of the conflict (Pfetsch 1990: 105). This argument has a multifaceted feature. It, foremost, refers to internal conflicts. A polity which possesses institutional arrangements for the channeling of disputes from bottom up and from top down is better equipped for peaceful solutions than one that reacts only with repressive measures. In other words, democratic regimes are internally more peaceful than authoritarian systems.
- If an agreement is not a compromise, the probability of a new conflict about the same issue is high (Trautner 1997: 77) or, in many cases: 'a war ends and the conflict goes on' (Pfetsch 1994).

Third parties

- Third parties should keep equidistance and should not be too closely related to either party (Pfetsch 1990: 107). Impartiality is a precondition to be accepted by all the participants. Equidistance does not, however, mean neutrality. Some kind of interest of the mediator is always given.
- To be successful a third party should possess bargaining power (Pfetsch 1990: 107). Effective mediation is a matter of resources not of impartiality (Bercovitch 1986: 160).

- The smaller the difference in power inequality, the greater the influence of a mediator (Liska 1962; Young 1967: 44). This coincides with the statement that in situations with clear imbalance, the stronger party will reject any compromise proposals (Lall 1966).
- The greater the economic interdependence of the conflicting parties, the greater the chances for successful mediation (Frei 1976: 73).
- Mediation has a better chance of success when the adversaries are recognized as the legitimate spokesmen for their parties (Bercovitch 1986: 160), and the more clearly defined and accepted the parties are and the less they are fragmented (Frei 1976: 73; Pfetsch 1990). A representative with weak support from his constituency cannot make concessions on foreign-policy issues.
- A mediator improves his chances when he manages to keep ideological elements out (Kelman 1965). A conflict is easier to resolve, the less the parties attach values to the objects in dispute (Randle 1973; Holsti 1967; Grewe 1964; 1970: 560).
- The process of settling a conflict is facilitated when there is more than one conflicting item; this allows for package deals or linkage (Pfetsch 1990).
- A deadlock in which neither party finds an acceptable way out is a favorable situation for the mediator (Zartman 1985).
- Mediation has a higher chance of success, the more the background powers are willing to cooperate (Pfetsch 1990). Since mediation is mostly done in international conflicts the behavior of external powers is decisive.
- Third parties have a higher chance to succeed when negotiations take place on a neutral side (Trautner 1997: 162).
- In the mediation process, powerful states are more likely to use manipulative means than less powerful states (Trautner 1997: 162).
- A third party from the same cultural realm has a higher chance to succeed than mediators assigned to the region, i.e. coming from an international organization (Trautner 1997: 324).
- Great powers mediate foremost on the basis of their own interests (Billing 1995: 321; Trautner 1997: 324).

The testing of theories

Democratic peace theory

This was the first theory to be tested. It states that democratic systems are more peaceful than dictatorial systems. Looking at the list of states that have been involved in conflicts since 1945, we see that the 'old democracies', the United Kingdom, the US and France, are on top. They are followed by the authoritarian states, the USSR and China. This evidence seems to contradict the theoretical postulate; it must be tested against a variety of conflict cases, and differentiated in interpretation and qualification according to types of conflicts and their intensity.

This argument, however, has also been applied to international disputes. Kant argued that Republican regimes are peaceful because, when asked, the individual does not want to go to war and will, therefore, not decide against his own interests. The assumption of this statement refers to a situation in which the individual member of a polity is asked whether it will go to war or not. Kant, therefore, refers to a fully democratic regime with participation by all its members. Many authors do not agree with the statement that democratic regimes are more peaceful in their external relations. Our data suggest that the regime character in general does not indicate the war proneness of a state. Democratic regimes have shown peaceful behavior only in their relations with other democracies, but not in their relations with other regime types (see descriptive findings above).

This does not necessarily contradict Kant's statement since the type of regime Kant had in mind did not exist before. Only in the more recent periods have democratic regimes shown more resistance to war. An example is the Vietnam war, which was stopped by internal opposition. The above-mentioned states are all dominant; some have been regarded as great powers for centuries. By definition, great powers are more engaged in global politics than less powerful states. The violent conflicts that were counted in our list are predominantly international or internationalized conflicts; here, great powers have more at stake than small powers.

The picture changes when we separate the participation of states by domestic and international conflicts, the political system of these states and the intensity of the conflicts. Now we can show that authoritarian systems have been engaged more often in violent conflicts than democracies; it is safe to say that, first, democracies among themselves have fought no wars; second, democracies, because of their international power position, have fought as many wars as authoritarian systems. Third, democracies seem to have a greater capacity to handle internal conflicts. Since democratic regimes are tied closer to the behavior of internal groups, even in international conflicts the regime character remains a determining factor (Rittberger 1987; Risse-Kappen 1994).

Aggressor theory

This theory can be falsified with our data. We have listed more than forty states without any conflict involvement and there are states or even regions of no-war zones. Most violent conflicts have been initiated by a very small number of states. In many conflicts, states have been initially challenged by opposition groups and not vice versa.

Weak-state theory

The weak-state theory (Holsti 1996) proposes that violent conflicts will more likely occur in weak states rather than in or among strong, authoritarian or legitimately governed states. Thus war-related studies should focus on the birth of states and the degree of legitimacy in the relation between the people and its rulers. By help of the state-conflict lists, we found that, on the whole, transitory regimes have been highly affected by conflicts. The examples of Lebanon, Somalia or Ethiopia may illustrate this theory. However, this theory does not give a satisfactory explanation for the zones of peace in and among South American countries. Other factors have to be taken into consideration such as long-time independence from colonial rule, stabilizing influence by the United States or a particular conflict culture.

Cold war theory

This can be tested by analyzing the encounters between the superpowers. During more than 40 years of the East–West conflict, there was no direct violent confrontation between the two giants. One reason for the avoidance of direct clashes of the superpowers could be their exhaustion after the Second World War. A stronger thesis proposes that nuclear deterrence kept the superpowers at a safe distance from each other. The effects of the end of the East–West conflict on violent conflicts were limited to those conflicts that were directly related to the dissolution of the communist block and to peripheral communist states in the Southern hemisphere, like Vietnam or Nicaragua.

Statistically, these conflicts are comparatively small in number when compared to those violent conflicts that started before the end of the East–West conflict. Also, based on our empirical findings, very few international conflicts during the East–West conflict can be interpreted as truly ideological wars for a better system. The same must be said for so-called wars-by-proxy; while often one superpower hampered one regime in opposition and rivalry against the other superpower's patronage of another regime, both superpowers were very sensitive to the possibility of serious escalations. In some cases, the superpowers even resided together on one side against both parties in a conflict, as in the Suez crisis against France and Great Britain.

Chaos or turbulence theory

This is the reverse of the Cold War theory. Since most violent conflicts were and are in areas outside the spheres of interest of the superpowers, we can deduce that the superpowers contained conflicts in their respective hemispheres, and, in consequence, the 'true nature' of the international system was still chaotic.

Issue theory

The issue theory assumes that the disputed issues influence the parties' conflict behavior. We can show that conflicts about ideology have led to more violence than conflicts about material or economic issues. This can be explained by the fact that economic goods are more open to negotiation and bargaining techniques. Environmental degradation as an issue by itself has not been coded, but it should be considered as an increasingly important issue in conflicts in the future (Rohloff 1998; Biermann, Rohloff and Petschel-Held 1998).

Clash of civilization theory

Our databank has not coded civilizations as labels to the parties in conflict for a test of this theory. However, some geographic regions that we used correspond to civilizational aggregates, e.g. Europe and North America belong to the Western civilization and most of the Middle East and Maghreb countries belong to the Islamic civilization. Our data hint at the fact that there have been at least as many clashes within the same civilization than between them.

Theory of liberal institutionalism

This tells us that institutions and international organizations and regimes strengthen the cooperative relations between states and make them more peaceful. By accepting the premises that the current world order is anarchic and in turbulence, there is need for liberal institutionalists to establish international regimes and institutions to give a framework for calculated action in a non-hierarchic structure. Norms and rules of behavior determine expectations of the actors, and by this, they stabilize the system. This produces a more durable frame of cooperative relations and, therefore, prevents aggressive confrontation.

For a test of this theory, our data show the high involvement of international organizations in international conflicts. Even if it is almost impossible to measure the success of these organizations, it can be deduced that without their functioning as a third party in conflict management and conflict resolution there would be much more violent conflict. As an example, NATO as a political defense alliance has certainly contributed to keeping peace between Turkey and Greece.

Ethno-political approaches

In these types of conflicts, we have observed a proportional increase of domestic conflicts and conflicts that involve ethnic, religious or regional autonomy. This issue has become the dominant cause for violent conflict today.

Conflict-ending theory

This says that the modalities of ending a conflict determine its further development. Only when a conflict is resolved by consensual agreement on all issues by all parties involved and without reservation, is there a realistic chance of a durable peace. This means that resolutions that are dictated by force or threat do not last; situations created by force will be revised as soon as circumstances allow a return to the status quo ante. Our data suggest the following conclusion: in more than two-thirds of all wars since 1945, this war was not the end to the conflict, but it induced another war.

Negotiated peace theory

This states that today the international community has more management instruments at its hands than during the state-centric system before 1945. One approach to prove the theory and to weigh the impact of the international community is to calculate the probability of conflicts in relation to the increase in the number of states entering the world state system after 1945. We have shown that the rate of conflict increase did not follow the rate of increase of states entering the world system. Also, what has been said earlier about the evolution of a new conflict resolution culture can support the theses. We have a slightly optimistic outlook on the future for an overall strengthened international conflict resolution capacity.

Predicting future conflicts

The application of theories and hypotheses to concrete cases, and the positive verification of their validity enable social scientists to take the risk of predictions. The analysis of data can give only partial answers to specific questions, since the causes and developments of conflicts are far too complex. The development from the beginning of a conflict to its end is affected by a multitude of structural, behavioral and interdependent variables. Therefore, on the one hand, it is possible to predict only the probabilities of alternative developments in the process of the conflict. Such predictions can only be made in an 'if-then' syntax. As an example, if the superpowers continue to cooperate, the international system of the northern hemisphere can function within a favorable framework. On the other hand, we can deduce some general conclusions from longer historical developments to future developments. Internal political conflicts, by experience, last longer than international conflicts; they are more violent and escalate easily. Since many of the civil wars in the Middle East and in other parts of the world have carried on over the years, and since they occur in an internally and externally highly complex environment, a sudden end of the hostilities is unlikely; even a cease-fire is no guarantee of a political settlement. The same is true for minority or nationality conflicts. For other conflicts, we can only hint at possible developments. Rivalries for power and dominance are often rooted in personal ambitions; therefore a reasonable prediction is hardly possible.

To a certain extent these results are useful for practical purposes, i.e. the foreign policy makers can be advised to strengthen democratic developments in the world or to make use of international organizations with their management capabilities in situations of conflicts. Conflict databanks such as KOSIMO may help to identify potential crises by pointing at high probabilities for a conflict escalation. The databank can also be the basis for a case-based reasoning method. By using a substantial number of conflicts, a machine-learning system can single out similar cases (Petrak *et al.* 1994).

Need for further research

The discussion of quantitative empirical research has led to various shortcomings which must be taken into consideration in further research. Further aspects of the reality of political conflict such as the personality and psychology of individuals and geographic or cultural characteristics have not been operationalized to a satisfactory extent in our project. Yet, in many cases, these factors have to be considered in order to explain certain developments and specifics of a conflict. For example, the most violent region in the world since 1945 is certainly the Middle East. A difference between this and other regions is its richness in crude oil. On the basis of our data, we could neither prove nor explain whether oil resources and high frequencies of violent conflict are actually related. A similar case is the 'big man' phenomenon in many developing states and its influence on conflict frequencies and violence. Long-serving statesmen such as Arafat for the Palestinian cause, Mubarak for Egypt or Mobutu for Zaire seemingly have more influence on the course of conflicts in their respective regions than factors such as 'political system' or 'behavior of neighbor states'. In this sense, KOSIMO is limited in its capacity to explain conflicts.

Still, the advantages of KOSIMO outweigh its limitations. The twenty-eight variables that were considered in the databank can be used in general support of psychological or cultural theses on conflict behavior. Also, knowledge of the frequencies of certain aspects of conflict over a fifty-year period may indicate important regional or global trends that by other means may have remained blurred.

The empirical evidence, especially for the years since 1989–90, unravels an increasing number of subnational conflict constellations in which the state is no longer the primary address for protest. Instead, rival societal groups, gangs, tribes, migrating peoples, organized or spontaneous formations of peoples enter into violent conflict among themselves. There are diminishing dividing lines between individual criminals, organized crime and political violence on a societal level. Instead, new, fragile and changing mixtures of potentially violent actors with quasi-political interests are rising and decomposing. These new forms of societal conflict will become a challenge in the future for systematic, empirical research. What is needed are adapted typologies and indicators that close the widening gap between traditional, criminal behavior based on non-political motives and societal group conflicts that are not addressed at the national level and in which the state is not directly involved as a conflict party.

From our analysis of old and new conflict patterns and the possible effects on a new conflict resolution culture, we suggest the following propositions for an extended research agenda:

- Strengthen the study of the impact of international and transnational private and official organizations on national foreign policies and conflict culture, and – as a consequence – the search for linkages between foreign policy analysis and international relations theory.
- Extend the categorization and analysis of new forms of violent conflict like the privatization of violence, and – as a consequence – the search for linkages between classical conflict research and theories on social movement.
- Shift from a dogmatic fixation of interstate conflict towards the inclusion of internal and subnational conflict constellations.
- Link research on political conflicts to negotiation theory in order to empower decision-makers with adequate instruments of conflict resolution.
- Finally, reconsider conventional basic terms and concepts of conflict research and keep adapting to ever-changing conflict patterns.

Appendix: KOSIMO conflicts 1945–95 by regions in chronological order

We have listed only five out of 28 variables. The current version of the entire databank with conflicts up to 1998 can be downloaded at http://www.kosimo.de

Note that the variable 'issue' is a basket category that can comprise more than the actually observed issues.

Sub–Saharan Africa

Name	Start	End	Issues	Intensity
Eritrea I (Annexation)	1946	1952	Ethnic, regional or religious autonomy	Severe crisis
India–South Africa (Apartheid)	1946	1959	Ideology, system	Latent conflict
Namibia I	1946	1966	Decolonization, national independence, territory, border, sea border	Latent conflict
Togo (independence)	1947	1957	Decolonization, national independence	Latent conflict
Malagasy Republic (independence)	1947	1960	Decolonization, national independence	War
Ethiopia–United Kingdom (Gadaduma I)	1947	1963	Territory, border, sea border	Latent conflict
Somalia–Ethiopia (border)	1950	1961	Territory, border, sea border	Severe crisis
Kenya (independence, Mau Mau)	1952	1956	Decolonization, national independence	War
Sudan (autonomy for Southern region)	1955	1963	National power	War
Cameroon (independence)	1955	1967	Decolonization, national independence	Severe crisis
Rwanda–Burundi (independence)	1958	1964	Ethnic, regional or religious autonomy, national power	Severe crisis
Malawi (independence)	1959	1964	Decolonization, national independence	Severe crisis
Ghana–Togo (Volta-Region I)	1960	1960	Territory, border, sea border, ethnic, regional or religious autonomy	Crisis
Mali–Senegal (federation)	1960	1960	Decolonization, national independence	Crisis
South Africa (Sharpeville)	1960	1960	Ideology, system, national power	Severe crisis
Zaire–Belgium (Belgian intervention)	1960	1960	National power, international power	War
Ethiopia (Somalis)	1960	1961	Territory, border, sea border	Severe crisis
Mali–Mauritania (border)	1960	1963	Territory, border, sea border	Severe crisis
Zaire (Katanga secession (Shaba))	1960	1963	Ethnic, regional or religious autonomy, ideology, system	War
Botswana, Lesotho, Swaziland	1960	1968	Decolonization, national independence	Latent conflict
Mali (Tuareg I)	1961	1964	National power	Severe crisis
Rhodesia (constitution 1961)	1961	1965	Decolonization, national independence, ideology, system	Latent conflict
Eritrea II (declaration of independence)	1961	1967	Decolonization, national independence	Severe crisis
Angola (independence)	1961	1974	Decolonization, national independence	War
Cameroon–Nigeria (Bakassi peninsula III)	1961	1981	Territory, border, sea border	Latent conflict
Gabon–Congo (soccer revolt)	1962	1962	Territory, border, sea border	Severe crisis
Somalia–Ethiopia (Ogaden I)	1962	1964	Territory, border, sea border	Severe crisis

Conflict	Year	Year	Issues	Outcome
Rwanda (Bugesera invasion)	1963	1964	Ethnic, regional or religious autonomy, national power	Severe crisis
Kenya–Somalia (Northern Frontier District)	1963	1964	Territory, border, sea border	Severe crisis
Zanzibar (massacre)	1963	1964	National power	Severe crisis
Benin–Niger (border)	1963	1965	Territory, border, sea border	Severe crisis
Kenya–Somalia (Shifta)	1963	1963	Territory, border, sea border	Severe crisis
Ethiopia–Kenya (Gadaduma II)	1963	1963	Territory, border, sea border	Latent conflict
Angola (border)	1963	1963	Territory, border, sea border	Severe crisis
Guinea-Bissau–Portugal (independence)	1963	1974	Decolonization, national independence	Severe crisis
Djibouti (Afars-Issas I)	1963	1977	Decolonization, national independence	Latent conflict
Ethiopia–Somalia (Shifta)	1964	1964	Ethnic, regional or religious autonomy	Severe crisis
Zaire (Stanleyville hostages)	1964	1964	National power, ethnic, regional or religious autonomy	Severe crisis
Ethiopia–Sudan (ELF)	1964	1964	Ethnic, regional or religious autonomy	Severe crisis
Niger–Ghana (Subversion)	1964	1965	International power	Crisis
Zaire (civil war)	1964	1965	Ethnic, regional or religious autonomy, national power	Severe crisis
Ghana–Upper Volta (border)	1964	1966	Territory, border, sea border	Latent conflict
Mozambique (independence)	1964	1975	Decolonization, national independence	War
Ghana–Togo (territorial claims I)	1965	1965	Others	Crisis
Ghana (francophone Africa)	1965	1966	Ideology, system	Latent conflict
Rhodesia (UDI)	1965	1966	Decolonization, national independence, international power	Severe crisis
Kenya (Shifta attack)	1965	1967	Ethnic, regional or religious autonomy	Severe crisis
Zambia–Rhodesia (border)	1965	1987	Territory, border, sea border, decolonization, national independence, ideology, system	Severe crisis
Ghana–Guinea (hostages)	1966	1966	Others	Crisis
Guinea-Ivory Coast (threat of invasion)	1966	1966	National power	Severe crisis
Rwanda–Burundi (Tutsi terror)	1966	1967	National power, ethnic, regional or religious autonomy	Severe crisis
Zaire (Katanga mercenaries)	1966	1967	National power	Severe crisis
Mozambique (border)	1966	1974	Territory, border, sea border, decolonization, national independence	Severe crisis
Chad I	1966	1975	National power	War
Namibia II (SWAPO)	1966	1990	Decolonization, national independence, ideology, system	Severe crisis
Guinea-Ivory Coast (hostages)	1967	1967	Ideology, system, international power	Latent conflict
Tanzania–Malawi (border)	1967	1967	Territory, border, sea border	Latent conflict
Nigeria (Biafra secession)	1967	1970	National power, ethnic, regional or religious autonomy, resources	War

Name	Start	End	Issues	Intensity
Eritrea III (civil war)	1967	1993	Ethnic, regional or religious autonomy	War
Equatorial Guinea–Spain (flag removal)	1969	1969	Decolonization, national independence, national power	Crisis
Zaire–PR Congo (claims of invasion attempts)	1969	1970	International power	Severe crisis
Portugal–Guinea (invasion Conakry)	1970	1970	National power	Severe crisis
Guinea (invasion)	1970	1974	National power	Crisis
Namibia (Caprivi)	1971	1971	Decolonization, national independence, international power	Severe crisis
Portugal–Zambia (economic sanctions)	1971	1971	Others	Latent conflict
Gabon–Equatorial Guinea (Corisco bay islands)	1972	1972	Territory, border, sea border, resources	Severe crisis
Uganda–Tanzania (invasion)	1972	1972	National power	Severe crisis
Burundi I (genocide)	1972	1973	National power	War
Rhodesia (civil war)	1972	1979	Decolonization, national independence	War
Rhodesia–Zambia (closure of border)	1973	1973	Decolonization, national independence, international power	Severe crisis
France–Malagasy Republic (Glorieuses Islands)	1973	1990	Territory, border, sea border	Latent conflict
Libya–Chad	1973	1994	Territory, border, sea border	Crisis
Burkina-Faso (Upper Volta)–Mali (border I)	1974	1975	Territory, border, sea border, resources	Severe crisis
Ethiopia ('red terror')	1974	1978	Ideology, system	Severe crisis
Ethiopia (Tigray)	1974	1991	Ethnic, regional or religious autonomy, national power	War
Angola (civil war I)	1975	1976	National power	War
Rhodesia–Mozambique (attempt at destabilization)	1975	1979	Decolonization, national independence, international power	Severe crisis
Chad II	1975	1979	National power	War
Mauritius–Malagasy Republic–France (Tromelin)	1976	Cont.	Territory, border, sea border	Latent conflict
Rhodesia (Nagomia attack)	1976	1976	National power, international power	Severe crisis
Rhodesia (Operation Thrasher)	1976	1976	National power, international power	Severe crisis
Uganda–Kenya (territorial claims)	1976	1977	Territory, border, sea border	Crisis
Somalia–Ethiopia (Ogaden II)	1976	1978	International power	War
Angola (civil war II)	1976	1991	National power, resources	War

Conflict	Begin	End	Items in dispute	Intensity
South Africa (ANC, PAC)	1976	1994	Ideology, system, national power	Severe crisis
Rhodesia (Mapai occupation)	1977	1977	Territory, border, sea border, national power, international power	Severe crisis
Rhodesia (Operation Tangent)	1977	1977	National power, international power, territory, border, sea border	Severe crisis
Sudan–Ethiopia	1977	1977	Territory, border, sea border, international power	Severe crisis
Zaire (Shaba II)	1977	1977	National power	Severe crisis
Rhodesia (Chimoio Tembue attacks)	1977	1978	Decolonization, national independence, international power	Severe crisis
Ethiopia (Oromo)	1977	1991	Ethnic, regional or religious autonomy, national power	Severe crisis
Namibia–South Africa (Walefishbay)	1977	1994	Territory, border, sea border	Latent conflict
Zaire (Shaba III)	1978	1978	National power	Severe crisis
Uganda–Tanzania (border war)	1978	1979	Territory, border, sea border, national power, international power	War
Ethiopia (Ogaden, WSLF)	1978	1988	Ethnic, regional or religious autonomy	Severe crisis
Mozambique (civil war; RENAMO)	1978	1994	National power, international power	War
Mauritius–United Kingdom (Diego Garcia)	1980	Cont.	Territory, border, sea border	Latent conflict
Chad III	1980	1980	National power	War
Zaire–Zambia I (Lake Mweru)	1980	1982	Territory, border, sea border	Severe crisis
Malawi–Zambia (Eastern Province)	1981	1986	Territory, border, sea border	Crisis
Uganda (Obote)	1981	1986	National power	Severe crisis
Cameroon–Nigeria (Bakassi peninsula I)	1981	1987	Territory, border, sea border	Crisis
Senegal (Casamance)	1982	Cont.	Ethnic, regional or religious autonomy	Severe crisis
Zimbabwe–South Africa (border incident)	1982	1982	Territory, border, sea border	Crisis
Chad IV	1982	1983	National power	Severe crisis
Zaire–Zambia II (Mweru Lake)	1982	1982	Territory, border, sea border	Latent conflict
Chad–Nigeria (Islands in Chad-Sea)	1983	1983	Territory, border, sea border	Latent conflict
Zimbabwe (Matabele massacre)	1983	1987	National power	Severe crisis
Chad V	1983	1990	National power	War
Burkina-Faso–Mali (border II)	1985	1985	Territory, border, sea border, resources	Severe crisis
Uganda–Kenya (border incidents)	1987	1987	Territory, border, sea border	Severe crisis
Burundi II (Hutu)	1988	1988	National power	War
Somalia (civil war I)	1988	1991	Ethnic, regional or religious autonomy, national power	War
Uganda–Kenya (border incidents)	1989	1989	Territory, border, sea border	Crisis
Zaire–Belgium	1989	1989	Others	Latent conflict
Mauritania–Senegal (tensions)	1989	1990	Territory, border, sea border, resources	Severe crisis

Name	Start	End	Issues	Intensity
Liberia (civil war)	1989	1995	National power, resources	War
Mali (Tuareg III)	1990	Cont.	Territory, border, sea border, ethnic, regional or religious autonomy	Severe crisis
Rwanda (civil war)	1990	1994	National power, resources	War
South Africa (ANC–Inkatha)	1990	1994	Ethnic, regional or religious autonomy	Severe crisis
Niger (Tuareg II)	1990	1995	Territory, border, sea border, ethnic, regional or religious autonomy	Severe crisis
Angola (secession Cabinda)	1991	Cont.	Territory, border, sea border, resources	Crisis
Ethiopia (Oromo II)	1991	Cont.	Ethnic, regional or religious autonomy, national power	Crisis
Sierra Leone (civil war)	1991	Cont.	National power, resources	War
Somalia (civil war II)	1991	Cont.	National power	War
Somalia (Somaliland secession)	1991	Cont.	Ethnic, regional or religious autonomy	Crisis
Chad VI	1991	Cont.	National power	Severe crisis
Zaire (regime crisis)	1991	Cont.	Ideology, system, national power	Severe crisis
Zaire (autonomy Shaba IV)	1991	Cont.	Ethnic, regional or religious autonomy, resources	Crisis
Djibouti (Afars–Issas II)	1991	1994	Ethnic, regional or religious autonomy, national power	Severe crisis
Togo (regime crisis)	1991	1994	Ideology, system, national power	Severe crisis
Kenya (Rift Valley)	1991	1995	National power, resources	Severe crisis
Sudan–Uganda	1992	Cont.	Ideology, system, international power	Severe crisis
Chad (autonomy Southern Provinces)	1992	Cont.	Ethnic, regional or religious autonomy, resources	Severe crisis
Angola (civil war III)	1992	1994	National power, resources	Severe crisis
Burundi III (civil war)	1993	Cont.	National power	War
Cameroon–Nigeria (Bakassi peninsula II)	1993	Cont.	Territory, border, sea border	Crisis
Nigeria (Ogoni)	1993	Cont.	Ethnic, regional or religious autonomy, resources	Severe crisis
Zanzibar (autonomy)	1993	Cont.	Ethnic, regional or religious autonomy	Crisis
Togo–Ghana (border violation)	1993	1994	Territory, border, sea border, ideology, system	Crisis
Congo (regime crisis)	1993	1995	National power	Severe crisis
Ethiopia (Ogaden II)	1994	Cont.	Ethnic, regional or religious autonomy	Crisis
Rwanda (Hutu refugees)	1994	Cont.	National power, resources	Severe crisis
Ghana (Konkomba)	1994	Cont.	Ethnic, regional or religious autonomy, resources	Severe crisis
Sudan–Eritrea	1994	Cont.	Ideology, system, national power	Crisis

Middle East and Maghreb

Morocco (independence)	1944	1956	Decolonization, national independence	War
Algeria (independence I)	1945	1946	Decolonization, national independence, international power	Severe crisis
France–Syria, Lebanon (Levant)	1945	1946	Decolonization, national independence	Severe crisis
Iran (Kurds I)	1945	1946	Decolonization, national independence, ethnic, religious or regional autonomy	Severe crisis
Iran–USSR (Azerbaijan)	1945	1946	Territory, border, sea border, national power, resources	Severe crisis
Turkey (Russian claims)	1945	1947	Territory, border, sea border, international power	Crisis
Israel I (independence)	1946	1948	Decolonization, national independence	Severe crisis
Sudan (independence I)	1946	1953	Decolonization, national independence, territory, border, sea border	Crisis
Afghanistan–Pakistan (Paschtunistan I)	1947	1963	Territory, border, sea border, international power, ethnic, religious or regional autonomy	Severe crisis
Yemen AR (civil war I)	1948	1948	National power	War
Israel II (Palestine war)	1948	1949	Territory, border, sea border, ethnic, religious or regional autonomy	War
Yemen–United Kingdom (Aden I)	1948	1963	Decolonization, national independence, territory, border, sea border	Severe crisis
Syria–Iraq	1949	1949	Ideology, system	Crisis
Syria–Lebanon	1949	1949	Others	Crisis
France–Egypt (status of foreigners)	1949	1950	Others	Latent conflict
Jordan–Arab States (Expansion West Bank)	1949	1950	Territory, border, sea border, international power	Crisis
Libya (Cyrenaica)	1949	1951	Decolonization, national independence	Latent conflict
Israel–Arab States (cease-fire)	1949	1956	Territory, border, sea border	Severe crisis
Saudi Arabia–Abu Dhabi (Buraimi I)	1949	1975	Territory, border, sea border, resources, international power	Crisis
Tunisia (independence)	1950	1956	Decolonization, national independence	Severe crisis
Saudi Arabia–Abu Dhabi (Buraimi II)	1951	1952	Territory, border, sea border	Severe crisis
Iran (oil nationalization, change of government)	1951	1953	Resources	Crisis
Egypt (1st Suez crisis)	1951	1954	Decolonization, national independence	Severe crisis
Sudan (independence II)	1953	1955	National power	Severe crisis
Algeria (independence II)	1954	1962	Decolonization, national independence	War

Name	Start	End	Issues	Intensity
Oman (Imam–Sultan conflict)	1954	1971	National power, resources	Severe crisis
Saudi Arabia–Abu Dhabi (Buraimi III)	1955	1955	Territory, border, sea border, international power, resources	Severe crisis
Turkey–Syria (border)	1955	1957	International power, ideology, system	Severe crisis
Iraq–Egypt, Syria (Baghdad Pact)	1955	1959	International power, ideology, system	Crisis
Tunisia–Egypt (Ben Yussuf)	1955	1961	International power	Crisis
Egypt (Suez war)	1956	1957	Territory, border, sea border, decolonization, national independence, international power	War
Jordan (Arab Legion)	1956	1957	National power	Severe crisis
Yemen–United Kingdom (Aden II)	1956	1958	Territory, border, sea border, decolonization, national independence	Severe crisis
Morocco (French troops)	1956	1958	Decolonization, national independence, international power	Severe crisis
Morocco (Western Sahara I)	1956	1976	Decolonization, national independence, international power, resources	Latent conflict
Tunisia (weapon sales)	1957	1957	Decolonization, national independence, international power	Crisis
Tunisia–France (Algerian border)	1957	1957	Decolonization, national independence	Severe crisis
Morocco–Spain (attempt at expansion)	1957	1958	Territory, border, sea border, decolonization, national independence	Severe crisis
Mauritania (independence I)	1957	1961	Decolonization, national independence	Latent conflict
Israel III (border)	1957	1967	Territory, border, sea border, international power	Severe crisis
Iraq–Jordan (Arab Federation)	1958	1958	Others	Latent conflict
Lebanon (1st civil war)	1958	1958	National power	Severe crisis
Tunisia (Remada)	1958	1958	International power	Severe crisis
Tunisia (Sakiet)	1958	1958	International power	Severe crisis
Egypt–Sudan (Wadi Halfa)	1958	1959	Territory, border, sea border	Crisis
Iraq (Mossul revolt)	1958	1959	National power, ideology, system	Severe crisis
UAR–Jordan	1959	1965	International power, others	Crisis
Jordan–Israel (Jordan water I)	1959	1967	Resources	Severe crisis
Morocco–Spain (Chute and Melissa)	1961	Cont.	Territory, border, sea border, decolonization, national independence	Latent conflict
Pakistan–Afghanistan (Bajaur)	1961	1961	Territory, border, sea border, international power	Severe crisis
Syria–Egypt (end of VAR)	1961	1961	Resources	Crisis

Case	Year	Year	Issues	Type
Iraq–Kuwait I (independence)	1961	1963	Territory, border, sea border, international power	Crisis
Tunisia (Biserta)	1961	1963	Decolonization, national independence, international power	Severe crisis
Iraq (Kurds I)	1961	1970	Ethnic, religious or regional autonomy	War
Morocco–Mauritania	1961	1970	Territory, border, sea border, international power	Latent conflict
Tunisia–Algeria (Sahara)	1961	1970	Territory, border, sea border	Latent conflict
Yemen AR (civil war II)	1962	1968	National power	War
Morocco–Algeria (Tindouf I)	1963	1963	Territory, border, sea border, resources	Severe crisis
Morocco–Algeria (Tindouf II)	1963	1970	Territory, border, sea border, resources	Latent conflict
Sudan (civil war I)	1963	1972	Ethnic, religious or regional autonomy, national power	War
Yemen PR–Oman (Dhofar uprising)	1963	1979	Decolonization, national independence, international power, national power	Severe crisis
Morocco–Spain (Ifni)	1964	1969	Territory, border, sea border, decolonization, national independence	Latent conflict
Saudi Arabia–Kuwait (islands)	1965	Cont.	Territory, border, sea border, resources	Latent conflict
Yemen PR (independence)	1965	1967	Decolonization, national independence	Severe crisis
FRG (Arab–German tensions)	1965	1972	Others	Latent conflict
Bahrain–Qatar I (sea borders)	1967	Cont.	Territory, border, sea border, resources	Latent conflict
Egypt–Israel (6-day war)	1967	1967	Territory, border, sea border, international power, resources	War
Egypt–Israel (confrontations)	1967	1973	Territory, border, sea border, international power	Severe crisis
Yemen PR (borders)	1968	1973	Territory, border, sea border	Severe crisis
Iraq (Shi'ites I)	1968	1978	Ideology, system, national power	Latent conflict
Iran–Iraq (Shat-al-Arab)	1969	1975	Territory, border, sea border	Severe crisis
Jordan–Israel (Jordan water II)	1969	1976	Resources	Severe crisis
Iran–United Kingdom (Bahrain independence)	1970	1971	International power, decolonization, national independence	Latent conflict
Iran–UAE I (islands)	1970	1971	Territory, border, sea border, resources	Crisis
Jordan (Black September)	1970	1971	National power	Severe crisis
Iran–UAE II (islands)	1971	1971	Territory, border, sea border, resources	Severe crisis
Yemen AR–Yemen PR I	1972	1972	Ideology, system	Severe crisis
Iraq–Kuwait II (border)	1973	1973	Ethnic, religious or regional autonomy, international power, resources	Severe crisis
Israel IV (Yom–Kippur war)	1973	1973	Territory, border, sea border, international power	War

Name	Start	End	Issues	Intensity
Afghanistan–Pakistan (Paschtunistan II)	1973	1978	Ethnic, religious or regional autonomy, decolonization, national independence, territory, border, sea border	Crisis
Libya–Malta	1973	1986	Territory, border, sea border, resources	Latent conflict
Libya–US I	1973	1989	International power	Severe crisis
Israel–Lebanon I	1974	1974	Territory, border, sea border	Severe crisis
Iraq (Kurds II)	1974	1975	Ethnic, religious or regional autonomy	Severe crisis
Iraq–Kuwait III (border)	1975	1975	Territory, border, sea border	Severe crisis
Lebanon I	1975	1975	National power	War
Lebanon II	1975	1976	National power	Severe crisis
Lebanon III	1976	1976	National power	Severe crisis
Lebanon IV	1976	1979	National power, resources	Severe crisis
Morocco (Western Sahara II)	1976	1979	Decolonization, national independence, international power	Latent conflict
Tunisia–Libya	1976	1988	Territory, border, sea border, resources	Severe crisis
Egypt–Libya	1977	1977	Ideology, system, territory, border, sea border	Latent conflict
Oman–UAE (territory)	1977	1981	Territory, border, sea border, resources	Latent conflict
Jordan–Israel (Jordan water III)	1977	1994	Resources	Latent conflict
Israel–Lebanon II (Litany operation)	1978	1978	Resources, ethnic, religious or regional autonomy, others	Crisis
Tunisia (uprisings)	1978	1978	Ideology, system, national power	Severe crisis
Afghanistan I (civil war I)	1978	1979	National power, ideology, system	Severe crisis
Iran (Islamic revolution I)	1978	1979	National power, international power	Severe crisis
Yemen PR–Yemen AR II	1978	1979	Ideology, system, resources, others	Severe crisis
Afghanistan–Pakistan (Paschtunistan III)	1978	1986	Ethnic, religious or regional autonomy	Crisis
Iran–UAE III (islands)	1979	Cont.	Territory, border, sea border, resources, international power	Latent conflict
Saudi Arabia (occupation of mosque)	1979	1979	National power, ethnic, religious or regional autonomy	Severe crisis
Iran (Islamic revolution II)	1979	1981	National power	Severe crisis
US–Iran (hostages)	1979	1981	Ideology, system, others	Severe crisis
Lebanon V	1979	1982	National power, resources	Severe crisis
Iraq (Kurds III)	1979	1986	Ethnic, religious or regional autonomy, national power	Severe crisis
Afghanistan II (Soviet intervention)	1979	1988	National power, ideology, system, international power	War
Iran (Kurds II)	1979	1988	Ethnic, religious, regional autonomy	Severe crisis
Iraq (Shi'ites II)	1979	1991	Ideology, system, national power	Crisis

Morocco (Western Sahara III)	1979	1991	Decolonization, national independence, international power	Severe crisis
Tunisia (Gafsa)	1980	1987	National power	Severe crisis
Iran–Iraq I (Gulf war)	1980	1988	Territory, border, sea border, ideology, system, international power	War
Iran (Islamic revolution III)	1981	1983	National power	Severe crisis
Yemen PR–Oman (border)	1981	1992	Territory, border, sea border	Crisis
Syria (February uprising in Hama)	1982	1982	National power	Severe crisis
Lebanon VI	1982	1984	Resources, national power, ethnic, religious or regional autonomy	War
Israel–Lebanon III	1982	1985	Others	Severe crisis
Sudan (civil war II)	1983	1988	National power, ethnic, religious or regional autonomy	War
Turkey (Kurds I)	1984	1989	Ethnic, religious or regional autonomy, ideology, system, decolonization, national independence	Severe crisis
Lebanon VII	1984	1989	National power, ethnic, religious or regional autonomy	War
Bahrain–Qatar II (sea borders)	1986	1986	Territory, border, sea border, resources	Severe crisis
Yemen PR (Aden civil war)	1986	1986	National power	War
Yemen PR–Yemen AR (unification) I	1986	1990	National power	Latent conflict
Bahrain–Qatar III (sea borders)	1986	1991	Territory, border, sea border, resources	Latent conflict
Iran–Saudi Arabia (pilgrims I)	1987	1987	Ethnic, religious or regional autonomy, ideology, system	Severe crisis
Israel V (Intifada)	1987	1993	Territory, border, sea border, ethnic, religious or regional autonomy, decolonization, national independence	Severe crisis
Egypt (Islamists vs. government)	1988	Cont.	National power, ideology, system	Severe crisis
Iran–Iraq II	1988	Cont.	Territory, border, sea border, ideology, system	Crisis
Iran–Saudi Arabia (pilgrims II)	1988	Cont.	Ideology, system, international power	Latent conflict
Algeria (October uprisings)	1988	1989	National power	Severe crisis
Lebanon (Shi'ite militia)	1988	1990	National power, ideology, system	War
Afghanistan III (civil war II)	1988	1991	National power, ideology, system	War
Turkey (Kurds II)	1989	Cont.	Ethnic, religious or regional autonomy, national power	War
Sudan (civil war III)	1989	Cont.	Ethnic, religious or regional autonomy, resources, national power	War
Lebanon VIII	1989	1990	National power	War
Algeria (Islamists vs. secularists I)	1989	1992	National power, ideology, system	Severe crisis
Qatar–Saudi Arabia (border)	1990	Cont.	Territory, border, sea border	Crisis

Name	Start	End	Issues	Intensity
Lebanon IX (FATAH militia)	1990	Cont.	International power, others	Severe crisis
Turkey–Syria, Iraq (water)	1990	Cont.	Resources	Crisis
Iraq–Kuwait IV	1990	1990	Territory, border, sea border, resources	Crisis
Iraq–Kuwait V (annexation)	1990	1991	Territory, border, sea border, resources, international power	Severe crisis
Iraq–Kuwait VI (US intervention)	1990	1991	Territory, border, sea border, resources, international power	War
Tajikistan (civil war I)	1990	1992	National power, ideology, system, ethnic, religious or regional autonomy	Severe crisis
Iraq (Kurds IV)	1991	Cont.	National power	Severe crisis
Iraq (Shi'ites III)	1991	Cont.	Ideology, system, national power	Severe crisis
Yemen (unification) II	1991	Cont.	National power, ideology, system	Severe crisis
Libya–US II	1991	Cont.	International power	Crisis
Armenia–Azerbaijan (Nagorny-Karabakh II)	1991	1994	Ethnic, religious or regional autonomy, decolonization, national independence	War
Iraq–Kuwait VII	1991	1994	Territory, border, sea border, international power, resources	Severe crisis
Sudan (SPLA split)	1991	1994	National power	Severe crisis
Algeria (Islamists vs. secularists II)	1992	Cont.	National power, ideology, system	Severe crisis
Iran (opposition)	1992	Cont.	National power	Severe crisis
Iran (Rushdie affair II)	1992	Cont.	Ideology, system, others	Latent conflict
Saudi Arabia–Yemen (border)	1992	Cont.	Territory, border, sea border, resources	Crisis
Morocco (Western Sahara IV)	1992	Cont.	Decolonization, national independence, international power	Severe crisis
Sudan–Egypt (border, Islamists)	1992	Cont.	Territory, border, sea border, resources	Severe crisis
Tajikistan (civil war III)	1992	Cont.	Ethnic, religious or regional autonomy	Latent conflict
Turkey–Russia (Bosporus)	1992	Cont.	Others	Severe crisis
Uzbekistan (student uprisings)	1992	1992	National power	Severe crisis
Afghanistan IV (civil war III)	1992	1993	National power, ethnic, religious or regional autonomy, ideology, system	War
Tajikistan (civil war II)	1992	1993	National power, ethnic, religious or regional autonomy	War
Afghanistan V (civil war IV)	1993	Cont.	National power, ethnic, religious or regional autonomy, ideology, system	War
Israel–Lebanon IV (Hizbollah vs. government)	1993	Cont.	Territory, border, sea border, ideology, system	Severe crisis

Armenia–Azerbaijan (Nagorny-Karabakh III)	1994	Cont.	Ethnic, religious or regional autonomy, decolonization, national independence	Crisis
Russia (oil exploitation Caspian Sea)	1994	Cont.	Territory, border, sea border, decolonization, national independence, international power, resources	Latent conflict
Yemen (70-days war)	1994	1994	National power, ideology, system	War
Eritrea–Yemen (Hanish Islands)	1995	Cont.	Territory, border, sea border, international power, resources	Crisis

Asia and Oceania

India I (independence)	1942	1947	Decolonization, national independence	Severe crisis
India II (partition)	1942	1948	Decolonization, national independence, ethnic, religious or regional autonomy	War
China (civil war)	1945	1949	Ideology, system	War
Indonesia (independence)	1945	1949	Decolonization, national independence	War
Mongolia (status)	1945	1950	Territory, border, sea border, international power, decolonization, national independence	Crisis
Indochina Ia	1945	1954	Decolonization, national independence, international power	War
Philippines (Luzon, HUK)	1945	1954	Ideology, system	Severe crisis
Japan–USSR/Russia (Kurils)	1945	Cont.	Territory, border, sea border	Latent conflict
China–Nationalist China	1947	1947	National power	Severe crisis
India III (Junagadh)	1947	1948	Territory, border, sea border, decolonization, national independence	Crisis
India IV (Kashmir I)	1947	1949	Decolonization, national independence, ethnic, religious or regional autonomy, territory, border, sea border	War
Korea I	1947	1950	Ideology, system, international power	Severe crisis
Indonesia (Darul Islam separation attempt)	1947	1991	Ethnic, religious or regional autonomy	Severe crisis
India V (Hyderabad)	1948	1948	Ethnic, religious or regional autonomy, national power	Severe crisis
India VI (Mahe)	1948	1954	Decolonization, national independence	Severe crisis
Burma–China (border)	1948	1960	Territory, border, sea border	Latent conflict
India VII (Indus channel)	1948	1960	Resources	Latent conflict
Malaya (independence)	1948	1960	Decolonization, national independence, ideology, system	War
Burma/Myanmar (minorities)	1948	Cont.	Ethnic, religious or regional autonomy, ideology, system	War

Name	Start	End	Issues	Intensity
Burma (Chinese troops)	1949	1961	Ideology, system	Severe crisis
India VIII (Kashmir II)	1949	1964	Territory, border, sea border	Severe crisis
China (Tibet I)	1950	1951	National power	Severe crisis
Nepal I	1950	1951	Ideology, system, national power	Crisis
Korea II (Korean War)	1950	1953	Ideology, system, national power, international power	War
Indonesia (West Irian I)	1950	1960	Territory, border, international power, resources	Crisis
India IX (Goa I)	1950	1961	Decolonization, national independence	Crisis
India X (Nagas)	1950	1964	Ethnic, religious or regional autonomy	Severe crisis
Indonesia (uprising in Southern Sulawesi)	1950	1965	National power	Severe crisis
Indonesia (South Moluccas)	1950	1965	Ethnic, religious or regional autonomy	War
Indonesia (Ulama movement in Aceh I)	1953	1961	Ethnic, religious or regional autonomy	Severe crisis
Laos I	1953	1961	Ideology, system, international power	Severe crisis
Thailand–Cambodia I (border)	1953	1991	Territory, border, sea border	Crisis
Korea III (partition)	1953	Cont.	Ideology, system, others	Latent conflict
China–Taiwan (Quemoy I)	1954	1954	Territory, border, sea border, ideology, system	Severe crisis
USSR–US (Chinese Sea, piracy)	1954	1954	Territory, border, sea border	Latent conflict
USSR–US (air-traffic incident)	1954	1954	Others	Latent conflict
China (Tibet II)	1954	1959	Ideology, system, ethnic, religious or regional autonomy	War
China–India (Aksai Chin)	1954	1962	Territory, border, sea border	Severe crisis
China (Tachen Islands)	1955	1955	Territory, border, sea border, ideology, system	Severe crisis
Indonesia (separation attempt II: PRRI rebels in Sumatra)	1955	1958	Ethnic, religious or regional autonomy	Severe crisis
Indochina Ib	1955	1973	Ideology, system, international power, others	War
China–Burma	1956	1956	Territory, border, sea border	Severe crisis
Sri Lanka (Ceylon, Tamils I)	1956	1958	Ethnic, religious or regional autonomy, ideology, system	Severe crisis
North Vietnam (land reform)	1956	1960	Ideology, system	Crisis
India XI (Rann of Kutch I)	1956	1964	Territory, border, sea border, decolonization, national independence	Severe crisis
Cambodia (border)	1956	1970	International power	Severe crisis
China–Taiwan (Quemoy II)	1958	1958	Territory, border, sea border, ideology, system	Severe crisis
USSR–US (Soviet airspace)	1958	1958	Others	Latent conflict

Crisis			Issues	Severity
Thailand–Cambodia II (border)	1958	1959	Territory, border, sea border	Crisis
Nepal II	1959	1961	Territory, border, sea border	Severe crisis
China (Tibet III)	1959	1965	Ethnic, religious or regional autonomy, ideology, system	Severe crisis
Nepal III	1960	1960	National power	Severe crisis
US–USSR (downing of RB-47)	1960	1960	Others	Crisis
US–USSR (U2 plane shooting)	1960	1960	Others	Crisis
Vietnam (civil war)	1960	1961	Ideology, system, national power	War
Indonesia (West Irian II)	1960	1969	Territory, border, sea border, international power, resources	Severe crisis
China–USSR (tensions)	1960	1991	Ideology, system, international power	Crisis
India XII (Goa II)	1961	1961	Decolonization, national independence	Severe crisis
Malaysia–Philippines	1961	1977	Territory, border, sea border	Latent conflict
Brunei (uprising)	1962	1962	Decolonization, national independence, national power	Severe crisis
Taiwan–China (invasion attempt)	1962	1962	Territory, border, sea border, ideology, system	Crisis
Laos–Thailand–US (Nam Tha crisis)	1962	1962	Ideology, system, international power	Crisis
China–India (war)	1962	1963	Territory, border, sea border	War
China–Pakistan–India (border)	1963	1963	Territory, border, sea border	Latent conflict
South Vietnam (Buddhists)	1963	1963	Ethnic, religious or regional autonomy, national power	Severe crisis
Malaya–Indonesia (Sarawak/Sabah)	1963	1966	Territory, border, sea border, national independence	War
Laos II (civil war)	1963	1975	Ideology, system, international power	War
China–India (border)	1963	1993	Territory, border, sea border	Latent conflict
India XIII (Mizo)	1964	1972	Ethnic, religious or regional autonomy	Crisis
Indochina II (Vietnam war)	1964	1973	Ideology, system, national power, international power	War
India XIV (Kashmir III)	1965	1965	Territory, border, sea border, decolonization, national independence	Severe crisis
India XV (Rann of Kutch II)	1965	1969	Territory, border, sea border, international power, resources	Severe crisis
India XVI (Kashmir IV)	1965	1970	Territory, border, sea border,	War
Thailand (communism)	1965	1980	Ideology, system, national power	Severe crisis
China–USSR (diplomats)	1966	1966	Ideology, system, international power	Latent conflict
Pakistan (Bangladesh I)	1966	1970	Ethnic, religious or regional autonomy	Crisis
North Korea–US (*Pueblo* incident)	1968	1968	Others	Crisis
Thailand–Cambodia III (border)	1968	1969	Territory, border, sea border	Severe crisis
Cambodia I	1968	1970	Ideology, system, national power	Crisis
Philippines (uprising of 'National Front')	1968	Cont.	National power	Severe crisis

Name	Start	End	Issues	Intensity
China (cultural revolution)	1969	1969	National power, ideology, system	Severe crisis
China–USSR (Ussuri conflict)	1969	1969	Territory, border, sea border	Severe crisis
North Vietnam (intervention Laos)	1969	1969	International power	Severe crisis
Indonesia (West Irian III)	1969	1982	Decolonization, national independence, ethnic, religious or regional autonomy, resources	Severe crisis
Cambodia II	1970	1975	Ideology, system, national power	War
Philippines (Moros in Mindanao and Sulu)	1970	Cont.	Decolonization, national independence, ethnic, religious or regional autonomy	Severe crisis
India XVII (Bangladesh III)	1971	1971	International power, decolonization, national independence	War
Pakistan (Bangladesh II)	1971	1971	Decolonization, national independence	Severe crisis
Sri Lanka (Ceylon) (uprising)	1971	1971	National power	Severe crisis
Bangladesh (Chittagong Hill Tracts)	1971	Cont.	Ethnic, religious or regional autonomy	Crisis
Pakistan (Belushistan)	1973	1976	Ethnic, religious or regional autonomy	Severe crisis
Indochina II (cease-fire)	1973	1976	Ideology, system, national power, others	War
China–Vietnam (Spratly I)	1974	1974	Territory, border, sea border, resources	Severe crisis
Indonesia (East Timor (civil war I))	1974	1975	Territory, border, sea border, decolonization, national independence	War
US–Cambodia (Mayaguez)	1975	1975	International power, territory, border, sea border	Crisis
Papua New Guinea (Papua)	1975	1975	Decolonization, national independence, ethnic, religious or regional autonomy	Crisis
Indonesia–FRETILIN (East Timor II)	1975	1976	Territory, border, sea border, decolonization, national independence, national power	Severe crisis
Papua New Guinea (Bougainville I)	1975	1977	Decolonization, national independence, ethnic, religious or regional autonomy, resources	Crisis
Bangladesh (Chakma, Marma)	1975	1987	Ethnic, religious or regional autonomy	Severe crisis
China–Vietnam (Spratly III)	1975	1987	Territory, border, sea border, resources	Latent conflict
Laos–Thailand (border)	1975	1992	Territory, border, sea border	Crisis
China–Laos	1975	1993	Territory, border, sea border	Latent conflict
Indonesia (East Timor III)	1976	Cont.	Decolonization, national independence, national power	War
Indochina IIIa	1977	1978	Territory, border, sea border, international power	War
Pakistan (civil war in Karachi)	1977	Cont.	Ideology, system	Severe crisis

Crisis/case	Onset	Termination	Issues		
Indochina IIIb	1978	1991	Ideology, system, national power, international power	War	War
China–Vietnam (war)	1979	1979	International power, territory, border, sea border	War	War
China–Vietnam (emigrants)	1979	1991	Territory, border, sea border, ideology, system	Crisis	Crisis
Vanuatu (attempt at secession)	1980	1980	Decolonization, national independence, ethnic, religious or regional autonomy	Severe crisis	Severe crisis
Vanuatu (independence)	1980	1980	Decolonization, national independence	Latent conflict	Latent conflict
Vanuatu–France	1981	1981	Others	Latent conflict	Latent conflict
India XVIII (Khalistan/Punjab)	1981	Cont.	Ethnic, religious or regional autonomy, decolonization, national independence	Severe crisis	Severe crisis
Indonesia (West Irian IV)	1982	Cont.	Decolonization, national independence, ethnic, religious or regional autonomy, resources	Crisis	Crisis
China–United Kingdom (Hong Kong)	1983	1984	Territory, border, sea border	Latent conflict	Latent conflict
India XIX (Assam I)	1983	1984	Ethnic, religious or regional autonomy, national power	Severe crisis	Severe crisis
Sri Lanka (Tamils II)	1983	1987	Ethnic, religious or regional autonomy	War	War
France (New Caledonia I)	1984	1985	Decolonization, national independence, resources	Crisis	Crisis
Philippines (Aquino–Marcos)	1984	1986	Ideology, system, national power, international power	Severe crisis	Severe crisis
New Zealand–US	1984	1990	International power, national power	Latent conflict	Latent conflict
India–Pakistan (Siachen glacier)	1984	1991	Territory, border, sea border	Severe crisis	Severe crisis
India XX (Ayodhya)	1984	Cont.	Ethnic, religious or regional autonomy	Severe crisis	Severe crisis
France (New Caledonia II)	1985	1988	Decolonization, national independence, national power, international power, resources	Crisis	Crisis
France (Tahiti uprisings)	1987	1987	Decolonization, national independence, national power, international power	Crisis	Crisis
Vanuatu–Australia	1987	1987	Others	Latent conflict	Latent conflict
Sri Lanka (Tamils III)	1987	1995	Ethnic, religious or regional autonomy, national power	War	War
China (Tibet IV)	1987	Cont.	Ethnic, religious or regional autonomy	Crisis	Crisis
India XXI (Assam II, Bodoland)	1987	Cont.	Ethnic, religious or regional autonomy, resources	Crisis	Crisis
Nepal IV	1987	Cont.	National power, ideology, system	Crisis	Crisis
France (New Caledonia III)	1988	1991	Decolonization, national independence, resources, international power, national power	Latent conflict	Latent conflict
Burma/Myanmar (democratization)	1988	Cont.	Ideology, system	Crisis	Crisis
Vietnam–China (Spratly II)	1988	Cont.	Territory, border, sea border, resources, international power	Crisis	Crisis

Name	Start	End	Issues	Intensity
India XXII (Kashmir V)	1988	Cont.	Territory, border, sea border, decolonization, national independence	Severe crisis
Papua New Guinea (Bougainville II)	1988	Cont.	Ethnic, religious or regional autonomy, resources	Severe crisis
China (student uprisings)	1989	1989	Ideology, system	Severe crisis
India–Nepal	1989	1990	International power, others	Crisis
China–Kazakhstan	1990	1993	Territory, border, sea border	Latent conflict
China–United Kingdom (status Hong Kong)	1990	Cont.	Decolonization, national independence	Latent conflict
Indonesia (GAM movement in Aceh II)	1990	Cont.	Decolonization, national independence	Severe crisis
Thailand (democratization)	1991	1992	Ideology, system	Crisis
North Korea–IAEA	1991	1994	International power, others	Crisis
Indochina IV (power struggle after peace treaty 1991)	1991	Cont.	National power	Severe crisis
China–Taiwan (Chinese maneuvers)	1993	Cont.	Territory, border, sea border, ideology, system	Latent conflict
France (Tahiti uprisings after atomic tests)	1995	1995	Ethnic, religious or regional autonomy	Latent conflict
Sri Lanka (Tamils IV)	1995	Cont.	Territory, border, sea border, national power, resources	War

Europe

Name	Start	End	Issues	Intensity
Greece (civil war I)	1944	1945	Ideology, system	Severe crisis
Poland (communism)	1945	1947	Ideology, system, national power	Crisis
Spain (guerilla)	1945	1950	Ideology, system, national power	Severe crisis
Yugoslavia–Italy (Trieste)	1945	1954	International power	Crisis
Austria (state treaty)	1945	1955	International power, decolonization, national independence	Latent conflict
GDR–FRG (division)	1945	1990	Territory, border, sea border, ideology, system, international power, national power	Latent conflict
USSR–Norway (Spitzbergen)	1945	1991	Territory, border, sea border, international power, resources	Latent conflict
Albania–United Kingdom (Corfu)	1946	1949	Territory, border, sea border, international power	Crisis
Greece (civil war II)	1946	1949	Ideology, system, international power	War
Hungary (communism)	1946	1949	Ideology, system, national power	Crisis
CSSR (communism)	1948	1948	Ideology, system, national power, international power	Crisis

Conflict	Year	Year	Issues	Severity
USSR–Finland I	1948	1948	International power	Crisis
GDR–FRG (Berlin I, blockade)	1948	1949	International power, ideology, system, territory, border, sea border	Crisis
Greece–Albania	1948	1949	Territory, border, sea border, ideology, system	Crisis
United Kingdom–Norway (fishery dispute)	1948	1951	Territory, border, sea border	Latent conflict
USSR–Yugoslavia	1948	1956	Ideology, system, international power	Crisis
Eastern Europe (human rights)	1949	1950	National power	Latent conflict
Netherlands–FRG (border)	1949	1963	Territory, border, sea border	Latent conflict
FRG–France (Saarland status)	1950	1957	Territory, border, sea border, resources	Latent conflict
France–United Kingdom (Minquiers and Ecrehouse)	1951	1953	Territory, border, sea border	Latent conflict
Hungary (C-47 plane shooting)	1951	1954	Territory, border, sea border	Latent conflict
USSR–Sweden (Catalina affair)	1952	1952	International power	Crisis
Eastern Europe (US interference)	1952	1953	Ideology, system	Latent conflict
Iceland–United Kingdom (fishery conflict I)	1952	1956	Territory, border, sea border, resources	Latent conflict
CSSR (air-traffic incident)	1953	1953	Others	Latent conflict
GDR (17 June 1953)	1953	1953	Ideology, system, international power	Crisis
Cyprus I (independence)	1954	1960	Decolonization, national independence	Severe crisis
Bulgaria (air-traffic incident)	1955	1955	Others	Crisis
Iceland (US troops)	1956	1956	Others, national power	Latent conflict
Poland (October uprisings)	1956	1956	Ideology, system, national power	Severe crisis
Hungary (revolt)	1956	1957	National power	Severe crisis
Netherlands–Belgium (border)	1957	1959	Territory, border, sea border	Latent conflict
GDR–FRG (Berlin II, status)	1958	1959	International power, ideology, system, territory, border, sea border	Crisis
Iceland–United Kingdom (fishery conflict II)	1958	1961	Territory, border, sea border, resources	Latent conflict
Spain (Basque autonomy)	1960	Cont.	Ethnic, religious or regional autonomy, ideology, system	Severe crisis
Albania–USSR (tensions)	1960	1991	Ideology, system	Latent conflict
Italy (South Tyrol)	1960	1992	Ethnic, religious or regional autonomy	Latent conflict
GDR–FRG (Berlin III, wall)	1961	1961	International power, territory, border, sea border	Crisis
USSR–Finland II (crisis)	1961	1961	International power	Crisis
Denmark–United Kingdom (fishery conflict)	1961	1964	Territory, border, sea border, resources	Latent conflict
Cyprus II (civil war)	1963	1964	Ethnic, religious or regional autonomy, national power	Severe crisis

Name	Start	End	Issues	Intensity
Spain–United Kingdom (Gibraltar)	1964	Cont.	Territory, border, sea border, decolonization, national independence, international power	Latent conflict
Turkey–Greece	1964	1965	Others	Latent conflict
USSR–Romania (tensions)	1964	1968	International power	Latent conflict
Cyprus III (crisis)	1967	1967	Ethnic, religious or regional autonomy, national power	Crisis
Greece (democratization)	1967	1975	Ideology, system	Crisis
Northern Ireland	1968	Cont.	Decolonization, national independence, ethnic, religious or regional autonomy	Severe crisis
CSSR (Prague spring)	1968	1968	Ideology, system, international power	Severe crisis
GDR–Denmark (border)	1969	1988	Territory, border, sea border	Latent conflict
Sweden–USSR (Baltic Sea)	1969	1988	Territory, border, sea border	Latent conflict
Iceland–United Kingdom (fishery conflict III)	1971	1973	Territory, border, sea border, resources	Crisis
Greece–Turkey (Aegean Sea I)	1973	1976	Territory, border, sea border, resources	Crisis
Portugal (democratization)	1973	1983	Ideology, system, national power	Crisis
Cyprus IV (Turkey invasion)	1974	1974	Ideology, system	War
France (Corsica)	1975	Cont.	Ethnic, religious or regional autonomy	Latent conflict
Cyprus V	1975	Cont.	Ethnic, religious or regional autonomy, territory, border, sea border	Latent conflict
Iceland–United Kingdom (fishery conflict IV)	1975	1976	Territory, border, sea border, resources	Latent conflict
Spain (democratization)	1975	1982	Ideology, system	Crisis
Poland–GDR (Stettin bay)	1977	1989	Territory, border, sea border	Latent conflict
Sweden–Denmark (Hesseloe)	1978	1984	Territory, border, sea border	Latent conflict
USSR (Volga Germans)	1979	1991	Ethnic, religious or regional autonomy	Latent conflict
Poland (democratization)	1980	1990	Ideology, system	Crisis
Hungary (democratization)	1983	1990	Ideology, system	Latent conflict
USSR (perestroika)	1985	1991	Ideology, system	Latent conflict
USSR (Estonia, Latvia, Lithuania)	1986	1991	Ethnic, religious or regional autonomy, decolonization, national independence, resources	Crisis
Greece–Turkey (Aegean Sea III)	1987	Cont.	Territory, border, sea border, resources	Crisis

Greece–Turkey (Aegean Sea II)	1987	1987	Territory, border, sea border, resources	Crisis
USSR (Nagorny-Karabakh I)	1987	1991	Ethnic, religious or regional autonomy, decolonization, national independence	Severe crisis
USSR (Krim Tatars)	1987	1991	Ethnic, religious or regional autonomy	Latent conflict
Yugoslavia (Serbia: Kosovo)	1988	Cont.	National power, ethnic, religious or regional autonomy, decolonization, national independence	Severe crisis
USSR/Russia–Moldavia (independence)	1988	Cont.	Ethnic, religious or regional autonomy, decolonization, national independence	Crisis
Georgia (Abchasia)	1989	Cont.	Ethnic, religious or regional autonomy, ideology, system, decolonization, national independence	Severe crisis
Georgia (Adcharia)	1989	Cont.	Ethnic, religious or regional autonomy	Crisis
Georgia (Gamsachurdia)	1989	Cont.	National power	Severe crisis
USSR (Uzbekistan)	1989	1989	Ethnic, religious or regional autonomy, decolonization, national independence	Severe crisis
CSFR (democratization)	1989	1990	Ideology, system	Crisis
GDR (democratization)	1989	1990	Ideology, system	Crisis
Albania (mass flights)	1989	1991	Ideology, system	Crisis
Iran–United Kingdom (Rushdie affair I)	1989	1991	Others	Crisis
Romania (revolt)	1989	1991	Ideology, system	Severe crisis
USSR (Karelia)	1989	1991	Ethnic, religious or regional autonomy, decolonization, national independence	Latent conflict
USSR (Nachizewan)	1989	1991	Ethnic, religious or regional autonomy, decolonization, national independence	Severe crisis
USSR (Ukraine independence)	1989	1991	Ethnic, religious or regional autonomy, decolonization, national independence	Latent conflict
USSR (Belorussia)	1989	1991	Ethnic, religious or regional autonomy	Latent conflict
Hungary–Slovakia (Gabchikowo power-plant)	1989	1994	Territory, border, sea border, resources	Crisis
Liechtenstein–Czech Republic–Slovakia (real estate)	1990	Cont.	Territory, border, sea border	Latent conflict
Romania (minorities)	1990	Cont.	Ethnic, religious or regional autonomy	Crisis
CSFR (division)	1990	1993	Decolonization, national independence	Crisis
Georgia (South Ossetia)	1991	Cont.	Ethnic, religious or regional autonomy, national power	Severe crisis
Yugoslavia (Serbia Sandchak)	1991	Cont.	Ethnic, religious or regional autonomy	Crisis

Name	Start	End	Issues	Intensity
Russian Federation (Ingushia–North Ossetia)	1991	Cont.	Territory, border, sea border, decolonization, national independence, ethnic, religious or regional autonomy, national power	Severe crisis
Russia (Chechnya)	1991	Cont.	Territory, border, sea border, decolonization, national independence	War
USSR (attempted *coup d'état*)	1991	1991	Ideology, system, national power	Severe crisis
Ukraine–Russian Federation (fleet, atomic weapons)	1991	1994	Territory, border, sea border, decolonization, national independence, national power, resources	Crisis
Croatia (occupation East Slavonia)	1991	1995	National power	War
Greece–Macedonia (name)	1991	1995	Others	Latent conflict
Russian Federation (attempted *coup d'état*)	1992	1993	National power	Severe crisis
Bosnia–Herzegovina (Serbs–Croats)	1992	1994	Territory, border, sea border, ethnic, religious or regional autonomy, national power	War
Bosnia–Herzegovina (Muslims–Croats)	1992	1994	Territory, border, sea border, national power	War
Russian Federation (Tartastan)	1992	1994	Territory, border, sea border, decolonization, national independence	Crisis
Iceland–Norway (fishery zones)	1993	Cont.	Territory, border, sea border, resources	Crisis
Bosnia–Herzegovina (Muslims–Muslims (Bihac))	1993	1994	Territory, border, sea border, ethnic, religious or regional autonomy, national power	Severe crisis
Bosnia–Herzegovina (re-conquest Krajina/West Slavonia	1995	1995	Territory, border, sea border, national power	War

The Americas

Peru–Ecuador (Amazon river I)	1942	1960	Territory, border, sea border	Latent conflict
Honduras–US (Swan island)	1945	1991	Territory, border, sea border	Latent conflict
Bolivia (teachers' strike)	1946	1952	Ideology, system	Severe crisis
Dominican Republic (invasion attempt)	1947	1947	Ideology, system	Crisis
Paraguay (*coup d'état*)	1947	1947	National power	War

Costa Rica (opposition)	1948	1948	National power	Severe crisis
Peru (APRA uproar 3.10.48)	1948	1948	Ideology, system, national power	Severe crisis
Chile–USSR (Russian wives)	1948	1949	Others	Latent conflict
Costa Rica (exiled people)	1948	1949	National power	Severe crisis
Colombia (Violencia I)	1948	1953	National power, ideology, system	War
Peru–Colombia (Torre Asyl)	1948	1954	Others	Latent conflict
Dominican Republic (LUPERON)	1949	1949	Ideology, system, others	Crisis
Haiti–Dominican Republic	1949	1950	Others	Crisis
Puerto Rico–US (status I)	1950	1952	Decolonization, national independence	Latent conflict
Dominican Republic–Cuba (sailors)	1951	1951	Others	Crisis
Colombia–Venezuela (Monjes islands)	1952	Cont.	Territory, border, sea border, resources	Latent conflict
British Guyana (independence)	1953	1966	Decolonization, national independence	Latent conflict
Guatemala I (intervention)	1954	1954	Ideology, system, international power	Severe crisis
Colombia (Violencia II)	1954	1957	Ideology, system, national power	Severe crisis
Liechtenstein–Guatemala	1955	1955	Others	Latent conflict
Nicaragua–Costa Rica (exiled people I)	1955	1956	Ideology, system, others	Severe crisis
Cuba–Dominican Republic	1956	1956	Ideology, system, others	Latent conflict
United Kingdom–Argentina–Chile (Palmer)	1956	1958	Territory, border, sea border	Latent conflict
Antarctic	1956	1959	Territory, border, sea border, resources	Latent conflict
Haiti I	1956	1959	National power	Crisis
Cuba (revolution)	1956	1959	Ideology, system	War
Honduras–Nicaragua (border I)	1957	1957	Territory, border, sea border, resources	Severe crisis
Honduras–Nicaragua (border II)	1957	1961	Territory, border, sea border, resources	Latent conflict
Guatemala–Mexico (Shrimp boat)	1958	1959	Territory, border, sea border, resources	Crisis
Paraguay (Argentine support for rebels)	1958	1961	Ideology, system	Crisis
Colombia (guerilla I)	1958	1962	Ideology, system	Severe crisis
Argentina–Chile (Palena dispute)	1958	1966	Territory, border, sea border	Latent conflict
Argentina–Chile (Beagle I)	1958	1972	Territory, border, sea border, resources	Crisis
Haiti II (exiled people)	1959	1959	Ideology, system	Crisis
Nicaragua (exiled people II)	1959	1959	National power	Crisis
Panama (revolutionaries)	1959	1959	National power	Crisis
Cuba–US	1959	1961	International power	Severe crisis
Dominican Republic I	1959	1962	Ideology, system, national power	Latent conflict
Cuba–US (Guantanamo)	1960	Cont.	Territory, border, sea border, international power	Crisis
Nicaragua (invasion attempt)	1960	1960	National power	

Name	Start	End	Issues	Intensity
Venezuela (guerilla)	1960	1969	Ideology, system	Severe crisis
Venezuela–British Guyana (Essequibo I)	1960	1970	Territory, border, sea border	Crisis
Guatemala II	1960	1972	Ideology, system	War
Guatemala–Belize I (UK)	1960	1977	Territory, border, sea border	Crisis
US–Cuba (bilateral relations)	1961	Cont.	International power	Latent conflict
Guatemala–Mexico	1961	1961	Others	Latent conflict
Cuba (Bay of Pigs)	1961	1961	Ideology, system	Severe crisis
Cuba ('Cuban Missile Crisis')	1962	1962	International power	Severe crisis
Bolivia–Chile (Lauca river)	1962	1964	Resources, territory, border, sea border	Crisis
Brazil–Paraguay (Parana)	1962	1985	Territory, border, sea border, resources	Latent conflict
Puerto Rico–US (status II)	1962	1993	Decolonization, national independence	Latent conflict
Dominican Republic–Haiti (April–May)	1963	1963	Ideology, system	Crisis
Haiti III (intervention August 1963)	1963	1963	Ideology, system	Severe crisis
Bolivia–Peru–Chile (Tacna and Arica)	1964	Cont.	Territory, border, sea border	Latent conflict
Panama (channel I)	1964	1967	Territory, border, sea border	Severe crisis
Colombia (guerilla II)	1964	1972	National power	Severe crisis
Uruguay (Tupamaros)	1964	1972	Ideology, system, national power	Severe crisis
Dominican Republic II (intervention)	1965	1965	International power, ideology, system	Severe crisis
Peru (guerilla)	1965	1966	Ideology, system	Severe crisis
Argentina–United Kingdom (Falklands I)	1965	1982	Territory, border, sea border	Latent conflict
Bolivia (Che Guevara 23.3.67–10.10.67)	1967	1967	Ideology, system	Severe crisis
Haiti IV (exiled people)	1968	1968	Ideology, system	Crisis
Honduras–El Salvador (soccer war I)	1969	1970	Others, territory, border, sea border	War
Argentina–Uruguay (Rio de la Plata)	1969	1973	Territory, border, sea border, resources	Crisis
US–Peru, Ecuador (Tuna)	1969	1974	Resources, territory, border, sea border	Latent conflict
Argentina (Montoneros)	1969	1977	Ideology, system	War
El Salvador–Honduras (soccer war II (aftermath))	1969	1980	Territory, border, sea border	Latent conflict
Panama (channel II)	1970	1979	Territory, border, sea border, international power	Latent conflict
Argentina–Chile (Beagle II)	1972	1977	Territory, border, sea border, others	Latent conflict
Guatemala–Belize II (UK)	1975	1975	Territory, border, sea border	Severe crisis
Canada–France (St Pierre and Miquelon)	1975	1992	Territory, border, sea border	Latent conflict
Nicaragua I (revolution)	1977	1979	Ideology, system	War

Conflict	Start	End	Issues	Status
Argentina–Chile (Beagle III)	1978	1979	Territory, border, sea border, resources	Severe crisis
Colombia (guerilla III)	1978	1984	Ideology, system	Severe crisis
Nicaragua–Colombia (San Andres Archipelago)	1979	Cont.	Territory, border, sea border	Latent conflict
Argentina–Chile (Beagle IV)	1979	1985	Territory, border, sea border, resources, international power	Crisis
Guatemala III	1980	Cont.	Ideology, system	War
Peru (Illuminated path)	1980	Cont.	Ideology, system	War
El Salvador–Honduras (border)	1980	1992	Territory, border, sea border	Latent conflict
Guatemala–Belize III	1981	Cont.	Territory, border, sea border	Latent conflict
Ecuador–Peru (Amazon River II)	1981	1981	Territory, border, sea border, resources	War
Canada–US (Gulf of Maine)	1981	1984	Territory, border, sea border, resources	Latent conflict
Nicaragua II (Contras)	1981	1990	Ideology, system, ethnic, religious or regional autonomy, international power	War
El Salvador (civil war)	1981	1992	Ideology, system	War
Argentina–United Kingdom (Falklands III)	1982	Cont.	Territory, border, sea border, resources	Latent conflict
Venezuela–Guyana (Essequibo II)	1982	Cont.	Territory, border, sea border	Latent conflict
Argentina–United Kingdom (Falklands II)	1982	1982	Territory, border, sea border, resources	War
Argentina (after Falklands defeat)	1982	1986	Ideology, system	Crisis
US–Grenada	1983	1983	International power	Severe crisis
Colombia (guerilla IV)	1985	Cont.	Ideology, system, national power	Severe crisis
Chile–Argentina (Campo de Hielo)	1985	1994	Territory, border, sea border	Latent conflict
Brazil (constitution)	1986	1986	Ideology, system	Latent conflict
Surinam I ('jungle-war')	1986	1992	Ideology, system, national power	Severe crisis
Colombia (drug cartel)	1989	Cont.	Others	Severe crisis
Panama (power struggle and US intervention)	1989	1990	National power	Severe crisis
Canada (secession attempt by Quebec)	1990	Cont.	Ethnic, religious or regional autonomy	Latent conflict
Nicaragua III (Recontras)	1990	1994	Ideology, system, national power	Severe crisis
Haiti V (military government vs. President Aristide)	1991	1994	Ideology, system, national power	Severe crisis
Cuba–US (refugees)	1993	Cont.	Others	Crisis
Mexico (Chiapas)	1994	Cont.	Ethnic, religious or regional autonomy	Severe crisis
Surinam II ('Toekayana')	1994	Cont.	Ethnic, religious or regional autonomy	Severe crisis
Ecuador–Peru (Amazon River III)	1995	Cont.	Territory, border, sea border, resources	Latent conflict

Notes

Preface

1   The Heidelberg Institute for International Conflict Research is a non-profit organization associated with the Institute of Political Science at the University of Heidelberg. The Institute publishes yearly *Konfliktbarometers* and links to the current version of the KOSIMO databank on its interactive Website at http://www.kosimo.de

Chapter 1

1   For a much longer time period Samuel P. Huntington (1991) refers to three waves of democratization. For a concise discussion of democratic transition and consolidation processes see Linz and Stepan (1996). Regime change is not always directed toward democratization but also toward authoritarianism (Huntington 1991, Pfetsch 1991).

2   The evolving field of negotiation theory is documented in the new journal *International Negotiation* (since 1996) and in books like Berton *et al.* (1999).

Chapter 2

1   There has by now been published a vast amount of literaure on the emergence, development and resolution of conflicts. It can be categorized into several groups, depending, for example, on the level of analysis the authors choose. Structural theories are placed on a macro level focusing internationally on discrepancies between states as actors in a conflict process and domestically on social strata or groups. On a micro level there are theories which focus on the decision-makers as individuals and their personal interests and values. On an intermediate level studies concentrate on the institutional frame which determines the role of the decision-makers and its impact on their decisions.

2   There are at least seven sources for the legitimization of a rule or regime:

- ethnicity, religion, cultural heritage as the constituting elements of group identity
- economic welfare: he who increases economic wealth is legitimated

- charismatic leadership or power politics, i.e. consensual or coercive personal capacities of political leaders which give support
- effective governance, bureaucracy performance, strategic thinking, efficient management of conflicts, effective use of the military
- through democratic processes: elections, plebiscite
- through the production of political outcomes, i.e. laws which become accepted
- through a constitution to which rules and norms politicians or citizens can refer to but the legality of constitutional law is only a source if the constitution is accepted, i.e. legitimized.

3   Databank projects from a survey at the Inter-university Consortium for Political and Social Research (ICPSR) at http://www.icpsr.umich.edu/
   International conflicts: Alker/Sherman: International conflict episodes 1945–1979 (1982), Azar, Sloan: Dimensions of interaction 1948–1973 (1975), Butterworth: Interstate security conflicts 1945–1974 (1976), Coplin/Rochester: Dyadic disputes 1920–1968 (n.a.), Feierabend/Feierabend/Chambers: Transactional databank of international conflict and amity events (1972), Huth, Gelpi, Bennett: Escalation of great power disputes: deterrence versus structural realism 1816–1984 (based on COW and Polity data, 1993), Huth/Bennett, Gelpi: Initiation of militarized disputes among great power rivals 1816–1975 (based on COW and Polity data 1993), Leng: Behavioral correlates of war 1816–1979 (1987), Levy: Great Power wars 1495–1815 (1988), Organski/Kugler: War ledger data 1870–1974 (n.a.), Richardson: Statistics of deadly quarrels 1809–1949 (1960), Rummel: Foreign conflict behavior 1950–1968 (n.a.), Singer/Small: Wages of war 1816–1980 Augmented with Disputes and Civil War data (update 1997).
   Internal conflicts: Banks: Domestic Conflict behavior 1919–1966 (1978), Bloomfield, Beattie: Cascon project: Local conflict data 1945–1969 (1971), Bratton, van de Walle: Political regimes and regime transition in Africa 1910–1994 (1996), Brecher, Wilkenfeld: International crisis behavior project (1977), Feierabend, Feierabend, Kelly: Databank of minority group conflict 1955–1965 (n.a.), Feierabend, Feierabend, Nesvold: Political events project 1948–1965 (1971), Feierabend, Feierabend, Nesvold: Systemic conditions of political aggression (SCOPA) project 1955–1964 (1975), Gurr, Bishop: Civil strife conflict magnitudes 1955–1970 (n.a.), Gurr, Giles: Conflict and society (n.a.), Gurr: Causal model of civil strife 1961–1965 (1971), Gurr: Civil strife events 1955–1970 (n.a.), Rummel, Tanter: Dimensions of conflict behavior within and between nations 1955–1960 (1971).
   Other datasets not at ICPSR: Blechmann/Kaplan: Force without war: US Armed Forces as a political instrument (1978), Brogan: World conflicts (1989), Butterworth: Managing interstate conflicts (1976), Day: Border and territorial disputes (1987), Dingemann: Bewaffnete Konflikte seit 1945 (1983), Gantzel/Schwinghammer: Die Kriege seit 1945 (1995), Kende: Wars of ten years 1967–1976 (1982), Maoz: Paths to conflict: International dispute initiation 1816–1976 (1982), Zacher: International conflicts and collective security 1946–1977.

Chapter 3

1 Quoted from UN (URL: http://www.un.org/members; 10 Oct. 1997).
2 Note: KOSIMO has not included *coups d'état* in its counting.

Chapter 4

1 We did not attribute an initiator to the conflict over the territorial rights in the Antarctic region. Therefore one case is missing in the analysis of political systems by the conflict initiators.

Chapter 5

1 According to Bercovitch (1984) a mediator shows the following characteristics:

- He is accepted voluntarily by the adversaries; he cannot function without trust and cooperation of the adversaries.
- He must be perceived as independent and credible by the parties; he must be sufficiently impartial.
- He enters an international dispute in order to affect, change, influence, or modify it in some way.
- He employs only peaceful means in order to let the conflicting parties agree to one or another proposal.
- He turns an original dyad into a triadic interaction.
- His engagement is perceived by all concerned as temporary.
- In most cases a mediator is not a disinterested party but pursues own interests especially when the mediator is a state.

Furthermore, a mediator should meet these qualifications:

- in-depth knowledge about the issues
- ability to understand the positions of the antagonists
- active listening
- sense of timing
- communication skills
- procedural skills.

2 The idea of United Nations peacekeeping is a similar pragmatic reaction to the existing gap between the principle of collective self-defense and widespread violence without clearly identifiable aggressors.

Bibliography

Publications related to the KOSIMO databank

Biermann, Frank, Petschel-Held, Gerhard and Christoph Rohloff 1998: 'Umweltzerstörung als Konfliktursache?' in *Zeitschrift für Internationale Beziehungen 1999/2*, pp. 273–308.

Billing, Peter 1992: *Eskalation und Deeskalation internationaler Konflikte. Ein Konfliktmodell auf der Grundlage der empirischen Auswertung von 188 internationalen Konflikten seit 1945.* Europäische Hochschulschriften Reihe XXXI. Frankfurt: Campus.

Heidelberger Institut für internationale Konfliktforschung 1992, 1993, 1994, 1995, 1996, 1997, 1998, 1999: Konfliktbarometer.

Klotz, Sabine 1996: 'Gelungene Friedensschlüsse und Konfliktregelungen' in V. Matthies, Ch. Rohloff and S. Klotz: *Frieden statt Krieg.* Interdependenz no. 21, Bonn, pp. 33–48.

Petrak, I., Trappl, R. and Fürnkranz, I. 1994: *The Potential Contribution of Artificial Intelligence to the Avoidance of Crises and Wars: Using CBR Methods with the KOSIMO Database of Conflicts.* Vienna: Austrian Institute of Artificial Intelligence, TR-94-32.

Pfetsch, Frank R. and Peter Billing 1994: *Datenhandbuch nationaler und internationaler Konflikte.* Baden-Baden: Nomos.

Pfetsch, Frank R. 1990: 'Conditions for Nonviolent Resolution of Conflict' in E.-O. Czempiel, L. Kiuzadjan and Z. Masopust: *Nonviolence in International Crises.* European Coordination Centre. Vienna, pp. 99–123.

Pfetsch, Frank R. 1990: 'Krieg und Frieden in neuerer Zeit. Konflikte in und zwischen Staaten' in *Wie Kriege entstehen.* Published by Volksbund Deutsche Kriegsgräberfürsorge und Landeszentrale für politische Bildung. Baden-Württemberg. Stuttgart, pp. 9–40.

Pfetsch, Frank R. 1992: *Internationale und nationale Konflikte nach dem Zweiten Weltkrieg.* PVS 38, pp. 258–85.

Pfetsch, Frank R. 1993: 'Der verstehende und der erklärende Ansatz in der internationalen Konfliktforschung' in O. W. Gabriel (ed.) *Verstehen und Erklären von Konflikten.* Munich: Minerva, pp. 33–53.

Pfetsch, Frank R. 1993: 'Die Bewältigung nationaler und internationaler Konflikte' in *Spektrum der Wissenschaft*, June, pp. 103–6.

Pfetsch, Frank R. 1994: *Internationale Politik.* Stuttgart: Kohlhammer.

Rohloff, Christoph 1996: 'Frieden sichtbar machen! Konzepte und empirische Befunde zu Friedenserhaltung und Friedenssicherung' in V. Matthies, Ch. Rohloff and S. Klotz: *Frieden statt Krieg.* Interdependenz no. 21, Bonn, pp. 18–32.

268   *Bibliography*

Rohloff, Christoph 1998: 'Empirische Konfliktforschung und Umweltkonflikte: Methodische Probleme' in A. Carius and K. Lietzmann: *Umwelt und Sicherheit.* Berlin.
Trautner, Bernhard J. 1997: *Konstruktive Konfliktbearbeitung im Vorderen und Mittleren Orient. Ansätze der Deeskalation und Beilegung nationaler und internationaler Konflikte 1945 bis 1995.* Band 2 der Heidelberger Studien zur Internationalen Politik. Münster: Lit.

References and further reading

Aristoteles 1991: *Metaphysik.* Stuttgart: Reclam.
Azar, Edward E. 1993: *Conflict and Peace Data Bank* (COPDAB), 1948–1978, 3rd edn, Ann Arbor, MI: Inter-university Consortium for Political and Social Research.
Bächler *et al.* 1996: *Kriegsursache Umweltzerstörung.* Zürich: Ruegger.
Barandat, Jörg (ed.) 1997: *Wasser: Konfrontation oder Kooperation: ökologische Aspekte von Sicherheit am Beispiel eines weltweit begehrten Rohstoffs.* Baden-Baden: Nomos.
Bendix, Reinhard 1971: Modernisierung in internationaler Perspektive' in W. Zapf (ed.): *Theorien des sozialen Wandels.* Cologne/Berlin: Kiepenheuer & Witsch, pp. 505–12.
Bercovitch, J. 1984: *Social Conflicts and Third Parties: Strategies of Conflict Resolution.* Boulder, Colorado.
Bercovitch, J. 1985: 'Third Parties in Conflict Management: The Structure and Conditions of Effective Mediation in International Relations', *International Journal* 40, 4, pp. 736–52.
Bercovitch, J. 1986: 'International Mediation: A Study of the Incidence, Strategies and Conditions of Successful Outcomes', *Cooperation and Conflict*, XXI, pp. 155–68.
Berton. P., Kimora, H. and Zartman, I. W. (eds) 1999: *International Negotiations.* New York: St Martin's Press.
BICC (Bonn International Conversion Center) 1996: 'Conversion Survey 1996: Global Disarmament, Demilitarization and Demobilization' at http://bicc.uni-bonn.de, Aug. 1998.
Biermann, Frank, Petschel-Held, Gerhard and Rohloff, Christoph 1998: 'Umweltzerstörung als Konflikturache? Theoretische Konzeptionalisierung und empirische Analyse des Zusammenhangs von "Umwelt" und "Sicherheit"', *Zeitschrift für Internationale Beziehungen* 5:2, pp. 273–308.
Billing, Peter 1992: *Eskalation und Deeskalation internationaler Konflikte. Ein Konfliktmodell auf der Grundlage der empirischen Auswertung von 288 internationalen Konflikten seit 1945.* (Europäische Hochschulschriften, Reihe XXXI, Politikwissenschaft) Frankfurt: Lang.
Billing, Peter 1995: 'Zuckerbrot und Peitsche: Vermittlungsaktionen der Supermächte in internationalen Konflikten' in N. Ropers and T. Debiel (eds): *Friedliche Konfliktbearbeitung in der Staaten- und Gesellschaftswelt*, pp. 112–31.
Blechman, B. M. and Kaplan, S. S. 1978: *Force Without War: US Armed Forces as a Political Instrument.* Washington DC.
Borchardt, U. 1986: 'Die Kriege der Nachkriegszeit', *Vereinte Nationen* 34, 2, pp. 68–74.
Brecher, M., Wilkenfeld, J. and Moser, S. 1988: Crises in the Twentieth Century, vol. 1. *Handbook of International Crises*, vol. 2. *Handbook of Foreign Policy Crises.* Oxford/New York: Pergamon.
Brock, Lothar 1997: 'Den Frieden erwirtschaften' in Dieter Senghaas (ed.): *Frieden*

machen. Frankfurt a.M.: Suhrkamp edition, pp. 397–420.

Burton, J. W. 1972: 'The Resolution of Conflict', *International Studies Quarterly,* 16, pp. 5–29.

Butterwegge, Christoph 1997: 'Jugendgewalt als neue Austragungsform des Generationskonflikts?' in W. Vogt (ed.): *Gewalt und Konfliktbearbeitung,* pp. 162–79.

Butterworth, R. L. 1976: *Managing Interstate Conflict, 1945–1974.* Data with Synopses. Pittsburgh.

Butterworth, R. L. 1978a: 'Do Conflict Managers Matter?', *International Studies Quarterly* 22, 2, pp. 195–214.

Butterworth, R. L. 1978b: *Moderation from Management. International Organizations and Peace.* Pittsburgh.

Coplin, W. D. and Rochester, J. M. 1972: 'The Permanent Court of International Justice, the League of Nations and the United Nations: A Comparative Empirical Survey', *APSR 66,* pp. 529–50.

Cukwurah, A. 1967: *The Settlement of Boundary Disputes in International Law.* Manchester.

Cusack, Thomas R. and Eberwein, Wolf-Dieter 1982: 'Prelude to War: Incidence, Escalation, and Intervention in International Disputes, 1900–1976', *International Interaction* 9:1, pp. 9–28.

Czempiel, E.-O. 1981: *Internationale Politik, Ein Konfliktmodell.* Paderborn: UTB/ Schönigh.

Czempiel, E.-O. 1986: *Friedensstrategien, Systemwandel durch internationale Organisationen.* Paderborn.

Dahrendorf, Ralf 1958: 'Toward a Theory of Social Conflict', *The Journal of Conflict Resolution,* 2, pp. 170–83.

Debiel, Thomas 1995: 'Demokratie und Gewalt in einer Welt des Umbruchs: Zur friedenspolitischen Relevanz politischer Herrschaftsformen in den 90er Jahren' in N. Ropers and T. Debiel (eds): *Friedliche Konfliktbearbeitung in der Staaten- und Gesellschaftswelt.* Bonn.

Debiel, Thomas and Zander, Ingo 1992: 'Die Friedensdividende der 90er Jahre. Chancen und Grenzen der Umwidmung von Militärausgaben zugunsten ziviler Zwecke'. *Reihe Interdependenz* no.11. Bonn: Stiftung Entwicklung und Frieden.

Deitchman, S. J. 1964: *Limited War and American Defense Policy.* Washington.

Deutsch, K. W. and Senghaas, D. 1970: 'Die Schritte zum Krieg. Eine Übersicht über Systemebenen, Entscheidungsstadien und einige Forschungsergebnisse', *apuz B47/70,* Nov. 21, p. 23.

Dingemann, R. 1983: *Bewaffnete Konflikte seit 1945. Zwischenstaatliche Auseinandersetzungen, Befreiungskriege in der Dritten Welt, Buergerkriege.* Duesseldorf.

Doyle, Michael, W. 1980: 'Liberalism and World Politics', *AOSR 80,* pp. 1151–69.

Eisenstadt, Shmuel 1964: 'Social Change, Differentiation and Evolution', *ASR,* 29, pp. 375–86.

Elias, Norbert 1976: *Über den Prozeß der Zivilisation: soziogenetische und psychogenetische Untersuchungen.* Frankfurt: Suhrkamp.

Enzensberger, Hans Magnus 1993: *Aussichten auf den Bürgerkrieg.* Frankfurt/M: Suhrkamp.

Fisher, R. 1978: *International Mediation.* International Peace Academy, NY.

Fisher, Roger and Ury, William 1981: *Getting to Yes.* Boston: Houghton Mifflin.

Freedom House 1999: The Annual Survey of Political Rights and Civil Liberties 1998–9 at http://freedomhouse.org/survey99

Frei, D. 1975: 'Erfolgsbedingungen für Vermittlungsaktionen in internationalen

Konflikten', *PVS 16*, 4, pp. 447–90.

Frei, D. 1976: 'Factors Affecting the Effectiveness of International Mediation', *Peace Science Society (International) Papers* 26, pp. 67–84.

Fukuyama, Francis 1994: 'Die Zukunft des Krieges', *Frankfurter Allgemeine Zeitung Magazin*, Heft 772, 16.12.1994, 16–22.

Galtung, Johan 1968: 'Friedensforschung' in E. Krippendorf (ed.): *Friedensforschung*. Cologne/Berlin, p. 520.

Gantzel, K. J. and Meyer-Stamer, J. (eds) 1986: *Die Kriege nach dem Zweiten Weltkrieg bis 1984*. Munich.

Gantzel, K. J. and Schwinghammer, T. 1995: *Die Kriege nach dem Zweiten Weltkrieg 1945–92*. Münster: Lit.

Geller, Daniel S. and Singer, David J. 1998: *Nations at War. A Scientific Study of International Conflict*. Cambridge: Cambridge UP.

Gleditsch, Nils Petter 1998: 'Armed Conflict and the Environment: A Critique of the Literature', *Journal of Peace Research*, 35:3, pp. 381–400.

Goedeke, P., Stuckmann, E. and Vogt, M. 1983: *Kriege im Frieden*. Braunschweig.

Greaves, F. V. 1962: 'Peace in Our Time – Fact or Fable?', *Military Review* (Dec. 1962), 55–8.

Grewe, W. G. 1964: 'Die Arten der Behandlung internationaler Konflikte' in Iklé, F. C.: *Strategie und Taktik des diplomatischen Verhandelns*, 11–14. Guetersloh.

Grewe, W. G. 1981: *Spiel der Kräfte in der Weltpolitik*. Frankfurt: Ullstein.

Gurr, T. R. 1970: *Why Men Rebel*. Princeton: Princeton UP.

Gurr, T. R. 1993: 'Why Minorities Rebel: A Global Analysis of Communal Mobilization and Conflict Since 1945', *International Political Science Review*, 14, 2, pp. 161–201.

Gurr, T. R., Jaggers, K. and Moore, W. H. 1990: 'The Transformation of the Western State: The Growth of Democracy, Autocracy, and State Power Since 1800', *Studies in Comparative International Development*, 25, 1, pp. 73–108.

Haas, E. B. 1968: *Collective Security and the Future International System*. Denver.

Haas, E. B. 1983: 'Regime Decay: Conflict Management and International Organizations, 1945–1981', *International Organizations*, 37, 2, pp. 189–256.

Haas, E. B., Butterworth, R. L. and Nye, J. S. 1972: *Conflict Management by International Organizations*. Morristown.

Hauchler, J. (ed.) 1998: *Global Trends*. Franfurt: Fischer Taschenbücher.

Holsti, Kalevi J. 1969: 'Resolving International Conflicts: A Taxonomy of Behavior and Some Figures on Procedure', *JCR*, 10, 3, pp. 272–6.

Holsti, Kalevi J. 1983: *International Politics: A Framework for Analysis*. Englewood Cliffs.

Holsti, Kalevi J. 1991: *Peace and War. Armed Conflict and International Order, 1648–1989*. Cambridge: Cambridge UP.

Holsti, Kalevi J. 1996: *The State, War, and the State of War*. Cambridge: Cambridge UP.

Homer-Dixon, Thomas F. 1994: 'Across the Threshold: Empirical Evidence on Environmental Scarcities as Causes of Violent Conflict', *International Security*, 19, 1, pp. 5–40.

Huntington, Samuel P. 1991: *The Third Wave. Democratization in the Late Twentieth Century*. Norman and London: Oklahoma UP.

Huntington, Samuel P. 1996: *The Clash of Civilizations*. New York: Simon & Schuster.

ICPSR (Inter-university Consortium for Political and Social Research) 1998: 'Conflict, Aggression, Violence, Wars' in http://www.icpsr.umich.edu/archive1.html, December 1998.

Iklé, Fred Charles. 1964: *How Nations Negotiate*. New York.

Jackson, E. 1972: *Meeting of Minds*. New York.
Jones, D. M., Bremer, S. A. and Singer, J. D. 1996: 'Militarized Interstate Disputes, 1816–1992. Rational Coding Rules and Empirical Patterns', *Conflict Management and Peace Science*, 15, 2, pp. 163–213.
Juette, R. and Grosse-Juette, A. (ed.) 1981: *The Future of International Organizations*. London.
Kant, Immanuel 1979: *Zum ewigen Frieden* (1795). Stuttgart: Reclam. Engl.: *Inevitable Peace*. Cambridge: Harvard UP (1948).
Kaplan, Robert 1996: 'Die kommende Anarchie', *Lettre international*, 32, pp. 52–61.
Kaufman, Johan 1962: *How United Nations Decisions Are Made*. Leyden.
Keck, Otto 1993: 'The New Institutionalism and the Relative-Gains-Debate' in F. R. Pfetsch (ed.): *International Relations and Pan-Europe*. Münster: Lit, pp. 35–62.
Keith, Jaggers and Gurr, T. R. 1996: *Polity III. Regime Change and Political Authority 1800–1994*. 2nd ICPSR version. Ann Arbor MI: Inter-university Consortium for Political and Social Research.
Kelman, H. C. (ed.) 1965: *International Behavior; A Social-Psychological Analysis*. New York.
Kende, I. 1971: 'Twenty-Five Years of Local Wars', *JPR*, 1, pp. 5–22.
Kende, I. 1978: 'Wars of Ten Years (1967–1976)', *JPR*, 15, 3, pp. 227–41.
Kende, I. 1982: 'Über die Kriege seit 1945', *Friedens- und Konfliktforschung* 16.
Keohane, Robert and Nye, Joseph 1977: *Power and Interdependence: World politics in Transition*. Boston and Toronto: Little Brown.
Konfliktbarometer, December 1998, Heidelberg: HIIK (Heidelberger Institut für internationale Konfliktforschung e.V.) http://www.konflikte.de/hiik.
Krasner, Stephen, D. (ed.) 1987: *International Regimes*. Ithaca, N.Y.: Cornell UP, rev. edition.
Krause, Joachim 1998: *Strukturwandel der Nichtverbreitungspolitik. Die Verbreitung von Massenvernichtungswaffen und die weltpolitische Transformation*. Oldenbourg.
Krippendorff, Ekkehart 1985: *Staat und Krieg. Die historische Logik politischer Unvernunft*. Frankfurt: Suhrkamp.
Lall, A. 1966: *Modern International Negotiation*. New York.
Leiss, A. C. and Bloomfield, L. P. 1967: *The Control of Local Conflict. A Design on Arms Control and Limited War in the Developing Areas*, 4 vols. Cambridge.
Levine, E. P. 1971: 'Mediation in International Politics', *Peace Research Society Papers*, 13, pp. 23–43.
Linz, Juan J. and Stepan, Alfred 1996: *Problems of Democratic Transition and Consolidation*. Baltimore and London: The Johns Hopkins UP.
Liska, G. 1962: *Nations in Alliance: the Limits of Interdependence*. Baltimore.
Luard, Evan 1986: *Conflict and Peace in the Modern International System*. London: Macmillan.
Luard, Evan 1986: *War in International Society*. London.
Maoz, Z. 1982: *Paths to Conflict. International Dispute Initiation, 1816–1976*. Boulder.
Matthies, Volker (ed.) 1996: *Frieden statt Krieg*. Bonn: Stiftung Entwicklung und Frieden, pp. 7–11.
Mearsheimer, John 1990: 'Back to the Future', *International Security*, 15:1, pp. 5–56.
Miall, Hugh 1992: *The Peacemakers. Peaceful Settlement of Disputes since 1945*. Oxford: Macmillan.
Morgenthau, Hans 1948: *Politics Among Nations: The Struggle for Power and Peace*. New York: McGraw-Hill.

Northedge, F. S. and Donelan, M. D. 1971: *International Disputes. The Political Aspects*. London.

Parsons, Talcott (ed.) 1961: *Theories of Society*. 2 vols, New York.

Parsons, Talcott 1964: 'Evolutionary Universals in Society', *American Sociological Review*, 29, pp. 339–357.

Pasierbsky, Fritz 1983: *Krieg und Frieden in der Sprache*. Frankfurt: Fischer.

Petrak, I., Trappl, R. and Fürnkranz, I. 1994: *The Potential Contribution of Artificial Intelligence to the Avoidance of Crises and Wars: Using CBR Methods with the KOSIMO Database of Conflicts*. Vienna: Austrian Institute of Artificial Intelligence, TR-94-32.

Pfetsch, Frank R. 1990: 'Conditions for Nonviolent Resolution of Conflict' in Ernst-Otto Czempiel, L. Kiuzadjan and Z. Masopust (eds): *Nonviolence in International Crises*. Vienna: European Coordination Centre, pp. 99–123.

Pfetsch, Frank R. (ed.) 1991: *Konflikte seit 1945*. 5 vols, Freiburg/Würzburg: Ploetz.

Pfetsch, Frank R. 1992: 'Nationale und internationale Konflikte nach 1945', *PVS 2*, pp. 258–85.

Pfetsch, Frank R. 1994: *Internationale Politik*. Stuttgart: Kohlhammer.

Pfetsch, Frank R. and Billing, Peter 1994: *Datenhandbuch nationaler und internationaler Konflikte*. Baden-Baden: Nomos.

Pfetsch, Frank R. (ed.) 1996: *Globales Konfliktpanorama 1990–1995*. Münster: Lit.

Putnam, Robert D. 1988: 'Diplomacy and domestic politics. The logic of two-level games', *International Organizations*, 42, 3, pp. 427–60.

Randle, R. F. 1973: *The Origins of Peace*. New York.

Richardson, L. F. 1960: *Statistics of Deadly Quarrels*. Pittsburgh.

Risse-Kappen, T. 1994: 'Demokratischer Frieden? Unfriedliche Demokratien? Überlegungen zu einem theoretischen Puzzle' in Gerd Krell and Harald Müller (eds) *Frieden und Konflikt in den internationalen Beziehungen*. Frankfurt/M., pp. 159–89.

Rittberger, Volker 1987 (Oct.): 'Zur Friedensfähigkeit von Demokratien' in *Aus Politik und Zeitgeschehen*, Bonn.

Rittberger, Volker (ed.) 1995: *Regime Theory and International Relations*. Oxford: Clarendon.

Rohloff, Christoph 1996: 'Frieden sichtbar machen! Konzepte und empirische Befunde zu Friedenserhaltung und Friedenssicherung' in V. Matthies, Chr. Rohloff and S. Klotz: *Frieden statt Krieg* in Interdependenz no. 21, Bonn, pp. 18–32.

Rohloff, Christoph 1998: 'Konfliktforschung und Umweltkonflikte: Methodische Probleme' in Alexander Carius and Kurt M. Lietzmann (eds): *Umwelt und Sicherheit. Herausforderungen für die Internationale Politik*. Berlin, Heidelberg: Springer, pp. 155–78.

Ruggie, John Gerald 1983: 'International Regimes. Transactions and Change. Embedded Liberalism in the Post-War Economic Order' in Krasner (ed.) 1983, pp. 195–231.

Ruloff, D. 1987: *Wie Kriege beginnen*. Munich.

Rummel, Rudolph 1983: 'Libertarianism and International Relations', *JCR*, 27, pp. 27–71.

Schindler, Hardi 1998: *Konflikte in Südamerika*. Münster: Lit.

Schmitt, Carl 1932 (1979): *Der Begriff des Politischen*. Nachdruck der 2. Aufl. Berlin.

Seeley, John 1902 (new edition): *Introduction to Political Science*. London.

Senghaas, Dieter 1995: 'Hexagon-Variationen: Zivilisierte Konfliktbearbeitung trotz Fundamentalpolitisierung' in N. Ropers and T. Debiel (eds): *Friedliche Konfliktbearbeitung in der Staaten- und Gesellschaftswelt*, pp. 37–54.

Simkim, W. E. 1971: *Mediation and the Dynamics of Collective Bargaining*. Washington.

Singer, David John 1979: *The Correalates of War I: Research Origins and Rationale*. New York.

Singer, David John 1980: *The Correlates of War II: Testing Some Realpolitical Models*. New York.

Singer, D. J. and Small, M. 1972: *The Wages of War 1816–1965. A Statistical Handbook*. New York.

SIPRI 1995: *Yearbook*. Oxford/New York: Oxford UP.

SIPRI (Stockholm International Peace Research Institute) 1997: Yearbook. http://www.sipri.se and Stockholm.

Siverson, R. M. and Tennefoss, M. R. 1982: 'Interstate Conflicts: 1815–1965', *International Interactions*, 9, 2, pp. 147–78.

Small, M. and Singer, D. J. 1982: *Resort to Arms*. Beverly Hills.

Small, M. and Singer, D. J. 1981: 'The War-proneness of Democratic Regimes', *Jerusalem Journal of International Relations*, 1, 2, pp. 50–69.

Snyder, S. and Glenn, H. 1972: 'Crisis Bargaining' in Ch. F. Hermann (ed.) *International Crises*. New York, pp. 217–256.

Sorokin, P. A. 1957: *Social and Cultural Dynamics*. New York.

Steinweg, R. (ed.) *1987 Kriegsursachen*. Frankfurt: Suhrkamp.

Tetzlaff, Rainer 1996: *Weltbank und Währungsfonds – Gestalter der Bretton-Woods-Ära: Kooperations- und Integrations-Regime in einer sich dynamisch entwickelnden Weltgesellschaft*. Opladen.

Trautner, Bernhard 1997: *Konstruktive Konfliktbearbeitung im Vorderen und Mittleren Orient. Ansätze der De-eskalation und Beilegung nationaler und internationaler Konflikte 1945–1995*. Münster: Lit.

UNIDIR (UN Institute for Disarmament Research) 1995: *Managing Arms in Peace Process: The Issues*. New York/Geneva.

Vanhanen, Tatu 1984: *The Emergence of Democracy. A Comparative Study of 119 States, 1850–1979*. Helsinki: The Finnish Society of Sciences and Letters.

Vasquez, John A. 1995: 'Why do neighbors fight? Proximity, interaction or territoriality', *Journal of Peace Research*, 32, 3, pp. 277–93.

Vogt, Wolfgang R. (ed.) 1997: *Gewalt und Konfliktbearbeitung. Befunde – Konzepte – Handeln*. Baden-Baden: Nomos.

WBGU 1996: *Jahresgutachten 1996*. Heidelberg: Springer.

Wehr, P. 1979: *Conflict Regulation*. Boulder.

Wood, D. 1968: *Conflict in the Twentieth Century*. London (Adelphi Papers No. 48, IISS).

Wright, Quincy 1942 (1960): *A Study of War*. 2 Vols. Chicago: UP.

Young, O. R. 1967: *The Intermediaries: Third Parties in International Crises*. New Jersey.

Zacher, M. W. 1979: *International Conflicts and Collective Security, 1946–77*. New York.

Zartman, I. W. 1985: *Ripe for Resolution. Conflict and Intervention in Africa*. New York.

Zartman, William 1995: *Collapsed States: The Disintegration and Restoration of Legitimate Authority*. Boulder: Lynne Rienner.

Zartman, I. W. (ed.) 1996: *Elusive Peace. Negotiating an End to Civil Wars*. Washington D.C.: The Brookings Institution.

Index

For Product Safety Concerns and Information please contact our EU
representative GPSR@taylorandfrancis.com
Taylor & Francis Verlag GmbH, Kaufingerstraße 24, 80331 München, Germany